In this vo
scribes Jewis
the expansio
ascendancy
explains ho
sions, and ⟨
of popular
slowly r
cultu⟨
⟨out
⟨n
⟨eth⟨
⟨era⟨
⟨ast ⟨
⟨and
⟨pp⟨
⟨he
⟨x⟨

⟨h
⟨r

⟨e⟨

A SOCIAL AND RELIGIOUS
HISTORY OF THE JEWS

High Middle Ages, 500–1200: Volumes III–VIII

VOLUME IV

MEETING OF EAST AND WEST

A SOCIAL
AND RELIGIOUS
HISTORY OF
THE JEWS

By SALO WITTMAYER BARON

Second Edition, Revised and Enlarged

High Middle Ages, 500–1200: Volumes III–VIII
VOLUME IV
MEETING OF EAST AND WEST

COLUMBIA UNIVERSITY PRESS 1957

New York

LIBRARY OF CONGRESS CATALOG CARD NUMBER: 52-404

© COPYRIGHT 1957 BY COLUMBIA UNIVERSITY PRESS, NEW YORK

PUBLISHED IN GREAT BRITAIN, CANADA, INDIA, AND PAKISTAN
BY THE OXFORD UNIVERSITY PRESS
LONDON, TORONTO, BOMBAY, AND KARACHI

MANUFACTURED IN THE UNITED STATES OF AMERICA

CONTENTS

A SOCIAL AND RELIGIOUS HISTORY
OF THE JEWS: HIGH MIDDLE AGES

MEETING OF EAST AND WEST

WESTERN CHRISTENDOM

REEMERGING, after their temporary eclipse during the seventh century, into the full light of history, the West European Jewish communities gradually rose to positions of leadership in the socioeconomic and cultural life of their people. The Golden Age of Muslim Spain communicated itself to Christian Spain, southern France, and southern Italy, especially through the numerous refugees from Almoravid and Almohade persecutions. Despite the basic differences in their political and economic status and in the general outlook of their neighbors, Spanish, Provençal, and Italian Jewries long continued the intellectual traditions evolved in Moorish Spain and North Africa. Even the Arabic language continued to be spoken or at least understood by many segments of the Jewish population.

Living in the borderlands between Islam and Christendom, these communities suffered considerably from the unceasing conflicts in that divided world. But they also helped to build those intellectual and socioeconomic bridges which in the long run were to bring its hostile members more closely together. At the same time they performed the great historic function of connecting the rising Jewish intelligentsia of Christian Europe with the older centers of Arabic-speaking Jewry. Through their memorable work, especially of translating Arabic classics, Jewish and non-Jewish, into Hebrew, they made the fruits of Greek and Near Eastern thought and science accessible to the young and, though intellectually still circumscribed, alert and rapidly advancing Jewries of northern France, England, and the Germanies.

Nonetheless, the differences in mores and outlook between the northern and southern communities led to a new and permanent division into Sefardim and Ashkenazim. The origin of these names, or rather of the application of these two biblical designations to the inhabitants of Spain and Germany, has long puzzled scholars, and no wholly satisfactory explanation has as yet been offered. It

appears that with the gradual shift of the Jewish geographic outlook to the western lands some biblical students were impressed
by the similarity of sound between Hesperia and Sefarad, between
Saxony or "As-Skandz" and Ashkenaz. The identification of Sefarad
with Spain appears fairly well established already in geonic writings. That of Ashkenaz with Germany did not appear in literature
until after the first millennium, when the emergence of a special
group of Jews living north of the Alps and Pyrenees and endowed
with customs and rituals of their own had become an established
fact. Nurtured by the uninterrupted flow of traditions from the
ancient Roman Empire, the northern Jews maintained steady contacts with the surviving centers of Roman civilization in Italy and,
more indirectly, with Palestine. The Sefardim, on the other hand,
long included in the vast Muslim civilization and generally and
Jewishly centered in Babylonia, fell heirs to the Babylonian outlook and lore. Ashkenazic Jewry's divergences from its southern
neighbors thus continued on a novel plane the ancient dichotomy
between Palestine and Babylonia.[1]

Italian Jewry, itself divided between the Peninsula's central and
northern sections, which permanently remained the focus of Latin
Christianity, and the southern provinces, long dominated by Byzantines or Muslims, developed many peculiar characteristics. It
held the middle way between the emergent new groupings. Nu-
merically, the Jewish communities of Rome and the republics in
the north of Italy lagged far behind the Jewish masses inhabiting
the Near East and Spain and even the sparser settlements in the
northern countries. Nevertheless they played a major role in shaping the cultural forms and political destinies of all European Jewry.
The Roman community was in direct contact with the Papacy,
which at that time embarked upon its most ambitious career as
both a spiritual and temporal power in Christendom. As in other
phases of papal history, therefore, many purely local developments in the city of Rome assumed European importance.

Some of the Italian republics, on the other hand, especially
Venice, Genoa, and Pisa, then entering the period of their greatest
imperial and economic expansion, became powerful factors in
international trade and in the great political transformations of
the entire Mediterranean basin. Whether as competitors of Jew-

ish merchants in the Levantine trade or as imperial masters of
numerous Jewish communities on the Italian mainland and in
the eastern colonies, they began playing a role in Jewish history
which was far out of proportion with the percentage of world
Jewry living under their flags. These interrelations were to reach
their full fruition only during the late Middle Ages and early
modern times, but foundations were fully laid during the tenth
to twelfth centuries. In any case, the destinies of Italian Jewry, in
both the north and the south, measurably influenced the evolution of the whole people.

THE ROMAN CHURCH

Ecclesiastical views on Jews and Judaism had been formulated
by Church Fathers and early popes, especially Gregory the Great,
with a degree of finality. Yet within that general framework there
was room for differences of opinion and even significant innovations in detail which at times fundamentally affected Jewish life
in western Europe. There still was fairly general agreement that
toleration of Jews to the end of days presupposed the prohibition
of forcibly converting them to Christianity. True, the manifold
expulsions of the seventh century and the subsequent outbursts
of extreme intolerance in Byzantium left their imprint on the
Church too. In fact, a churchman, Cyril of Alexandria, had been
the first to introduce this method of settling the Judeo-Christian
controversy. Nevertheless, even in Visigothic Spain, ecclesiastical
opinion at first condemned Sisebut's forced conversions, and only
gradually acquiesced in the subsequent less stringent royal decrees.
Gregory even more sharply condemned efforts to bring Jews into
the Christian fold by forcible means of any kind.

On the other hand, once converted, even if under nonphysical
duress, neophytes had no right to return to their former faith.
Hadrian I (772–95) set the pace for the entire, increasingly casuis-
tic, canonical jurisprudence on this subject when he failed to ap-
prove the aforementioned decision of the Nicean Council of 787,
which denied communion to repentant converts and refused baptism to their children. Although this was the last truly "universal"
council, with the participation of Western as well as Eastern

churches, the pope felt that such "leniency" should not be applied in the West. Since the disappearance of the Visigothic kingdom, insincere converts no longer appeared as a major, unassimilable mass in any western country, until the emergence of the Marrano problem in Spain. The Western churches could, therefore, more readily afford to insist on the "indelible character" of the sacrament of baptism, even if unlawfully performed. Gregory IV (827–44) stated the official position in his succinct injunction to the bishops of Gaul and Germany in 828: "Jews are not to be forced to adopt the faith, but if they accept it, however unwillingly, they ought to be forced to adhere to it." More broadly incorporated in Gratian's *Decretum* (I, dist. xlv, c. 5, in *Corpus juris canonici,* ed. by Friedberg, I, 161 f.) on the basis of Toledan canons, this doctrine was never seriously challenged by canon jurists.

Later, a distinction began to be drawn between forced conversion and expulsion. In his significant reply to an inquiry by Frederick, Archbishop of Mayence in 937–38, as to whether "it is better to force them [the Jews] to submit to the sacred faith, or else to expel them." Pope Leo VII declared,

You should never cease preaching to them, with all the sagacity, prudent counsel and reverence toward God, the belief in the Sacred Trinity, and the mystery of the Lord's incarnation. If they wholeheartedly wish to believe and become baptized, we shall offer thanks and high praise to the omnipotent God. Should they, however, refuse to believe, you shall expel them from your states with our permission. For we ought not to associate with the Lord's enemies, as the Apostle says: "Be ye not unequally yoked together with unbelievers: for what fellowship hath righteousness with unrighteousness? . . . or what part hath he that believeth with an infidel?" [II Cor. 6:14–15]. But you must not baptize them by force, and without their wish and request. For it is written: "Give not that which is holy unto the dogs, neither cast ye your pearls before swine, lest they trample them under their feet" [Matthew 7:6].

Powerless and ineffectual as this pope may have been in his own domain, an authority of this kind, given to a Christian ruler and buttressed by Scriptural hermeneutics, however tenuous, set a dangerous precedent. Curiously, the popes never expelled the Jews from Rome, which has therefore become the oldest Jewish community in Europe with an uninterrupted history of some two

mans, led by the Pierleoni family, loyally supported him until
his death eight years later. But a strong faction sided with Innocent II, who had simultaneously been elected by a minority of influential cardinals. This disputed election immediately became
the playball of international power politics. Innocent's partisans,
led by the great preacher Bernard of Clairvaux, seized on Anacletus' Jewish origin, as well as his alleged personal faults, as a
pretext for refusing him allegiance. Bernard, who throughout his
life combined strong anti-Jewish prejudices with sharp repudiation
of forced conversions, argued in a letter to Emperor Lothar that
"it is well known that Jewish offspring now occupies the see of
St. Peter to the injury of Christ." Innocent II himself was further
aroused by the behavior of the Roman Jews who, contrary to their
general hostility toward apostates and the latter's descendants but
in keeping with the prevailing sentiments among their Christian
neighbors, rendered faithful services to his rival. Ultimately supported by Germany, France, and England, Innocent became the
more widely recognized pope. Yet, with the aid of Roger II, whom
he crowned the first "king" of Sicily, Anacletus held out in Rome
to the very end. In fact, as J. B. Villars observed, the decision came
only after Anacletus' early death. Had he survived his competitor,
he would doubtless have secured fairly universal recognition, and
Innocent would have come down in history as the "antipope"
and schismatic. In any case, the racial issue was seized upon by
Anacletus' enemies as an excuse for, rather than as a major cause
of, their opposition.[8]

Nevertheless, Innocent II's hostile gesture upon his entry into
Rome in 1138, must have filled Jewish leaders with grave forebodings. Had not the pope seven years earlier condemned the entire opposition as dominated by the "furor of Jewish infidelity"?
The news about the pope's vindictiveness against Anacletus' former
partisans must also have traveled far and wide; it even evoked
the censure of Bernard, his most ardent and effective champion.
Only his punitive expedition against Roger was frustrated by his
defeat in the field and his capture by the Norman army. It is small
wonder, then, that his convocation of a great "ecumenical" council in 1139, a year after Anacletus' death, while the emotions still
were running high, caused widespread consternation among the

Jews of all western countries. According to the chronicler Shem-Tob Sonzolo, this convocation "inspired fears in all Jewish communities, and they fasted for three consecutive days. God showed them favor, however, and they [the members of the Council] spoke only kindly words about the Jews." The latter statement cannot be verified, for we have but scanty reference to the proceedings of that important assembly, attended by some five hundred ecclesiastical leaders. But no anti-Jewish canons were adopted, not even of the kind promulgated forty years later by the Third Lateran Council. Evidently, in so far as the Jewish question was raised, calmer counsels prevailed.[9]

Despite the wide publicity given the Anacletus-Innocent controversy in the contemporary letters and diplomatic negotiations, the specific background of Innocent's animosity toward the Roman Jews was speedily forgotten. Posterity remembered only his harsh reply to the Jewish deputation, and gradually made it part of a regular ceremony. Before long every new pope was greeted by Jewish communal elders and rabbis with prayers and scrolls of law, and replied with that standardized rebuke. Some popes underscored the Jewish inferiority by disdainfully dropping to the ground the scroll handed them by the deputies. The Jewish community often was also in a serious quandary as to whether to pay homage to one or another of competing popes. As a rule, it tried to steer clear of controversy, and swore allegiance to each rival upon his entry into the city. It also greeted in the same way a victorious emperor (for instance, Henry V). To Gregory X it paid homage again on his reentry from exile in 1238. In time, these ceremonies became ever more elaborate, the scrolls of law ever more richly adorned. Many a pope felt tempted to keep these precious souvenirs, some of which are still preserved in the Vatican Library.[10]

FISCAL VICISSITUDES

Another complication in Judeo-Christian relations characteristic of Western Christendom, though affecting the Papal States only indirectly, caused many popes to intervene for the benefit of the Catholic clergy in other lands. The local churches derived much of their revenue from the ecclesiastical tithe which, in emulation of the biblical *ma'aser,* was collected for the support of priests. Unlike its biblical model, however, this tax was imposed also upon urban land. By general agreement Jews as such were not called upon to contribute to the support of a non-Jewish ecclesiastical establishment. Yet, when real estate originally owned by Christians was transferred to Jewish owners, the local parishes were suddenly deprived of a substantial source of revenue. Since during the tenth to twelfth centuries Jewish land ownership constantly expanded, in part through involuntary foreclosures, the local clergy began agitating for the enactment of laws forcing Jewish owners to continue paying the accustomed tithes from lands acquired from Christians. At times a monastery, like that of St. Edmundsbury, expressly stipulated in its land grants that the new owners must not transfer their rights to clerics or Jews. Successful in persuading Charles the Simple to confiscate such property from the Jews of Narbonne in 898–99 and in having pertinent provisions inserted in such local custumals as the *Fueros de Aragon,* the Church often encountered stiff resistance on the part of secular authorities, who increasingly viewed all Jewish property and taxes therefrom as their own preserve. An inquiry addressed by the bishop of Auxerre to Innocent III in 1207 illustrates well the dilemma of the churches; they could neither force recalcitrant Jewish tithe payers through unwilling secular administrators, nor threaten them with ecclesiastical censures, "which they despise." Innocent advised the bishop that, failing to secure redress by an appeal to the prince, he ought to warn Christians, under threat of excommunication, to refrain from all commercial relations with delinquent Jewish taxpayers. Retaliatory boycotts of this kind were soon thereafter incorporated by the Fourth Lateran Council of 1215 in a canon of international scope.[11]

Of course, in the Papal States the sovereign could use his secular powers to enforce such payments. But perhaps for that very reason Jews apparently were not subjected there to the ecclesiastical tithe. At least Benjamin of Tudela was amazed to find that the 200 Jewish families living in Rome, "the head of the kingdoms of Christendom," occupied an honorable position and paid "no tribute to any man." He evidently found there none of the specific Jewish poll taxes and other imposts so familiar in other lands. In more orderly times the Papacy drew much of its revenue from voluntary contributions by pious Catholics all over Europe, while in anarchical periods the treasury collected all it could extort from Christians and Jews alike. It so happened that during Benjamin's visit Rome had for some time been enjoying the relative peace and security of Alexander III's powerful regime. In contrast thereto, an earlier penitential poem by Solomon the "Babylonian" (a synonym for "Roman"; lived about 970–1020) movingly describes the heavy yoke of taxation resting upon the shoulders of the community. The poet sang:

> Destroy the Jew! despoil him! is the cry,
> Thine own true servants are uprooted so.
> To blot us out their aim. They villify,
> And tax, and spoil, and fleece, to bring us low.

This complaint does not necessarily reflect the existence of special Jewish taxes, but rather that Jews, as the most defenseless subjects, were particular victims of the existing fiscal anarchy.[12]

Here we perceive the frequent dichotomy between the Papacy's attitude toward the Jews and that of the local and provincial leaders of the Church, since the interests of the provinces often were at variance with the policies of the central organs. The temper of the local population, both friendly and inimical to Jews, likewise more readily communicated itself to the parish priests and even bishops, than to the central authorities in Rome. Only the Papacy could maintain, therefore, a more or less unbroken line of continuity in its Jewish policies, whereas the provincial clergy was often swayed especially by the anti-Jewish feelings of its constituents in periods of great tension. At times parish priests and monks were even prone to join the ranks of extreme Jew-baiters. On the other hand, when relations between Jews and Christians became "too friendly," as they appeared under the early Carolingians, bishops like Agobard and Amulo viewed with alarm what they called "Jewish insolence" and the ensuing menace to Christian orthodoxy.

Socioeconomic conflicts of provincial origin loomed large also in the deliberations of the three twelfth-century "universal" councils. The most important of these international gatherings, the

Third Lateran Council, contributed nothing to the religious and theological Judeo-Christian debate, except in so far as in its canon 26 it renewed and sharpened the old prohibition for Jews and Saracens to employ Christian servants. Pope Alexander III, the Council's chairman, further elaborated that prohibition by adding the specific outlawry of Christian women nursing Jewish children in Jewish homes. "For the mores of Jews in no way agree with our mores," and hence frequent friendly relations with them might conceivably "incline simple souls to their superstition and unbelief." [13]

Curiously, neither pope nor Council made any reference to that other perennial Church grievance, the frequent employment of Jewish officials by Christian princes. This issue, which had engaged the attention of Gregory VII and his associates in the midst of their struggle for church supremacy, was to become more burning in the thirteenth century, when the growing complexity of economic and fiscal relations, as well as the greater availability of capable Jewish candidates, made such employment extremely desirable. At that time various ecclesiastics fulminated in vain against this breach of old laws, and popes themselves had to issue special dispensations. Even earlier Alexander III himself had employed Jewish officials, according to the generally trustworthy Benjamin of Tudela. Among the papal administrators Benjamin found Yeḥiel, grandson of Nathan the lexicographer, "a handsome young man of intelligence and wisdom, who has the entry of the pope's palace; for he is the steward of his house and of all that he has." [14]

The Council had to take cognizance, however, of the relatively novel protection of Jewish financial interests by princes viewing all Jewish property as their own. To safeguard that property, some rulers went the whole length of giving preference to the testimony of Jewish over Christian witnesses, and of depriving Jewish converts to Christianity of all their property rights. By becoming Christian, many rulers believed, the converts unlawfully withdrew their possessions from under royal control. In the welter of medieval feudal conflicts the old protective devices for converts, already included in the Theodosian Code, had often gone into total discard.

For this reason canon 26 adopted by the Third Lateran Council also stated expressly,

We order that the testimony of Christians against Jews be admitted in all cases, just as Jews make use of their own witnesses against Christians; and we decree that those who might wish to give preference to Jews over Christians in this matter should be excommunicated, for it is but fitting that Jews be placed below Christians and favored by the latter only for the sake of humanity. If some of them, moreover, under divine inspiration, convert themselves to the Christian faith, they should by no means be deprived of their property. For it is but fitting that converts should enjoy a better status than the one they had before accepting the faith. In the case of contrary proceedings, however, we enjoin the princes and authorities of those places, under pain of excommunication, to cause the full restoration of their hereditary portion and their possessions [to these converts].

Here again the ecclesiastical leaders had strong incentives to preserve the converts' property and hereditary rights, lest they become public charges on the frequently strained episcopal treasuries. Alexander III once more went further than the Council, and in an epistle of unknown date added the stringent prohibitions for Jews to cite clerics before secular courts, and for judges in mixed Jewish-Christian litigations to rely upon the testimony of but a single witness. The pope insisted on the testimony of no less than two or three witnesses "of respectable life and intercourse." Alexander clearly wished to censure not only the Jews' "overbearing" behavior, but also the conduct of many secular authorities who, in his opinion, were bent on favoring the Jewish against the clerical litigant and accepted the testimony of one witness or even mere documents.[15]

Under the feudal clashes in medieval society, many protective devices for both the clergy and Jewish converts were thus discarded. The remedial provisions of the Lateran Council and its presiding officer likewise proved quite ineffective. Innocent III had frequent occasion to censure bishops for their lack of solicitude for the support of penniless converts. In his letter to the king of France on January 16, 1205, he also sharply protested against the widespread disregard of other provisions of the Lateran Council. Jews, he claimed, brazenly employed Christian servants and nurses, "with whom, at times, they commit such abominations as are more fitting for you to punish than for us to detail." Similarly, French courts, Innocent asserted, gave general preference to Jewish over Christian witnesses. These accusations were repeated by his successors on many later occasions. Alexander III's insistence that clerics not be hailed before secular courts was even more widely observed in its breach. If carried out, it would have created a deadlock, since Jewish litigants, with the aid of their royal supporters, successfully resisted being hailed before ecclesiastical judges in civil matters. They had obvious reasons to fear discriminatory treatment there in any case involving a clerical opponent. In fact, during the decades immediately following the Lateran Council, the clergy frequently appeared among both defendants and plaintiffs against Jews in the numerous court records extant from medieval England and other countries.[16]

Understandably, provincial councils responded more directly to local pressures. Following in the footsteps of their Visigothic and Merovingian predecessors, they often betrayed far greater anti-Jewish bias than did the central organs of the Church. In many respects, their utterances and enactments illustrate more clearly changing environmental power constellations than traditional Church policies.

It is not surprising, therefore, that at times Jews looked to the popes for protection against local rulers, particularly bishops subject to direct papal supervision. Jacob bar Yequtiel, a Lotharingian rabbi, appeared as such a delegate of Jewish communities before a pope (Joannes XVIII or Sergius IV, 1007–10). Individuals, too, often sought redress for their private grievances by appealing to Rome. Owing to the progressive feudalization of Europe, loans extended to subjects of another feudal baron frequently proved uncollectible. One of two Jewish creditors, finding that their own ruler had failed to support their claim against a debtor living in a neighboring locality, was said to have journeyed to Rome to secure papal intervention with the debtor's master, probably a bishop. Far more urgent appeared some direct Jewish intervention before the meeting of the Second or Third Lateran Council.[17]

The growing stability and power of the Church also found expression in the codification of canon law. Begun in ancient times under Jewish influence in such collections as the *Didaché* and the Apostolic Canons, this process led to a number of medieval summaries like the *Collectio veterum canonum ecclesiae hispanae* (*Hispana*), which influenced all canon law in the western lands. Although a private collection which included a number of non-Spanish canons, it lent considerable weight to the resolutions of the Toledan councils of the Visigothic age. In this way the growingly anti-Jewish sentiments of the seventh-century Spanish Church permeated the teachings of canon jurists all over Europe, far beyond the role played by the Spaniards before the *reconquista* in the entire structure of the Roman Church. Since the Merovingian councils were only a shade less unfriendly to Jews, a collection of their enactments concerning Jewish status must likewise have underscored their anti-Jewish animus. This was undoubtedly the tenor of a compilation prepared by Agobard for Louis the Pious in 826–27. Charles the Bald was under even greater ecclesiastical pressure when in 845 he was formally presented by the important Council of Meaux with an anti-Jewish collection of Roman imperial decrees and conciliar canons, including resolutions adopted in Toledo and Laodicaea. Amulo increased that organized pressure by an appeal to the masses (846). Although evidently set aside by the kings, these codifications of anti-Jewish enactments must have continued to agitate the minds of canon jurists in the following generations. On the other hand, we do not know whether Pope Hadrian I fulfilled Charlemagne's request for a general summary of conciliar resolutions. If compiled, such a summary must have placed the Jewish position in a better perspective within the general structure of canon law.[18]

Fortunately for the Jews, the memory of Gregory I's decisions loomed in undiminished brightness in the annals of Church legislation and contributed to the generally more balanced ecclesiastical position. When in 1148 Gratian compiled his *Decretum,* which though likewise the work of an individual author soon achieved the rank of a semiofficial code of canon law, this balance was fully maintained. Calling his comprehensive work the *Concordantia discordantium canonum,* the famous jurist made his way through the bewildering maze of conflicting, often outrightly contradictory, laws enacted by church councils or popes to meet different exigencies of the moment. He achieved it by a process of judicious selection, extensive omission, and reasoning harmonization. For example, in restating the old prohibitions of Jewish ownership of Christian slaves or other forms of control over Christians, Gratian formulated the general principle "that master and serf ought to belong to the same religious persuasion. Hence, if a Jew acquires a Christian slave, he ought to set him free even against his will under the authority of judge or bishop." In support of this view the codifier quoted a letter by Gregory the Great and expatiated on a point enacted at the Twelfth Toledan Council of 681. He used a decision of the Third Council of 589 to document his view that "Jews must not be entrusted with public office through which they might have the opportunity of imposing penalties on Christians." However, he refrained from citing the far harsher canons of other Visigothic councils at the height of their "bigotry"—this word itself perhaps being but a derivative from "Visigoth." Gratian's *Decretum* so effectively eclipsed all previous efforts at codification that it laid the foundations for a new evolution of canon jurisprudence and casuistry. The subsequent collections of "decretals" issued by individual popes and of conciliar canons merely served as its supplements, to form together the comprehensive *Corpus juris canonici,* until its fresh recodification under papal authority in 1918.[19]

In Gratian's *Decretum* the Roman Church consolidated its position and summarized its juridical thinking up to the twelfth century. In essence, however, this entire period from the death of Gregory I to the rise of Innocent III marked but an intermediate stage between the foundations laid for the ancient Church by its apostles, fathers, and early popes, and the more or less definitive formulations of Church doctrines and laws through the great popes, councils, and teachers of the thirteenth through the sixteenth centuries. Only in the powerful imperial regime of Innocent III, the great theological restatement of the religious fundamentals by Thomas Aquinas, the tireless efforts of generations of Dominicans, Franciscans, and Jesuits, and the official reformulation of Church doctrines and rituals at the great Council of Trent, did medieval Catholicism reach the acme of its power and self-realization. This period happened to coincide with the shift of the center of gravity of the Jewish people to the Christian West. With the reintegration of Spain, Portugal, and Sicily into Western Christendom, the Jewish masses living in these countries, which before 1200 easily outnumbered the rest of West European Jewry, again came under the sway of the Church. Achieving ever greater cultural ascendancy over the stagnating Jewries of the Near East, European Jewry now began shaping the destinies of the entire people. Its fascinating, if sometimes tragic, interaction with the Roman Church in the later Middle Ages and early modern times, illumined by a rich flow of documentary evidence, will, when described more extensively in our forthcoming volumes, shed much additional light also on our intermediate period.

ITALY

Papal control extended directly over only the States of the Church, although even there it often had to contend with popular factions within and self-assertive imperial overlordship from without. In the neighboring Italian territories, papal influence varied under individual popes and changing local constellations. On the whole, as in ancient times and in the days of Gregory the Great, most Jewish settlements clustered in the southern sections, and but relatively few Jews established themselves permanently in the northern provinces despite, or rather because of, the speedy rise of the great merchant republics in that area.

Notwithstanding constant changes in imperial control, Sicily and the neighboring parts of the mainland continued to harbor affluent and intellectually advanced communities. An unbroken series of inscriptions in Venosa, in particular, shows the continuity of Jewish life from ancient to medieval times. Jewish influence is attested also by certain incidents, as when Grimoaldo, duke of Benevento, in 793 divorced his sterile wife *more hebraico;* that is, in accordance with Jewish law allowing such divorces after ten years of childless marriage. During the two centuries of Muslim rule, filled though these were with inner dissensions and intermittent warfare, the Jews enjoyed the usual status of *dhimmis* and were drawn into the general orbit of the pulsating economic and intellectual life of the world of Islam. Palermo became the capital of a

Muslim realm, and it assumed many characteristics of an Arab city, with Arabic speech predominating in many streets flanked by typically oriental buildings. Next to Arabic, however, Greek retained widespread currency; Latin was pushed underground, to be revived later by immigrants from the Peninsula. All along, Jews retained their peculiar forms of life, and the Hebrew tongue belonged to the more influential literary and business media. Even later the city custumal of Palermo expressly provided for the full legal validity of Hebrew, as well as of Arabic or Greek, deeds issued by Jewish, Saracen, or Greek notaries.[20]

This situation continued for a while under the Norman domination, especially during the height of its power under Roger II, who had received from the "Jewish" pope, Anacletus II, the resounding sovereignty over "the kingdom of Sicily, Calabria, and Apulia, and the Principate of Capua, with the homage of Naples and the support of the men of Benevento." After 1138 he made peace with Innocent II, but turned against the Byzantine emperor. From a raid on Corfu, Corinth, and Thebes in 1147, his commander George of Antioch, himself a renegade Greek, allegedly brought back "all Jews of that land," including a number of dyers and silk weavers. He thus strengthened the previous foundations for an important Jewish industry in the West. About the same time southern Italian Jewry was reinforced by an influx of Spanish refugees. Attested in Trani in 1144, this immigration must have substantially increased after the Almohade conquest of Spain four years later.[21]

At the end of his life, to be sure, Roger is said to have relinquished many of his secular endeavors, and to have labored with all means to convert Jews and Saracens to the Christian faith. The chronicler Romualdus, however, to whom we owe this information (*Annales,* ed. by W. Arndt, in *MGH,* Scriptores, XIX, 426 f.), evidently tried to exonerate the king from the accusation of excessive secularism. He also sought to put the blame on some of the royal advisers—the invariable expedient of governmental apologists. According to Romualdus, a prominent eunuch, Philipp, "hated the Christians, often associated with pagans [Muslims], entered without invitation God's churches, more frequently visited the synagogues of the evildoers, and gave them oil for their illumination and other necessaries." Clearly, such fraternization, for which

Philipp suffered death by burning, was less popular with the ecclesiastical judges and chroniclers than it was in the upper reaches
of bureaucracy, and probably also among the masses.

Ultimately, under the Hohenstaufen rulers (after 1187), Sicilian
Jewry found itself drawn into the net of far-flung imperial policies,
and was also affected by the gradually crystallizing concept of Jews
as "serfs" of the imperial Chamber. Royal mastery over Jews had
long been an accepted premise of state legislation. Typical of the
recognized freedom of disposal of the royal revenue from Jews
was Roger I's donation in 1090 to the archbishop of Salerno of
"the entire Jewish quarter of this our city of Salerno with all the
Jews living in it now or in the future." In fact, such transfers belong to the earliest records of the Norman administration relating to Sicilian Jewry. One need not imagine, however, that such
sweeping assertions conveyed to contemporaries any idea of outright Jewish serfdom. Even when the brilliant last scion of the
Hohenstaufen dynasty, Frederick II, handed over in 1210 the Jews
of Palermo, together with their courts and their dyeing factory,
to the Church of that city "for ever," he did not mean to entrust
the recipients with the physical possession of Jews, nor did he intend to relinquish the ultimate royal overlordship over them.
Though he repeated the same phrase, "for ever," in another document a year later (evidently the original transfer did not seem
definitive enough), he again donated the Jews to the Church four
years later for a period of six years. Such a gift for a limited time
was more reassuring than an unrestricted donation which enabled
the monarch to interfere immediately in the affairs of his Jewish
"serfs," a technical term occuring for the first time two decades
later in another decree of the same emperor.[22]

In all essentials the legal status of Jews remained unimpaired.
The cities maintained much of their traditional independence,
and, as before, the city custumals, like the *Consuetudines Palermi-
tanae*, affected the local population as much as did the royal legislation. At times the cities' struggle for the preservation of their
traditional rights assumed bizarre forms, as when Palermo provided that kings could not increase the customary taxes of "whores,
both public and private, innkeepers, butchers, and Jews, whether
citizens or foreigners, however ignominious or sordid a life these

may be living." Even the mention of Jewish burghers (*cives*) was not inadvertent. To all intents and purposes, Jews enjoyed a considerable measure of equality with the Christian burghers, although the legislators of both state and cities long endeavored to disqualify Jews, as well as Saracens and heretics, from testifying against Christians. As the Palermitan custumal quaintly argued, "Jews ought to be separated from the community of the faithful because of the false testimony they had presented against Christ." From Muslim times the Norman administration had also inherited the system of special Jewish taxation. Originally imposed on all *dhimmis*, the poll tax remained a permanent source of revenue from Jews, while Christians were speedily exempted. In time this tax lost its personal features, however, and was converted into a regular impost on the Jewish community. Its size bore only a remote resemblance to the rise or fall of the Jewish population. More significantly, in a privilege allegedly granted by Roger II to the city of Messina in 1129 in recognition of its signal services in the campaign against the Saracens, Jews were specifically mentioned as enjoying the same rights and immunities as the Christian burghers. While the text of that privilege was undoubtedly tampered with and extensively interpolated in later years (the present version is indubitably a fabrication of later elders bent upon extending their city's self-government), the section relating to Jews must have been included in the original decree. There certainly was no reason for the Messinians living in the subsequent less tolerant period to enlarge upon the rights of Jews. In any case, even in a city like Capua, with its strong heritage of Byzantine law and culture, the ancestors of the chronicler Aḥimaaz could live a prosperous and socially respected life under both Muslim and Christian domination. One of them, Samuel ben Palṭiel, was entrusted by Capua's Muslim rulers "to supervise their treasury, and to exercise control over their city, ports, and market tolls, as well as over their currency and other governmental revenues." [23]

With the continued flowering of Hebrew literature and science, personally fostered by Roger II and Frederick II, Jews could view the two centuries of Norman and Hohenstaufen rule as but a prolongation of their Golden Age under the Muslim regime. Curiously, the largest concentration of Sicilian Jewry, both in size and in geographic distribution, was to come in the subsequent two centuries under the far less friendly Aragonese domination. During the Norman regime, Jews hardly amounted to 3 percent of the population, although in many cities they exceeded that ratio. In Palermo, where Benjamin found 1,500 Jewish families, in Salerno and Naples with their 600 and 500 families respectively, they may have numbered one tenth or more of all inhabitants. The community of Salerno, in particular, seems to have contributed greatly to the rise of the famous medical school which was vitally to influence the development of European medical science. The figures given here appear modest by modern standards, yet in the aggregate the Jewish population of the Norman kingdom may well have outstripped that of any other Christian country except Spain. The Jews of these three cities and of the important mainland communities of Bari (temporarily interrupted by the city's destruction in 1156), Otranto, Trani, and Capua far overshadowed in economic power and intellectual achievement the rest of Italian Jewry. Together with the smaller southern communities, they comprised the majority of the approximately 40,000 Jews estimated to have lived in Italy during the eleventh and twelfth centuries— about one half of one percent of the population.[24]

Curiously, among the communities visited by Benjamin, that of Amalfi embraced only twenty Jewish families. Although only a shadow of its former self, Amalfi retained enough economic opportunity to have attracted a larger number of Jewish settlers, had the burghers not seen in the Jews unwelcome competitors. Ironically, Amalfitans shared with Jews and Lombards from Bari the questionable distinction of being excluded from Venetian shipping to Byzantium by an edict of emperors Basil II and Constantine VIII in 992. The meaning of this law has often been misunderstood. It may not actually have originated at all from Venetian commercial jealousies, but rather from the wish of the Byzantine administration to restrict to Venetian merchants alone the benefits of the privileged status accorded them by treaty. At the same time, it underscored the inferior competitive position of Jewish traders, who had no political or military means of retaliation.[25]

More directly inspired by Venice's commercial hostility was Doge Petrus II Candiano's effort, in 932, to persuade the German emperor Henry I and the Diet of Erfurt to follow the Byzantine example and force the Jews to adopt Christianity. The less certain we are of the authenticity of Romanos Lekapenos' decree, the more serious appears the doge's intervention. Even more obviously aimed at Jewish competition was his suggestion that the emperor forbid Jews to touch the sign of a cross on any object made of metal or cloth. Though couched in terms of extreme Christian sensitivity, the doge's recommendation could not conceal his intention to place insuperable obstacles in the way of Jewish traders in handling merchandise, which often bore the sign of the cross in its commercial markings. In 945 the republic forbade all its captains to transport Jews or their merchandise in Oriental waters. At the same time, the Venetians themselves seem to have tolerated some Jews in their midst. One of their city's islands still bears the name of Giudecca. First recorded in a document of 1252, this name has long been associated by scholars with an original Jewish settlement included in the city. However, the figure of 1,300 Jews allegedly living there in 1152 is almost certainly a gross exaggeration.[26]

All other contemporary estimates, including the fairly reliable ones given by Benjamin, show that even in the twelfth century there existed only small and struggling Jewish communities north of the Papal States. Jews evidently still suffered from the after-effects of the intolerant enactment of Perctarit in 661, and possibly also from some hostile measures adopted by Emperor Louis II in 855. The following summary of Louis' alleged decree is perfectly plain:

Concerning Jews We ordain that none should remain within the kingdom of Italy beyond the first of October. They should be properly informed that they all must leave before that deadline, and [proceed] wherever they wish with no one interfering. Should any of them be found there after the first of October, he may be seized by any person and brought before Our presence together with all his possessions.

Nevertheless, its authenticity has rightly been questioned. Such a sweeping decree enacted by a powerful emperor for an entire kingdom would certainly have left behind more reliable and detailed traces than this passing mention by an anonymous chronicler. But there must have been sufficient hostility toward Jews in northern Italy to prevent the growth of any community of major size for several centuries. On one occasion Bishop Ratherius of Verona took the initiative in trying to expel the Jews from that city (931–38), applying in practice what Archbishop Frederick of Mayence was authorized to do about the same time.[27]

Even in Lucca, whose famous academy had become the matrix of Jewish learning in France and Germany and where in the 1140's Abraham ibn Ezra had received many an intellectual stimulus for his scientific work, Benjamin found only forty Jewish families two decades later. Neighboring Pisa, one of the great merchant republics of the time, accommodated only half that number. In Genoa, Pisa's great commercial rival, whose population allegedly inhabited "about 10,000 turreted houses for battle in times of strife," the Jewish community, rather substantial before the end of the sixth century, had dwindled to the families of two brothers, apparently recent arrivals from North African Ceuta. But there doubtless were many more Jews among the Oriental merchants, who helped the city carry on its intensive trade with the Levant. Small Jewish settlements were also recorded in Siena, Bologna, Ferrara, and Modena, in Padua, Verona, Mantua, Treviso, and Milan—most of them destined to play major roles in Jewish cultural and economic history in later centuries. Before 1200, however, they were mentioned principally in connection with some such religious controversies as the disputation of Pavia in 774, reported by Alcuin, or the Church Council of Ticino which, in 850, fulminated against the current employment of Jews as toll collectors and even as judges in litigations among Christians of that district. In the unceasing anti-Jewish attacks, included in his book *De qualitatis conjectura* (966), Bishop Ratherius of Verona only reiterated the old arguments of Agobard of Lyons. Yet there must have been enough Jews in Verona at that time to lend some actuality to such fulminations. Even earlier the Jewish religious influence had made itself sufficiently felt, in the northeastern district of Friuli, for a Church council meeting there in 796 to deplore the widespread abstention from work on the Sabbath by local farmers.[28]

Sporadic attempts at total exclusion of Jews are likewise recorded. The Jews of Bologna, then the greatest center of juridical learning, are said to have been formally expelled in 1171. But this decree, if authentic, may never have been carried out. Possibly some Jews had become involved in a local political struggle and suffered reprisals by the victorious party. This had decidedly been the case, for example, in the southern community of Lanciano. There a political upset brought to power in 1156 a rebel party opposed by Jews who had remained loyal to King William I. The ensuing expulsion was not revoked until 1191, when eighty Jewish families were readmitted under clearly defined stipulations. This form of admission by a treaty between the city and a group of Jews, later frequently called *condotta,* was to become very popular in the fourteenth and fifteenth centuries. Its effect was to replace the previous vagueness by clearly defined, but easily revocable, stipulations.[29]

SPANISH SETTLEMENTS

Even more than Italy, Christian Spain was under the influence of confusing cross currents with respect to Jewish status. On the one hand, there was the heritage of the intolerant Christian Roman Empire and the anti-Jewish persecutions during the last century of Visigothic rule. The Visigothic code had retained its validity not only in the few remnants of the country which, because of their inaccessibility in the mountain recesses of the Pyrenees, had retained their independence, but also among the Christian subjects of the Caliphate of Cordova and its successor states. As soon as any additional section of the country was reconquered by the rulers of Navarre or Leon, of Castile, Aragon, or Barcelona, the former Mozarab population became the ruling group and restored much of the Visigothic law and traditions.

On the other hand, the new evolution in the Carolingian Empire exerted a lasting influence also on conditions south of the Pyrenees. Frankish conquerors actively intervened in Spain's international affairs, for a time establishing a regular Hispanic march as a rampart against the Moors. French knights and princesses in the Spanish armies and courts served as a vanguard for the deep penetration of the feudal way of life and feudal institutions. The new equilibrium, however shaky, between the feudal estates was bound to affect deeply the Jewish status. The same is true of the new religious and cultural trends, and especially the movement toward Church reform emanating from Cluny, which were carried into Spain by French or French-trained Spanish churchmen.

Nor were traditions of Muslim rule completely forgotten. At first the economic, cultural, and military superiority of the Muslim regions was so clearly marked that the northern rulers would have had to adopt some administrative and strategic concepts from their Muslim neighbors even if their own "liberated" subjects had not long since become inured to Moorish ways of life, and many of their own advisers had not received earlier training in the Muslim bureaucracy. One need but compare the Christian and Muslim libraries of the tenth century to note the great cultural disparity between the two areas. The former embraced at the most 200 books, whereas the catalogue of the famous Cordovan Library listed some 400,000 volumes. The continued presence of a fairly large and prosperous Muslim population, whether of original Arab, Berber, or native Iberian descent, imposed on the new rulers severe limitations unknown to other Christian monarchs, except the Norman conquerors of Sicily and Naples. The old Visigothic capital of Toledo had been, as E. Lévi-Provençal remarked, "a town of Mozarabs under Islam, [and] was a town of Morescos for quite a long time after its return to Christianity" in 1085. In 1135, Alphonso VII was crowned in Leon in the presence of the king of Navarre, the counts of Toulouse and Barcelona, and some Muslim princes under the high-sounding title of "emperor of Spain and king of the men of the two religions." He was surpassed by Ferdinand III (1217–52), who called himself "king of the three religions," placing Jews on a par with his Christian and Muslim subjects.[30]

As in most other periods of their history, Jews benefited greatly from not being the sole or even the principal minority. In fact, in the constant internal and external struggles, which characterized the northern Christian courts almost as much as those of the southern "petty princes," Jews could be considered the Crown's most reliable allies. They shared neither the Muslims' natural

irredentist leanings, nor the Christian nobles' penchant for joining opposing court factions and hostile neighbors. The same reasons which made Samuel ibn Nagrela more acceptable to the
Berber rulers of Granada than Muslim counselors of Arab descent,
also encouraged many Christian monarchs to employ Jewish agents
in their domestic and foreign affairs. Certainly the personal appearance of able and persuasive envoys from Muslim courts, such
as Ḥisdai ibn Shaprut on his diplomatic mission to Navarre and
Leon, invited emulation. Ḥisdai's medical expertness, too, must
have encouraged not only Queen Tota to look for some gifted
Jewish physician-diplomats.

Equally important were the practical needs of these backward
and depopulated areas. New settlers, and particularly an intelligent and industrious group like the Jews, were an obvious source
of economic and political strength. With the experiences accumulated in the flourishing southern regions, Jews could indeed
pioneer equally well in opening up new lands for agricultural exploitation, as in introducing new methods of industrial production and commercial exchanges. We shall see that, unlike their
coreligionists of other European countries, Spanish Jews permanently remained a highly differentiated economic group. The story
told in the famous *Poem of the Cid,* in which that great national
hero of the Spanish legend (his real name was Roderigo Diaz de
Bivar, about 1040–99) outwitted two Jewish moneylenders of
Burgos, is more descriptive of twelfth-century literary tastes and
folklore than of the true class structure of Spanish Jewry, then or
later. More characteristic were the various localities called *mons
Judaeorum,* or *villa judaica,* and the like, which probably reflected
close Jewish agricultural settlements. As elsewhere, Jews also
proved useful minters. Gold coins produced by one Bonnom ebreo
are recorded in deeds of 1019 and 1030, while a partnership of one
David bar Jacob and two Christians acquired in 1067, for a period
of five years, the silver mint of Barcelona.[31]

One would look in vain, however, for any consistent policy
toward Jews under the resuscitating Christian regimes. In the
welter of battles, court intrigues, and assassinations, in the endless succession of victories and defeats, there emerged an almost
chaotic variation of laws and usages which often defy generaliza-

tion. Apart from royal ordinances, sometimes issued on the spur of the moment, there grew up numerous local customs and observances which, when ultimately codified in one or another formal *fuero* conferred on a city by the monarch, became independent sources of law. Here local and temporary exigencies played an even greater role.

Sometimes Muslim cities surrendering to Christian conquerors concluded formal treaties, akin to those, actual or fictitious, made by the early Muslims with conquered "infidels." Even in their breach these treaties served as another source of existing law. On submitting, for instance, to the occupation of their city by Alphonso I of Navarre in 1115, the Muslims of Tudela stipulated among other matters that Jews not be allowed to exercise control over Moors, to insult them, or to acquire Moorish captives. Similar provisions were inserted in the treaty between Alphonso and the Muslim population of Saragossa in 1118, and in that between Count Ramon Berenger IV of Barcelona and the surrendering Muslims of Tortosa in 1148. On the other hand, in another treaty, simultaneously concluded with the Jews of Tudela in 1115, Alphonso I invited all Jewish refugees to return to the city under favorable conditions which included the prohibition for Muslims and Christians to occupy Jewish houses. This treaty, like the former, evidently composed in both Latin and Arabic though preserved only in Latin copies, appeared so favorable to the Tudelan Jews that they secured its formal confirmation by Charles II of Navarre as late as 1355. In Tortosa, too, the count reassured Jews that they would not be placed under Moorish control. In order to attract new Jewish settlers, he set aside for them a large plot of land for a housing development to accommodate sixty buildings, and assigned to them orchards, vineyards, and olive groves from the properties left behind by Moors. The residential provisions here, as well as in the treaty with Tudelan Jewry, did not mean that Jews had to be enclosed in a ghetto of their own, but rather signified a concession to them that they did not have to tolerate members of other faiths in their midst, unless they so desired.[32]

Stipulations of this kind reflect the mutual hostility among Jews and Muslims, heightened by the Almoravid and Almohade persecutions in the Muslim parts of Spain. Perhaps only Ramon

Berenger IV's resentment of the equal mistreatment of Christians in the Almohade empire made him drop the provision against the appointment of Jewish officials over the Moriscos of Tortosa. Probably in less tense periods there was less mutual hatred. Had not during the earlier Almoravid invasion even some Moorish princes sided with the Christian monarchs, according to Ibn al-Qama, the well-informed Moorish chronicler of Valencia? On the other hand, the growing intolerance of the Muslim regimes heightened the solidarity among their Mozarab and Jewish subjects, which was bound to influence favorably the Judeo-Christian relations in the northern principalities as well. In this respect the ruthless Almohade regime not only forced a great many Jews and Christians to seek refuge in the north, but also helped forge certain fateful links among these refugees themselves and their respective coreligionists in Castile or Aragon.[33]

Not that Jews accustomed to the cultured, if intrinsically corrupt, ways of life in the Muslim south easily decided to settle in the backward northern regions. True, the general feeling of cultural superiority, which had animated such Muslim writers as the Qadhi of Toledo Ibn Sa'id in the tenth century, had gradually receded with the cultural advances of the Spanish Christians in the subsequent two centuries and their gradual absorption of many formerly Moorish areas. Yet, even in the early twelfth century, there must have been many maladjusted Jewish newcomers in the northern communities of the type of the great poet Moses ibn Ezra. Forced to leave his native Granada in 1095, five years after its Almoravid occupation, Ibn Ezra wandered about for forty years (he is recorded to have lived in Saragossa, Barcelona, Portugal, and even remote Estella on the French border), although his brothers Joseph and Isaac seem to have found no difficulty in reestablishing their shattered fortunes in Toledo. During these four decades Moses complained unceasingly of his fate, which "at the end of my days had thrown me into a strange and distant land, and I feel like a prisoner in jail, or like one put away in a grave." His undying nostalgia for the old life in Granada permeated many of his immortal poems. In one he sang:

> How far must my feet, at Fate's behest,
> Bear me o'er exile's path, and find no rest?

Oh, if indeed, the Lord would me restore
To beautiful Granada-land, my paths
Would be the paths of pleasantness once more;
For in that land my life was very sweet—
A kindly Fate laid homage to my feet,
And deep I quaffed at Friendship's fount; . . .
Though hope be long deferred, though heart be faint,
  On God I wait,
Unto whose mercy there is no restraint—
  And whose decree
Can break the shackles and unbar the gate,
And set the prisoner of exile free.

In these complaints he was encouraged by his younger friend, Yehudah Halevi who, although himself a native of Toledo (or Tudela) and a resident of Christian Spain in his youth, returned there only reluctantly for a brief sojourn in later years.[34]

In the course of the twelfth century, however, Christian Spain made remarkable progress in all domains of cultural life, while Muslim areas were suffocating under Almohade totalitarianism. There even the orthodox writings by Al-Ghazali were publicly burned, merely because the great thinker had dared to attack the ecclesiastical spokesmen of the Mosque. For these and other reasons, even before the great *reconquista* of the thirteenth century, the Jewish center of gravity was constantly moving into the northern sections.

Awakened scientific curiosity among the ruling circles of Christian Spain made even ecclesiastical leaders more amenable to the influx of Jewish settlers of Ibn Ezra's type. In the twelfth century Spanish Jews began playing a significant role as transmitters of Eastern science and philosophy. They were particularly active in the prodigious work of translation into Latin of Arabic classics, whether original or mere renditions from the Greek or Syriac. It is small wonder, then, that Archbishop Raymond of Toledo (1126–51), one of the leading patrons of learning in his day, assembled around him a band of translators, which included at least such baptized Jews as John Avendeath (Ibn Daud). In the privilege he granted to the town of Alcala de Henares he specifically provided that "every Jew who may wish to reside in Alcala and its vicinity, may do so; while any one not desiring to stay, shall proceed with good luck wherever he pleases." [35]

Numerical growth and cultural advances of Spanish Jews and Christians accounted also for the ever increasing flow of records relating to all phases of Jewish life. Until the beginning of the eleventh century we are often limited to the stray information yielded by occasional epitaphs. Some inscriptions, probably dating in part from the tenth century, have been discovered in the vicinity of La Palloza, along a river traditionally called Arroyo de los Judíos, and particularly in the Montjuich cemetery of Barcelona. Many can only approximately be dated from the much-disputed Hebrew palaeographic evidence. We are on safer ground with the epitaph commemorating the death of one Mar Jacob ben R. Isaac ibn Qutb, assassinated in Sahagun in 1026, and that from 1100 of one Joseph, son of 'Aziz, a bronze worker; both were found in Puente del Castro in Leon. Of course, inscriptions furnish as a rule only names of persons and, occasionally, glimpses of the religious beliefs of survivors. Unlike the ancient inscriptions in Roman catacombs and elsewhere, they are rarely adorned by Jewish religious symbols. Even those who disagree with the extreme interpretations suggested by E. R. Goodenough for these ancient symbols, will concede the over-all importance of this material, which is sadly lacking in most medieval tombs. Certainly, the few verbal references to resurrection and the messianic hope merely document doctrinal stereotypes of the Jewish faith.[36]

On the other hand, the cemetery of Montjuich has preserved a number of skeletons which lend themselves to anthropological exploration. While some of the 171 graves uncovered in 1945 undoubtedly stem from a period closer to 1391, when the Jewish necropolis went into disuse, a few doubtless go back to the eleventh and twelfth centuries. Neither the age and sex distribution of the 114 corpses heretofore recovered (there were 57 adult males, 33 females, and 24 minors), nor their cranial and other measurements, for the most part resembling the so-called Mediterranean type, are in any way conclusive. Yet they offer rare material for the investigation of some socially significant phases of medieval Jewish life.[37]

Somewhat more informative are a number of extant governmental and private documents. A letter addressed by Charles the Bald to Barcelona in 876–77 informed the city that he had heard from a Jew, Judah, about its inhabitants' loyalty to him. In an autograph postscript the emperor also told the bishop of Barcelona that he was transmitting, through Judah, ten pounds of silver for the repair of the local church. From that time Barcelona remained a major center of Jewish life, maintaining its position of leadership to the catastrophic year of 1391, and in part to the expulsion of 1492. A considerable number of Hebrew deeds, still extant, testify to its Jewry's economic vigor and fine legal discernment. Not by mere coincidence, a Barcelona rabbi of the eleventh century, Yehudah bar Barzillai, produced a "Book of Deeds," long recognized as a classic in its field. On the other hand, there is decided exaggeration in the assertion of the Arab chronicler, Ibn 'Abd al-Mum'in al-Ḥimyari, that in his day (eleventh century) there were as many Jews as Christians in Barcelona. An extant list of householders of 1079 records only some sixty Jewish names. But the intellectual life of the community seems to have been vigorous enough even earlier for it to maintain direct relations with the great academies in Babylonia.[38]

During all that time the Barcelona community suffered from recurrent warfare. After a temporary Moorish occupation in 985, a sufficient number of Jews was victimized in neighboring Mogoria for the count to sell their landed property fifteen years later. These Jews may have left no heirs behind, and the count exercised his right of eminent domain without regard to possible claims of the Jewish community. Perhaps these particular victims had been accused, rightly or wrongly, of conspiring with the Arab invaders —just as other Jews had been accused of complicity with Moorish raiders in 850—and the count had confiscated their property. Some Jews also became involved in such court intrigues as the romance of Raymond, son of Count Berenger, with a Narbonese woman (1054–55). Similarly exposed to invasions and concomitant suspicions were the Jews of such other frontier communities as neighboring Tarragona, which in 1152 the great geographer Idrisi called a "Jewish city," undoubtedly with much exaggeration.[39]

At one time or another almost all Spanish and Portuguese cities were frontier communities, and the settlement of Jews in what had largely become underpopulated, if not empty, spaces appeared desirable to their rulers on strategic as well as economic grounds. The first record relating to the Jews of Portugal, dating back to 900, already mentions vineyards, owned still earlier by Jews in Coimbra. That district had been reconquered by Alphonso III the Great of Leon (866–910), in whose earlier possessions, too, Jews constantly increased in number.[40]

Internal security also left much to be desired. Apart from factional strife, there was much highway robbery, as well as pillage and murder in the cities, which the weak feudal regimes were unable to prevent. Because of their religious disparity, Jews were choice targets for attack. That is why one of the earliest recorded privileges of Castilian Jewry, that granted to the city of Castrojeriz in 974 by Count Garcia Fernandez, provided that the penalty for the assassination of a Jew should equal that for the murder of a Christian. This sanction did not prevent the burghers of that city, after the death of Sancho the Great in 1035, from attacking neighboring Mercatello, killing sixty Jews along with four royal guards, and forcing the other Jews to remove to their city. Other decrees, too, often set the *wergeld* for Jews quite high, although not always on a par with that of Christians, who, moreover, often varied among themselves according to their corporate status.[41]

Self-help often proved more effective. Sometimes Jews settled in fortified quarters, called *castra Judaeorum*. A communal ordinance in the community of Estella, still recorded in the late thirteenth century in one of Ibn Adret's responsa, forbade the weakening of the walls. Such voluntary ghettos—Christians, too, for example in Jacca in 1063, were sometimes assigned separate quarters by their own rulers—did not prevent mass attacks upon Jews. But they undoubtedly gave their inhabitants a greater sense of security, and an opportunity to stave off minor attacks. The defensive character of the Jewish quarter is emphasized also in the provision inserted by Sancho VII the Wise of Navarra into his privilege for Tudela Jewry of 1170. After the removal of the Jews into the castle the king wrote: "If, however, perchance some one should invade and attack you in that castle, and as a result some persons should be hurt or killed, the Jews should not for that reason be accused of homicide nor pay damages, whether [the incident] happens in day time or at night." [42]

Jews were often called upon to defend their quarters also against foreign invaders. At times, they seem to have enlisted in regular armed forces under their own banners. The oft-repeated legend of their participation at the great battle of Zalaqa in 1086 with a force of 40,000 soldiers, as well as the derivative legend about the surrender of a Jewish wing in the subsequent battle of Ucles (1109), are undoubtedly grossly exaggerated. But they reflect the historic reality of the active participation of Spanish Jewry in their countries' wars. This phenomenon deeply impressed even foreign Jews, and the twelfth-century German rabbi Eliezer bar Joel ha-Levi tersely observed, "it still is a general practice in Spain for the Jews to go out to war together with the king." This statement was repeated verbatim a century later by Isaac Or Zaru'a of Vienna.[43]

ROYAL ALLIANCE

Such military and economic power was put to good use by the rulers who increasingly considered the Jews their special preserve. Many Jewish fiscal and diplomatic advisers, especially, began serving Christian masters, as they had long served Muslim overlords. Alphonso VI, the conqueror of Toledo, employed his personal physician, Joseph ibn Ferrizuel (Cidellus), and the latter's nephew, Solomon ibn Ferrizuel, in many important domestic and international negotiations. The more frequent and intimate the relations with the neighboring Moorish states became, the greater were the services Jewish officials could render through their intimate knowledge of the Arabic language and diplomacy and their familiarity with the internal conditions in these principalities.[44]

Even the mere command of the intricate Arabic epistolary style and a beautiful Arabic handwriting served these royal counselors in good stead, as it did their counterparts at Muslim courts. Yehudah ibn Tibbon advised his son to study Arabic calligraphy and pointed not only to the example of Samuel ibn Nagrela in Granada, but also to that of Sheshet bar Solomon Perfet (Profet) who earlier in the twelfth century had successfully served as *alfaquim* (secre-

tary-interpreter) of Count Ramon Berenger III of Barcelona.
"By means of it [Arabic]," Ibn Tibbon observed, "he [Sheshet]
paid his debts, met all his large expenses, and made charitable gifts." Sheshet, his sons (especially Saltiel), and other members of his family are indeed recorded in many contemporary
public and private transactions. At times monarchs and Jews
entered business partnerships, as when Ramon Berenger IV gave
his Jewish court physician, Abraham, the right to erect jointly
with him the only public baths in Barcelona, in return for a permanent share of one third of its revenues. This bathhouse remained
in the possession of Abraham's family for almost forty years
(1160–99). Even the Knights Templar, who had come to Spain
animated with the crusading spirit against infidels, employed Jewish officials. In the city of Lerida, jointly controlled by them and
the counts of Barcelona, the Jewish community had to give up its
synagogue, converted into a church in 1173. But a Jewish "bailiff,"
Jafia ben David of Monzon, often figured in official documents, in
part connected with the redistribution of land made necessary
by the transition from Muslim to Christian rule. Apparently because of his expert knowledge of land measurements and surveying, the famous Jewish mathematician and astronomer Abraham
bar Ḥiyya likewise served in an official capacity, although his title
saḥib ash-shurta more generally designated a combination of police commissioner and district attorney. On the distaff side we
hear of a Jewish mistress of the powerful King Alphonso VIII of
Castile (1158–1214). According to his grand-nephew, Alphonso X,
author of the *Estoria de Espanna,* the king became so infatuated
with Fermosa (Raquel) that for nearly seven years he completely
neglected his wife, Leonora of Acquitaine, daughter of Henry II
of England, "and paid no heed to the government or any other
matter." [45]

Understandably, the position of Jewish dignitaries created considerable resentment among the Christian churchmen. Doubtless
it was on their initiative that Gregory VII, as we recall, sternly
warned Alphonso VI against the employment of Jews in positions
of power—to no avail. On their part, the masses lent a willing ear
to rumor mongers who revived the old accusation of Jews conspiring with Muslim enemies abroad. Buttressed by memories of the

original Muslim invasion of the Peninsula, such an accusation appeared doubly credible, as Christian princes and grandees often allied themselves with Muslim rulers to combat foreign or domestic coreligionists. After the death of Alphonso VI in 1109, serious anti-Jewish riots spread from Toledo to many communities of Castile and Leon. Cidellus himself seems to have been affected by these disturbances, and especially by the miscarriage of a court cabal relating to the marriage of Alphonso's daughter, Urraca, in which he had actively participated. But when that princess ascended the throne he was again mentioned in a prominent capacity in a document of 1110.[46]

Nor was the rise of a few individuals to power necessarily beneficial to the Jewish community as a whole. True, the rulers' self-interest in attracting Jews was heightened by the services rendered by these Jewish advisers. Maintaining close social contacts with Christian nobles and patricians, Jewish officials, businessmen, and landowners often helped to dispel suspicions nurtured by the Jews' religious disparity and different mode of life. Jewish grandees were also extremely important in patronizing Jewish men of letters and promoting the spread of Jewish culture. As in the south, much of Jewish poetry assumed the character of "court poetry." Without that type of patronage the Golden Age of Spanish Jewry could hardly have been achieved in Muslim Spain, and still less could it have been maintained on the same high level in the more barbarous northern environment. Strong communal controls, buttressed by the influence of these councilors at royal courts, also helped to foster communal unity. Because of the power wielded by Jewish dignitaries for three successive generations, Spanish Jewry staved off those deep internal cleavages which had been occasioned by the spread of the Karaite sect in the Arab Near East and Byzantium.[47]

On the other hand, these very factors also tended to lend undue preeminence to certain individuals in communal affairs, doubly irksome when royal favorites secured from the kings special tax immunities, relieving them and their children from their share in communal taxation. At times the community actually had to make regular payments, in cash or in kind, to powerful and well-connected families. For instance, two pounds of meat had to be delivered daily from the Jewish slaughterhouse in Saragossa to Alaçar, the financial manager of the royal household (1135). Only after a protracted struggle did the community of Huesca in Aragon secure from Pedro II in 1212 a decree abolishing all tax exemptions, as well as transfers of revenue from individual Jewish taxpayers to churches, and restoring this much-needed income to the communal treasury. The king even forbade future attempts by influential Jews to secure immunities of this kind, allowing the community to excommunicate and stone the culprits. Only in the case of stoning did the community have to pay 1,000 solidi to the king as an indemnity for the loss of a taxpayer.[48]

We must bear in mind, however, that the very text of the Alaçar privilege indicates that even before 1135 he had been collecting the two pounds of meat daily from the Jewish slaughterhouse, probably as a voluntary contribution from the community. Similarly, in his decree of 1212 Pedro also had to annul tax exemptions previously granted to Jewish individuals by their own community. Evidently Jewish communal leadership itself could not resist the prevailing trend toward special privilege for individuals and groups.

State treasuries had long been accustomed to receive indemnities for the murder of a Jew. Apart from the inequalities in the amount of the *wergeld*, there was a difference in regard to its recipients. According to the *Fuero* of Sepulveda, a Jewish murderer of a Christian was to be executed and his property confiscated; one third each was the share of the family, the king and judge, and the alcalde. A Christian killer of a Jew had to pay out 100 maravedis to be distributed in the same way. This distribution was unusual. In most local laws the Christian victim's family received all, or at least half, the fine, the other half going to the Treasury; in the case of Jews the king was the sole beneficiary. We need not see therein a conscious attempt at lowering the dignity of Jews. On the contrary, this arrangement may have met with Jewish approval, since the effectiveness of royal protection of life and limb increased with the fine the rulers expected to collect for each slain Jew. Of course, in moments of mass frenzy even these devices proved of little avail. Eighteen years after the massacre and pillage of 1109, Alphonso VII was forced to issue a general amnesty for the perpetrators of these crimes, as well as for the arsonists who had burned and plundered of their furnishings the royal palaces in Saldaña, Cea, Carrion, Valle de Anebra, and the neighboring communities. Even earlier, in the new privilege granted to the Mozarabs, Castilians, and Franks of Toledo in 1118, the king also specifically "forgave them all sins" they had committed by the slaying of Jews and the appropriation of Jewish possessions. Perhaps because of the recurrence of violent attacks on the relatively defenseless Jews as well as the burghers, Pedro II of Aragon included them all, together with their possessions, in the royal truce he proclaimed in 1199.[49]

The Toledan privilege of 1118 illustrates the king's equal concern for the protection of all subjects. Protection of Jews against individual assaults was doubly imperative, as, apart from the general insecurity of life in the Middle Ages, they had already encountered considerable animosity among Christian fellow sufferers under Muslim domination. The Coimbra monk, Theophilo, had not been alone in refusing, as we recall, to exchange greetings with them. The rulers were doubly obliged now forcefully to maintain public order in the midst of the aroused passions of the age of Crusades. The Toledo decree provided, therefore, that within the confines of the city and in a radius of five miles around it the murderer of any person was "to die a most heinous death by stoning." Because of the prevailing feeling for communal responsibility, entire cities were often held responsible when the slayers of a Jew remained undetected, just as Jewish communities were collectively held responsible for the *wergeld* owed a Christian family by a Jewish criminal. If in some local laws Jewish parties were either disqualified from settling legal disputes by resort to the ordeal of dueling, or else forced to send Christian substitutes, the reason was neither an alleged Jewish inferiority in combat, nor a studied attempt at lowering Jewish prestige, but rather the recognition that such an ordeal might cast reflection on the Christian religion. The underlying conception of these ordeals was that God would help the righteous fighter, even if he happened to be physically weaker. But in the case of a duel between members of different faiths, the combat might assume the character of a battle between opposing deities. The victory of a Jewish combatant could be interpreted by naive onlookers as that of his Jewish God.[50]

Along with many other aspects of feudal life, Teuton legal concepts and procedures penetrated the Iberian Peninsula under the combined impact of the Visigothic heritage and the neighboring Carolingian Empire. Among these novel feudal concepts was also that of royal control over Jews, not in the sense of Jewish servitude, long proclaimed by the Seventeenth Toledan Council in consonance with old patristic doctrines (694), but rather in the favorable meaning of the special protection extended by the royal power to its Jewish clients. The full implications and manifold ramifications of this complex institution will become clearer in connection with its later historic evolution in the countries north of the Pyrenees. But one of its early clean-cut formulations in Spain unmistakably carried this positive connotation. In the famous *Fuero* of Teruel of 1176, which was soon thereafter imitated in Cuenca (1190–91) and many other Spanish cities, the legislator tried to justify the Treasury's collection of Jewish *wergeld* by stating succinctly: "For the Jews are serfs of the king, and always assigned to the royal *fiscus*." [51]

Otherwise, too, the legislators made an overt endeavor to place the relations between Jews and Christians on the foundations of justice and fairness, at least in so far as this was possible in the religiously overcharged medieval environment. As time went on and the reconquest of the Peninsula progressed, there was growing liberalization of the laws. Even two of the three crucial paragraphs included in the original custumal (*Usatges*) of Barcelona (1053–71) evinced a desire to secure fair procedural rights for Jewish litigants. They provided that:

Jews hurt or wounded, captured, enfeebled or even slain should be paid for at the discretion of the authorities [Art. 11].

Jews shall take an oath for Christians; Christians, however, shall never swear for Jews [Art. 51].

. . . if a litigation should arise between Christians and Jews, two witnesses shall suffice for either side to prove their contention, namely one Christian and one Jew. This shall be done in the following fashion: if the evidence favors the Christians, both witnesses shall testify, and the Jewish party shall take an oath, but if it favors Jews, both witnesses shall similarly testify and the Christian party shall take the oath [Art. 129].

Some scholars have viewed the first provision as a declaration of Jewish rightlessness, whereas it connoted only the withdrawal of assaults on Jews from the city's jurisdiction. The sovereign alone was to set the penalties on crimes against Jews. On the other hand, the extremely long formula of the oath *more judaico* (Art. 171) is an obviously late insertion, probably dating from 1241.[52]

Even more outspoken was Ramon Berenger IV's aforementioned privilege in favor of the city of Daroca (1142). It succinctly stated that "Christians, Jews, and Saracens shall have the same legal procedure [*forum*] in assaults and criminal prosecutions [*calumniis*]." Elsewhere the specific regulations differed in accordance with local traditions, temporary exigencies, and changing constellations of power. On the whole, kings tried to enlarge upon the rights of their Jewish protégés, while the burghers attempted to assert their own superiority and local controls.

Remarkably, by contrast with the Visigothic period, the Church was rather inactive in these political and legal controversies. At times even papal proddings proved to no avail. Within half a century after the Muslim occupation, Pope Stephen III (IV, 768–72) expressed to the bishops of Spain and Septimania his deep regrets over the numerous acquisitions by Jews of urban and rural estates and the extensive employment thereon of Christian workers. Later on, during the expansion of Christian rule, the Spanish Church actively collaborated with both princes and Jews in the common task of the economic upbuilding of the country. Occasionally, as a result of internal strife, churchmen had to turn to Jews for help. In his letter to the bishops of Leon of 1199, Innocent III himself bitterly complained of the effects of his interdict which had forced the local clergy "not only to beg, but even to do menial labor and serve the Jews, to the shame of the Church." Finally, in 1205, Innocent threatened Alphonso VIII of Castile with dire ecclesiastical punishments if he continued to allow Jews to expand their possessions, and to force the Church to redeem Saracen slaves of Jews turning Christian at prices far in excess of the canonically prescribed fees. The outcome, according to the pope, was that "while the Synagogue grows in power, the Church becomes weaker." [53]

Generally, the Spanish Church sought to influence only the legislation relating to its own interests. Ever since the Council of Elvira, the problem of segregating Christians from Jews loomed large in the minds of ecclesiastical leaders. The Church had indeed every reason to fear imitation of Jewish ways of life by the then economically and culturally backward Christian masses. The important Castilian Council of Coyanza (Oviedo) of 1050 legislated, therefore, that no Christian should live in a house, or partake of a meal, with Jews. On the other hand, the heads of the Spanish Church were praised by Alexander II for their effective defense of Jews against Spanish crusaders (1063). The Church Council of Gerona in 1068 referred only to the obligation of Jewish landowners to pay the ecclesiastical tithes, "for it is unjust that the Church should lose these tithes, it being manifest that it had owned them before the arrival of Jews here." Ten years later another Council, likewise meeting in Gerona, repeated that injunction, only adding a few harsh words about "the infidel Jews' execrable ferocity [saevitia]." In contrast to this reticence of canon jurists, the *fueros* in both Aragon and Castile constantly elaborated the provisions concerning Jews, thus reflecting the latter's growing role in the economic and social life of the country from the twelfth century on.[54]

THE CAROLINGIAN EMPIRE

While Spanish Jewry was thus gradually transferring its center of activity to northern Spain and Portugal and implanting Sephardic Judaism with its immemorial Eastern connections in a Western Christian environment, Jews north of the Pyrenees slowly developed new cultural patterns of their own. Largely isolated from the great Eastern centers and forced to rely on their own religious and intellectual resources, the Ashkenazic Jews of France, Germany, and England continued on a new creative plane the life of the ancient Roman dispersion. This evolution was facilitated by the great Carolingian Renaissance. Through the efforts of Odo of Aquitaine and Charles Martell of Austrasia (721–37), the Franks successfully contained the Moorish expansion. Although Saracen raids continued for several decades thereafter, the Carolingians now went over to the offensive and, before long, incorporated formerly Visigothic and Moorish Septimania and Catalonia into their own possessions. In the century following Pepin's coronation in 751 the Carolingian Empire extended from the English Channel and the Atlantic to the Adriatic, and from the Oder to the Ebro. Although broken up in the Peace Treaty of Verdun in 843, it, like the Caliphate, left a permanent imprint on its successor states. From the standpoint of Jewish history, too, the institutions developed under Charlemagne and Louis the Pious, in however tentative and fragmentary a fashion, largely survived the subsequent political divisions and decisively shaped the later destinies of European Jewry.

Pirenne's long-debated theories concerning the impact of the rise and expansion of Islam on the European evolution may have been greatly modified by more recent investigations. Yet there is no question that the separation between the Muslim and Christian worlds was even more sharply felt in the West than in the Byzantine Empire. With the Mediterranean littoral largely under Muslim control, and with navigation greatly impeded by mutually hostile and piratical navies and merchant marines, the importance of inland communications increased rapidly. This transition greatly facilitated the shift of both commerce and culture to the newly developing urban centers along the northern waterways and land routes. At the same time the need for maintaining at least minimal contacts with the Mediterranean world fostered the entry of a great many Jews. We shall see how, as a result of the two-world system, Jews gradually displaced the Christian Syrians as the main commercial mediators between East and West.[55]

Unfortunately, the extant sources furnish few illustrations of Jewish contributions to the intellectual phases of the Carolingian Renaissance. Certainly the great period of Jewish intellectual mediation between East and West was to come only in the twelfth and thirteenth centuries. However, Raban Maur recorded his consultations with a Jewish expert in the Law while preparing his biblical commentaries. Among the numerous Jewish merchants in "spices" doubtless there were also some distributors of new oriental drugs and medicines. We shall see that the occasional abuses which crept into this branch of trade soon induced Shabbetai Donnolo to compose an important treatise on drugs. When sometime between 792 and 796 Alcuin sent a *negotiator* to make purchases for him in Italy, he undoubtedly included orders for manuscripts from this older center of civilization. There is no reason for assuming that Jews failed to participate in this significant and profitable branch of business.[56]

Symbolic of this new world status was the role played by the Jew Isaac in the renowned embassy sent by Charlemagne to Harun ar-Rashid in 797. The Frankish king, who was soon to be crowned Holy Roman Emperor, doubtless anticipated serious objections from the Byzantine successors of the ancient Caesars, and he tried to secure some understanding with the caliph, Byzantium's hereditary enemy. He readily overlooked the religious disparity and entrusted to a Jew, together with two Christian nobles, the delicate task of traveling to Baghdad and negotiating there a treaty of friendship with the spiritual as well as political head of the rivaling faith. Among the Franks but few could match the Jew's knowledge of conditions in foreign countries, or even of the complex methods of travel, to avoid the pitfalls of both Mediterranean piracy and Byzantine interception. One such Jew, who had "frequently visited" Palestine, was used by Charlemagne personally to play a trick on the vain and credulous Archbishop Richulf of Mayence. It happened that the two Frankish noblemen died on the journey, while Isaac returned home in 802, bearing precious gifts from Baghdad and Jerusalem. Even if we discount any of the purported commitments by the caliph, the Jewish messenger's mission in the Orient seems to have set in motion forces which, in the long run, led to French involvement in the affairs of the Holy Land and the Near Eastern Latin Christians.[57]

Among the caliph's gifts was, according to legend, a Babylonian scholar, Makhir, who established a famous Jewish academy in Narbonne, subsequently the fountainhead of much French-Jewish scholarship. Although there is no reason to doubt the presence of a Baghdad Jew in Isaac's entourage, this story has become imbedded in various confused accounts concerning the growth of the important community of Narbonne which cast a shadow on its veracity. Having played a certain role in Visigothic times when the city had often served as the royal capital, the Jewish population of Narbonne must have increased considerably during the brief Moorish occupation (720–59). It became a factor in the city's surrender to the Franks. The fullest description of that surrender, offered by "Philomena," has long intrigued scholars. Because of its late date (it was probably composed early in the thirteenth century) and its obvious romanticizing features, its historical credibility has rightly been questioned. On the other hand, it shows excellent familiarity with the general topography of Narbonne and its Jewish quarter, and it evidently includes genuine historical recollections. Unfortunately, the paucity of other pertinent sources does not allow us completely to disentangle the true facts from the fictional strains.[58]

Of particular importance is the story of negotiations between "Charlemagne" and a Jewish delegation, headed by one Isaac, and of the final terms agreed upon and proclaimed by the new rulers. Having reached the conclusion that their city could no longer hold out, we are told, and yet unable to persuade the Saracen "King" Matrand to give up the struggle, the Jewish leaders addressed themselves to the French commander, promised him to let him enter through their section of the city's fortifications, and stated:

Sire, do not believe that we are committing treason. For Matrand has no power over us, nor do we hold anything from him except that, in return for the protection he extends to us, we are paying him a certain sum annually. Besides, we ask you that there should always be in Narbonne a king of our nation, because there ought to be one in the future, just as there is one today. It is on his order that we have come to you; he is of the family of David hailing from Baghdad.

The Frankish ruler is said to have acceded to this demand and, after the conquest, assigned one third of the city to the count, one third to the archbishop, and one third to the Jews under their own "king." We need not take literally speeches ascribed to various historical personalities even in authentic medieval historical works, yet it does appear that the Narbonne Jews considered their status as "protected subjects" under Islam as a contractual agreement which could be terminated by either party. They seem to have joined the Goths in delivering the city to the Franks, and to have obtained in return a promise of full autonomy under their own *nasi* (prince). Later generations, evidently confusing three historically independent events, namely Charlemagne's transfer of a member of the Kalonymide family from Lucca to Mayence, the arrival in Spain (about 772) of the exiled prince of captivity, Natronai bar Habibai (he was a scion of the house of David from Baghdad), and Makhir's settlement in France in 802, connected them all with the Frankish conquest and sincerely believed in the Davidic descent of the Narbonne *nasi*. Still another legend combined the self-sacrificing rescue of Emperor Otto II by a Jew with the conquest of Narbonne. Four centuries later Benjamin still encountered there a leader named Kalonymos, son of the *nasi* Todros, "of the seed of David, whose pedigree is established. He possesses hereditaments and lands given him by the ruler of the city, of which no man can forcibly deprive him." [59]

Concessions of that magnitude naturally enough alarmed the Church. Its fears were nurtured by the recollection, doubtless kept alive by the writings of Archbishop Julian of Toledo, of the short-lived revolt against the Visigothic King Wamba in 673, during which many Christians in Gallia Narbonensis had converted themselves to Judaism. The cosmopolitan character of the population, moreover, consisting of Gallo-Romans, Visigoths, Greeks, and Italians, as well as Saracens and Jews, militated against all segregationist efforts. Understandably, therefore, Pope Stephen III (IV) became "frightened to death" by various reports from Narbonne's Bishop Aribert about the new regime. Unable to protest against the general political and military arrangements made by Pepin, the Papacy's great protector against the Langobards, the pope, apparently writing in 769 at the Narbonne episcopate's instigation, concentrated his shafts on certain practices which had traditionally been condemned by the Church. In his letter to Aribert (or Daniel) and other prelates of Septimania and the Spanish March, he therefore deplored the fact that "the Jewish mob, always rebellious against God and derogatory of our ceremonies," was allowed to own hereditary *allodia* in villages and suburbs, employ thereon Christian workers, and live in the cities together with Christian men and women, who were thus exposed "day and night to their blasphemous speeches." [60]

The papal protest remained without effect. Narbonne became a great center of Jewish learning, from which, as Benjamin was to observe, the Torah went out to all countries. In Benjamin's day, in fact, a Narbonne ordinance concerning the return of a dowry to the family of a wife who died without issue within a year after her marriage served as the model for a resolution adopted by the distinguished northern synod which met at Troyes with Jacob Tam as its leader (1160). Other of the southern communities including Marseilles, Arles, and Montpellier, joined Narbonne in assuming the burden of cultural leadership for European Jewry. Lunel allegedly had a predominantly Jewish population. This assertion is probably no more exaggerated here than in some Spanish cities, for Lunel's Jewish inhabitants, who because of the equation between *luna* and *yerah* (moon) were often surnamed *yarhi*, amounted to some 300 families in the days of Benjamin. If we accept the latter figure, the Jews may indeed have amounted to half the population. Only thus can we understand Benjamin's other statement that "students that come from distant lands to learn the Law [there] are taught, boarded, lodged, and clothed by the congregation so long as they attend the house of study." [61]

These southern communities' economic and cultural standing within the Empire seems also to have influenced favorably the Carolingian rulers' attitude toward other Frankish Jews. In their effort to foster the economy of their far-flung dominions, and especially to promote the much-needed importation of advanced industrial products from abroad, Charlemagne and Louis the Pious made a special effort to attract Jewish traders to their northern French and German possessions. The texts of only three charters, issued by Louis some time before 825, have come down to us; they had been granted to (1) Rabbi Donatus and his nephew Samuel; (2) David, Joseph, and their associates in Lyons; and (3) Abraham of Saragossa. But doubtless many more privileges had been issued to other individuals and groups. Their contents and phrasing had become so standardized that we owe the preservation of our three texts, which are largely repetitious of one another, to their inclusion by later jurists among collections of Carolingian formularies.[62]

Among their most important provisions was the promise of imperial protection for the lives, limbs, and property of the beneficiaries. In one charter the emperor specifically prescribed the high fine of ten gold pounds for the slaying of a Jew, or even the mere incitation thereto. Jews were allowed undisturbedly to own slaves and to import them from abroad, but not to sell them to foreign countries. Attempts at converting such slaves to Christianity were severely discouraged. At the same time, contrary to ecclesiastical demands, Jews were allowed to employ free Christians. Christian plaintiffs against Jews had to produce three Jewish as well as three Christian witnesses, just as Jewish plaintiffs had to be supported by three Christian witnesses. Jews could not be subjected to the ordeals of fire or scalding water, nor punished by flogging, unless one could prove that these procedures were permissible "according to their own law." These provisions were supplemented by such specific enactments as that relating to Jewish oaths, issued by Charlemagne himself. Here the Jew was told to hold the five books of Moses in Hebrew or, when unavailable, in Latin, and to swear, "So may God help me, the same God who gave the Law to Moses on Mount Sinai, and may the leprosy of Naaman the Syrian not afflict me as it afflicted him, and may the earth not swallow me as it swallowed Dathan and Abiram. [I swear that] I have committed no wrong against thee in this matter." [63]

In these Carolingian charters and decrees, the effective application of which was entrusted to a special high official called *magister judaeorum,* was adumbrated the entire legal status of Jews in medieval France, Germany, and England. We have noticed repercussions of these legal concepts and procedures even in those parts of northern Spain and Norman Italy which had never been occupied by Carolingian troops. Directly or indirectly, Carolingian institutions deeply pervaded all of European feudalism.[64]

These early Carolingian Jewish charters were already deeply colored by feudal concepts. In his charter addressed to Abraham of Saragossa, Louis clearly stated that Abraham "had entrusted himself [*se commendavit*] unto Our hands, and after an oath We have received and hold him under Our protection." In other words, through handshake and oath, Abraham assumed the character of a royal vassal. Since the formula of the oath of fidelity had not yet become standardized, the Jew could readily evade the Christological terms which later were to become such a major obstacle to his assumption of many a public responsibility. Like other vassals he was also given the right to represent those persons, not necessarily Jews, who had entrusted themselves to his protection, that is become his vassals in turn. To underscore this protective relationship, the high fine of ten gold pounds for the murder of a Jew, set at a time when gold had become increasingly scarce and been replaced by silver currency, was paid to his imperial protector. Here, too, the Jews themselves doubtless gladly enlisted the ruler's self-interest in their personal security. Wherever local authorities were unwilling or unable to secure justice for them, Jews could appeal to imperial officials and thus force recalcitrant witnesses to testify in their behalf. As an ultimate recourse they could bring their law suits before the emperor himself. In return, they were expected to show their recognition for that protection by regular payments to the court. In some cases, as in his charter for the Jews of Lyons, the emperor considered Jewish property so much his own, that he allowed the owners to exchange it for other holdings, but not to sell it. In short, they were to be allowed "to live quietly under Our tutelage and protection and faithfully to serve Our court [*partibus palatii nostri fideliter deservire*]," a phrase which was to recur in the charter given to the non-Jewish merchants.[65]

In this gradually evolving new feudal relationship, the Jews' dependence upon and alliance with the royal power became the mainstays of their entire legal structure. After the sudden decline of Jewish population and influence in the seventh century, the Carolingian communities made a fresh start. The memories of their former status as Gallo-Romans under the Theodosian Code and its derivatives were not completely expunged, but the new approach bore striking resemblance to the legal concepts governing the relations of aliens who, completely rightless under the primitive Teuton laws, were wont to seek the protection of local rulers in return for more or less regular payments. Despite their different origin and numerous differences in detail, the status of Jews and that of aliens were sufficiently alike to reinforce the growing medieval conviction, nurtured from theological preconceptions, of the "alien" character of Jews.[66]

Clearly, such legal status was full of ambiguities and open to arbitrary interpretation. On principle, it created a new group of royal vassals, somewhat akin to Christian nobles. By shifting the center of gravity to royal protection, however, and basing it overtly on mutual self-interest, it threatened to alter the long-established relationships between the Jewish and the Christian worlds, and to make them vary in accordance with the changing constellations of power and economic needs. This transformation could not go unchallenged by defenders of the old system. Some churchmen feared that the old segregationist objectives of canon law, long ago adopted by Theodosius and other secular legislators, would now be undermined by the chaotic diversity of personal and group relations developing under the new order.

Of course, most Carolingian rulers were pious Christians, Louis himself often being called the "royal monk." None of them consciously wished to abrogate accepted fundamentals of Church doctrine. Nor did they completely overlook the dangers to the state, too, emerging from the great feudal diversity of legal doctrines and local usages, the prevailing acceptance of the personal principle which allowed each tribal group to be governed by its own laws, and the constant *ad hoc* legislation to meet temporary needs. In their initial efforts to secure over-all legal unity, Louis and his advisers enlisted the support of such influential Church leaders as Archbishop Agobard of Lyons, whose principal aim was to secure the continued application of canon concepts and traditions. Agobard was particularly distrustful of the innovations in Jewish status, which he viewed as a serious menace to Christianity. For this reason he, together with the Archbishop of Vienne and the Bishop of Châlons, constantly invoked the decisions of earlier Frankish rulers and Church councils in attacking "Jewish superstitions" (826–27). Like most of the contemporary French bishops, Agobard had reached the height of his career as an administrator and ecclesiastical politician, rather than as a saint or theologian. His writings, correspondingly, were far more concerned with the general sociopolitical conditions shaped by the new system than with purely religious or ritualistic aspects. His anti-Jewish pamphlets injected, therefore, many novel economic and social issues into the old religious polemics. But kings, ever conscious of the Old Testament sanctions and hence also of both the limitations of their sovereignty and the king's supremacy over the priest, long resisted these encroachments successfully.[67]

Negatively, too, the Carolingian legislation left a permanent imprint on Jewish life in Europe through Agobard's anti-Jewish outbursts, which it had provoked. Returning from a visit to the court, where he could directly observe the Jewish influence on the emperor and his councilors, this militant churchman first attacked the prohibitions aimed at stemming conversions of pagan slaves without their Jewish owners' permission. He considered such protection of Jewish slaveholdings a direct subversion of canon law. Before long his agitation drew a reprimand from the *magister judaeorum* and, ultimately, also from the imperial *missi*, many of them high ecclesiastics themselves. The Archbishop, however, refused to be silenced. On the contrary, he now expanded his attacks to the entire position of Jews. He regarded the "Jewish insolence" as a serious menace to the Christian faith and tradition. Not surprisingly, he was particularly aroused by the situation in Septimania, and he urged Archbishop Nibridius of Narbonne (before 829) to forbid Christians to associate with Jews. In the writings of Agobard and his disciples, the Carolingian Empire thus also contributed some significant new ingredients to the old Judeo-Christian controversy and deeply influenced the new anti-Jewish reactions evolving in feudal Europe.[68]

Agobard's apprehensions were seemingly confirmed by a dramatic incident toward the end of Louis' life. During the political dissensions and intrigues, even overt rebellions relating to the anticipated division of the empire among Louis' sons, most Jews seem to have sided with Empress Judith and her son against Louis' three older sons from an earlier marriage. In the midst of this turmoil and much ecclesiastical anarchy and moral dissolution, a deacon of the imperial court, Bodo (Botho), an Aleman noble by birth, took the fateful step of converting himself to Judaism (839). Almost all our information comes from hostile sources. But it appears that a pilgrimage to Rome and the close observation of constant dogmatic strife and low moral standards at the Papal, as well as the imperial, court persuaded this Teuton nobleman to desert his family and friends, emigrate to Saragossa, marry a Jewess, and by personal influence and writings persuade many Mozarabs to convert themselves to either Judaism or Islam. According to rumor, he also induced his nephew to join him in the new faith and sold many of his Christian attendants as slaves to Spanish Moors. The news of this conversion caused widespread consternation at the imperial court, and Louis, a man of deep mystic inclinations, long refused to believe it. To Jew-baiters of the school of Agobard, especially Amulo, this incident was but another illustration of the overweening pride and power attained by Jews in the Frankish Empire. Their wrath was by no means mitigated by Bodo's Spanish counterpart, Paulus Alvarus, who, perhaps after his own conversion to Christianity, addressed a series of interesting letters to Bodo trying to persuade him to return to his former faith. For churchmen of Amulo's type, conversion was to remain, as it clearly appeared in the laws of all Christian countries, a one-way street leading to, but not away from, the Church.[69]

FRANCE

Dissolution of the Carolingian Empire affected Jewish status adversely. While there was little change in basic approach, the empire, and especially its western part out of which was to emerge the Kingdom of France, lost entirely its centralized, vigorous leadership. Within a century it saw governmental authority diffused among a mass of feudal lords, ecclesiastical and secular, each of whom could deal with the Jews of his area according to his own lights. Since in that state of dissolution the Church remained relatively the most uniform and consistent factor, its point of view gradually predominated over the more secular approaches of either the Roman-Merovingian legal tradition or the newer Carolingian charters. Only in that period, one may state with some exaggeration, "royal ordinances in Jewish affairs contained nothing that was not of ecclesiastical origin" (Anchel). Apart from its far-reaching economic effects, feudalism thus greatly complicated Jewish life in western Europe by both its anarchical diversity and its strengthening of the Church's authority over Jews. At the same time the central and provincial organs of the Church significantly contributed to Jewish security by their continued insistence on basic toleration, their strengthening of the royal power through emphasis on the divine right of kings, their injunctions to kings to rule justly, and their tireless propagation of compacts aimed at establishing the "divine truce" for the more defenseless groups in the population, including clerics and Jews.[70]

For these reasons Amulo, Agobard's disciple and successor in the metropolitan see of Lyons (841–52), could with greater effectiveness pursue his master's segregationist policies. Agobard himself may have lost "face" when the rebellion of Louis' sons, supported by him, petered out after 833 under a popular revulsion in favor of the emperor. For three years (835–38) he was out of office. Amulo did not have to live down his master's defeat. Generally overshadowed in the contemporary dogmatic disputes by his deacon, Florus, he felt doubly prompted to assert his leadership in the Jewish question.

In his anti-Jewish tract composed in 846, Amulo appealed to his readers to abstain from physical attacks on Jews and their property. But he urged the French bishops to join him in persuading, or forcing, "the princes in all their possessions to apply in that matter what had been ordained by the sayings of our saintly fathers, their actions and edicts." Just as the bishops ought to proclaim these principles faithfully, he contended, so must the rulers accept them "with Christian piety," for they would ultimately have to render account to the "King of kings and Lord of lords" for the behavior of all their serfs and underlings, including infidels (Amulo's *Contra Judaeos*, XLV ff., in *PL,* CXVI, 172 ff.). Without neglecting the socioeconomic issues, Amulo evinced particular concern about the Jewish control over Christian workers and ensuing damage to their orthodoxy. He mentioned a rumor that some Jews, unlawfully entrusted with the collection of tolls in a remote district, were allegedly raising or lowering tolls dependent on the degree of submissiveness to their anti-Christian teachings by the "poor and ignorant Christians" of the vicinity (*ibid.,* XLII, pp. 170 f.). Probably some minor incident was magnified here into a major Jewish proselyting effort.

Not satisfied with merely verbal exhortations, the old combination of churchmen of Lyons, Vienne, and Châlons, this time joined by the Bishop of Mâcon, proceeded actively to missionize among Jews. In a letter to the emperor, written by Amulo or, more likely, by his successor Remigius (some time after 852), the bishop spoke about the deep impression made by weekly sermons delivered by Catholic priests in synagogues. This seems to be the first record of such practice, mentioned here in passing, although it had doubtless encountered stiff resistance on the Jewish side. The rulers' failure to protect their Jewish protégés against such overt violation of their religious autonomy was in itself a sign of the ecclesiastical party's success in imposing its viewpoints on the secular authorities—a success facilitated by the unsettled state of affairs in Lyons under Duke Girard, Lothar's brother-in-law. The practical results must have been no less disturbing. Christian suasion apparently proved so effective among young boys that Jewish parents in the four communities, to the writer's chagrin, sent their children to Arles, where they enjoyed greater immunity from outside pressures. The bishop's letter was to induce the emperor not only to allow the missionaries to complete their work in the four cities, undisturbed by parents and authorities, but also to instruct the bishop of Arles to follow that example.[71]

Following old precedents, the ecclesiastical party also cast aspersions on Jewish loyalty to the country. According to chroniclers far removed in both time and space from the events, Jews were responsible for both the Danish raid on Bordeaux and the Saracen occupation of Toulouse (about 848). These writers forgot that Toulouse had never been taken by the Moors, and that Jews could hardly expect to gain anything from a Norman raid bent on murder and pillage. Clearly, Jewish disloyalty belonged to the accepted mystique of Judeo-Christian relations. In Toulouse it served as a rationale for the local custom of administering a public slap in the face to a Jew during the Easter holiday. At times, as in the story reported by a chronicler in 1018, the slap resulted in the victim's instantaneous death. Not until the beginning of the twelfth century was this barbaric spectacle replaced by annual payments by Jews for the benefit of the local clergy. Even without such a political rationale, the Easter season brought back to the minds of pious Christians the story of the Passion of Christ and the Jewish share therein. Exacerbated by appropriate sermons, the heightened tension often led to anti-Jewish outbreaks. In Béziers onslaughts were formalized, and the populace was given permission on the eve of Palm Sunday and during the following two weeks to stone the

Jewish quarter. Here, too, beginning in 1160, a single payment of
200 solidi to the bishop and an annual tax replaced this unbridled
license. That such customs developed in the relatively tolerant
south of France merely underscored the instability of Jewish fortunes and their dependence on panics generated by the recurrent
incursions of Normans and Saracens.[72]

Of a somewhat different order were the arrangements in the city
of Arles. Here the Jews, recorded from Roman times, formed in the
middle of the twelfth century a substantial community of some 200
families headed by a number of distinguished rabbis. Their regular
taxes were moderate, amounting in 1157 to but 8 solidi and 4
denarii. However, following an ancient custom, Jews were forced
personally to transport stones for public works on donkeys supplied
by them. Apparently, on Good Fridays the performance of this
duty often gave rise to scenes of violence between Christian teen-
agers and Jewish workers. Finally in 1178, the Jewish community
made an agreement with the archbishop and the city's consuls by
which this corvée labor was replaced by a one-time payment of
50 solidi and an annual tax of 20 solidi. The contracting parties
promised to protect the Jews, so that they would suffer "no harm
in their persons or their houses, nor were they to be tormented or
blamed in any manner. . . . Should, however, as formerly, the
youth and the people persecute the Jews and attack their homes,
and the consuls be unable to punish the transgressors and to restore
order, the aforesaid Jews would not be obliged to pay the 20 solidi."
The Arelate Jews were evidently willing to triple their annual
taxes for the sake of peace during the Easter season.[73]

While these proceedings, however distressing, could still be
explained by age-old rancors nurtured on the New Testament tradition, the hierarchy, often enjoying political power as well, felt
free occasionally to depart from the canonical doctrines of basic
toleration of Jews. For some obscure reason (the chronicler himself
speaks vaguely of *certa de causa*) Archbishop Ansegisus of Sens expelled both Jews and nuns from his city after 876. With the current
penchant for generalization, a single case of unchastity between a
Jew and a nun may have sufficed to engulf both groups in a vehement popular reaction. Rumors played even greater havoc with
Jews in various parts of France in 1007–10, when news about the

intolerant outbursts of the Faṭimid Caliph Al-Ḥakim began reaching Europe. As was usual, Jews were blamed for the destruction of Christian churches, and particularly for that of the Holy Sepulcher in Jerusalem. For some reason the community of Orléans was singled out as the alleged instigator of that decree. The four more or less contemporary records relating to this event are evidently confused. But it appears that there were widespread anti-Jewish riots, and that, under popular clamor, many rulers wished to force the Jews to adopt Christianity. In 1010, Adhémar de Chabannes tells us, Bishop Alduin of Limoges forced the Jews to adopt Christianity or else to leave the city. He also ordered the local professors of theology to engage in regular religious disputations with the Jews, who undoubtedly proved to be reluctant partners. He thus helped develop the pernicious system of forcing Jews to attend missionary sermons, aimed at debasing Judaism and at glorifying the Church, which was to be greatly refined in the later Middle Ages. The threatened communities allegedly secured delay until their messenger, Jacob bar Yequtiel, could appeal directly to the Holy See. According to a Hebrew source, Jacob persuaded the pope to dispatch an envoy bearing a papal order "not to kill, injure or rob Jews, nor to deprive them of their religion." This envoy supposedly spent four years visiting all the endangered communities, while Jacob and his family, except for one son whom he had left behind as a hostage, remained in Rome where they were hospitably entertained by the Jewish leaders. Ultimately about 1024 Jacob is said to have settled in Arras (?), Flanders, and to have died shortly thereafter and been buried in Reims.[74]

Perhaps some explanation of this obscure, international episode may be derived from the time lag between Ḥakim's persecution of Christians and Jews in the Faṭimid Empire. Both the Hebrew and the Latin sources indicate the date of 1007–9, which had marked, indeed, the beginning of the persecution of the Egyptian and Palestinian Christians, but not yet of Jews. The caliph's initial friendliness toward Jews undoubtedly helped fan the flames of western accusations of Jewish betrayal. The Orléans letter, allegedly intercepted, need not have contained more than a simple inquiry about one of the recurrent messianic movements similar to that addressed by the Rhenish Jews to Palestine in 960, according to Isaac bar Dorbelo's later report (about 1140). Certainly the millenarian agitation throughout Europe and its frustration during that period must have nurtured such curiosity among Jews, too. Because of the international and principally religious character of this alleged Jewish involvement in an action against the Church of the Holy Sepulcher, we may readily understand the intensity of the widespread Western reaction, emphasized by both Glaber and the Hebrew chronicler. The decisive turn for the better in the West may not have come until 1012, when the sudden persecution of Jews in the Faṭimid Empire must have demonstrated to the Christian world the baselessness of the alleged Judeo-Muslim conspiracy.[75]

In calmer periods, churchmen, like kings and barons, were principally interested in the amount of revenue they could secure from Jews. In Narbonne, as we recall, Jews were economically as well as politically too firmly entrenched to be deprived of their landholdings. The hierarchy could only, with the pope's assistance, demand the payment by Jews of tithes from property they had acquired from Christians. This Narbonne controversy led the Church to insist on the Jews' paying ecclesiastical tithes, especially in newer areas of their settlement, like northern France or Spain, where—so the argument ran—all their landed estates must have been at some time or other acquired from Christian taxpayers.

That this problem was less frequently debated in contemporary writings or legal enactments was doubtless owing to the variety of titles under which the Church managed to secure revenue from Jews. Under the feudal atomization of France during the tenth and eleventh centuries, many bishops were overlords of Jews and, like other masters, could tax them freely. In some localities, like Narbonne or Marseilles, the entire city was divided between a secular and an ecclesiastical lord, and the Jewish quarters located in the two sections paid taxes to their respective rulers. In 1143, Archbishop Pierre de Lubières authorized the settlement of Jews in Aix in return for an annual tax of two pounds "of the best pepper." On many occasions churches succeeded in securing, here as in Spain and elsewhere, grants of Jews and their possessions from kings. Charles the Simple's donation of some lands of Jews around

Narbonne to its archbishop set the pace for many such gifts thereafter. Several recorded royal grants (about 880, 921, 1147, 1154) entrusted the mastery over the Jews of Arles to the local archbishops. The abbey of Saint-Denis obtained, in the same fashion, from Louis VI full judicial control over the formerly royal Jews of its town (1112) along with "each person living within the city limits of Saint-Denis." The king himself could only complain to the abbot and litigate before the court of the abbey. This provision is the more remarkable as the king generally sought to submit the clergy to royal jurisdiction. Distant Frederick Barbarossa, especially, utilized his supreme powers to confer new, or reaffirm old, rights on Jews held by the churches in Marseilles, Avignon, and Arles. His privilege of 1177 in favor of Archbishop Raymond de Bollène of Arles stated specifically:

We generously add as a gift of our benevolence the extension of his and his successors' power over the Jews residing in the city of Arles who belong to Our Chamber. We firmly state that no one shall dare for any reason whatever to impose upon them his rule through any exactions without his [the Archbishop's] consent and counsel. Anyone running counter to this statute and order of Our Majesty should know that he will without any doubt fall under Our ban, be peremptorily excluded from Our grace, and be subject to a fine of forty pounds of gold of the best alloy, of which one half shall be paid to Our Treasury, and the other half to the offended Archbishop.

On some occasions it was the Papacy which promised its protection for Church holdings. In 1147, for instance, Pope Eugenius III promised to protect the property of the monastery of Jumièges in the bishopric of Paris, including land of a *Villa Judei*.[76]

Even where royal grants mentioned transfers or mortgages of Jewish persons as well as property, they amounted in substance only to the cession of their fiscal contributions, but did not involve any physical mastery over them. In two cases of individual transfer recorded in France in the eleventh and early twelfth centuries, and one in Spain, a Christian burgher was ceded (or exempted from the cession) together with the Jew. All these transactions were consciously ambiguous. But, except for some emergency periods, they established a reasonably satisfactory *modus vivendi* for both sides, which enabled the Jews to settle in ever new communities, to increase in number, and to make signal contributions to Jewish learning. Benjamin of Tudela's comment on the "great city" of Paris mirrors conditions in other communities as well. "Scholars are there," the visitor observed, "unequaled in the whole world, who study the law day and night. They are charitable and hospitable to all travelers, and are as brothers and friends unto all their brethren the Jews." Not that the community was very large by modern or contemporary Muslim standards. "The Rue de la Juiverie," rightly observes U. T. Holmes, Jr., "extended for a single block, in the modern sense. There was a large synagogue (to be converted later into the Madeleine Church) on the northeastern corner; apparently there were twenty-four houses occupied by Jews. . . . Many Jews came to own buildings occupied by Christian clerics." [77]

Next to the Crown and the Church, a new factor began shaping the political as well as economic destinies of Jews. Without ever achieving the full sovereignty of the Italian republics, the French, like the Spanish, English, and German, cities began playing an increasingly powerful role, and in part served as a counterweight to the feudal lords. They often shared royal protection with the Jews, and were frequently allied with the Crown against the overweening pride and power of barons. Yet, in the economic sphere, the burghers increasingly found themselves competing with Jews. Jews had contributed greatly to the rise and historic evolution of the medieval cities, but once firmly established, the latter's ruling classes felt free to dispense with their services, or at least to restrict them to some economically or socially undesirable occupations. Before long, spokesmen of the burghers class, unrestrained by the canonical traditions of limited toleration of Jews, became the harshest Jew-baiters.

Anti-Jewish propaganda of this kind was to crystallize particularly after the twelfth century. In the earlier period, even most city custumals, here as in Spain, merely echoed the restrictions long demanded by the Church. Even if more detailed and specific than the ecclesiastical regulations, their provisions, too, were mainly aimed at segregating Jews and keeping them in their "place." Typical of these urban statutes is that of Arles, in part going back to the middle of the twelfth century. Here Jews were forbidden to work on Sundays and Christian holidays with open doors or in any other way noticeable to Christian onlookers. Each offense was punishable by the high fine of twenty solidi. Jews were also prohibited from selling meat slaughtered by them to Christians, or from slaughtering animals in Christian houses, the underlying rationale being that it was beneath the dignity of Christians to consume meat ritualistically rejected by Jews. We also find here a lengthy formula of the Jewish oath, which doubtless includes accretions of later date. In general, French custumals, even more than the Spanish *fueros*, were subject to considerable editorial sharpening in the period of growing tension between burghers and Jews after 1200.[78]

All these slowly smoldering hatreds produced a major eruption in 1182, when Philip II Augustus issued a decree expelling Jews from the royal dominions. Apart from frequent popular outbreaks, such as those which characterized particularly the period of the Crusades (the Crusaders' attacks on Jews will be more fully discussed in the next chapter), keen observers could have sensed serious portents in the Archbishop's expulsion of Jews from Sens after 876, and in the popular agitation of 1007–10. But throughout these tense moments the French kings persisted in protecting their Jewish subjects. None of them emulated Emperor Louis II's sharply intolerant Italian decree of 855. Louis VII, for example, in cooperation with the other feudal lords, in 1144–45 merely outlawed relapse to Judaism under the penalty of death and mutilation. But this decree did not affect professing Jews. That is why the abrupt change in 1182 caught the Jewish community entirely off guard.[79]

Despite his youth (he was then but seventeen years old) Philip II revealed all the characteristics of calculating ruthlessness and perseverance which were to make him one of the chief architects of French unity. His sudden revocation of Jewish toleration is usually ascribed to the influence of his ecclesiastical advisers, his biographer, Rigord, associating particularly the name of a hermit, Bernard, with this decision. The Church's exclusive responsibility is controverted, however, not only by the generally more moderate policies of the contemporary French hierarchy, but also by its recorded earlier disagreements with the young king. Like his father, Philip had at first refused to implement the decisions of the

Third Lateran Council of 1179 relating to Jewish employment of Christian servants. Obviously economic and fiscal considerations loomed uppermost in Philip Augustus' mind. Rumor had it that, through mortgages and foreclosures, Jewish creditors had already seized control of over half the real estate of Paris. Following the then prevailing custom of *Einlager,* many Christian debtors, including members of the upper classes, were said to have been detained by Jewish lenders and made to stay in the latter's homes in a semiservile state. In his decree, therefore, the king enjoined the Jews to leave his realm within some two months (before June 24, 1182), and canceled all debts due them, only demanding from the debtors the payment of one fifth to the treasury. In this way Philip Augustus hoped at the same time quickly to fill his own coffers and to secure wide popular support for his difficult and costly program of restoration of the old Carolingian glory.[80]

In time, however, the king and his advisers realized that such immediate gains were more than nullified by the ensuing permanent losses. The emigration of Jews helped enrich the feudal rulers outside the royal domains; many of them were Philip Augustus' overt rivals. His also was an abrupt departure from policies and precedents set by Charlemagne in attracting Jews to his empire.

For these reasons Philip II, who only seven years previously had allegedly ordered the burning of some eighty Jews at Bray-sur-Seine, and who was soon to help set in motion the sanguinary anti-Albigensian crusades, cold-bloodedly reversed himself. In 1198 he decided to recall the Jews, "against the opinion of all," according to his chaplain, William Armoricus. He merely established a so-called *produit de Juifs,* a department in the Treasury along English models, to supervise Jewish moneylending activities. Eight years later, once again following the example set across the Channel and acting in cooperation with the Countess of Champagne and Guy of Dampierre, he appointed notaries in every major commercial center to record debts owed to Jews. More significantly, in 1198 he also concluded an unprecedented treaty with Count Thibaut of Champagne (a short time after the latter had taken his oath of fealty) and followed it up by similar treaties with the counts of St. Paul and Nevers (1210). Through these compacts he sought to secure the forcible return of those Jewish exiles from the royal possessions who had found new homes in the adjacent provinces. Beyond such immediate return, the counts had to promise to extradite all future Jewish settlers arriving from lands under royal control. On the other hand, Jews born in Champagne had no right to leave that province and settle in Paris or Orléans. Although the king promised complete reciprocity, it was obvious that, at least for a time, he would profit more from such forced repatriations. To reinforce those treaty provisions, he also forced some Jews to swear on the scroll and deposit a bond that they would not depart from the country (about 1204). While mouthing pious phrases, the king and his advisers, including some distinguished ecclesiastical leaders, undisguisedly began applying to the Jewish question simple considerations of the *raison d'état*. Even more overtly utilitarian were such regional treaties as that concluded in 1195 by William III, count of Montpellier, with the bishop and viscount of that city—all pledging equal treatment to Christian, Muslim, and Jewish merchants.[81]

By this decree of expulsion, its revocation, and the ensuing treaties, Philip II adumbrated a new concept of Jewish status based upon a more literal interpretation of Jewish "serfdom." Despite the ancient origins of that term, born from ecclesiastical and homiletical preconceptions, Jews had theretofore enjoyed untrammeled freedom of movement. Now their treatment began to be more akin to that of villeins. Although not entirely *glebae adscripti*, or bound to specific localities, they were to be irrevocably attached to the domains of their political masters. Understandably, Jewish leadership contested the legality of that one-sided alteration of a long-accepted status. While fully recognizing the validity of the laws of the countries in which they dwelt, the rabbis qualified this principle by applying it only to laws legitimately enacted by the government. The great Tosafist, Isaac bar Samuel of Dampierre (Rashi's great-grandson), who had witnessed Philip II's decree of expulsion but probably not its revocation, clearly expressed this view. Discussing the obligation of purchasers of estates left behind by Jewish expellees to restore them to their rightful owners, R. Isaac wrote:

This case is not in the nature of the "law of the kingdom" [which must be respected], but rather in that of the "robbery of the kingdom."

For we have seen in the countries around us that Jews have had the right to reside wherever they wished, like the nobles, the law of the kingdom being that the ruler should not seize the property of Jews who left his town. This was indeed the practice in all of Burgundy. Therefore, if there is a regime which tries to alter the law and make a new law unto itself, this is not to be considered the "law of the kingdom," for this is not a proper law at all.

Resistance of this type not only prevented the Jews' acquiescence in servile status, but in the long run effectively undermined all attempts to attach them permanently to any province or country. In their own consciousness, and as we shall see, also in historic reality, they never sank to the status of villeins.[82]

GERMANY

In the eastern part of the Frankish Empire, which emerged from the Treaty of Verdun, Carolingian traditions continued to shape all aspects of public life. As a Holy Roman Empire, the Germanies assumed the burdens and privileges of Western leadership along patterns set by Charlemagne, whose personality dominated there the minds of men even more than in the other successor states. Ultimately the name of the idealized monarch penetrated deeply into German Church liturgy, and through Germany became the byword for "king" in many Slavonic languages. Curiously, unlike the Alexander romances, the numerous legends concerning Charlemagne left little imprint on Jewish folklore. Whatever traces may still be detected in later Hebrew and Yiddish letters seem to be outright literary borrowings of a later day, rather than vivid recollections from the Carolingian era. This folkloristic reticence offers another testimony to the real break in continuity of Jewish life in Germany from Roman times. It seems that the Jewish settlements reappearing at the end of the ninth and during the tenth centuries (Metz 888, Mayence 906, and others) represented in the main fresh starts. The nuclei of older Jewries may have helped maintain some measure of stability, but they left in their wake few spiritual influences. Nonetheless, in the Jewish question too, Germany revealed from the first a degree of continuity unseen in atomized France and Italy, although the policies of the central organs were often tempered by varying powers of feudal lords, changing relations between church and empire, and the rise of the medieval cities. In the midst of these ever changing power constellations Jewish communal leadership, which after R. Gershom bar Yehudah of Mayence ("the Light of the Exile") included in each generation a brilliant array of scholars and religious devotees, tried to steer a more or less consistent course.[83]

As in France, the growth of civilization at first greatly enhanced the economic and cultural functions of the Jewish communities. At the same time it stimulated the rise of rival forces, especially among the growing class of burghers. The latter's increasing enmity injected serious complications into Judeo-Christian relations, and ultimately these reduced greatly the area of Jewish usefulness to society at large. Thus the main factors shaping the rise and decline of medieval German Jewry made themselves felt already in the vitally formative period between the tenth and twelfth centuries. However, more consistently than in France, Germany's royal power adhered to the Carolingian tradition of protecting Jews. Hence feudal delegations of power to barons and ecclesiastical lords constituted an imminent threat to Jewish security in Germany, too. In fact, the most important early enactments by German emperors concerning Jews related to transfers of control over them to the ecclesiastical heads of Magdeburg and Merseburg. In the case of Magdeburg, Otto II merely confirmed for the benefit of the archbishop a previous privilege of Otto I (965), which had granted the monastery of St. Moritz founded by him exclusive jurisdiction over all "merchants or Jews" as well as over the city's unfree inhabitants. Six years later the emperor added the power of ban and enlarged the archbishop's hold over all inhabitants "of whatever status." The provision for Merseburg was even more sweeping. Here Otto II gave the bishop "everything included in the walls of Merseburg with the Jews and merchants" (973). In the following three decades the bishops forfeited their control by voluntary exchanges. Nonetheless, Henry II restored all merchants and Jews to the archbishop in 1004. The emperors generally respected also feudal rights, such as custom duties received by local barons from merchants. In the Raffelstetten toll ordinance of 906, Louis the Child reassured the bishops, abbots, and counts of Bavaria that the customary duties theretofore paid by merchants, "that is Jews and other merchants from wherever they may come," would remain undisturbed.[84]

Notwithstanding these grants, the emperors evidently considered themselves permanent overlords and protectors of Jews, even if they handed over their Jewish revenue to new beneficiaries. As overlord, Henry II felt entitled to undo the intervening transactions and restore the Merseburg Jews, or rather the revenue from them, to the bishop. All emperors seem unwaveringly to have adhered to this bilateral arrangement which was accruing to the benefit of both the empire and the Jews. Although subjected to the combined pressures from Constantinople, Rome, and Venice, Henry I and his associates at the Diet of Erfurt, as we recall, adopted no hostile measures against Jews (932–36). Only Archbishop Frederick of Mayence contemplated at that time the expulsion or forced conversion of Jews, but he consulted the pope, rather than the emperor, probably expecting little cooperation from the secular authorities.

Under the date of 1012, to be sure, a well-informed Saxon chronicler reported that "an expulsion of Jews was instituted by the emperor [Henry II] in Mayence, while the insanity of some heretics was refuted." This obscure reference has been interpreted to mean that Henry II, on learning in Mayence in November–December 1012 of the conversion of a cleric Vecelin to Judaism, issued a decree of expulsion. But he revoked this decree early in 1013, and even permitted the forced converts to return to their former faith. This reconstruction has been effectively challenged, however. The record makes it more likely that Vecelin converted himself in 1005 or 1006. Perhaps Henry's outburst was but a delayed reaction to the alleged Jewish involvement in the anti-Christian persecution in the Faṭimid Empire. Henry may indeed have been persuaded, during his sojourn in Mayence, to institute a general expulsion of Jews. This may have been a mere threat, or a decree speedily revoked, possibly as a result of the papal intercession secured by Jacob bar Yequtiel. In any case, here as elsewhere this decree, even if issued, need not have been the cause of the departure or conversion of more than a handful of Jews, the majority quietly persisting until the decree was either formally revoked or informally allowed to sink into oblivion. Be this as it may, this single record, unconfirmed by any other evidence and full of obscurities, cannot in any way controvert the emperors' generally protective attitude toward the German Jews.[85]

It does illustrate, however, the sovereign's inability to stem the rise of those hostile forces which threatened to submerge German Jewry. The growing popular animosity, combined with the increase in the number and diffusion of Jews, doubtless called for some clearer definition of Jewish status and its imperial guarantees, made doubly necessary by the break between the German episcopate and Henry IV during the War of the Investiture. While the evidence for new legislation is largely limited to the two communities of Spires and Worms, we may assume that similar enactments were issued also in favor of other communities, especially that of Mayence, which not unjustifiedly claimed to have combined "Torah and greatness, wealth and honor." With their predilection for punning, Mayence Jews often spoke of their city, called *Magenṣa* (from Moguntia) in Hebrew, as the *magen veṣinnah* (shield and armor) of all German Jewry. We shall see that in the great crisis of 1096 it was indeed one of its representatives who secured the emperor's intervention in behalf of all German Jewry. Any attempt, however, at reconstructing the Mayence privilege from those given to Spires and Worms—a perilous undertaking at best—is further aggravated by certain significant variations between the latter two themselves, and by their availability only in later copies doubtless considerably altered during subsequent renewals as well as by careless or biased copyists. No less dubious is the restoration of a Ratisbon privilege, apparently issued by Henry IV in 1097, on the basis of its renewal by Frederick I in 1182. It is small wonder, therefore, that these texts have been the subject of extended scholarly controversies over the last seventy years, and that many important juridical and historical problems connected with them still await solution. Nevertheless they allow for some legitimate generalizations concerning the status of German Jewry at the end of the eleventh century.[86]

Already in 1074 Jews appear alongside the other burghers of Worms as beneficiaries of Henry IV's privilege freeing them from paying certain customary duties. The emperor, who upon reaching maturity a few years earlier had found his treasury in a state of utter penury and who all his life suffered from a shortage of funds to finance his ambitious undertakings, probably issued that privilege in return for some tangible support from both burghers and Jews. In asserting his direct supremacy, however, he intentionally snubbed the bishop. In his later decree for the Jews of Worms (about 1090), he was even more outspoken on this score.

For We wish [he wrote] that in all judicial matters they [the Jews] should turn to Us only. We ordain on the authority of Our royal dignity that neither the bishop nor [his] chamberlain, neither the count nor [his] bailiff, nor anyone else except he whom they would themselves elect, should presume to treat with or against them in any matter or in the application of any kind of justice. Only he who, as has been mentioned, as a result of their election is placed over them by the emperor [shall be entitled to do so.] It has thus pleased Us because they belong to Our chamber.

On the other hand, in Spires, whose Bishop Rüdiger-Huozmann had been Henry's loyal adherent, the bishop was allowed to share in the control over the Jewish community. In fact, Henry's Spires privilege, which was clearly based on Carolingian models and in turn served as a prototype for other privileges including that for Worms issued shortly thereafter, seems to have been recommended to the emperor by the bishop himself a few days before his demise.[87]

By following a well-established tradition from Carolingian times, this privilege appears as but a link in one of those legal chains of evolution which were so characteristic of the Middle Ages. It served, in turn, as a basis for the privilege of Worms which was subsequently formally renewed by the still more powerful Emperor Frederick I in 1157—in fact, we possess only the text of that renewal from which we must reconstruct the original grant— and broadened in scope by Frederick II to govern the position of all German Jewry (1236). Frederick II's decree was to serve, in turn, as a model for many later privileges, and vitally to affect the legal status of Jews in most central and eastern European Jewish communities to the eighteenth century.[88]

Among the most important provisions of both privileges were those relating to the security of Jewish persons and property, the owners' freedom to dispose of their possessions as they saw fit, and freedom of travel through the length and breadth of the Empire.

Jews were to be protected against unlawful exactions, the conversion of their children or slaves against their will (even adults had to wait three days before they were to be baptized), and any interference with the sale of their pagan slaves. For the first time *bona fide* Jewish purchasers of stolen goods were enjoined to restore them to former owners only after receiving full indemnity for their investment. The old Carolingian exemption from ordeals and the requirement of witnesses of both faiths in mixed Judeo-Christian litigations were amplified here by specific provisions in favor of the internal Jewish administration of justice and law enforcement. Only in exceptionally difficult litigations "among or against them" were they to repair to the bishop himself (in Spires) or to the emperor (in Worms). The Worms text also spelled out the right of Jews to engage in money changing operations throughout the city. It provided further that the murder of a Jew or instigation thereto and conversion of Jewish children without their parents' consent were to be punished by the high fine of twelve gold pounds, and that Jews were freely to employ Christian servants, maids, and nurses. "Let neither bishop nor any cleric controvert that." Apparently in Spires, where the bishop shared the revenue from Jews, the emperor was prepared to accept a considerably smaller fine in silver. Probably by mere oversight Henry did not repeat in Worms the provision of the Spires privilege that an assailant of a Jew unable to pay the prescribed fine was to be punished by blinding and the amputation of his right hand. By citing here a precedent, set by his father Henry III in an unnamed locality, the emperor probably wished to lend it wider application. On the whole, the Jews of Worms enjoyed to all intents and purposes all the civil rights of "burghers," as they were reiteratedly called in thirteenth-century documents. Their failure to partake of such political rights as elections to city councils was the natural result of their communal separation, rather than of the legislators' discriminatory intent.[89]

Neither Henry nor the Jews realized at that time how soon these pledges of imperial protection would be put to a severe test. Although symptoms of popular Jew-baiting became clearly noticeable long before 1096, neither the Rhenish communities nor the authorities took the necessary precautions against popular outbreaks. True, Jews were expected to help the authorities in the pursuit of criminals, to assist in the defense of their cities against foreign attack, and to defend themselves, especially on their ever perilous journeys both on water and on land. For these reasons, they frequently bore arms and were trained in their use. Contemporary rabbis discussed such equipment as a matter of course, and were merely concerned with its legal effects on the Sabbath rest commandment. The great mystic, Eleazar of Worms, reminisced of the time when his city had been besieged "by large armies" (he probably referred to the siege of 1201), and he had permitted the carrying of weapons on the Sabbath. However, like most other urbanites, especially merchants, Jews did not serve as regular soldiers, nor did they take part in any offensive wars. In this respect, as Eliezer bar Joel and Isaac Or Zaru'a were to observe, the Spanish Jews played a far more active military role. At the same time imperial legislation was increasingly veering away from the old Teuton treatment of assault and battery as essentially private offenses, to be prosecuted only at the instance of the injured party and usually to be punished only by a fine. Hence there gradually evolved the system of "peace" proclamations, often by compacts between kings and lords, whereby all acts of violence were outlawed during certain periods, or against certain classes of the population. Jews who had not previously been included in such proclamations, except incidentally under the category of merchants, now were specifically mentioned in the significant treaty concluded in January of 1103 by Henry IV with the lords of the empire. The contracting parties pledged themselves for the following four years to uphold the peace toward "churches, priests, monks, laymen, merchants, women (lest they be raped), and Jews." [90]

This was a fateful step. Despite its overtly pro-Jewish objectives, this agreement became another milestone in the development of Jewish "serfdom." Clearly, none of the persons here mentioned belonged to the class of unfree villeins. The only criterion was their relative defenselessness in a lawless society. Yet it highlighted the Jews' dependence on imperial protection, and helped to forge further links in their attachment to the Crown, as well as in the latter's self-seeking expectation of ever greater revenues from them. Promoted by the constant increase in Jewish population, the deterioration in general Judeo-Christian relations and the growing anarchy under the recurrent civil wars, these privileges and peace ordinances could well be construed, at least on the part of emperors and their advisers, as a mark of that particular Jewish "bondage" which the Church had been preaching from time immemorial.

Bondage here never assumed the bizarre features of the French treaties of extradition, however. Apart from retaining their general overlordship over Jews, the emperors specifically guaranteed the latter's right to move freely from place to place. In so far as there was a limitation on their choice of residence, this depended more on admission by the local Jewish communities than on the arbitrary decisions of local lords. This communal discretion led, as we shall see, to an elaborate legislation concerning the *herem ha-yishub* (residence permit), which went far beyond its talmudic antecedents and may even have helped to shape certain legal requirements (for instance, a temporary residence of twelve months before final admission) among neighboring non-Jews. The very fact, moreover, that the overwhelming majority of German Jews lived in cities militated against their serfdom ever being equated with the peasants' villeinage. Even fugitive villeins settling in a city, as a rule, immediately secured freedom.[91]

Full rationalizations of this peculiar status were not to evolve until the thirteenth century. At first, most of the emperors, especially such superior persons as Frederick I Barbarossa (1152–90), viewed that relationship between the Crown and its Jewish protégés as a matter of duty, as much as one of right. To forestall the usual automatic expiration of medieval privileges at the death of their originator, Frederick in 1157 renewed Henry IV's privilege for Worms Jewry and specifically declared its perpetual validity. Without arranging for another compact with the lords of the whole empire, he participated in such regional arrangements as that of Rhenish Franconia in 1179 which proclaimed a universal "truce" for only four days a week but provided that "Jews who belong to the Emperor's Chamber . . . should enjoy peace on every day." Most outspoken was Frederick's privilege for the Jews of Ratisbon. Enacted in 1182, possibly as a renewal of a decree first issued by Henry IV, it started with a solemn preamble which evidently was Frederick's own contribution. It proclaimed:

It is the duty of Our Imperial Majesty, as well as a requirement of justice and a demand of reason, that We rightly preserve his due to everyone of Our loyal subjects, not only the adherents of the Christian faith, but also to those who differ from Our faith and live in accordance with the rites of their ancestral tradition. We must provide for their persevering in their customs and secure peace for their persons and property. For this reason We announce to all faithful subjects of the Empire, present and future, that, deeply concerned with the welfare of all Jews living in Our Empire who are known to belong to the imperial Chamber by virtue of a special prerogative of Our dignity, We concede to Our Ratisbon Jews and confirm with Our imperial authority their good customs which their ancestors had secured through the grace and favor of Our predecessors until Our time.

For the first time the principle was clearly enunciated here that the emperor was to be responsible for the peace and well-being of all his Jewish subjects throughout the empire.[92]

Perhaps this emphasis was more needed then, because, concurrently with the imperial overlordship, various local forms of control over Jews had begun to develop in many parts of Germany. Although, unlike the French kings, twelfth-century German emperors retained great authority over their country's Jewry, decentralization even in this field progressed inexorably and at an ever accelerating pace. Occasionally we learn of actions taken by local counts; for instance, the burgrave of Cologne, who, for the annual payment of ten marks and six pounds of pepper from the Jewish community, conducted safely all Jewish travelers to and from the city through the archdiocese. In far-off Bohemia, Moravia, and Austria the local rulers exercised the main jurisdiction over their Jewish subjects. Duke Leopold V of Austria (1177–94) employed a Jewish mintmaster, Schlom, and allowed him not only to own real estate, but also to employ Christian servants. Probably the same rights were given to other Jews of Vienna, whose synagogue is first recorded in 1204. Such local authority could be exercised without completely undermining the community's nexus with the rest of imperial Jewry. Even in the western compacts concerning "peace" the local lords had to be treated as full-fledged partners.[93]

Paucity of information concerning the rights and activities of Germany's dukes and barons in regard to Jews during the eleventh and twelfth centuries contrasts sharply with conditions in contemporary France and Spain, as well as in latter-day Germany herself. The large majority of German Jews of that period lived in cities under the control of bishops, rather than secular lords. Almost all our extant records, including those relating to the blood baths during the Crusades, relate to such episcopal sees. On his return journey through Germany, Benjamin of Tudela enumerated Jewish communities exclusively in centers of ecclesiastical power (Verdun, Metz, Treves, Coblenz, Andernach, Bonn, Cologne, Bingen, Münster, Worms, Strasbourg, Würzburg, Mantern, Bamberg, Freising, and Ratisbon). "In these cities there are many Israelites, wise men and rich." Benjamin's list is evidently incomplete; it does not even include the principal community of Mayence, nor those of Spires, Halle, and others. However, all these cities, too, were controlled by bishops. Only a negligible minority of twelfth-century German Jewry seems to have lived outside these major centers.[94]

In the administration of Jewish affairs in their dioceses, however, the German bishops acted far more as secular lords than as religious leaders. True, Frederick of Mayence consulted the pope as to how to proceed in the Jewish question, and acquiesced only when a compilation of canonical precedents prepared for him by a cleric convinced him of the legitimacy of tolerating Jews. But his was an exceptional behavior. The alleged expulsion of Jews from Mayence in 1012 was attributed to the emperor, rather than to Frederick's successor. In general, the German episcopate was for a long time intimately allied with the imperial office, and it served as a mainstay in the troubled periods of the eleventh and twelfth centuries. Not even during the War of the Investiture did all bishops side with the popes against the emperors. In their attitude to Jews they also largely followed the emperors' lead in trying to preserve the security of Jewish lives and possessions. We shall see that in critical moments, as during the onslaughts of Crusaders, some of them proved ineffectual defenders of Jews. The archbishop of Mayence who, at least in the thirteenth century, was supposed to serve as protector of all imperial Jewry during the emperor's absence from the country, was unable to protect Jewish refugees in his own fortress. But these princes of the Church

merely yielded to strong pressures out of weakness or general cal-
lousness, and not because of personal conviction or any conscious
change in the Church's accepted policy.[95]

Among the most successful protectors of Jews during these tragic
events was John, Bishop of Spires (1090–1104). He followed thus
in the footsteps of his predecessor, Rüdiger-Huozmann, who had
in 1084 attracted many Jews from Mayence to his city. As loyal
partisans of Henry IV, both these churchmen probably also helped
to shape the entire imperial policy with respect to Jews. The aforementioned privilege for the Jews of Spires of 1090 was doubtless
formulated in cooperation with the bishop, whose own statute,
issued six years previously, belongs among the classic utterances
on the Jewish question in medieval Germany. "When I converted
the village of Spires into a city," the bishop wrote, "I believed to
increase the dignity of our locality a thousandfold if I assembled
there Jews, too." For this reason he assigned to the Jewish community a separate district surrounded by a wall, "lest they be
easily disturbed by the insolence of the mob," and gave them a
cemetery of their own. He also extended to them many privileges,
modeled more after the Carolingian edicts than after provisions
of canon law. He allowed them, for example, to employ Christian
nurses and male servants, and to sell to Christians ritualistically
forbidden meat. He also tried to facilitate their commercial transactions—doubtless the main objective of his legislation—and to
safeguard their full autonomy in internal affairs. In return, Jews
had to pay in perpetuity three and one-half silver pounds to the
episcopal treasury, and to take part in the defense of the city by
repelling, together with their servants, enemy attacks on their
quarter. "As the highest expression of my good will I have conceded that they should enjoy the most favorable legal treatment
accorded the Jewish people in any city of the German Empire."
While no other bishop went the whole length of Rüdiger's pro-
Jewish legislation, the German hierarchy of that period, on the
whole, effectively supported the imperial legislation relating to
Jews and greatly facilitated the growth of the Jewish communities in the Rhinelands and southern Germany.[96]

Far less uniform was the attitude of burghers. On the whole,
the relations between the Jews and their Christian neighbors were

fairly amicable. As a class the burghers had not yet reached that state of affluence and political self-assertion which later enabled them to seek complete domination over their cities. Most burghers still were satisfied with their extended autonomy in municipal affairs, and were prepared to view the equally autonomous Jewish community as a distinct and independent group under the direct control of their joint sovereign. Economically, too, most Christian merchants still regarded Jews as welcome collaborators. On the other hand, Jewish wealth often provoked the jealousy of the underprivileged groups. Jewish moneylenders also incurred the enmity of many debtors. Nor was religious disparity as readily glossed over among the masses as it was sometimes among the more sophisticated upper classes. For these reasons in critical moments, the "lower" classes were more prone to lend a willing ear to the preaching of fanatics. In general, nevertheless, the Christian burghers seem to have acquiesced in the pro-Jewish legislation emanating from the imperial and episcopal chanceries. Whatever discords existed between them and their Jewish neighbors, they did not yet play that fateful role in Jewish history which was to be theirs in the following centuries.[97]

ENGLAND AND NORMANDY

Cities and nobles also played an increasing role in English affairs, and ultimately affected Jewish status in a decisive fashion. In many ways Angevin England anticipated the Continental evolution. Here, before anywhere else, Jews were converted into a class of "royal usurers," whose main function was to provide credit for both political and economic ventures. After accumulating great wealth through the high rate of interest, these moneylenders were forced to disgorge it in one form or another for the benefit of the royal treasury. The prolonged well-being of many Jewish families, the splendor of their residence and attire, and their influence on public affairs blinded even experienced observers to the deep dangers lurking from the growing resentment of debtors of all classes, and the exclusive dependence of Jews on the protection of their royal masters. With the monarchy itself often embroiled in sharp internal and external struggles, this support ultimately

proved to be but a broken reed. Rumblings of discontent, cul-
minating in violent outbreaks in 1189–90, presaged the final
tragedy: the expulsion of 1290. The meteoric rise, and even more
rapid decline, of English Jewry in the brief span of two and a
quarter centuries (1066–1290) brought into sharp relief the fundamental factors shaping the destinies of all western Jewries in the
crucial first half of the second millennium.

Whatever progress Jewish settlement on the British Isles may
have made in the Roman period, and again immediately after the
Anglo-Saxon conquest (there is reason to believe that some Jews
were found in both the Roman camps and the newly arising
Anglo-Saxon cities) reliable historical data begin flowing only
after the Norman invasion in 1066. Our records increase in number from the middle of the twelfth century, and assume truly
substantial proportions in the nine decades preceding the expulsion. In 1893 Joseph Jacobs claimed that his collection of sources
pertaining to the period of 1066–1206 would be dwarfed in a
ratio of some 20:1 by similar excerpts covering the remaining
eighty-four years. Since that time many more thirteenth-century
documents have come to light. Because the country was spared de-
structive foreign invasions, the continuity of traditions in many
of its leading families and churches and the keen historical sense
revealed by such chroniclers as William of Malmesbury and William of Newbury helped to preserve the memory of medieval English Jewry far more adequately than was the case in any of the more
populous and culturally more influential Continental communities.[98]

Most of these English records, to be sure, refer only to economic and social aspects of life. In endless reiteration they perpetuate the memory of specific business transactions, principally
relating to loans, and their repayment or forfeitures. Another large
group of entries in official registers relates to taxes, fines, and other
revenues of the Exchequer from Jewish sources. Our information,
on the other hand, about the manifold intellectual interests and
activities of medieval Anglo-Jewish authors is largely derived from
Continental sources, since post-expulsion England evinced little
interest in preserving such scholarly writings. But this very dis-
proportion served as a corrective to the frequent imbalance in

political and socioeconomic sources pertaining to most Continental Jewries. On the whole, these details add up to a fairly comprehensive picture of a community which, shortly before 1200, consisted in the aggregate of about 2,500 persons, or about one tenth of one percent in the population. Because its financial resources helped satisfy the crying needs for capital in an upsurging economy, and also to furnish the sinews for internal and foreign wars, its socioeconomic influence appeared wholly out of proportion to its numbers.[99]

This important, though limited, function may have been in William the Conqueror's mind when he invited (according to William of Malmesbury), or at least allowed, Jews from his duchy of Normandy to follow him across the Channel. We know very little about the Jewish communities of eleventh-century Normandy, but it seems that Jacob bar Yequtiel, the effective envoy to the pope in the early eleventh century, was a native of Rouen, where he had allegedly escaped the wrath of Duke Richard only by a miracle. The Conqueror's successor, William Rufus (1088–1100), treated the Jews on both sides of the Channel so well as to incur the displeasure of ecclesiastics who resented his general irreligiosity and venality. According to a tradition recorded by William of Malmesbury, the king not only allowed some remorseful Jewish converts in Rouen publicly to revert to their Jewish faith (about 1090; the chronicler may have confused this action with happenings in the aftermath of the First Crusade), but also staged a religious disputation in London. If the Jews were to prove victorious over the bishops, he is reputed to have said jokingly, "he would join their sect." [100]

Since disputations between members of the two faiths recorded from that period were conducted in a rather friendly spirit, this story must have arisen from the general resentment of the allegedly excessive royal favoritism shown to Jews. Such resentment was expressed also when the Constitution of Clarendon of 1164 sought to curtail the jurisdiction of ecclesiastical courts, and a spokesman of the clergy demanded for churchmen the freedom from ordeals previously granted to burghers and Jews. "Would it not seem to thee unworthy," he wrote, "unless the clergy were granted a privilege which is indulged to lay citizens or Jews?" [101]

Henry I (1100–1135) took the initiative, regulating more clearly the status of Jews. "Cool-headed, clear-sighted, and patient," he was characterized by William John Corbett, "a methodical man of business, and for a prince well educated, he hated all waste, violence and disorder." Although the text of his privilege regulating the position of his Jewish subjects is not preserved (it is merely referred to in a decree by his great-grandson John in 1201), its general tenor may perhaps be reconstructed from Richard the Lion-Heart's confirmation in 1190 of a privilege issued by his father, Henry II (1154[1150]–89). While the verbiage and even individual provisions were doubtless modified to suit the needs of the later age, Richard's and John's decrees seem in essence to reflect the thinking of the early twelfth century as well. They aimed at allowing Jews to "reside in our land freely and honorably." Among their main provisions were the protection of Jewish property, including loans which were to be safeguarded beyond the lifetime of creditor or debtor; the insistence on the primacy of documentary evidence, and wherever unavailable, on the testimony of Jewish as well as Christian witnesses in mixed litigations; the trial of Jewish defendants before their "peers" only; the Jewish creditors' right freely to dispose of pledges held for a year and a day; and the Jews' freedom to move together with their chattels, throughout the realm "just like our own goods, and let no one keep them or prevent them." Most significantly, the decree concluded, "And we order that the Jews through all England and Normandy be free of all customs and of tolls and of modiation of wine, just like our own chattels, and we command and order you to ward and defend and protect them." These provisions were far from revolutionary; they followed well-established Continental patterns. But there is a new emphasis upon the protection of Jewish moneylending, which reflected the increasing concentration of English Jewry on this one occupation, and the primary interest of the Crown in its promotion for the benefit of the Exchequer.[102]

Neither the dates nor the particular circumstances which led the two Henrys to issue these charters are known. They largely followed Carolingian patterns, long familiar all over western Europe. Richard's charter was addressed to "Isaac, son of Rabbi Joce, and his sons and their men," as if this had still been the time of

Louis the Pious' capitularies. The English king, even less than his Frankish predecessor, wished to limit the application of his charter to that family only. John may indeed have been the first to abandon this long-established formula and address his decree "to all the Jews of England and Normandy."

Outwardly English jurisprudence still sneered at usury in all its forms. An interpolator of the latter part of the twelfth century inserted into the so-called "Laws of Edward the Confessor" a sharp condemnation of usury, "the root of all vices." At the same time he or some other contemporary attributed to that revered figure of the pre-Norman age the most sweeping formulation of the specific nexus between the Jews and the royal power.

It should be known [he declared] that all Jews, wheresoever in the realm they be, ought to be under the guard and protection of the king's liege. Nor ought any of them to place himself under any mighty man without the king's license. For the Jews and all theirs belong to the king. And if any detain anything of theirs, let the king ask their money back as if it were his own.

Although nothing prevented the transfer of control over Jews to the king's vassals, a procedure so frequently applied in the Continental countries, the English Crown retained its direct control to the very end. In theory, after the death of a Jewish subject the king could take over his entire estate. But such expropriation is recorded only in the case of Aaron of Lincoln, who had apparently died childless. Otherwise the charter of 1201, based on that of Henry I, expressly provided that "when a Jew dies, his body shall not be detained above earth, but his heirs shall have his money and his debts." True, the Treasury collected an estate tax. But a similar tax was also paid by the heirs of a royal vassal, since the king also claimed the right of eminent domain over all of England's land. In general, there was little to distinguish a Jew from a knight, except for the latter's military service and active participation in public affairs.[103]

Royal protection was indeed fairly effective. With the exception of the massacres of 1189–90, which caught the royal authorities completely unprepared, public order was more or less satisfactorily maintained. Even in the later, more violently anti-Jewish, period Jewish lives were rarely jeopardized. This sense of security was not seriously affected even by the recurrent blood accusations, although entire communities were denounced as participants in the ritual murder of young boys (Norwich in 1144, Gloucester in 1168, Bury St. Edmunds in 1181, Bristol in 1183, and others). True, the anti-Jewish emotions were stirred not only immediately after the events, but for many years later, especially among the pious pilgrims attracted to the shrines erected in honor of such "martyrs." Nevertheless there is no record that this new complication in Judeo-Christian relations, which rapidly spread from England to the Continent, entailed much loss of Jewish blood on the British Isles.[104]

It is small wonder, then, that England began attracting numerous Jewish settlers from the European Continent and North Africa. The list of recorded Jewish names in twelfth-century England, compiled by Jacobs some sixty years ago, includes residents hailing from Spain, Italy, and even Morocco and Russia. Several years before the large influx of French Jews, occasioned by Philip Augustus' decree of expulsion of 1182, the number of Jews in the provincial communities had increased to such an extent that they secured from Henry II a generic permission to establish their own cemeteries outside the walls of any English city (1177). If we may take a clue from an obscure passage in the chronicle of Gervase of Canterbury, Frederick Barbarossa's ambassadors, seeking an alliance with the king of England in 1168, complained of the excessive departures of the emperor's Jewish subjects to England. "For the sake of these ambassadors," we are told, "the King caused the richer Jews to remove themselves from England, and exacted from the rest 5,000 marks." Even if this rather tenuous interpretation be correct, one could not see in this compliance of the English king anything resembling the treaties of extradition concluded by the French rulers three or four decades later.[105]

Such royal "favoritism," of which contemporary chroniclers often complained, was secured at a high monetary price. In his famous "Dialogue of the Exchequer" (ed. by C. Johnson, pp. 99 ff.) Richard, son of Nigel, stated that "of the amercement of the Jews and the ransom of the moneyer the Queen has her share on the same scale as of voluntary offerings." He thus intimated their largely voluntary character. But this situation speedily changed.

The small English community served in this respect, too, as the earliest object of far-reaching experimentation. Almost literally applying the concept of royal mastery, the administration at first tried to promote Jewish business ventures to the utmost of its capacity. It felt that, by enriching the Jews, it indirectly acquired their accumulated treasures for its own benefit. In time, however, Jewish moneylending was bound to embroil the kings in constant controversies with the Jews' debtors, who included many influential nobles, clergymen, and burghers. Anxious as these borrowers were to secure the original loans, they bitterly resented their rapidly mounting indebtedness under the then prevailing high rates of interest. In the twelfth century the royal imposts still were relatively moderate. Of course, at times Jews were victimized by both parties to civil strife, as in the struggle between Matilde and Stephen in 1141. Perhaps because they had paid Matilde an "exchange" of money, the Jews of Oxford were forced by Stephen to deliver to him three and one-half "exchanges" under the threat of having their houses burned. Apart from such emergencies, however, the taxes seemed quite bearable for Jews and remunerative for the Crown. Only on the occasion of the so-called Saladin tithe of 1188, raised to finance the forthcoming Third Crusade, the Jews were asked to contribute the enormous sum of £60,000, figured at the exorbitant rate of one quarter of their entire property. In fact, this Jewish impost, assessed at Guildford in 1187 and preceded by some two years by another more moderate tax for aid of the Holy Land, paved the way a year later for the tithe, which in the case of other inhabitants really amounted to but ten percent, the first full-fledged property tax in English history. By assuming that the Jewish revenue alone would amount to £60,000, as against the rest of the country's contributions of only £70,000, the assessment undoubtedly overestimated the value of Jewish property as approximating one fourth of the national wealth (£240,000 out of a total of £940,000). But Jewish capital was more readily convertible into cash. The government itself must have realized the inequity of this distribution of the tax burden. Considering also the intervening loss of Jewish lives and property during the massacres, it demanded from English Jewry a contribution of only 5,000 marks toward the ransom of 100,000 marks for Richard the Lion-Heart in 1194. But even that contribution far exceeded that of the 1,500 marks expected from the City of London.[106]

Aggregate Jewish communal wealth had, moreover, been greatly depleted by the confiscation in 1185 of Aaron of Lincoln's estate, which followed a similar confiscation of the possessions of William Cade, a Flemish Christian usurer, in 1166. The liquidation of the far-flung business dealings of Aaron, who had included among his customers and debtors the king of Scotland, the archbishop of Canterbury, the count of Brittany, and many other dignitaries of state and church on both sides of the Channel, proved an extremely difficult task. A special liquidating department of the Treasury, the so-called Exchequer of Aaron, closed down after sixteen years of operation in 1201, with half the loans still uncollected.[107]

Such sporadic confiscations, however, as yet interfered but little with the growing concentration of capital in the hands of a few leading Anglo-Jewish families. Rapid accumulation of this kind was bound to have political as well as economic effects. When Richard Care "Strongbow" borrowed much-needed funds from Josce of Gloucester for his unauthorized expedition to Ireland in 1170, Henry II feared that the powerful though impoverished lord would, with the aid of such loans, seek to establish an independent Irish kingdom. That is why he fined Josce one hundred shillings for lending money "to those who against the King's prohibition went over to Ireland." Josce had evidently broken no law in lending money to a noble lord for purposes with which he had hardly been familiar. Similarly legal, but politically dangerous, was the loan of ten marks extended in 1164 by London Jews to Thomas Beckett for his flight to France on the security of Beckett's revenue from Waltham. In his anger Henry confiscated that revenue and the lender was still seeking redress nine years later. Such potential use of Jewish funds for independent military and political ventures must have opened threatening vistas for the government, and stimulated further tightening of administrative controls over the Jews.[108]

Political and fiscal considerations thus combined with efforts to appease an aroused citizenry to initiate a sharp regulation of Jewish moneylending. The royal ordinance of 1194 was designed both to protect the treasury against concealment of Jewish funds and to safeguard the debtors against excessive claims. It provided, according to Richard Howden's summary, that

all the debts, pledges, mortgages, lands, houses, rents, and possessions of the Jews shall be registered. The Jew who shall conceal any of these shall forfeit to the King his body and the thing concealed, and likewise all his possessions and chattels, neither shall it be lawful to the Jew to recover the thing concealed.

Likewise six or seven places shall be provided in which they shall make all their loans, and there shall be appointed two Christian and two Jewish lawyers, and two legal registrars, and before them and the clerks of William of the Church of St. Mary's and William of Chimilli, shall their loan contracts be made.

And charters shall be made of their contracts by way of indenture. And one part of the indenture shall remain with the Jew, sealed with the seal of him to whom the money is lent, and the other part shall remain in the common chest.

In addition, Jews were made to swear on the scroll of law that they had declared all their property. All persons, including fellow Jews, were ordered secretly to denounce to the justices any concealed property, as well as each case of forgery or coin clipping. With this ordinance and the establishment of the special Exchequer of the Jews, began a new and ever more complex chapter in the relations between the Anglo-Jewish community and the royal administration.[109]

These police measures were not only emulated in France, but used also as a basis for a general introduction of chirograph indentures among Christians as well as Jews, thus giving rise to a new class of English records (1195). Although with respect to the evils of interest accumulation they were bound to be mere palliatives, for a time they seem to have satisfied the popular clamor. Whatever ill feeling the Jews' usury and intimate alliance with the Crown still generated among the disaffected groups, no anti-Jewish attitude crystallized. The clergy, often blamed by modern historians for the anti-Jewish discrimination in law and society, was merely adhering to its long-established segregationist policies. In the twelfth century, at least, it was responsible for few new anti-Jewish actions. Even in the frenzy generated by blood accusations, the local clerics seem rather to have followed the lead of the aroused masses than to have inspired them. This restraint did not prevent them, of course, from exploiting such incidents by creating for themselves additional sources of revenue from pilgrims to the newly created shrines.

Like other debtors, clerics enjoyed receiving loans, but they were weary of repaying them. No less than seven Cistercian monasteries in the north were built with funds provided by Aaron of Lincoln, who also claimed to have built the shrine of St. Alban. On one occasion, Pope Alexander III, doubtless prompted by the monks of St. Augustine at Canterbury, intervened with the king to safeguard the monastery's interests in its business dealings with Jews (1179). Churches and monasteries frequently served as repositories for Jewish valuables, which facilitated visits by Jews with higher and lower churchmen. So intimate were the Jews' contacts with the clergy, that at times they dared to interfere in the churches' internal affairs. When a protracted quarrel broke out in 1187, between the monks of Christ Church and those of St. Augustine in Canterbury, the Jews, together with most of the city's Christian inhabitants, sided with the former. Even after the cathedral was surrounded by the archbishop's troops, who sought to starve the monks into submission, the Jews not only offered prayers in their synagogue in behalf of the beleaguered monks, but also clandestinely supplied them with food. The chronicler of these events, Gervase, observed: "The Archbishop did not cease to take away, nor the Jews to give. The Archbishop excommunicated, the Jews prayed. A strange inversion, indeed!" [110]

At times such involvement ended tragically for the Jews. In a conflict between William, sacristan of the Abbey of St. Edmunds, and his associate Samson in 1182, the Jews and the rest of the townspeople sided with William, who, according to the chronicler Joce de Brakelond, "was called their father and their patron." Eight years later Samson came to power and, utilizing the anti-Jewish feeling running high in the country, secured the expulsion of Jews from Bury St. Edmund. Although he had mainly demanded that Jews, like the rest of the community, should belong to the Abbey rather than to the king or else be ejected from the town, he thus set a dangerous precedent for local exclusions of Jews. The Church's stiffening anti-Jewish bias also came to the fore, as we shall see, in the progressively sharp anti-Jewish polemics. However, even in the thirteenth century the clergy offered rationalizations for movements essentially generated by the real spearheads of the anti-Jewish propaganda, the burghers.[111]

In the twelfth century even the emergent patrician leadership in the rapidly growing urban centers still refrained from demanding outright exclusion of Jews. Jewish wealth and its frequent display doubtless created much envy among Christians of all classes. The outward contrast between the flimsy frame dwellings inhabited even by the wealthier burghers and the imposing stone structures erected by some Jewish bankers must have been galling to many contemporaries. Jews may merely have persisted in their ancestral habits brought over from Palestine, where stone quarries had been abundant and stone structures best fit the climate, or, what is less likely, they may consciously have sought shelter behind stone walls against sudden assault. Some of these stone structures, like Aaron of Lincoln's home or the synagogue of Bury St. Edmunds, have defied the storms of ages and lasted into the twentieth century, bearing mute testimony to the affluence and grandeur, however short-lived, of some Jews in Angevin England. One can still sense the jealousy of their non-Jewish compatriots in the remark of the chronicler Ralph of Coggeshall about their "houses which had been erected as if they had been palaces of kings." This widespread envy contributed to the massacres at the inception of Richard's reign, although it did not yet give rise to an organized anti-Jewish movement, such as was to emerge in the thirteenth century and result in the progressive elimination of Jews from a number of English cities—ultimately from the whole country.[112]

On the whole, twelfth-century English Jewry must have appeared to contemporary observers as relatively secure and prosperous. Still free to move throughout the length and breadth of the realm, which until 1206 included large parts of France; allowed to control real estate, both urban and rural, and build enduring stone mansions; enjoying extensive self-government and substantial educational opportunities, it must have been envied by the increasingly harassed Continental communities. For its size it included also a substantial number of scholars and writers, both native and foreign born. But its good fortune was not to last.

As the most typically "medieval" Jewish community of the time, its speedy rise and fall epitomized the changing destinies of all medieval Jews under Western Christendom.[113]

BETWEEN HAMMERS AND ANVILS

In the crucial half-millennium embracing the eighth to twelfth centuries, European Jewry emerged as an increasingly influential factor in the historic evolution of the whole people. Shattered by the barbarian invasions and the wave of intolerance which had engulfed most of its communities during the seventh century, Western Jewry began slowly to reconstruct its economic and cultural life in the more favorable clime of the Carolingian Renaissance. Western Europe itself was in need of both manpower and capital, in need of new techniques and sciences. An enterprising, experienced, and industrious population like the Jews could only accrue to the benefit of these reborn civilizations.

With their fortunes undermined by the growing dissolution of the Great Caliphate and the ensuing political and economic anarchy in the world of Islam, many eastern, North African, and Spanish Jews on their part heeded the call of these backward but promising countries. In ever increasing numbers they established themselves in France, Germany, England, and northern Spain under mutually advantageous conditions. Even when the Jews were not formally admitted under clearly spelled-out stipulations, the prevailing understanding was that they would live their independent life as a sheltered minority, in accordance with their own traditions. To be sure, as "infidels," they were to suffer from certain major disabilities. But even the Church recognized their unique claim to continued existence as a separate and distinct ethnic-religious group, endowed with certain basic rights and duties. Enjoying fundamental safeguards for the security of their persons and property, considerable freedom of movement and worship, and a vast autonomy in religious, educational, and even judicial affairs, Jews were given the opportunity to play a significant role in the rise of these young and vigorously expanding nations.

Despite local difficulties, the Western communities grew by

leaps and bounds, and in the twelfth century they began making their influence felt in all of world Jewry. Foundations were indeed laid then for the transfer of the world Jewish center from the decaying east to the dynamically expanding west, an evolution which became an incontestable reality before the end of the following century. Notwithstanding temporary outbreaks of popular intolerance and monarchial arbitrariness, Jewish life in the west still appeared fairly prosperous. A biased chronicler like William of Newbury could comment that "the Jews who were living in England under King Henry the Second, by a preposterous proceeding had been made happy and more famous above the Christians." (IV.9, ed. by Howlett, I, 317; trans. by Stevenson, IV, 568.)

Of course this was a gross oversimplification. "Christians" were not all of the same kind; each class had a legal and social life of its own. The well-being of the individual Christian depended far more on his status within his special group than on his faith or political allegiance. This was, in fact, one of the main strengths —and weaknesses—of medieval society. The progress of European feudalism led not only to increasing territorial subdivisions, but also to an ever deeper separation of the various "estates," each with a status and outlook of its own, many of them still fluid and ill-defined. Separated from all these estates and mixing with none, Jews soon found themselves placed in the midst of an ever sharper struggle for power.

Circumstances forced the Jews into an alliance with the monarchy, which necessarily accrued to the greater advantage of the royal power than to that of its Jewish "serfs." It was an alliance between unequal partners, since the kings could arbitrarily set the terms and even abrogate the entire compact. Jews could only appeal to the humanity and self-interest of their masters. But that very alliance often antagonized classes temporarily or permanently in conflict with kings or the monarchy as such. Because of the kings' primarily fiscal interests in their Jewish subjects, this mutual relationship often degenerated into a crass exploitation of the Jewish taxpayers, and the latter's enforced economic exploitation of other classes via moneylending.

What happened in England in the twelfth century was bound to happen everywhere else sooner or later. The Jew increasingly served as the "royal usurer," whose main function consisted in sucking up the wealth of other classes through high rates of interest, and being in turn squeezed dry by the royal treasury. For a while Jews deluded themselves into believing in the permanence of their speedy successes; many enjoyed the luxuries of great wealth and power. But sooner or later the royal appetites were whetted beyond the possibility of appeasement, while the resentments of the exploited masses grew into deep-seated hatreds. Only a few contemporaries realized how many communities were thus permanently living on a powder keg whose violent explosion threatened to eliminate them, either through extralegal massacres or by legally unimpeachable decrees of expulsion.

AGE OF CRUSADES

IN many ways 1096 marked a turning point in Jewish history. The trail of blood and smoldering ruins left behind in the Jewish communities from France to Palestine, by the crusading mobs even more than by the regular armies, for the first time brought home to the Jewish people, its foes and friends, the utter instability of the Jewish position in the Western world. Since the great wave of expulsions and forced conversions of the seventh century, Jews had encountered occasional outbreaks of intolerance, even murderous riots which caused some loss of life. But these "incidents" invariably were local and sporadic in nature, lacked premeditation and widespread concerted action. From the First Crusade on, anti-Jewish persecutions exercised a dangerously contagious appeal, which in periods of great emotional stress degenerated into a mass psychosis transcending national boundaries. Much beyond the number of direct victims, therefore, the massacres of 1096–99 left a permanent imprint on the Jewish, as well as the Christian, evaluation of Judeo-Christian relations. Alienage and insecurity, theretofore mainly theoretical concepts which affected the lives of individual Jews to but a limited extent, now became the overpowering concerns of all thinking persons on both sides.

The apprehensions of the Jews were heightened by the uncontrollable fury of the new forces which manifested themselves in these sanguinary outbreaks. In the past, Jewish leaders had believed that, by negotiating compacts with the ruling powers of state and church, their constituents were assured of a more or less durable state of peaceful coexistence with their Christian neighbors. True, it always had been necessary to reckon with uncertain personal equations, temperamental outbursts of highly placed individuals, and particularly with changes in succession. Yet individual skill in negotiations could always be relied upon, while financial resources made possible, wherever necessary, both increased fiscal contributions and clandestine bribes to influential counselors. But the new events showed the impotence of established authority in the face of the unleashed frenzy of fanatical mobs who, combining the quest for a religious ideal with ordinary human greed and sadism, cold-bloodedly committed unspeakable atrocities. Human life generally counted for very little in those harsh ages of constant warfare, both foreign and domestic. But here an opportunity was given for the oppressed masses to give vent to cumulative grievances and hatreds through acts of violence cloaked as meritorious deeds in behalf of a religious ideal. What E. Barker said about the crusading knight applied with undiminished force also to the crusading mobster: "He might butcher all, till he waded ankle-deep in blood, and then at nightfall kneel, sobbing for very joy, at the altar of the Sepulcher—for was he not red from the winepress of the Lord?" Had not Pope Leo IV, more than two centuries before, promised heavenly rewards to all those who fell in battle in the Church's defense? This clear reversal of the long-regnant pacifist doctrine of most Church Fathers in favor of an imitation of Islam's preachment of Holy War necessarily victimized the Jewish people caught in a vise between the two world civilizations.[1]

Remarkably, the growing feeling of estrangement and instability did not prevent masses of Jews from settling in western lands during the twelfth century. In fact, the center of gravity of the whole people was moving slowly but inexorably to those harsh but vigorous and enterprising young nations who were beginning to shape the future of all mankind. Despite the tremendous difficulties facing them in these new lands, some Jews were irresistibly drawn to them by economic needs; others by their spirit of adventure and pioneering.

This westward movement was actually fostered by the Crusades. Until the end of the eleventh century, the Jewish communities in the three main areas of Jewish settlement, under Islam, Byzantium, and the Roman Catholic West, developed in almost complete independence of one another. The overwhelming majority of the people still lived under eastern or western Islam. It maintained but few tenuous contacts with the feeble Western centers and the struggling groups scattered among the possessions of the Eastern emperors and their Slavonic vassals. This mutual isolation now gave way to an awareness of the entire people of the community of its destinies in economics and politics as well as in culture. Theretofore largely separated from the mainstream of Jewish historic evolution, the Byzantine and Western communities found themselves drawn into the vortex of the memorable clash between East and West. The Crusades thus helped to reweave the three separate strands of Jewish history into a unitarian pattern, just as they helped to reunite the lines of evolution among the peoples of the entire Mediterranean world. At the same time they created a new tension between East and West, between Islam and Christendom, which deeply affected also the "neutral" Jewish subjects of both. Jews could not remain mere observers of this titanic struggle. As frequent victims and passionate, if unwilling, participants, they too were forced to respond to the new world crisis. In a multiplicity of forms, as we shall see, Jewish thinking of the period, especially in the Spanish border area between East and West, was a direct response to that great historic challenge.

RUMBLINGS OF HOSTILITY

In retrospect the events of 1096 appear as but a culmination of anti-Jewish trends gradually building up among the Western masses over several generations. But these hostile manifestations were geographically and chronologically so disparate and apparently so unrelated to one another, their immediate effects so local and temporary, that their threatening portents would have escaped the attention of Jewish leaders even if the latter had not wishfully lulled themselves into a false sense of security. Not all of these disturbances became known even to informed persons in distant communities, and they could be largely discounted as the result of some specific, more or less accidental causes. At most they seemed merely to demonstrate anew the general insecurity of life in that age of violence, and to serve as reminders for Jews that they lived in "exile."

Outbreaks in Metz in 888 must have been largely forgotten. More serious were the anti-Jewish repercussions of the Christian millenary movements, which were climaxed by widespread expectations of the second coming of Christ in the year 1000. Whether or not these expectations and the ensuing sense of frustration are to be considered direct antecedents of the Crusades, any heightened hope of an end of days must have sharpened Christian sensitivities toward both the Jewish share in the Passion of Christ and the Jewish "stubbornness" in resisting conversion to the very end. That is why, if we are to believe an anonymous romanticizing chronicler, a renegade, self-seeking Jewish swindler bearing the incredible name of Saḥoq ben Esther Israeli could readily persuade the ruler of Limoges in 992 that, by preparing an effigy of their ruler and heaping on it maledictions, Jews could bring about that ruler's death. Since sympathetic magic of this kind enjoyed wide credence, the informer needed but to "plant" such an effigy in the synagogue as proof of the Jews' evil intentions. As further evidence of their guilt, he challenged the Jewish leaders to a duel, thus allegedly giving them the opportunity to prove their innocence through the ordeal of combat. In vain did the Jews argue that "it is not now the custom of Israel to engage in combat, as do the Gentile nations." Their proffer of money was likewise rejected, and the Limoges authorities allegedly contemplated dispatching letters to all Christian countries urging them "to eliminate them [the Jews] from the surface of the earth." Despite the incomplete state of our fragment, its evidently romanticizing features, its literary borrowings from the book of Esther, and its indubitable exaggerations, we may indeed assume that the community of Limoges found itself in great danger as a result of the machinations of a faithless member. But even here the destruction of the Jewish community was envisaged in the traditional terms of governmental outlawry rather than unbridled popular attacks. Even more ominous must have appeared an alleged threat of expulsion of the Jews from Treves in 1066, although, occasioned by the then prevailing civil strife and governmental instability, it remained a dead letter.[2]

On the same plane were the more serious actions instituted by Robert I in France and Henry II in Germany in the years 1007–12, both of which, as we recall, seem to have been averted by the papal intervention secured by Jacob bar Yequtiel. Here, too, the populace still remained passive, even if deeply agitated, leaving retribution for alleged Jewish misdeeds in the Holy Land to the established authority. These, or some other, anti-Jewish governmental decrees also seem to have been mainly responsible for the sudden increase in the number of Jewish converts to Christianity during that period. The great leader of northern Jewry of the time, Gershom bar Yehudah, "The Light of the Exile," himself suffered a grievous loss when his only son joined the Christian faith. The rabbi's behavior on this occasion underscored his conviction that the son had acted under some sort of compulsion, although his pertinent penitential poems furnish no specific data. On the one hand, Gershom complained that "they forbid us to invoke the name of the Lord, / Our Redeemer, whose name is the Lord of Hosts," intimating some kind of governmental regulation. On the other hand, two stanzas seem to reflect mob reactions. Here the poet deplores the fact that

> When listening to my persuasive speeches,
>   They reply together by vengeful action;
> Their hands are filled with robbery and plunder
>   While their lips shout of murder and destruction.
> From its fine home, its tabernacle and shelter,
>   Thy community to all winds is scattered;
> Thy inheritance, mournful and deserted,
>   Lifts its eyes only to Thy help unfettered.

But even here emerges the image of some legalized expropriation and expulsion (probably that of 1007–12), rather than that of popular riots.[3]

These forebodings of the Crusades were heightened in Spain. Here the Christians were locked in never-ending warfare with the hosts of Islam. Much of that struggle bore the usual earmarks of power politics, with Christians and Muslims often arrayed on both sides. Nonetheless, at times the conflicts could be fanned into real religious wars. Particularly knights attracted to Spain from across the Pyrenees often played the role of warriors for the Lord, bent upon redeeming a formerly Christian land from the hands of infidels. These early crusaders, like their successors embarking on the redemption of the Holy Land, could readily give vent to their pent-up religious emotions by attacking Jews, as well as Muslims. There must have been sufficient disorders going beyond the usual belligerent excesses for Pope Alexander II to issue warnings in 1063 against attacks on Jews. This papal bull was addressed to "all the bishops of Spain," as well as to the archbishop and viscount of Narbonne. Buttressed by the need of Jewish assistance on the part of the reconquering Christian armies, the papal intercession proved effective. Few further incidents were recorded in the eleventh and twelfth centuries on the Iberian front.[4]

Ironically, Jews themselves contributed their share to the stimulation of crusading movements. For several centuries they had performed the great historic task of bridging the deep chasm between East and West through their mercantile endeavors and cultural mediation. By helping to keep at a high pitch the curiosity of Western nations about the fabulous lands of the East, and by whetting Western appetites for oriental luxury products, they strengthened the economic motivations which, together with religious zeal and political ambitions, accounted so greatly for the vigor and persistence of these expansive efforts. Their own undying attachment to the Holy Land also helped to keep alive the Palestinian ideal among their Christian neighbors. From ancient times the Jewish pilgrimages to Jerusalem found numerous imitators among pious Christians. Defying the great insecurity of maritime and land travel, and the hostility of Muslim rulers, a great many Christian and Jewish pilgrims succeeded in reaching the Holy Land. At times these pilgrims traveled in large groups. One pilgrimage headed by the archbishop of Mayence in 1064 is said to have included 7,000 participants. This feat was to be duplicated on a somewhat different level by Jews, when in 1211 three hundred rabbis traveled from western Europe to Palestine. Interference with pilgrims, as is well known, became a burning issue after the Seljuk occupation of Jerusalem in 1071 and set off the sparks which started the conflagration under Urban II's pontificate.[5]

THE FIRST CRUSADE

Mundane and spiritual factors combined to make the Crusaders' march from France to the Holy Land in 1096–99 one of the most memorable events in world and Jewish history. Widespread failure of crops and mass starvation greatly swelled the ranks of desperadoes and adventurers to whom plunder and burning of Jewish, and occasionally also non-Jewish, communities appealed as much as the arduous expeditions to the Near East. Weakness of imperial authority, undermined by the long War of Investiture, and the protracted absence of the emperor from Germany (Henry IV had resided in Italy since 1090) left the maintenance of public order to local authorities. Without a firm hand to direct uniform action, the local rulers were readily disoriented and unable to cope with the unprecedented emergency.

On its part, the papacy constantly raised its sights toward world domination. Having obtained notable successes in its struggle with the Western Empire, it now eagerly listened to appeals for help from the harassed Byzantine emperor, Alexis Comnenus. By marshaling effective military aid, it hoped not only to mend the breach with the Eastern churches and thus reestablish its hegemony over the entire Christian world, but also to plant the cross over the citadels of the Holy Land and break Islam's hold over the Near East. In thus preaching a holy war against Mohammedanism, the Church took over the latter's most effective instrument of expansion and combatted it on its own ground. Most significantly, the Crusades gave a new turn to the quest for salvation via penitence and martyrdom. The penitential pilgrimage had long been recognized in the Christian world as a major instrumentality for the remission of sin. Heightened by dangers of warfare, a crusading pilgrimage, which involved full preparedness for martyrdom in behalf of one's faith, was confidently expected to assure its participant a *novum salutis genus,* a new road to salvation.

Self-sacrificing penitential prepossessions dominated also the outlook of contemporary Jewry. In periods of heightened tension, especially, Jews were easily reminded of the Maccabean example; not so much of the Maccabean warriors as the martyrs and witnesses for their faith, glorified in the Apocryphal literature. The reverse was true of the Christians, who had long extolled the idea of Maccabean-like martyrdom but now received their main inspiration from the descriptions of that ancient *War* of religion.

The Apocryphal narratives so strongly influenced the regular crusading armies that these sincerely believed that they, too, would be aided in combat by angelic hosts, visible or invisible. They even succeeded in instilling that belief in their Muslim enemies. On one occasion the latter actually rejoiced in slaying a white-clad warrior because they thought to have thus disposed of St. George in person. Jews, on their part, remembered mainly Hannah and her seven "Maccabean" children, who had displayed great fortitude in sacrificing their lives for their faith. Commenting on the self-imposed martyrdom of a Mayence Jewess and her four children, the Hebrew chronicler, Solomon bar Simson, a typical spokesman of that age, emphasized that she had died, "as had the righteous one together with her seven children. It is to them that [the psalmist] referred when he spoke of the 'joyful mother of children.'" Nor was the example set by the rabbinic martyrs, especially R. 'Aqiba, lost on their medieval successors whose thinking was so deeply permeated with the teachings of Talmud and Midrash.[6]

It should be noted that the crusading movement as well as its victimization of Jews transcended class lines and also affected members of the weaker sex. In fact, women played a significant role both in urging the men to take up the cross, and in the self-sacrificing deeds of martyrs. The Mayence woman with the goose, whose willingness to join the expedition impressed the male population with their divinely inspired mission, had her Jewish counterpart in Minna, the Jewess of Spires, who was the first to point the way toward sacrificial self-immolation as an alternative to enforced baptism.[7]

Mental preparedness for religious martyrdom was heightened during that period by a widespread Western messianic movement, in part derived from a chronological computation. Jeremiah's messianic prediction, "Sing [ronnu] with gladness for Jacob, And shout at the head of the nations" (31:6) was interpreted to hint, by the numerical value of its first word, to the 256th lunar cycle of 19 years each, which began in 5846 (1095–96). It was indeed during the interval between the Council of Clermont which had proclaimed the idea of Crusade, and the spring of 1096 when the first regular detachments and armed bands began forming, that

Western Jews inquired, as we shall see, from their Byzantine coreligionists about rumors relating to an immediately forthcoming advent of the redeemer. Doubtless stimulated by the great enthusiasm generated by the crusading movement and the revivalist meetings among their Christian neighbors, these high-strung expectations deepened the religious tensions within the Jewish community too. They sharpened the preparedness of Jews for the great test which was to come when the year 1096, instead of bringing "gladness for Jacob," turned into a period of "sorrow and sighing, of wail and crying, and the people was afflicted by many evils enumerated in all the threatening admonitions [tokha-hot] written or unwritten." [8]

With these pathetic sentiments the principal Hebrew chronicler of these tragic developments, Solomon bar Simson, introduces his much-quoted tale of woe. Although written at least forty-four years after the events through a compilation of a variety of disjointed earlier records, his account has stood the test of subsequent investigations. It can be supplemented with a few data communicated by other contemporary chroniclers or poets, both Christian and Jewish.[9]

The few facts standing out in all these reports indicate that, although religious fanaticism was the main propelling force behind the Crusaders' attacks on Jews, the Church as such cannot be held responsible for the bloodshed. True, Pope Urban II remained remarkably silent when the news of the massacres reached him. But, if we are to judge only on the basis of extant sources, this silence may have been caused by the equally astonishing failure of Jews to seek papal intervention as Jacob bar Yequtiel had at the beginning of the century. Urban II had lingered in France for several months after the Council of Clermont, and he was within easy reach of the French and Norman communities. While German Jews may have felt some compunctions about sending a mission to an avowed enemy of their emperor in whom they confided, no such obstacle existed in the case of other threatened communities.

Of course, our information about the Jews of France or England at the end of the eleventh century is extremely limited. It is conceivable, therefore, that an approach was made to the pope or his chief representative, Adhémar de Monteil, bishop of Le Puy, and that the Jews were promised a measure of protection which may have served them in good stead in the following crucial months. Some such agreement with the Church may indeed be in the background of the letter from the French Jews to their German coreligionists which Peter the Hermit presented to the community of Treves upon his arrival in that city on April 10. Here the Jews were exhorted to "supply him [Peter] with food in all places where he would pass a Jewish settlement." In return Peter was to "speak kindly about the Jews, for he was a monk and his words were listened to." Although unconfirmed by any other source, this arrangement plausibly explains why the motley crowds assembled by this most effective evangelist of the First Crusade passed the Rhinelands in April without any untoward incident for Jews. It stands to reason that, as in most other matters, the Hermit cooperated here with the pope and his accredited representatives, who at times could not conceal their misgivings about the popular Frankenstein they had evoked. Remarkably, however, none of the contemporary chroniclers, Christian or Jewish, alludes to any such negotiations. Nor did Anti-Pope Clement III (Wibertus, 1080–1100), in his subsequent intervention of 1097–98 with the Bishop of Bamberg against relapsed Jewish converts, refer to any earlier efforts to prevent the bloodshed and to stem the wave of canonically inadmissible forced conversions. Most likely Urban II simply did not wish to take overt cognizance of "minor" incidents which might interfere with the realization of his grandiose plans. He reacted no more vigorously with respect to attacks on Christian cities, apparently preferring not to check the popular frenzy, that major propelling force in the entire movement.[10]

Most bishops, on the other hand, were often too deeply engrossed in the local struggles for power to care much for what happened to the relatively small Jewish communities under their jurisdiction. Only the youthful John, bishop of Spires, a loyal follower of the emperor, took seriously his obligation toward the latter's Jewish subjects. He enjoyed the support of the majority of burghers deeply appreciative of what he and his predecessor Rüdiger-Huozmann had done for the enhancement of the city

as a commercial center. No sooner did riots break out, which
entailed the loss of eleven Jewish lives, when the bishop appeared
with a substantial military force, quelled the outbreaks, and
punished some of the ringleaders by cutting off their arms. He
subsequently transported the Jews to fortified castles where they
successfully weathered the storms of that tragic spring. In neighboring Worms, on the contrary, neither bishop Adalbert, nor any
of the antibishops appointed by Henry IV after his contested
deposition of Adalbert in 1085, took effective action. The burghers,
moreover, had long been in opposition to their episcopal sovereign, and they now refused to support whatever remedial measures the latter may have adopted. Perhaps in recognition of his
own weakness, the bishop therefore seems merely to have advised
the Jews to accept the easy alternative of conversion to Christianity. In the largest of the three communities, Mayence, Archbishop Ruthard, as well as the burgrave and some of the leading
burghers, at first tried to protect the Jews gathered in the episcopal
palace, and sent some to apparent safety on a ship cruising on
the Rhine. The bishop's attitude was obviously lukewarm, however, and his action had to be secured by a substantial bribe
which, when it became known, defeated the moral force of his
exhortations.[11]

Moreover, neither he nor his confreres in other cities could rely
wholly on the active collaboration of the local citizenry, or of
their own soldiers. On many occasions, as noted by the Saxon
chronicler and the *Annales Patherburgenses*, "Christians did not
wish to fight against Christians in behalf of Jews." In Treves,
where the episcopal power was at a low ebb and where one of
Egilbert's predecessors was assassinated by his own *ministeriales*,
the bishop made an effort to protect the Jews who fled to his
castle, but was abandoned by his own guards and had to go into
hiding. All he could offer his Jewish subjects was the cheap advice
to embrace Christianity. Archbishop Hermann III of Cologne, on
his part, adopted a policy of dispersing Jews in the neighboring
villages. This merely meant that each group was attacked separately, the archbishop's military resources proving wholly inadequate against the aroused passions of Crusaders and local peasants
acting in unison. The ecclesiastical leaders of Metz, Ratisbon,

and other bishoprics proved no more effective. While none of them willingly cooperated with the assailants, they apparently made even less sustained efforts to salvage their Jewish protégés. In Ratisbon they evidently suffered the crusading mob to round up the entire Jewish community, force it into the Danube, and perform on it mass baptism. Whatever its canonical validity, this act at least saved the Jews from extermination and made possible the return of their majority to the Jewish faith after the storm blew over. Similarly in Prague, the story as related by the main chronicler shows Bishop Cosmas playing an active, if ineffectual, part in preventing the forced conversions. According to his account, only the absence of Duke Bratislav from the country was responsible for the authorities' failure to take vigorous measures against the rioters. The lower clergy, especially the parish priests, likewise remained, as a rule, on the side of law and order, only one monk Gottschalk being mentioned among the ringleaders of the riots.[12]

Even more ineffective were the efforts of friendly burghers. On the whole, the burghers' class, not yet in official control of the cities, had no legal obligation to protect Jews. Yet having had close business relations and also some social contacts with Jews, individual citizens extended a helping hand to their friends in need. Many leading burghers must also have feared the spread of disorders and plunder, once the unruly mobs got out of hand. That is why in Cologne and elsewhere many Jews found at least temporary shelter among their neighbors. In Mayence the burghers joined the militia of bishop and burgrave in fighting off the first assailants, until the latter's numbers and fervor overwhelmed all resistance. On the other hand, some inhabitants of the cities were from the first sympathizers, if not active participants, in the assaults on Jews for religious or economic reasons. Even friends of Jews were often persuaded to follow the herd, especially since some of them saw therein the opportunity to enrich themselves from the property entrusted to them by Jewish victims. It required more than usual prudence and *sang-froid* not to be affected by the prevailing mass psychosis, whose often irresistible nature was noted already by the chronicler Hugo of Flavigny.

It certainly seems amazing [he observed] that on a single day in many different places, moved in unison by a violent inspiration, such massacres should have taken place, despite their widespread disapproval and their condemnation as contrary to religion. But we know that they could not have been avoided since they occurred in the face of excommunication imposed by numerous clergymen [on those who took part in them], and of the threat of punishment on the part of many princes.

Such threats of retribution by state authorities were meaningful only if, as in the case of Spires, some of the rioters were immediately seized and punished. In most cases the hordes of the "people's crusade" marched on toward their ultimate goal, leaving behind many dead, maimed, or forcibly converted Jews. They had little to fear from punitive action by courts whose jurisdiction rarely extended beyond the confines of their locality and which could hardly prove the identity and extent of guilt of individual assailants. Threats of formal excommunication might have carried greater weight. But, apart from the fact that no such actual bans are recorded anywhere, most Crusaders doubtless felt that they were doing a thing pleasing to the Lord, and thus they could defy the clergy, whose declarations, they believed, had been secured only by Jewish bribes. Moreover, was not participation in the Crusade itself a sufficient expiation for all sins including bloodshed? [13]

Ecclesiastical leaders and sections of the more enlightened citizenry thus went through the motions of trying to save their Jewish neighbors, for the sake of humanity, in obedience to the established law and express orders of the emperor, or in response to substantial *douceurs*. The ravaging mobs, too, acted from a variety of motives. Many shiftless persons, adventurers, and even outright criminals joined the Crusade because they had little to lose and much to gain in the way of worldly goods. Attacking Jews seemed like the easiest road to riches, either through direct plunder or through the collection of ransom from the threatened communities. The rabble rousers could the more readily accept such payments, as the recognized rulers were known to have accepted similar protection money. All legitimate protectors of Jews, such as Bishop John of Spires, were accused by contempo-

raries and chroniclers of having acted only in response to tangible
Jewish appeals. As a matter of fact, in John's case all the evidence, including the Mayence Anonymus' direct assertion, points
to disinterested action. Nor were promises of immunity obtained
by the Jewish communities through great financial sacrifices considered altogether binding. Count Emicho and other ringleaders
could always blame subsequent outbreaks on the religious fervor
of their followers which they were unable to curb.[14]

In substance, the Crusades generally and their anti-Jewish
aspects specifically can be understood only against the background
of the extraordinary religious enthusiasm generated by revivalist
preachers. The unsophisticated marching bands, even more than
the regular armies, were readily persuaded by this simple
reasoning:

We are marching a great distance to seek our sanctuary and to take
vengeance on the Muslims. Lo and behold, there live among us Jews
whose forefathers slew him [Jesus] and crucified him for no cause.
Let us revenge ourselves on them first, and eliminate them from among
the nations, so that the name of Israel no longer be remembered, or
else let them be like ourselves and believe in the son of [Mary.]

Even a general of the stature of Godfrey of Bouillon adopted that
view until he was stopped by an express order of Henry IV,
abetted by a handsome gift of 500 silver marks from the communities of Mayence and Cologne. A distorted version of the
alleged self-condemnation of the Jews at Golgotha, "His [Jesus']
blood be on us, and on our children" (Matt. 27:25), likewise
made the rounds. It was believed that Jesus had said that "there
will come a day when my children will avenge my blood" on the
children of those guilty of the crucifixion. In the opinion of many
Crusaders, that time had come.[15]

Jewish reactions were no less frenzied. At first the Rhenish
communities which had long been spared overt persecutions
lulled themselves into believing that "it could not happen" to
them. Even the community of Mayence, which had experienced
some critical moments in 937 and about 1012, did not take early
precautions. Rhenish Jewry was apparently misled into thinking
that, like most of its French coreligionists, it would merely be
forced to supply the marching Crusaders with food and other

necessaries. When letters from French Jews reached the Rhine-lands, asking the German communities to extend similar hospi-tality to the Crusaders, the latter were fully prepared to shoulder that additional burden. They considered the new impost but an-other form of their manifold tributes on extraordinary occasions. They did not immediately realize, however, that they could not deal in this case with a unified command. If certain groups were pacified by such payments and moved on leaving the Jews undis-turbed, their followers did not feel in any way bound by them. Even the express imperial order secured the Jews but temporary respite, and it was obeyed only by leaders like Godfrey. It was disregarded even by such nobles as counts Emicho and Dithmar (Volkmar?); the latter allegedly vowed not to leave Germany before he had killed at least one Jew. Neither diplomatic skill nor substantial bribes were to prove adequate in the face of that extraordinary emergency.[16]

At times Jews took up cudgels in self-defense. In Mayence their armed young men, led by Kalonymos bar Meshullam, held off the assailants under Emicho until they were abandoned by the arch-bishop's soldiers and overwhelmed by far superior numbers. In another city, identified by N. Porges with Vishehrad near Prague, 500 young Jews, joined by a force of 1,000 men of the duke's army, defeated the assailing Crusaders, suffering only six casualties. According to a tradition preserved in the fourteenth-century Czech rhymed chronicle by "Dalimil," the duke encouraged the Jewish resistance, and "the Jews vanquished the Crusaders, slaying two hundred Germans." After the battle the Jews were transferred to a neighboring castle, and the community escaped the fate of most of its coreligionists.[17]

Even in connection with these two episodes the chronicler emphasized that the Jewish fighters had been weakened by pro-longed fasting. From the outset the Rhenish Jews had been ex-horted in letters from France to proclaim days of fast. Most of the victims had indeed placed their main reliance on divine inter-vention. When that expected supernatural help failed to mate-rialize, they saw therein but an opportunity granted them by God's inscrutable will to suffer martyrdom for their faith. They allegedly were forewarned by a ghost congregation on one night praying aloud in the Mayence synagogue behind closed doors. According to our chief chronicler, Solomon, the Jews of Mayence, seeing all avenues of escape closed,

declared with their whole heart and willing soul, After all one must not have any doubts concerning the ways of the Holy One blessed be He who had given us His Torah and the commandment to suffer death in behalf of the unity of His holy name. Happy are we if we fulfill His wish, and happy is he who is slain and slaughtered for the unity of His name. Such an one will be prepared to enter the world-to-come, to sit in company of the righteous men, R. 'Aqiba and his compeers who are the foundations of the world and who have died for His name. More, he will have exchanged the world of darkness for a world of light, a world of suffering for a world of joy, the transitory world for a world enduring for ever.

After this mutual self-exhortation, they proceeded to self-immolation. Imitating on a grand scale Abraham's readiness to sacrifice Isaac, fathers slaughtered their children and husbands their wives. These acts of unspeakable horror and heroism were performed in the ritualistic form of slaughter with sacrificial knives sharpened in accordance with Jewish law. At times the leading sages of the community, supervising the mass immolation, were the last to part with life at their own hands. Shemaryahu, a refugee from the holocaust of Mörs, resisted conversion even after he was removed from a grave where he had been buried alive; he accepted martyrdom, saying "this is the day to which I was looking forward all my life." Gone were the restraints of Jewish law and ethics, enjoining suicide and manslaughter in any form and extolling the merits of life as such. In the mass hysteria, sanctified by the glow of religious martyrdom and compensated by the confident expectation of heavenly rewards, nothing seemed to matter but to end life before one fell into the hands of the implacable foes and had to face the inescapable alternative of death at the enemy's hand or conversion to Christianity.[18]

Not all Jews in the communities under attack committed suicide. Many were killed by their assailants before they had a chance to participate in this act of self-extermination. Others lost their courage at the last moment and were slain by the rioters. Still others surrendered and accepted conversion to save their lives. Many were physically compelled to submit to baptism. On one

occasion, we are told, the Jews of Mörs were imprisoned overnight and carefully guarded lest they commit suicide. In the
morning they were dragged before the baptismal font. It is impossible even remotely to estimate the ratio of such converts,
voluntary or involuntary, to the number of dead. The Hebrew
chroniclers underplay the number of the weak-kneed, and stress
only the acts of heroism on the part of the resisters. If the figures
of 900–1,300 martyrs in Mayence and 800 more in Worms are
correct, these must have embraced the large majority of Jewish
inhabitants of those cities. In this case, the total number of German Jews who suffered martyrdom in 1096 may indeed have approximated 5,000, as estimated by the sixteenth-century historian,
Gedaliah ibn Yaḥya. But there is no way of ascertaining the real
number of victims, since the extant *memor* books apparently
recorded the names of only a minority. Nor can we tell how many
survived, either through conversion or because their own communities were not in the path of the crusading bands or were
more effectively protected by their governments. In fact, we know
too little about the total Jewish population of the Germanies in
that period to estimate how large was the majority of survivors,
which undoubtedly was very substantial.[19]

The tragedy had a tremendous impact on the minds of contemporaries. Before long their recollections assigned an ever
greater area to the massacres. The persecutions supposedly had
affected not only Germany and France, but also northern Italy,
where the name of at least one martyr, Moses of Pavia, was preserved. The fact, however, that the same source mentions among
the Lombard martyrs also Kalonymos (bar Shabbetai) of Rome,
one of the well-known victims of the Worms massacre, and that
another Hebrew author attributes the bloodshed in Italy to Godfrey of Bouillon, makes them both extremely suspect. Ultimately,
David Gans, the well-known sixteenth-century historian and astronomer, wrote with complete abandon that "in that year [1096]
there were persecutions and massacres in all sections of Germany,
France, Spain, England, Italy, Bohemia and Hungary. These persecutions were unprecedented in their savagery." [20]

Some of the forced converts probably remained within the new
fold after the Crusaders had moved away. The author of *Gesta*

Treverorum claims that a rabbi named Micheas of Treves explained to his coreligionists that it was better to accept Christianity "than thus to be subject from day to day to the danger to our lives and possessions." It was indeed with great personal danger that most of these converts, according to Solomon bar Simson, ate only ritually slaughtered meat, abstained from drinking prohibited wine, and only rarely attended church services. "The Gentiles themselves knew that they had not wholeheartedly accepted baptism." Their hopes of early return to their ancestral faith materialized sooner than most of them dared to expect. King William II of England-Normandy and Emperor Henry IV of Germany, defying the more rigid interpretations of canon law, declared the forced baptisms null and void and allowed the converts to profess Judaism in public again. Like Henry, William could disclaim all responsibility for the events of 1096, since Normandy had then been under his brother Robert's control. Both monarchs also disregarded such protests as were voiced by Anti-Pope Clement III in 1097–98. The unconverted Jews welcomed back the returning converts, and Rashi specifically permitted to drink of their wine, and even to allow them to perform the functions of priesthood. Ultimately, what stood out in the memory of subsequent generations were only the great acts of heroism and testimony for the faith of the martyrs. Their deeds were extolled in numerous penitential poems, many of which were incorporated in the permanent liturgical recitations of European synagogues.[21]

THE LATIN KINGDOM OF JERUSALEM

Solomon bar Simson evinced interest in what happened to the Crusaders after their departure from the Holy Roman Empire. Writing about half a century later (1140), he still reflects the glee with which the Jewish communities hailed the news about the destruction of the bands of *pauperes,* their chief enemies, in Hungary, the Balkans, or Asia Minor. With more vindictiveness than accuracy he described in graphic detail the scenes before the fortress of Wieselburg, unsuccessfully beleaguered by Emicho and his troops. The defeated count escaped during the night and returned to Germany, while his followers were slain by the Hungarians or sunk in the mud. According to Solomon, a bridge previously built by Peter the Hermit broke down, and "thousands upon thousands and myriads upon myriads drowned in the Danube, so that [their foes] crossed on their backs as one walks on land. When their remnant returned home bringing these tidings our heart rejoiced, for the Lord has shown His revenge on our enemies. In those days there was an eclipse of the sun." Such an eclipse was taken as an ill omen for the Christians, just as an eclipse of the moon in 1099 was considered by the invaders of Palestine as an encouraging sign of the approaching eclipse of the Crescent. Our chronicler also confused the destruction of detachments led by Volkmar and Gottschalk, the main agents in the mass conversions of Jews in Prague and Ratisbon, with that of followers of their more famous colleague, Peter the Hermit. In any case, even most survivors of the passage through Hungary and Bulgaria, where their brutality and proneness to plunder had quickly turned against them the friendly Christian peoples, did not last long after crossing the Byzantine territories into Asia Minor. Here in their first encounter with the Muslim army of the Sultan of Rum at Cibetum they were decisively defeated.[22]

In the meantime, the arrival in the Byzantine areas of some of these unorganized bands, followed by regular army units, and their progressive concentration in Constantinople, deeply impressed the Balkan population, both Christian and Jewish. Here many Crusaders continued with their riotous way of living. If we are to believe a French chronicler of the twelfth century, Baudri (Baldricus) of Bourgueil, the troops under Bohemund, upon arrival in Pelagonia (Macedonia), "justly burned all travelers, Jews, heretics and Saracens, whom everybody calls enemies of God." True, the source underlying this statement refers only to the massacre of Paulicians, and there were few, if any, Saracens in Macedonia. Yet news of such slaughter or wholesale captivity for ransom must have traveled far and wide.[23]

From obscure references in a Byzantine Hebrew epistle it appears, on the other hand, that these rumors gave new impetus to messianic expectations among the Jews of Salonica. Elijah was supposed to have appeared to some local leaders; the masses began neglecting their work. Other signs of the approaching Redeemer manifested themselves to an extent gaining credence even among Christians who previously had "hated the Jews immeasurably." Both governor and archbishop allegedly inquired, "O Jews, why do you remain in Salonica? Sell your homes and property and the Emperor will help you. . . . You have not yet set out, although we have definitely learned that your Messiah has appeared." The government supposedly ceased collecting capitation tax and the other levies, so that Jews could "sit garbed in prayer-shawls and not work." None of the original Salonican letters, from which these reports were culled, were available to the author of our epistle. We know still less about the reaction of their recipients in Constantinople, which set the pace for the whole Empire. But there seems to be enough substance in these reports to indicate that the Byzantine Jewish, as well as Christian, masses were seized by the messianic frenzy. The central government, however, maintained its equilibrium, provided the passing hosts of Crusaders with food and weapons, and sped them on to their destination. Afraid for its own safety, it did not allow them to dwell too long in the Balkans, and on the whole effectively maintained public order. That is why Byzantine Jewry seems, except for some local outbreaks such as that in Pelagonia, to have overcome the great crisis without serious losses.[24]

Eastern Jewries were less fortunate. Just as their Muslim neighbors, they did not seem at first to comprehend the nature and extent of the danger. The Muslim principalities continued with their perennial squabbles, unwittingly, and sometimes even consciously, playing into the hands of the invaders. As far as we can judge, Jews too carried on with their usual ways of living, at least until the enemy began knocking at their gates. But when the invasion materialized, they took sudden fright.

The state of mind of Syrian Jewry in the localities lying athwart of the marching Crusaders is well illustrated by a pathetic letter from an unidentified Syrian community. Mentioning briefly "the approaching misfortune, because of the fear of the Germans who are about to encamp among us, and because we are overwhelmed by the bad news from them," the elders requested the Damascus leaders both to institute prayers for them and to save them "without counting the cost." Like their western coreligionists, they placed their main reliance on fasts and ransom money, which might be expended to stave off an attack and to redeem captives from among the survivors. But, doubtless taught by the experience of their predecessors, many Jews must have fled before the approaching enemy to the safety of as yet unoccupied cities. They were joined by a great many Muslims. In the case of Ramleh, we are told by a Latin chronicler, the Crusaders found the city completely evacuated by the Muslim population. This movement was but slightly balanced by the arrival of Muslim volunteers eager to fight in the defense of Al-Quds (Jerusalem).[25]

The fears of the Muslim and Jewish populations proved wholly justified. Even the greatest Christian historian of the Latin kingdom, William, who was to serve as archbishop of Tyre from 1175–83, though writing some seven decades after the event, could not repress his shudder at the recollection of the carnage during the conquest of Jerusalem in 1099.

It was impossible [he wrote] to look upon the vast numbers of the slain without horror; everywhere lay fragments of human bodies, and the very ground was covered with the blood of the slain. It was not alone the spectacle of headless bodies and mutilated limbs strewn in all directions that roused horror in all that looked upon them. Still more dreadful was it to gaze upon the victors themselves, dripping with blood from head to foot, an ominous sight which brought terror to all who met them. It is reported that within the Temple enclosure alone about ten thousand infidels perished, in addition to those who lay slain everywhere throughout the city in the streets and squares, the number of whom was estimated as no less.

This indiscriminate slaughter was facilitated by the evacuation from the city of the entire Christian population shortly before the siege. Most Jews who had not escaped before the Crusaders' arrival—the country had been in a turmoil for several years before—either fell in battle, or were killed during the general massacre. According to the Muslim historian, Ibn al-Qalanisi, the conquerors, finding Jews assembled in their synagogue, set it afire. Apparently, on seeing the section of the wall defended by them breached by the invaders, many Jews of themselves sought solace in prayer at the synagogue. There is no reason to doubt the accuracy of this statement written by a well-informed historian in neighboring Damascus some fifty or sixty years after the event, although we have no additional evidence from either Jewish or Christian sources.[26]

Ibn al-Qalanisi did not claim that all Jerusalem Jews were burned. His statement, repeated a century later by Sibt ibn al-Jauzi, is therefore not controverted by the fact that quite a few Jews survived the city's fall. According to the somewhat unreliable chronicler, Baudri, even greedy Tancred sold many Jewish captives far below the current price for slaves of 33 gold dinars per head. He allegedly disposed of them at the rate of thirty men for one gold piece (dinar), in order to show their inferiority as compared with the price secured by Judas Iscariot. In fact, prices of slaves always dropped sharply after a campaign which greatly increased their supply, and they must have doubly declined in Palestine in 1099, because the new conquerors had their hands full in extending their conquests. Using the accepted technique of predicting for some distant future what he observed in his day, a more or less contemporary apocalyptic writer described the "coming" massacres among Muslims, the captivity of Muslim women and how the Crusaders "will sacrifice children daily to Jesus." He also mentioned that at that time, "the nations will rise against Israel, and slay a great many of them. Many of the illiterate will sin [apostasize], while many of the pious will be tortured with chains to make them give up the Lord's law." Probably some of these converts later escaped and returned to Judaism.[27]

We now have a remarkable confirmation in a Genizah letter describing the efforts of Jewish fund raisers in Egypt for the ransom of some remaining twenty captives held in Ascalon. According to the writer of that epistle, Isaiah ha-Kohen ben Masliah ha-Maskil (the Enlightened), these twenty survivors were only a minority of those who had reached Ascalon, then still in Egyptian hands. Many others had succeeded in escaping from captivity, abjured their faith, or been carried away to Antioch. Those previously liberated had become impatient, and because of their privations decided to leave for Egypt "without food or protection against the cold, and they died on the way. Others in a similar way perished at sea, and yet others, after having arrived here safely, became exposed to a 'change of air,'" that is, suffered from the pest which had been ravaging Egypt for a number of years. But many others had been ransomed, far below the market price, for some 500 dinars available to the charity group, and safely conducted to Egypt by a philanthropic coreligionist, agent of the Sultan in Ascalon. But apparently no professing Jew remained in Jerusalem, for the new regime decided to convert it into an all-Christian city, and prohibited infidels from setting foot in it. It is small wonder, then, that the Jerusalem carnage, even if it affected only a minority of Jews, caused their coreligionists in other parts of the country to resist more fiercely. They were the main defenders of Haifa, where they seem to have constituted the majority of the population. Although provided with heavy equipment for the siege, Albert of Aix tells us, the Crusaders were beaten back by the Jewish defenders, and after a fortnight of futile attacks "lost all courage and, in total despair, desisted from all further assaults." Only after the patriarch's personal intervention and the arrival of reinforcements did the besiegers take the city by storm.[28]

Who were the Jewish survivors of Jerusalem? It appears that, in their majority, they were members of the old-established Karaite community of the Holy City. The Rabbanites themselves may have worshiped in more than one synagogue. Certainly, the Karaites had a synagogue in their own quarter, which is not recorded as having gone up in flames during the holocaust mentioned by Ibn al-Qalanisi. The fact that the writer of the Genizah epistle signs his name ha-Maskil, which had long become almost a technical designation for a Karaite scholar, and that he felt that there was "no one in this country [Egypt] to whom we could write as we are writing to you," would by itself mark this action as resting primarily in Karaite hands. This impression is further confirmed by the relative smallness of the amounts raised in the still well-to-do and populous Jewish communities in Egypt, particularly when contrasted with the vast collection of 330 codices and 8 scrolls of law which the committee had succeeded in ransoming from the Crusaders. All these books, moreover, consisted exclusively of biblical manuscripts and scrolls. This concentration on Scripture would hardly have occurred in the case of a Rabbanite congregation, which at the end of the eleventh century would undoubtedly have possessed quite a few copies of the Talmud and other rabbinic writings. But such a large biblical collection may well have been the long-treasured possession of Jerusalem's Karaite synagogue and academy, previously a world center of Karaite learning. The departure of a great many members in the preceding, turbulent decades probably left that great library intact. It now fell into the hands of the conquerors, who were perfectly willing to preserve copies of Hebrew Scriptures and secure a good price for them.[29]

If this hypothesis should be borne out by further discoveries, we may also better understand some long-debated colophons on old Karaite scrolls of law. In one of them the original writer had threatened with dire penalties anyone who would steal, sell, or remove the scroll from Jerusalem. Yet a later hand noted briefly, "Removed by way of ransom from the spoils of Jerusalem, the Holy City, to the 'Jerusalem' Congregation of Fusṭaṭ." This scroll may actually have been included among the books rescued by the intervention of Isaiah ben Maṣliaḥ and his confreres. Nor was this literary salvage discontinued after 1099. According to the somewhat dubious colophon on another scroll of law, it was Solomon, the Karaite elder of Jerusalem, who in 1106 secured from King Baldwin I the return of all sacred books. Needless to say that this return, too, was obtained by some consideration, probably more than the 200 dinars paid for the entire former collection in the early rush of events. In all these negotiations the Karaites may have persuaded the Christian rulers that their ancestors, from whom, they claimed, the Rabbanites had separated in the days of King Jeroboam I, could not have taken part in the crucifixion of Jesus. Although such Karaite arguments are attested only from modern times, they may already have been advanced at this crucial first contact with the conquering Latins.[30]

Palestine Jewry, including its Karaite segment, recovered but slowly from this shock. True, the Crusaders were gradually acclimatizing themselves to the conditions of the country and seeking to restore its normal economic life. They had to learn to get along with the Muslim population, although the peace that followed the hostilities remained precarious and the huge defense budget constantly drained the Treasury's limited resources. For a while

Egypt still retained control over Gaza and Ascalon (not occupied by the Crusaders until 1153), where some Jewish refugees, as well as ransomed captives had found shelter during the invasion. From the outset the Crusaders treated the entire local population outside Jerusalem far more humanely. Isaiah ben Maṣliaḥ himself observed with amazement that the female captives had not been raped by the Frankish troops. Statesmanship replaced religious fanaticism, especially after the short-lived regime of Godfrey and his brother Baldwin's accession to the throne. Hence neither the Jews of Tiberias nor those of Tripolis, after its conquest by the Crusaders in 1109, seem to have suffered serious harm. Similarly, when Tyre finally surrendered in 1124, its large Jewish population was not molested. Some Jews were even allowed in 1243 to live in the newly established Venetian quarter. This policy, pursued during all later conquests, was more in keeping with the earlier treatment extended to Muslims and Jews, as well as to native Christian sectarians, during the Crusaders' long march through Syria before they reached Jerusalem.[31]

Economic pressures likewise favored the slow regeneration of Jewish life. Together with the feudalization of the country and development of an overseas commerce which largely lay in the hand of the Italian merchant republics, the conquerors established a number of royal monopolies to buttress the treasury's ever insufficient revenue. As in Sicily, the Norman rulers found it convenient to entrust the management of some of these industries to Jews. At least when Benjamin of Tudela visited the Holy Land about 1170, he found Jerusalem, though a "small city," fortified by three walls and inhabited by a polyglot population which included only four Jewish families. The city, he added, "contains a dyeing house for which the Jews pay a small rent annually to the king, on condition that besides the Jews no other dyers be allowed in Jerusalem." In neighboring Tyre, which in the preceding century had inherited the mantle of Jewish cultural leadership from Jerusalem and Tiberias, he found a sizable community of 500, including some skilled glass-blowers, "who make that fine Tyrian glassware which is prized in all countries." Somewhat later one of the Christian lords (Amelric?), falling ill in Acco, requested the association of physicians in Cairo to send him one of its members. They chose Maimonides, a fairly recent arrival. The great philosopher, whose fame as a physician was just beginning to spread, was unwilling, however, to return to Palestine, which he had left after a brief sojourn a few years before.[32]

All through that period the conquerors increasingly adopted the ways of life characteristic of the Near Eastern peoples. In fact, they speedily developed certain Levantine features which remained incomprehensible to their compatriots at home. Had not, as early as 1114, Patriarch Arnulf performed a marriage ceremony between a Christian and a Muslim woman? He drew for it a reprimand from Pope Paschal II. These factors accounted also for greater toleration of new or returning Jewish settlers. Nevertheless the enmity between Jews and the Crusaders persisted with sufficient intensity for the Muslim commander, Imad ad-Din Zangi, after his reconquest of Edessa, to settle there 300 Jewish families in 1146 as a replacement for Armenians accused of high treason.[33]

Remarkably, the growing Jewish communities in the Latin Kingdom did not suffer from the usual disabilities of their West European coreligionists, although the general feudal order introduced into the country by the conquerors followed rather closely western patterns. In fact, starting afresh with a conglomeration of inhabitants recruited from all over western Europe, though with a decided preponderance of Norman and French elements, the new realm developed certain new institutional forms which reciprocally influenced the subsequent evolution in the West. Surprisingly, therefore, we do not even hear of discriminatory taxation of Jews. It stands to reason that, continuing the system prevailing in the occupied countries before their conquest, the new regime imposed capitation and land taxes upon the religious minorities. The difference was that, as in Sicily, the Muslims became subject to that form of taxation, while the Latin Christians may have been freed from it. In a direct emulation of western procedures, Bohemund III of Antioch transferred in 1183 to Roger de Moulins and his brother Alexander many (*nonnullos*) "Greeks, Armenians, Latins and Jews," or rather the tax revenue from them. Perhaps the age-old local taxes were so much taken for granted that none of the legislators or chroniclers found it necessary to comment on them. Characteristically, in the great emergency of the 1180's the rulers imposed a national tax to be collected from all inhabitants alike. While moderate in size and roughly ranging from 1 percent of property to 2 percent of income, this tax as promulgated in 1183, "included Christians, Moslems, and Jews; Greeks, Italians, Franks, and Syrians." Even churches and monasteries, as well as nobles and their mercenaries, had to pay it. This tax, as J. L. LaMonte observed, was not only extraordinary in the annals of the Latin Kingdom, but "is the first national tax of which there is any record in the feudal period" in the West.[34]

Such absence of anti-Jewish discrimination may be accounted for not only by the smallness of the Jewish population and by the country's socioeconomic needs, but also, paradoxically, by traditions brought with them by the conquerors from those European countries which harbored mixed Jewish and Muslim minorities. We recall that eleventh-century Sicily had treated its religious minorities basically alike with the Christian majority. The Crusaders coming from other countries, too, started from common Carolingian traditions, and a background of the more or less favorable, if largely unformulated, Jewish status of the eleventh century. The great series of anti-Jewish laws, which was to be enacted in the course of the twelfth and thirteenth centuries, had little bearing on the constitutional developments in the Holy Land. Under these circumstances, Jews were allowed to cultivate their trade relations with both the East and the West, and to partake especially of the flourishing commerce developing in the coastal cities.

For this reason, even after Saladin's reconquest of Jerusalem in 1187, which to all intents and purposes presaged the end of the Latin Kingdom, relatively few Jews availed themselves of the opportunity to return there, though the new administration hastened to remove the Crusaders' outlawry of Jewish settlement and, according to Yehudah al-Ḥarizi, even issued a call to Jews to resettle in the Holy City. At its Egyptian headquarters many Jews, including Maimonides, played an influential role. To be sure, true to its general policy of rekindling the Muslim religious spirit by reviving the old Islamic institutions, the new regime restored many provisions of the so-called Covenant of 'Umar which had gone into desuetude under the more tolerant Faṭimids. Nevertheless most Jews doubtless shared the favorable opinion of Saladin voiced by a contemporary chronicler, Abraham bar Hillel, who called him "a righteous king, repairer of the breach, remover of fear and averse to bribery." In fact, on his visit to Jerusalem in 1218, Al-Ḥarizi already found there three functioning congregations of Jews from "Ascalon," the "West" (North Africa and Muslim Spain), and France (western Europe). The former group probably included natives from other Palestinian and Syrian communities, while the latter embraced a great many pilgrims only on a temporary visit to the Holy Land. But their combined number still was very small. The majority of Jews continued living in the thin coastal strip which remained under Christian control, where Acco soon assumed the undisputed leadership over the communal and spiritual affairs of all Palestinian Jewry. This overt preference for living under the domination of Crusaders not only underscored the importance of the economic factor and the intervening transformation in the rulers' attitude toward religious minorities, but also adumbrated on a small scale the great historic shift of the Jewish people's cultural center from the Muslim to the Christian world.[35]

THE SECOND CRUSADE

In the West meanwhile the relations between Jews and Christians suffered further deterioration. At first, to be sure, there was an apparent return to normalcy. In 1102, the Norman priest, Johannes, of the southern Italian city of Oppido, could embrace Judaism without causing immediate reprisals to the Jewish community around him; only he himself had to flee to the Near East. Mayence Jews who had succeeded in escaping to Spires returned to their city. In 1104, they solemnly dedicated the newly rebuilt synagogue, which, along with large parts of the city, had been destroyed during the riots by the sacrificial fire set by a martyr, Mar Isaac son of David, the community's elder. Henry IV instituted an inquiry concerning the whereabouts of the dispersed Jewish property, and found that relatives of Archbishop Ruthard had played a prominent role in its unlawful acquisition. Henry's partisan, "Anti-Pope" Clement III, pointed an accusing finger at the archbishop himself in connection with the disappearance of a gold cup which, originally the property of a Spires church, had come into Jewish, and later into the archbishop's, control. By first denying, and later confessing to its possession, Ruthard had shown that "he did not fear to commit theft combined with sacrilege." This entire prosecution soon became entangled in the political struggles of the day, the archbishop joining the opposition against Henry. Whatever property was thus recovered accrued to the benefit of the imperial treasury, rather than to the heirs of the original Jewish owners or the Jewish community at large. Nevertheless, the fact that even a semisovereign archbishop had to render an account of heirless Jewish property set an important precedent. Widely debated, it must also have served as a warning for future despoilers of Jews. Some Jews may also have recovered treasures hidden by their forefathers in cellars, as had Isaac bar David himself after the first massacre shortly before he committed that fateful suicide.[36]

In 1112, Henry V renewed the relief from tolls in all imperial possessions which his father had granted to the burghers and Jews of Worms. The Cologne community, too, seems to have recuperated quickly, and by 1121–23 some of its members, including women, could indulge in friendly religious debates with a local abbot named Rudolph. Communities which escaped destruction in 1096 made even more rapid progress. By 1105, the Jews of Nuremberg were said to have treasonably surrendered the city to the besieging Emperor Henry V. Subsequently they allegedly acquired the best locations in the market. Exaggerated as these reports by the fifteenth-century Nuremberg chronicler Sigmund Meisterlein undoubtedly are, they do reveal the presence there of a substantial Jewish community at the beginning of the twelfth century.[37]

More complicated was the situation of the surviving involuntary converts. Although permitted by Henry IV and William II to return to their ancestral faith, they must have realized the precariousness of their position in the face of the Church's consistent opposition to relapse after the sacrament of baptism had taken hold. This opposition had been unwaveringly maintained by the Church leadership since the days of Justinian, although occasionally some local churchmen had themselves deviated from that rule. In our period it was particularly Hermann, Cosmas' successor in the bishopric of Prague, who tolerated the reversion to Judaism of those forcibly baptized by Volkmar's rabble in 1096. On his deathbed he is reputed to have repented deeply that "sin" of toleration. It is small wonder, then, that the Jews of Prague, informed of Duke Vratislav's decision to leave the treatment of relapsed converts to the bishop's discretion, began in 1198 clandestinely to transfer their holdings to Hungary or Poland, doubtless in preparation of their own removal there. The duke became incensed, and sent soldiers to confiscate all Jewish valuables, leaving them only food. Advancing the spurious historical argument that after the fall of Jerusalem the Jews had left Palestine penniless and, hence, all their wealth was acquired in the country, he despoiled them of their riches. According to the chronicler waxing rhetorical, these far exceeded the riches carried away by the conquerors from burning Troy. This wholesale expropriation did not prevent the government nine years later from heavily taxing the Jews together with the other subjects for the ransom of Duke Sviatopluk. Some of the converts, on the other hand, doubtless remained within their new fold. Perhaps among these was one Jacob, who soon thereafter made a career in government service and reached the high rank of vicedominus. By 1124, however, he was accused of having returned to Judaism, destroyed a formerly Christian altar which had in the meantime been erected in the Jewish synagogue (possibly in an annex originally maintained by the forced converts and subsequently used for worship by Christian servants of Jews), and thrown the Christian relics into the sewer. This irrational act led not only to his imprisonment and the confiscation of his property, but also to an enormous "ransom" of 3,000 pounds of silver and 100 pounds of gold, paid by the Jewish community for his life. This ransom seems to have been but a fine imposed on the Jewish community, after a successful cabal by Jacob's enemies, who may well have fabricated his sacrilegious act. They thus forced the duke's hand against his favorite and then pacified him with this huge "ransom." [38]

All these were but pinpricks when compared with what was in store for the Jews during the Second Crusade in 1146. The religious fervor, especially in France and Germany, was no less deep than that which had manifested itself half a century earlier. Stimulated by an existing but endangered Latin Kingdom of Jerusalem, this Crusade attracted an even wider following. Kings Louis VII of France and Conrad III of Germany themselves took the cross. Precisely because it so greatly appealed to the ruling classes, its impact on Jewish-Christian relations all over Europe was even more profound and enduring.

One immediate effect of this more responsible leadership of the movement and the relative absence of unruly mobs was a far lesser loss of Jewish lives. Our main source, the "Book of Remembrance" by Ephraim bar Jacob of Bonn, who as a boy of thirteen had been among the Cologne refugees at the castle of Wolkenburg, reports mainly attacks on individuals and small groups. Most of these sufferers had ventured outside the castles to which they had been removed from threatened localities. Ephraim mentions larger figures, such as "about 150 souls" or "countless souls," only in connection with three distant communities, probably French, whose very identity appears dubious. He records here what he learned from hearsay, including a story of how the great Jewish scholar, Jacob ben Meir Tam, was wounded while resisting conversion, but was saved by a passing knight. Apparently the attackers, too, were not massed as during the First Crusade, but as a rule consisted of a few bloodthirsty individuals. It was enough for the Cologne Jews to retire to the Wolkenburg, and man it with the relatively few armed young men in their midst to stave off the attack. The chronicler specifically mentions that the commander, all his men, indeed all Christians, had left the castle by prearrangement. More, a Jewish farmer seems to have lived undisturbed in a village at the foot of that hill, and lost his two sons only when the latter out of curiosity walked up toward the castle. Their murderer was apprehended, blinded, and allowed to die within three days. A single Crusader attacked two Mayence Jews working on a wine press; he moved on without being detected. On the other hand, a young Jewish traveler from Mayence to Worms vigorously fought back his assailants, wounding three before he went down. Three Bachrach Jews, including the "reputable" scholar, Alexander bar Moses, left their refuge in the castle of Staleck and went back to the city "to attend to their loans and other business on the government's order" (May 6, 1147). They had apparently been in the castle for many months (most attacks had occurred in September–October, 1146), and their affairs brooked no further delay. Pursued by some Crusaders, they chose death rather than conversion. Only the community of Würzburg, which had refused to face the danger and escape into neighboring castles, was assailed by a group of Crusaders and a local mob. It lost twenty-two persons, the rest finding shelter in the houses of Christian neighbors and, on the following day, in the otherwise unidentified castle of Stuhlbach or Stuhlpitsch.[39]

Clearly, forewarned by previous experiences, both the Jews and the authorities took early precautions, especially in regions where the memory of the former bloodshed still was much alive. They did it apparently without the prompting of King Conrad, whose mind was fully preoccupied with domestic conflicts and soon also with the preparations for the Crusade. Not that there was a paucity of rabble rousers. Once again, it was a hermit who left his seclusion in order to evangelize for the Crusade and became the greatest scourge of German Jewry. Like Peter the Hermit, the Cistercian monk, Radulph, a most effective recruiting agent, was a man of strict religiosity, rather than intellectual attainments. Otto von Freising, the great historian and eye-witness of many negotiations, later claimed that Radulph had "heedlessly" (non vigilanter) inserted in his speeches a statement that "Jews residing in the various cities and hamlets ought to be killed as enemies of the Christian faith." Otto obviously underestimated the intent behind these "casual" remarks, whose incendiary character he himself admitted. Their very repetition shows that the preacher was bent on arousing his listeners to repeat the massacres of the First Crusade. He defied even the archbishop of Mayence, who found no other way of silencing the fanatical propagandist than to appeal to Bernard of Clairvaux. This outstanding homilist and theologian was not only the spiritual leader of the Crusade, enjoying a matchless reputation for both learning and saintliness throughout western Europe, but also exercised specific authority over the Cistercian monks. His position was made unmistakably clear in various sermons in which he preached that even heretics "should be won over not by arms, but by arguments." [40]

Yielding to such entreaties also from other quarters, Bernard sent letters to Germany and then undertook a journey there for the double purpose of preventing bloodshed of Jews and inducing Conrad to join the Crusade in person. He was successful in both endeavors. He admonished Radulph to desist, unless he wished to be guilty of the three sins of unlawful preaching, contempt for bishops, and incitation to murder. Defying an aroused populace in Mayence, Bernard persuaded Radulph to return to his monastery. The abbot of Clairvaux went further and addressed a circular letter to various cities in which he referred to the Church's long-established doctrine that "Jews must not be persecuted, killed, nor put to flight." He cited the psalmist's prediction "Slay them not lest my people forget" (59:12), and added, "They [the Jews] are living symbols for us, reminding us always of the Lord's Passion. For this reason they are dispersed to all lands so that while they expiate so great a crime, they may be everywhere living witnesses of our redemption. . . . When the time is ripe all Israel shall be saved." One might legitimately demand only that Jews not collect interest from debts owed them by Crusaders, in accordance with a moratorium on all such debts shortly before proclaimed by the pope.[41]

In this connection Bernard made a statement, perhaps unwittingly, which was destined in the long run to controvert his preaching of limited toleration. In trying to answer some popular accusations, he declared, "We are pained to observe that, where there are no Jews, the Christian moneylenders extort worse usuries [peius iudaizare], if these men may indeed be called Christians, and not rather baptized Jews." Here the abbot's essentially anti-Jewish animus, which had come to the fore during his struggle with Anacletus II and in some of his exegetical comments, as when, in one of his sermons, he called Jews immersed in the "night" of their perfidy, again broke through. The equation of Jew with usurer, just beginning to have a semblance of reality in his native France, but not yet in Germany, now received authoritative support.[42]

In substance, therefore, St. Bernard did not contradict what his compeer, Peter the Venerable, had just written in a rabidly anti-Jewish epistle to Louis VII. Such a vehement denunciation by a leading churchman of Jewish economic activities, though not specifically of Jewish usury, had not been heard anywhere in western Europe since the days of Agobard and Amulo. In verbiage even stronger than that used by the archbishops of Lyons three centuries before, the abbot of the famous monastery of Cluny urged his king to expropriate the Jews' ill-gotten wealth and to expel them from France. With special reference to the contemporary agitation for a new Crusade, he argued that Jews should contribute more than anyone else to the expenses of the holy war. In direct contrast to Pope Alexander II, Peter insisted that Jews were worse than Muslims, who at least believed in Jesus, if not in his divine nature. He suggested, therefore,

Let their [the Jews'] life be spared them, but their money taken away, in order that, through Christian hands helped by the money of blaspheming Jews the boldness of unbelieving Saracens may be vanquished! . . . All this, most gracious King, have I written to thee from the love of Christ, and of thee and thy Christian army, since it were foolish and displeasing, I believe, to God, if so holy an expedition, on which the property of Christians is to be spent as each can afford, were not assisted much more amply by the money of the ungodly.

True, this letter seems not to have been made public immediately. But Peter had previously circulated a polemical tractate "Against the Jews' Inveterate Obstinacy," in which he used substantially the same arguments. Able controversialist that he was, he knew that heaping mere negatives would prove ineffective. He intermingled therefore, from time to time, some sweetly "reasonable" appeals to Jews to abandon their obstinacy and convert themselves to Christianity:

Why are you not touched when you see that the entire strength of the Christian faith, the entire hope of human salvation, is derived from your books? Why are you not touched when you see that we have received from your people, from the descendants of the great Abraham, the patriarchs, the foretelling prophets, the preaching apostles, the exalted supercelestial Virgin, mother of Christ; yea Christ himself, our redeemer, whom your prophet had announced to the nations?

But he devoted most of the treatise to almost vulgar Jew-baiting.[43]

Much as we may wish to explain these temperamental outbursts by the abbot's keen disappointment because of the Jews' relative immunity in the face of Christendom's great crisis, their impact was felt long after the two kings returned from their ill-starred Crusade. The idea of a national tax had not yet been conceived, and the financing of the Crusade depended essentially on voluntary contributions, or on the individual Crusader's personal resources and willingness to part with them. Jews were not expected to make voluntary donations toward a cause which did not directly concern them. Nor were they purchasers of the promised indulgences which, for the payment of, say, 12 dinars promised a state of sinlessness for twelve months. Even the moratorium on debts and freedom from interest for debtors taking the cross was a sharp innovation. Little did Peter and his associates realize the grave losses this provision would entail for those Jewish lenders whose livelihood depended on their income from loans. Ultimately, the very capital often proved uncollectible, especially in France, where most loans were secured by neither pawns nor mortgages. To uninformed outsiders the only visible result of the Crusades was that Jews could sit back and watch with complete detachment the sacrifices in blood and money of their fellow citizens. Possibly, like many Christian businessmen, some Jews acquired valuable properties at the bargain prices occasioned by the sudden large supplies. It was easy to generalize that all Jews were parasites profiting from the misfortunes of their fellow men. At any rate, the upshot of all these debates was that the equation of Jew with usurer and exploiter now received through Bernard and Peter a respectability, which no Gottschalks or Radulphs could ever hope to give it.[44]

LATER CRUSADES

With the progressive secularization of the Crusades, these socioeconomic antagonisms made themselves strongly felt. The Third Crusade, following the fall of Jerusalem at the hands of Saladin, may have been started by the archbishop of Tyre's visit to the pope, but it was quickly taken over by the leading Western monarchs, Frederick I, Philip Augustus, and Richard Lion-Heart. It became a major part of European power politics. This secularization of the movement and the powerful leadership behind it assured, on the whole, a certain measure of tranquility to the Jews of France and Germany, where we hear of but relatively minor clashes between Crusaders and law-enforcement officers with respect to Jews. Only in England, where no outbreaks had occurred during the earlier Crusades, both the authorities and the Jews were taken by surprise when a riot, started for fortuitous reasons in London, soon spread like wildfire through the county and embroiled several Jewish communities.[45]

In contrast to the Continental massacres, those in England are known to us principally from non-Jewish sources. Even Ephraim of Bonn was able to include only two brief paragraphs relating to the tragedy of English Jewry in the Appendix to his "Book of Remembrance." Although based on hearsay, his report is fairly accurate. Two extant penitential poems by Menaḥem bar Jacob of Worms and Joseph bar Asher of Chartres mention several York martyrs by name, but otherwise add little to our factual information. But non-Jewish contemporaries, almost eye-witnesses, like Ralph de Diceto and William of Newbury, went into considerable lengths in describing these events. There is substantial agreement that the riots first broke out in London on the occasion of Richard I's coronation, to which a Jewish delegation, including at least two prominent Jews of York, came bearing gifts. The delegation was not admitted to the church where the coronation took place, lest it, like the women who were also excluded, cast a magic spell on the solemn performance. But when it was also refused admission to the palace where a post-coronation banquet was served, the Jewish leaders, long spoiled by their ready access to the throne under Henry II, apparently persisted. The ensuing riot quickly spread into other parts of town. Since the Jewish houses, although "stoutly besieged from 9 o'clock till sunset . . . could not be broken into owing to their strong build," the assailants finally set fire to their thatched roofs, starting a conflagration which consumed a number of Christian houses as well. Inmates escaping from their burning homes were slaughtered, while the mob now turned to pillaging the Jewish dwellings. The number of slain mounted to thirty, and included the famous Tosafist, Jacob of Orléans.[46]

According to the extant reports, no pretense was made here that this massacre was performed in pursuit of religious objectives. Only one of the two York delegates, Benedict, was forcibly converted and given the name William, but he quickly resumed his former faith and name. He seemingly even secured the approval of the intolerant Archbishop Baldwin of Canterbury, who allegedly declared "He does not wish to be a Christian, let him be the Devil's man." The attack largely reflected the accumulated hatred against Jewish moneylenders, whose credit transactions had so long been lovingly fostered by Henry II. Richard, who had often opposed his father and even once wounded him in a personal encounter, did not wish to start his regime with overt favoritism toward Henry's protégés. That is why his punishment of the perpetrators of the London massacre was perfunctory, and his edict guaranteeing peace to Jews proved effective for only five months.[47]

In February and March of 1190, mobs led by Crusaders being recruited for Richard's expedition attacked the Jews of Norwich, Lynn, and especially York and St. Edmunds. The massacre in York involved the largest number of victims, estimated by contemporaries at between 150 and 500. It also added another bloody chapter to Jewish martyrology through the self-immolation of a great many Jews under the leadership of the Continental scholar, R. Yom Tob bar Isaac of Joigny. On the other hand, the Jews of Lincoln and, to a lesser extent, of Stamford escaped destruction by a timely withdrawal to a castle, while those of Winchester and probably also Gloucester, Canterbury, Northampton, Bristol, Kent, Oxford, Cambridge, and several other localities were never attacked. The anti-Jewish chronicler Richard of Devizes explained the restraint of his fellow townsmen by saying: "Winchester alone, the people being prudent and circumspect, and the city always acting civilly, spared her vermin. It never did anything over-hastily; fearing nothing more than to repent, it considers the effects before the commencement." Except at York, the assailants did not attack fortified places, although Jews hardly possessed the necessary equipment for a protracted defense, and had generally been disarmed by the "Assize of Arms" of 1181. This law may not have had any anti-Jewish animus, but been intended merely to increase the supply of weapons for the royal army. Yet in its effects it made the Jewish communities more defenseless than they otherwise might have been. As a rule, the heroes of anti-Jewish riots preferred to assail helpless victims without any danger to themselves.[48]

Only in York the better organized assailants laid siege to the York castle. This siege showed that, despite the unfavorable laws, Jews were still able to defend themselves in emergencies. The record of the York massacre includes also the epic story of the defense by the Jews of Clifford's Tower. According to William of Newbury, that tower "was stoutly besieged for several days" and had to be captured by the use of machines. The Jews seem to have been its sole defenders; on one occasion they even refused readmission to the Warden, whom they distrusted. This self-reliance, bred on desperation, reminds one of the all-Jewish defense of the Wolkenburg castle near Cologne in 1147.

Among the active besiegers of Jews in the castle of York was another "hermit," an unnamed Premonstratensian monk, who was killed by a stone thrown by one of the Jewish defenders. But when a group of Jews who had chosen conversion rather than suicide surrendered and emerged from the castle, their assailants "seized them as enemies, and though they demanded the baptism of Christ, those cruel butchers destroyed them" (William of Newbury). The economic motive was paramount. No sooner did the York Jew-baiters accomplish their sanguinary task, than they proceeded to the cathedral and, under severe threats, forced the guardians to deliver to them the records of Jewish loans kept in the Church's custody. Having secured these deeds, probably the original objective of the attack, they staged a bonfire, hoping thus to be rid of debts. The amounts involved must have been temptingly large, if one recalls the ramified credit transactions of Aaron of Lincoln alone but a few years earlier. If most Crusaders as such, belonging to neither nobles nor the mercantile classes and hence rarely indebted to Jews, stood to benefit little from such destruction of evidence, they were stimulated to acts of violence by their general envy of Jewish wealth and conspicuous consumption. They must have been particularly impressed by the irate reasoning "that the enemies of the cross of Christ . . . should possess so much, when they [the Crusaders] had not enough for the expenses of so great a journey. They considered themselves entitled to extort from them [the Jews] as unjust possessors whatever they could apply to the necessary uses of the pilgrimage they had undertaken." William of Newbury, who recorded that reasoning in connection with the attacks on Stamford Jewry shortly after the event (he died in 1198), also made it clear that many Crusaders were foreign to the localities in which they helped to stage the riots, and that hence they could easily depart with their loot without fear of detection. On the other hand, "the nobles of the city [of York] and the more weighty citizens," who must have included some of the Jews' more substantial debtors, refused to participate in these mass murders. But, according to our chronicler, they acted thus only out of fear of royal reprisals. That is why, for the most part, they merely refrained from actively abetting the disorders, but did not extend a helping hand to their Jewish neighbors, as had many upper class citizens in the German cities during the earlier upheavals.[49]

Royal retribution came, "too late and too little." The disorders probably could have been averted, had it not been for the king's protracted absence from the country. Although the combined Anglo-French forces under his and Philip Augustus' command were not to start marching until July 4, 1190, Richard had moved to Normandy three months after his coronation. During the crucial weeks before Easter his chancellor, William Longchamp, bishop of Ely, was with him on the Continent.

When the news of the massacres reached him, Richard grew extremely irate, and he ordered Longchamp to institute a sharp investigation, especially in York. Of course, the burghers placed the blame entirely on the Crusaders who had since departed, while some of the guilty ringleaders escaped to Scotland. The investigation was resumed after Richard's return from his Crusade and captivity in 1194. However, this punitive action lost much of its moral force when it was noted that Longchamp had imposed the severest fines on members of the Pudsey and Percy families. These families were undoubtedly involved through Richard de

Malbys (Malebisse), whom a decade earlier a Hebrew writer, punning on his name, not inappropriately nicknamed, the "evil beast." But Longchamp's severity could now be explained by his personal bias against political opponents. Similarly, the almost exclusive concentration of punishments on fines could be attributed to the Treasury's quest for self-enrichment, rather than its sense of justice. As a matter of record, there were but few executions, which, however, was quite in line with the fine of but 20 shillings for the murder of a single Jew in Cambridge in 1155. The smallness of that fine suggested, as Canon Stokes observed, "some riot or quarrel," which was considered an extenuating circumstance. Now, according to Ephraim, Richard ordered only that the guard at the palace, who had misinformed him about the nature of the noises coming from the street during his inaugural banquet, be tied to a horse's tail and dragged through the streets of London until he expired. Only three rioters were executed; they were convicted of also robbing and destroying houses of Christians. William of Newbury later expostulated that it was plainly impossible for Richard to "call to justice so indiscriminate and vast a multitude" of criminals—a lame excuse, indeed.[50]

Perhaps because of Richard's presence in Normandy, his measures to protect the Jews in his Continental possessions proved the more effective. According to the French chronicler of Laon, Richard "dispatched messengers to Normandy and Poitou to prevent the slaying of Jews through a similar aberration." While Philip Augustus, who had expelled the Jews from all royal possession a decade before, did not require similar precautions, his French vassals had come doubly to appreciate the advantages accruing to their lands by the settlement of the king's Jewish subjects. They did not now tolerate any disturbances which might interfere with this accretion to their strength. Only one somewhat unclear episode in France, but indirectly connected with the Third Crusade, showed that French Jewry was not altogether safe even in those provinces where the exiles of 1182 had found refuge. According to the story told by Ephraim of Bonn, a Christian subject of Philip Augustus, "the same king who had previously expelled the Jews from his land," murdered a Jew in the small community of Bray-sur-Seine, then under the rule of a countess. After much suasion and the expenditure of money, the community of Bray secured the execution of the murderer on the day of Purim (March 12, 1191). In retaliation the king of France entered Bray, tried to force the Jews to adopt Christianity, and when they resisted burned some eighty adults but left children below thirteen unharmed. This story is confirmed by a substantially similar account by Rigord (giving the date of the cremation as of March 19, 1191), and by Guillaume Brita, the king's chaplain. The latter merely raised the number of victims to ninety-nine. However, despite the agreement between the Hebrew and the Latin chroniclers, the date is decidedly erroneous. In March, 1191, Philip Augustus was fighting the Saracens in the Holy Land. He only left Acre on his return journey on July 31. Moreover, all three accounts leave the question unanswered as to how the king could at any time indulge in such a punitive action against a Jewish community in semi-independent Champagne. In 1198, as we recall, Philip had to conclude a formal treaty of mutual extradition of Jews with Count Thibaut. All one can assert, therefore, is that sometime during the Third Crusade there occurred a persecution of the Jews in the small community of Bray, which probably was magnified out of all proportion by the contemporary chroniclers.[51]

Neither were serious incidents allowed in Germany, where Frederick Barbarossa, whose pro-Jewish sentiments had found expression in decrees issued as late as 1187, enjoyed enormous prestige. At the very beginning of the agitation for a new Crusade many Jews of Mayence, Worms, Spires, Strasbourg, Würzburg and other cities, escaped to neighboring castles, leaving their books and precious possessions in the custody of friendly burghers. Occasional individual lawlessness was sharply repressed by governmental organs, sometimes with the cooperation of humane priests and knights. Finally, a Jewish deputy, Moses bar Joseph ha-Kohen of Mayence, using the customary means of diplomatic and financial persuasion, supposedly secured from the emperor a decree stating that "he who attacks a Jew and wounds him, shall have his arm cut off; he who slays a Jew, shall die" (March 29, 1188). In addition the German bishops allegedly threatened to excommunicate all assailants of Jews, and declared that participation in the Crusade would avail them nothing before God. These steps seem to have been taken in connection with the Diet of Mayence which, during Easter of 1188, solemnly proclaimed the expedition to the East. Secure of domestic peace and order, Frederick soon left Germany, leading a well-equipped and well-disciplined army of more than 100,000 men to his and their ultimate disaster in Asia.[52]

Unlike the First Crusade, neither the Second nor the Third expedition seems to have produced any repercussions among the Jews of the Byzantine Empire and western Asia. Crusaders came and went, but they left undisturbed the Jewish communities which viewed the marching armies as mere episodes in the perennial struggle between East and West. Byzantine Jews could remain interested spectators even when their Greek neighbors staged popular uprisings against the local Latin colonies. They probably viewed with considerable detachment such spectacles as that of the head of a Latin patriarch being dragged at the end of a dog's tail through the streets of Constantinople in 1182. If they heard about it at all, they may have derived comfort also from the reciprocal doctrine expounded in Latin circles that it was just as meritorious a deed to attack Greek heretics as to attack Jews. Certainly their own safety was increased by such divisions among their powerful overlords.

For this reason even the fateful Fourth Crusade, which was to result in the establishment of the Latin Empire in Constantinople, left no imprint in Jewish letters. True, the sixteenth-century historians Joseph ha-Kohen and Gedaliah ibn Yaḥya vaguely refer to some difficulties at the inception of the Crusade in 1202, but they clearly have only Western countries in mind, and even there these allusions deserve little credence. In the East, too, we hear from the Byzantine chronicler Nicetas Choniates only that the great conflagration which consumed a large section of the capital on August 19, 1203, had started with a fire set by Flemish Crusaders. Aided by Pisans and Venetians, the latter burned a Saracen "synagogue," called by the people "Mitatos" (mosque). In any case, fires were nothing unusual in the Byzantine capital, and Jews suffered from them no more than the other inhabitants. On the other hand, Geoffroi de Villehardouin, a participant in that expedition who claimed not to know who the perpetrators of the crime were, merely described how the crusaders had spent a night "before the Tower [of Galata] and in the Jewry which is called Estanor [Stenon] where there was a very pretty and very rich suburb." There is no evidence that these riches had aroused the cupidity of the Crusaders and caused them to indulge in their frequent pastime of collecting "booty." [53]

Between these four major Crusades there occurred many lesser movements of armed pilgrims toward the Holy Land. Without this constant stream of reinforcements the Latin Kingdom of Jerusalem could not have lasted as long as it did. In a sense, the Crusades were a never-ending commotion which kept the Western world astir during the entire twelfth century. While the propelling force had increasingly become secular, and particularly economic, the religious impulse remained a powerful stimulant. It is doubly remarkable, therefore, how little Jews suffered directly from the religious fanaticism thus constantly kept at a high pitch. The aftereffects decidedly exceeded in importance the immediate results.

The same holds true also for the Crusades conducted on the European Continent. The various crusading expeditions conducted by the Germans, with papal encouragement, against the Slavonic Wends and other pagans, which in the course of the twelfth century led to the incorporation into Germany of important new territories along the Baltic, were of little Jewish concern. There were few Jewish settlements in that region. Only in time did the addition of these new lands, combined with the development of more intensive political and economic relations with the long-Christianized Poles, gradually shift the center of gravity of German Jewry from the Rhinelands to the central and eastern sections of the Holy Roman Empire.

More directly relevant were the Crusades, organized especially in France, to help drive the Muslims out of the Iberian Peninsula. Logically, as we recall, attacks on near-by Jews had seemed such an appropriate prelude to assaults on more distant Muslim infidels that they called forth Pope Alexander II's intercession in 1063. With the intensification of the crusading spirit from 1095 on, one might have feared more serious repercussions on Spanish

Jewry, too. Certainly, exhortations by the bishops of Toledo and Leon, such as are recorded in the contemporary *Chronica Adefonsi Imperatoris,* could have inspired attacks on Jews, too: "They absolve crimes . . . ; they promise to everybody the reward of both lives [in this and the future worlds]; they promise gifts of silver and the crown; they promise also whatever gold the Moors have." Yet, for reasons discussed in the preceding chapter, the Spanish rulers succeeded not only in keeping their own troops under control, but also in imposing restraints on the French Crusaders. Not even the conquest of Lisbon by the English Crusaders on their way to the Holy Land in 1147—together with the conquest of Tortosa, the only permanent achievement of the Second Crusade—seems to have resulted in any direct attacks on Jews, although these suffered severely when the Flemish and German soldiers staged a blood bath among the Saracen population. This massacre was followed by a severe pestilence. But the surviving Jews thus escaped the even heavier hand of the Almohades. As late as 1212, Spanish knights rose up in arms to prevent a massacre of Jews by their French allies in Toledo. This move was the more noteworthy, as passions were then inflamed by the simultaneous anti-Albigensian Crusade, and the Jews' alleged proheretical sympathies. Since the Provençal heresies were greatly stimulated by such foreign elements as the Bogomil missionaries and Crusaders returning from their stay in the Balkans, it was easy to ascribe to Jewish travelers, too, the spread of these alien doctrines, whether or not they bore any resemblance to Jewish teachings. During the conquest of Béziers in 1209, we are told, 200 Jews were massacred by the Crusaders, together with 20,000 Christians. Nevertheless Pedro II of Aragon, who professed at least verbal allegiance to the Pope, unwaveringly maintained the earlier favorable status of his Jewish subjects.[54]

GROWING ANIMOSITY

Almost worse than these outbreaks of mass fanaticism at climactic moments of the crusading élan, was the ensuing exacerbation of the mutual animosities between Christians and Jews. Human life counted for less and less in the Western world. The very atrocity propaganda conducted by the promoters of the Crusades to whip up the enthusiasm of prospective soldiers and financial contributors, combined with the insistent preachment of the high religious achievement of killing infidels, made acts of violence against unbelieving Jews at home a pardonable, if not meritorious, deed. When Eastern messengers spread blood-curdling rumors about Turkish atrocities, when they told, for example, that Turks liked to roast Christian babies on spits, they not only stirred up the thirst for revenge among the masses to the desired high pitch, but also awakened slumbering sadistic desires and the search for retaliation in kind. From the hoped-for mass killings of cruel Muslims to similar unrestrained extermination of the near-by Jewish "infidels" was an easy transition. Large-scale rioting, moreover, especially if combined with monetary gains and relative impunity, by itself invited emulation at other crucial junctures. The Jews, too, by keeping the memory of their martyrdom alive and constantly reciting the immortal deeds of their witnesses for the faith, did not let their neighbors forget. We shall see that, while some of these neighbors remembered their coreligionists' barbaric acts with a sense of shame, others were quite prone to put the blame on the Jewish victims themselves.

So convinced now became the Christian masses of the Jews' undying hostility toward them that they glibly believed any kind of rumor about Jewish assassinations of individual Christians. When, in 1179, some passengers on a Rhine boat detected the body of a Christian girl on shore, they immediately accused Jews traveling on another boat of murder, and followed them to the city of Boppard. There they wounded the alleged culprits and threw them into the river while still alive. Subsequently they dragged the corpse of one victim through many towns and villages as a demonstration of Jewish wickedness. The authorities seem not to have interfered with this gruesome display. At the end, Frederick I actually imposed a fine of 500 silver marks on the neighboring Jewish communities, to which the local bishop added another 4,200 marks. There is not the slightest indication of any regular prosecution, or trial, in the sources. Similarly, in 1195, the finding of the body of a Christian woman in the vicinity of Spires was sufficient for its populace to conclude without further evidence that Jews had been guilty of murder. In retaliation it first exhumed the body, then recently buried, of R. Isaac bar Asher ha-Levi's daughter and displayed it nude on the market place. To add to the ridicule, a mouse was placed on the corpse's head; only by a rather substantial bribe did the father secure from the authorities the right to rebury her. Instead of calming down overnight, the next morning the townspeople surrounded the rabbi's house, slew him and eight other occupants, and set fire to other Jewish houses. The rest of the community was saved only by retiring to the synagogue and pulling up a ladder, which alone made access to the upper story feasible. Temporarily relieved by some outside intervention, the survivors left the city during the following night. The raging mob burned down the synagogue, desecrated the scrolls of Law, and plundered the abandoned Jewish dwellings. True, in this case, there was swift retribution. Duke Otto, brother of the emperor, and later Henry VI himself imposed a severe fine on bishop and burghers, made them rebuild the synagogue and the Jewish houses, and pay an indemnity of 500 gold pieces to the Jewish community. But apparently here, too, there were no executions. Even worse consequences arose from the act of a Jewish maniac, who apparently without any provocation killed a Christian girl on the street of Neuss, near Cologne, in 1197. The enraged populace lynched him on the spot, together with six other Jews. Five days later the culprit's mother was seized and buried alive, while his brother was broken upon a wheel. Four Jewesses were forcibly converted. Worse yet, both bishop and count declared the community of Neuss, as well as several neighboring communities, guilty by association, and imposed severe fines upon them. Apparently no one thought of penalizing the assassins of the innocent Jewish bystanders.[55]

Episodes of this kind were symptomatic of the ever deepening conviction among the Christian masses that Jews hated all Christians with an indiscriminate, murderous hatred. With corporate responsibility pushed to the extreme on both sides, it was not only possible to hold entire communities responsible for proved misdeeds of individual members, but also to believe in planned communal revenge, or even gratuitous insults to the Christian faith. Against this background one may readily understand the rise of that fateful popular invention which was permanently to envenom the relations between Jews and Christians in many lands: the so-called "blood accusation." Although in many ways but a renewal of libels aimed first at Jews, and later at Christians, by Graeco-Roman pagans, the new accusation revealed so many novel features that one may doubt the existence of any historic continuity from ancient times.[56]

At its inception the main ingredient, namely the alleged Jewish ritual requirement of Christian blood for Passover, was altogether lacking. The first indictment of a Jewish community on this score, that of Norwich in 1144, is couched in the following terms by a more or less contemporary writer:

The Jews of Norwich bought a Christian child before Easter and tortured him with all the tortures wherewith our Lord was tortured, and on Good Friday hanged him on a cross in hatred of our Lord, and afterwards buried him. They supposed that this would stay hidden, but our Lord revealed that he was a holy martyr, and the monks took him and solemnly buried him in the church, and through our Lord he performed wonderful and various miracles, and he was called St. William.

This account is amplified in another medieval report which attributes the first assertion of the guilt of Norwich Jews to a Jewish convert, Theobald, then a monk in Cambridge. According to Theobald's yarn, "in the ancient writings of his fathers it was written that the Jews, without the shedding of human blood, could neither obtain their freedom, nor could they ever return to their fatherland." For this reason they must sacrifice a Christian every year. "Wherefore the chief men and Rabbis of the Jews who dwell in Spain assemble together at Narbonne, where the Royal seed [resides], and where they are held in highest estimation, and they cast lots for all the countries which the Jews inhabit." The particular country in turn designated by lot the locality where the child was to be crucified. In 1144, that Council had designated Norwich as the place, and William as the object, of that sacrifice. Here we have in a nutshell the combination of the ritual murder accusation with that of a Jewish world conspiracy. Yet no word is mentioned in either report of bloodletting for ritualistic purposes. Nor is there any evidence that a regular trial was instituted against the community or any individual perpetrators of that crime. Evidently the outgrowth of overheated popular fancy, this story, perhaps first created as a diversion by the child's family which had overhastily buried him while he was suffering from a mere epileptic fit, lent itself to much accretion and embroidery in subsequent retelling. Since, moreover, the "miracles" performed at William's shrine, as well as those of other such boy martyrs, attracted many pilgrims and became a substantial source of revenue for the respective monasteries, they soon created vested interests dependent on the perpetuation of these legends.[57]

Once given credence by a gullible populace, the story found imitators elsewhere. In 1168 a child, Harold, was found dead and mutilated in Gloucester. Without much ado the crime was ascribed to a Jewish family assembled at the feast of circumcision of a newly born baby. Rumor magnified this gathering into one of "Jews of all England." The chronicler admitted that "no Christian was present, who either saw or heard the torture, nor have we learned that anything had been betrayed by any Jew." Nevertheless the body was solemnly buried in the Church of St. Peter near the altar of Archbishop Edmund and the grave of King Edward the Confessor, where for generations after it was performing "miracles." Similar tales gained speedy currency in Bury St. Edmunds in 1181 where, as Jocelin summarized in his earlier treatise, "the holy boy Robert suffered martyrdom and was buried in our church, and many signs and wonders were performed among the common folk," and in Bristol in 1183. Here, however, it was a single murderer, Samuel, who had allegedly killed three other Christian boys as well. Even supposedly overcautious Winchester did not escape a similar tragedy in 1192. According to Richard of Devizes, who furnished an elaborate narrative of the Winchester events, the boy was supposed to have been of French birth and brought to England by an international Jewish cabal. None of these stories included as yet the later essential ingredient of the victims' blood being used for the baking of unleavened bread; they merely were supposed to have become objects of an annual Jewish ritual reenacting the Passion of

Jesus. The Winchester rumor alone led to some sort of prosecution, but the single Jewish defendant was acquitted, according to the chronicler because the judges had been won over by gold.[58]

For proper historical perspective we must bear in mind that all these accusations had few immediate effects on Jewish life. True, the absence of any reference to them in Anglo-Jewish letters of the period might be explained by the extreme paucity of extant sources. But they left no traces even in Continental writings, at a time when Jewish public opinion was keenly awake to all manifestations of Jew-baiting. None of the Continental chroniclers and poets, who so dolefully recorded the Jewish sufferings in England in 1189–90, made any allusion whatsoever to the menacing rumors spread about the Jews of Bury St. Edmunds, Bristol, or Winchester a few years before or after these tragic events. Nor did Richard and John in their charters of 1190 and 1202, doubtless secured by Jews, find it necessary to include any pertinent provision, similar to that inserted by Přemysl Ottokar II of Bohemia into his Statute of 1254. One cannot escape the impression that in these early stages the accusation was not taken too literally even by its exponents. Jews appear here more as shadowy enemies of Christianity than as the real Jews living in the affected localities. Hence came that ready acceptance of the fantastic canard about a Jewish international gathering designating a particular child for exquisite tortures, followed by no direct punitive action against local culprits.[59]

Much more serious were the consequences of similar charges for a Continental community. At its major appearance in France, the accusation lost whatever connection it had had in England with the Passover holiday, and the murder of a Christian child was attributed merely to the general Jewish hatred of Christians. The tragic affair in Blois took place in May, 1171, some two months after Passover without the recovery of any corpse. It arose from a servant's suspicion that he had seen a Jew drowning a child's body in the river. Unfortunately for the Jews, the investigation became entangled in Count Thibaut's love affair with a Jewess, Polcelina, the jealousy of Countess Alix, and the enmity of local officials toward the count's exacting lady friend. On the flimsy evidence of a water ordeal, with the accuser surviving after

being immersed in a tank of holy water, the community of some
forty souls was condemned to death by burning. In this early
auto-da-fé, thirty-two martyrs (including seventeen women) suffered death, after refusing the alternative of conversion to Christianity. This event left a lasting impression on French Jewry.
R. Jacob Tam immediately proclaimed Sivan 20 a permanent
fast day. "Let that fast," he declared, "be considered greater than
the fast of Gedaliah son of Ahikam, for it is a day of atone-
ment." Authors of penitential poems, perhaps written for recitation during that observance, elaborated on that theme. In his
informative and moving, rather than poetically inspired, verses,
Hillel bar Jacob, brother of Ephraim of Bonn, declaimed:

> When the order came to take them to the place of burning,
> Like brides to their canopies, they went hearts with joy astir,
> They sang, "Let us praise the Lord," with voices full of yearning,
> "Behold, thou art beautiful, my love, behold, thou art fair."
> May Jeshurun be inscribed for pardon and salvation,
> On this our atonement day, secure us consolation.
> May the martyrs' merit help appease God's indignation,
> Bring reprieve to the priests and assembled congregation.

The selection of the 'Alenu prayer by the martyrs was appropriate
to the occasion. Soon recited also in daily prayers (apparently by
order of Eleazar of Worms), this liturgical piece had long been
read with great solemnity on the High Holidays, because it
shouted defiance at attempted conversions. The Lord is praised
here because "He hath not made us like the nations of the
[various] lands, nor placed us on a par with the clans of the
earth. He hath not set our fate with theirs, nor cast our lot with
all their multitude." [60]

From these beginnings of almost unbelievable crudeness and
naiveté arose one of the most fantastic libels in human history.
For a long time these stories apparently failed to attract the attention of the more educated classes, and called forth no action
on the part of the constituted authorities. It took nearly a century before it spread to Germany, although anti-Jewish feelings
ran higher there than in any other country. Nor did it command
that minimum semblance of reality which can be found at the
root of most other folkloristic tales. The custom of burning the

effigy of Haman as part of the jocose Purim festivities, which is sometimes advanced as the reason for the mistaken belief that Jews reenacted the Crucifixion on or before every Passover, is not attested anywhere in western Europe at that time. Most remarkably, the accusation has persisted through the ages despite sharp denials by popes and monarchs, courts of justice and royal commissions, even the sworn testimonies of converted Jews. Born from the ancient conception of Jews as the *odium generis humani,* magnified beyond recognition in the crucible of the harsh age of Crusades, it found ready acceptance in a populace which expected from the persecuted Jews some such reaction to its own undying hatred.[61]

PSYCHOLOGICAL AFTEREFFECTS

The "blood accusation" was but one of the enduring heritages in Jewish history of the age of Crusades. The martyrdom of Blois, on the other hand, belonged to the category of generalizations, in which the whole Jewish community was blamed for misdeeds of individuals whether or not attested by valid evidence. It is more in line with the events in Boppard, Spires, and Neuss, which were soon to follow, than with those of Norwich or Gloucester which preceded it. Yet it too was symptomatic of what the Christian world thought of Jews, and of their plausible behavior. Before long there emerged the image of the Jew as the ally of Satan, who knew the truth of Christianity but obstinately repudiated it. Because of this association he often prospered in the world, could perform miracles of healing, and achieve magnificent results in many other undertakings. But he did it all as the enemy of God and of mankind, and always sought the detriment of his Christian neighbors. This purported alliance of the devil and the Jew removed the latter, too, into the irrational sphere, and created an impenetrable wall to all reasoning appeals for humanity and understanding.[62]

In part this expectancy of Jewish hostility, even criminality, was but a sublimation of the Western world's own sense of guilt. The massacres of 1096 and after left a permanent imprint not only on the victimized groups, but also on the majority from which the slayers had come. At first some of the Christian chroniclers of these events, such as Albert of Aix, expressed their indignation over the unprovoked bloodshed "of homeless Jews who, though Christ's enemies, were slaughtered in cold-blooded murder more from greed than from the fear of the Lord." Even German folklore reflected a modicum of popular remorse, when in 1123 it envisaged the ghosts of Emicho and his partners in crime wandering restlessly, and pitifully seeking forgiveness for the sins committed some twenty-seven years earlier. The majority, however, even then tried to gloss over the guilt of its compatriots and blame the events on the excessive zeal of a few misguided individuals. During the later massacres even that limited recognition of Christian responsibility was lacking. The otherwise moderate William of Newbury saw in the disturbances during Richard I's coronation only the good omen "that the fate of the blaspheming people ennobled the day and place of the King's consecration, that at the very beginning of his reign the enemies of the Christian faith began to fall and become weakened around him." Richard of Devizes spoke more sharply "of the sacrifice of the Jews to their father the devil" having commenced in London and spread to other cities which "with a like devotion despatched their bloodsuckers with blood to hell." Equally gloating were the rhymed exclamations of Robert of Gloucester:

> For the King was somewhat vexed, and took it for great shame,
> That from such unclean things as *them* any meat to him came.
> And bade them put it out of court, and to the wretches shame do
> There was many a wild serving-man that was ready thereto.
> And they went into Jewry and wounded and tore men *too*
> And robbed and burned houses, and many of them slew.

Not one word of condemnation of the assailants, none of pity for the sufferers! [63]

Ultimately, the very repetition of such attacks removed some of the stigma of lawlessness from their perpetrators. In the memory of the masses these butcheries appeared not as the result of human greed and sadism, but as wondrous deeds in the exalted struggle against infidels. Hallowed by the great religious enthusiasm which had led countless multitudes to leave their homes and families in quest of an ideal, these incidents lost much of their criminal character and became part of a behavior pattern considered quite normal in periods of high tension. A new method was thus introduced into settling the old Judeo-Christian controversy by the spontaneous action of the masses, which in those times of widespread recognition of the "right of the fist" invited constant emulation and even achieved a measure of respectability.

The immediate effect of the disturbances of 1096 was, as we recall, the tightening of security measures through the treaties of peace, beginning with that arranged by Henry IV in 1103. Temporarily effective, these new compacts only underscored the defenselessness of Jews and their utter dependence on the government's protective arm. As a consequence they were progressively disarmed and ultimately forbidden to bear arms. Four years after the enactment of the Assize of Arms an English Jew was fined the large sum of 40 marks, of which he was able to pay immediately but one-half, because his wife had accepted a hauberk in pledge (*Pipe Rolls*, 32 Henry II, p. 78). Such exclusive governmental patronage forged an ever more formidable alliance between the Jews and their royal masters, on the one hand reinforcing the factors tending toward full-fledged Jewish "serfdom," and on the other hand making Jews doubly vulnerable in periods of social unrest. They were bound to lose, whether the monarchs waxed stronger, and therefore ruled them with an iron fist, or grew weaker and hence could not offer them the much-needed protection against the newly arising forces of discontent. To some extent Jews tried to come to terms with both the nobility and the Church, although from the latter they could expect at best adherence to the principle of limited toleration, combined with a more or less persistent effort at conversion. But they neglected the growing class of burghers, and especially its lower echelons of craftsmen and workers. Of course, from the outset the increasing economic rivalries made such an understanding extremely difficult. With the tensions generated by the Crusades the two groups soon viewed each other as sworn enemies.

This growing mutual hostility was, indeed, the most portentous heritage of the crusading age. The ordinary Jew now saw in the average Christian, particularly one unknown to him personally, a potential assassin whose deep-rooted hatred of Jews and Judaism required merely a spark to break out into acts of unbridled savagery. After the traumatic experience of 1096, even the numerous instances of generous cooperation on the part of Christian neighbors, in whose houses many Jews and their property had found temporary shelter, were submerged in the general recollection of undisguised brutality. In his generally temperate recital of Jewish sufferings during the First Crusade, Solomon bar Simson, writing nearly half a century after the events, played down these acts of humanity and rather emphasized the frequent betrayals of victims by unscrupulous or frightened hosts.

In that religiously enthusiastic age, moreover, it seemed perfectly natural to attribute sufferings to human wickedness, and acts of kindness and life-saving to divine intervention. The very instances of law observance and human cooperation were largely ascribed to the intercession of some well-connected Jews, or to the bribing of powerful officials. It is with a deep sense of wonder, for example, that the Mayence Anonymus stresses the disinterested character of Bishop John's early military intervention which had nipped in the bud the Spires uprising. "It was through Moses [bar Yequtiel] the Elder," he wrote, "that Bishop John saved them [the Jews], for God had inspired his heart to save them without bribery. It was God's will to secure for us through him a remnant" in that city. This was indeed an exceptional occurrence. Elsewhere, almost invariably, direct pro-Jewish interventions had to be paid for at a very high price. The chroniclers never failed to underscore this nexus between the payment of "taxes" or "gifts," and practically all governmental measures to uphold the law. Since the Christians, too, took it for granted that every law-abiding official who insisted on the preservation of public order did so only under the prompting of Jewish *douceurs,* it is small wonder that the Jews increasingly viewed the accumulation of riches as their most effective means of defense. They were prone to forget that this very accumulation often was the major incentive to those acts of violence, against which these riches were to guard them.[64]

Payments for services rendered by governmental agencies were far from exceptional, however. The frequency of references to such payments in the Jewish sources may in part be explained by

the convic   r a high price constituted
bilateral (freely abrogate. That is
why in hi   Moses ha-Kohen did not
fail to mention that the favorabie proclamations by Frederick
Barbarossa and the bishops had "all been achieved by full payment," although he had previously stressed the Emperor's benevolence toward the Jews. On his part, Ephraim, too, expressed his
gratitude for God's mercy in averting the dangers arising from the
Boppard incident in 1179, by "giving our fortune as ransom for
our lives" (*Hebräische Berichte,* ed. by Neubauer and Stern, pp.
69, 78, 204, 219).

Mounting bitterness affected the general outlook of Jew and
Gentile alike. We recall Solomon bar Simson's gloating over the
downfall of the crusading bands during their march through the
Balkans and Asia Minor. He concluded this part of his narrative
with a paragraph as vindictive as any written by a contemporary
Jew-baiting chronicler.

The enemies [he wrote] have nonetheless not yet given up their evil
designs, and every day start out on another expedition to Jerusalem.
But the Lord has delivered them like sheep to slaughter, and set them
aside for the day of extermination. Mayest Thou "render unto our
neighbors sevenfold into their bosom," and inflict upon them Thy
retribution commensurate with their misdeeds. Give sorrow to their
hearts, place Thy curse upon them, "pursue them in anger and destroy
them under the heavens of the Lord," for "the Lord hath a day of
vengeance, a year of recompense for the controversy of Zion." At the
same time may "Israel be saved by the Lord with an everlasting salvation. Ye shall not be ashamed nor confounded" for ever and ever more.

Coming from a moderate writer like Solomon and interspersed
with long-standardized phrases from the psalms and Jewish liturgy,
this vindictive tirade doubly typified the prevailing mood among
Jewish intellectuals. Even less restrained, as usual, were the poets.
A lengthy poem of twenty-two stanzas, arranged in a reverse Hebrew alphabetical order and beginning, *Titnem le-ḥerpah* (Deliver Them to Shame), consists of little more than a bewildering
variety of synonyms relating to the same theme of vengeance and
destruction, borrowed from the rich and "juicy" vocabulary of the
ancient prophetic denunciations. It so sharply exemplified the
state of mind of the Jews of that time that it could soon be at-

tributed to the old and genteel scholar, Rashi, whose last years had been marred by the bloodshed of the First Crusade.[65]

Cries for vengeance were merely counterparts of the glorification of Jewish martyrs. The unprecedented nature of the mass attacks on Jews, combined with the renewed exaltation of religious martyrdom which underlay the entire crusading movement, would have brought back the ancient encomia of martyrs to the memory of Jewish contemporaries, even had there not been that unprecedented wave of mass suicides which put an indelible imprint on that period. Comparing such self-immolation, and especially the frequent slaughter of children by their fathers, with the Sacrifice of Isaac, the chroniclers, evidently reflecting the public's general reaction, exclaimed,

Please inquire and find out as to whether there ever was such a mass 'aqedah from the days of Adam; have there ever been eleven hundred 'aqedot in a single day, all of them like the 'aqedah of Isaac son of Abraham? A single one performed on Mount Moriah shook the world, as it is written, "Behold their valiant ones cry without; the angels of peace weep bitterly" and the skies darkened. But now what have they done? Why have the skies not become black, and the stars withdrawn their shining, and why have not sun and moon darkened in their courses, when on a single day, a Tuesday the third of Sivan were killed and slaughtered eleven hundred martyrs, including infants and children who had never sinned and souls of the innocent and humble? Willst Thou in the sight of these things withhold Thy anger?

The impact of this mass "sanctification of the name of the Lord" was so overwhelming that contemporaries forgot even the traditional Jewish self-accusation and the blaming of the disaster on the sins of the generation. Rather than commiserating with the sufferers, historians and poets uniformly extolled their achievement as securing for them eternal bliss. Almost with an undertone of envy Solomon bar Simson spoke of them as "the generation chosen before the Lord to be an offering unto Him, for they had the strength and heroism to stand in His sanctuary, to fulfill His commandment, and to sanctify His great name in His world!" He concluded: "Happy are they, and happy their portion for all are allotted life in the world-to-come. May my portion be with theirs!" These witnesses for their faith were held up as shining examples for all Jews to follow in moments of crisis. Each and every Jew was to hold himself in readiness to sacrifice his life, rather than to yield to threats or blandishments by assassins or missionaries.[66]

As a matter of fact, these tales of woe were not told by chroniclers and poets merely to satisfy the curiosity of readers. Many penitential poems were soon incorporated into the liturgy to be recited on such special occasions as the fast of Sivan 20, commemorating the martyrs of Blois, or the long-established fast day of the Ninth of Ab. Unlike R. Jacob Tam's instantaneous reaction to the Blois holocaust, the German rabbis refrained from proclaiming a special commemorative day for the Rhenish martyrs. Perhaps they were discouraged by the multiplicity of possible dates; perhaps they felt that by inserting new liturgical pieces into the traditional recitations of the Ninth of Ab they would bring home to the worshipers more effectively the magnitude of that tragedy, which many compared with the burning of the two Temples. Kalonymos bar Yehudah of Mayence, Samuel the Pious' nephew, who drew that comparison, added the legalistic reason, "One must not add a day to commemorate misfortune and fire." This certainly was not a binding principle, as is attested not only by Jacob Tam's action, but also by the numerous local fasts and *purims,* observed in many countries through the ages. But since most of the massacres had taken place in the spring months of Iyyar and Sivan, a heavy pall fell on the traditional period of the *Sefirat ha-'omer* (Counting of Sheaves) between Passover and the Festival of Weeks. Long observed through certain overt restraints because of the purported death of many pupils of R. 'Aqiba during that season (Naṭronai Gaon already had warned against contracting marriages then), this entire seven-week interval, with the exception of the thirty-third day (the *Lag be-'omer*), was now reemphasized as a protracted period of national mourning. Until today Orthodox Jews abstain from marrying or cutting their hair on these days, consciously or unwittingly helping to perpetuate the memory of the great martyrdom of 1096. That tragedy resulted in still another liturgical innovation. Many names of martyrs were now recorded in special congregational *memor* books for the recitation of prayers for their souls on festive occasions. Sometimes names were inscribed in more than one *memor* book, so that the recollection of their martyrdom might serve as an inspiration for generations of worshipers in many communities. In this way Jewish martyrology became, as in other periods of great crisis, an enormous source of strength and a means of preservation of the Jewish people.[67]

Consciously or unconsciously, the recital of these heroic deeds helped strengthen the solidarity of Jews and the control of communal organs over members. Only by preaching resistance to the point of self-sacrifice, could the leaders hope to maintain the continuity of a small minority struggling to preserve its identity and faith against tremendous odds. For this reason even the original leniency toward forced converts reverting to Judaism gave way to harsher judgments, as when Benedict of York's body was refused burial in the Jewish cemetery. The progressive change from deep compassion with the weakness of those yielding to irresistible pressures to ultimate condemnation, which on a larger scale was to manifest itself in the attitude of the sixteenth and seventeenth century rabbinate toward Marranos, is reflected in the pietistic writings of Eleazar of Worms and his disciple, Yehudah the Pious. Here the experience of a Jewish elder was to serve as an appropriate warning: When his community faced the choice between conversion and death, the elder supposedly advised it to accept the former, with the understanding that, at the first opportunity, each individual would revert to Judaism. "Because they were converted according to his advice," added Yehudah, "his own children became apostates, and he will pay the penalty [in the Hereafter], as if he had caused them all to sin." [68]

In these cruel days of unmitigated gloom and sufferings, the old lachrymose conception of Jewish history received a new impetus and profound reformulation. Apart from reliance on the supernatural compensations promised by tradition and reiterated by contemporary preachers, there evolved a new rationale for Jewish sufferings which must have filled contemporaries and successors with the glow of inner satisfaction. It strengthened the determination of the majority to carry on despite almost impossible odds.

Characteristically, the spokesman of that new rationale was Yehudah Halevi, a Spanish Jew, and not one of the fellow sufferers of the northern massacres. Perhaps a certain distance was necessary for better perspective. Having spent most of his life in both the Christian and the Muslim parts of Spain after the Christian conquest of Toledo in 1085, familiar with the Castilian as well as the Arabic language, Halevi perceived with greater clarity than anyone else in his day the meaning to Judaism of the great world crisis of the Crusades. To him the Jewish people's sufferings were an essential part of Jewish and human destiny. But rather than deplore them, he considered them the hallmark of all outstanding individuals and groups. In his memorable dialogue before the king of the Khazars, his spokesman readily admitted the Jews' political inferiority and their lack of power, but emphasized that these were compensated for by the great achievements of martyrs. Did not even Muslims and Christians, he argued, extol their martyrs far above their great rulers and military commanders? This is doubly true, therefore, in the case of an entire people of martyrs. "Israel amidst the nations," he exclaimed, "is like the heart amidst the organs of the body, it is at one and the same time the most sick and the most healthy of them." In essence, therefore, the Jewish people is indestructible; it has outlasted all its ancient oppressors, and will outlast its future foes as well. Its very exilic existence has had its important place in the divine scheme of life. He insisted that individual Jews had no more reason to despair of the ultimate salvation of their people, than of personal salvation, in spite of their sins. Combining a number of rabbinic doctrines, Halevi finally declared, "If his mind is disturbed by the length of the exile and the diaspora and the degradation of his people, he [the Jew] finds comfort first in 'acknowledging the justice of the [divine] decree' . . . ; then, in being cleansed from his sins; then in the reward and recompense awaiting him in the world to come, and the attachment to the Divine Influence in the world." In this proud and self-assertive formulation the lachrymose conception of Jewish history received a new dimension of deep morality and dignity, and as such became an eminent instrumentality of Jewish survival.[69]

TWELFTH-CENTURY RENAISSANCE

The practical effects of the age of the Crusades were far less significant. True, the loss of some five thousand members during the First Crusade, and of several hundred more during the

Second and Third Crusades, must have weakened the small and struggling communities of western Europe. Equally important must have been the drain on Jewish manpower, occasioned by conversions to Christianity, whether of the dramatic kind accompanying the massacres, or stemming from the latter's delayed effects. Probably quite a few of the forced converts did not avail themselves of the legal opportunity to revert to Judaism. Some others may have lost heart in the face of the great sufferings of their people, of which no end was in sight. We shall see that missionary activities never ceased, and that at least some of these proved successful.

Nonetheless, the European Jewish communities constantly increased in numerical, economic, and cultural strength. By telescoping the events of a whole century, modern observers often received a totally erroneous impression. When the Rhenish communities suffered, those in France and England were quiescent, and Blois or York had no contemporary counterparts in Germany. Most existing communities even in disturbed areas, as in England in 1190, escaped the assassins' hands by chance or precaution. That lack of simultaneity made possible speedy recovery even on the scenes of disaster. Of all the communities afflicted by massacres, only that of Bury St. Edmunds had no chance to recuperate, because within two years the survivors suffered from the first of a growing series of local expulsions, which were to eliminate the Jews from many English cities in the course of the thirteenth century. Even the community of York appears again in 1218, in a royal ordinance enjoining the local authorities to protect Jews against outside interference. The Rhenish communities more than recovered their original strength. In 1152, a German chronicler, narrating at some length the romantic attachment of a priest to a young Jewess, the ensuing Jewish cabal to expose him, and through him Christianity, to public contumely, and the miraculous silencing of the would-be accusers, referred to "a great many Jewish synagogues in the cities of eastern Franconia around the Rhine." At the same time there was a tremendous expansion of the Jewish population in Christian Spain, and in the newer sections of central and eastern Europe. Certainly, by 1200 many more Jews lived under Christendom than had in 1095.[70]

Such tenacity in the face of adversity and growing animosities can be understood only against the background of the vast economic and cultural changes throughout the Western world. The "multifaceted" twelfth century was anything but a period of unmitigated gloom even in Jewish history. While whipping up much religious fanaticism, the Crusades nevertheless bridged the gap between the divided worlds of Islam and Christendom. Jews, who had long served as mediators between East and West in both international trade and cultural exchanges, now found themselves confronted by a great many new competitors in the former, but also by numerous collaborators in the latter spheres. Even north of the Alps and Pyrenees many Jews maintained personal contacts with Christian scholars, merchants, and customers, and thus learned, as well as imparted the knowledge of, each other's human qualities which somehow did not conform with the stereotype patterns of literature, homily, or rumor. The progressive economic and cultural decline of the East, and the growth of the West, sufficed to overcome all psychological difficulties.[71]

Slowly but inexorably the focus of Jewish history was moving westward, for basic socioeconomic and cultural realities simply proved stronger than the psychological misgivings. Once again undismayed by its tragic experiences, the Jewish people, in pursuit of its historic destiny, overcame the enormous resistance of natural, as well as man-made, factors and opened a new era of its Western achievement.

XXII

ECONOMIC TRANSFORMATIONS

REFERENCE to economic factors has frequently been made in the preceding chapters. Of enormous importance in all human history, as will readily be admitted even by opponents of economic determinism, they were doubly significant in medieval Jewish history, since the very existence of Jews in certain countries entirely depended on their "usefulness" to the latter's economies and fiscal structures. Many political and legal developments affecting Jewish status were, therefore, deeply interrelated with these economic realities which, hitherto mentioned only more or less in passing, must now be more fully and independently analyzed. Even so, this rapid survey will necessarily gloss over many local and chronological variations; it will pay primary attention to major trends and causations.

During the seven centuries here under review the Jewish occupational stratification underwent a radical change. A people theretofore still largely deriving its livelihood from farming and handicrafts was being transformed into a predominantly mercantile population with a strong emphasis on the money trade. The climactic stage of that evolution was not to be reached until the later Middle Ages and, even then, was to be limited only to a few areas north of the Alps and the Loire. But the basic trends became fully manifest long before 1200. They operated most strongly under Western Christendom, and were constantly reinforced by the gradual transfer of the Jewish people's center of gravity from East to West, as well as by the slow infiltration of Western concepts and institutions into the Muslim areas. These economic readjustments deeply affected all Judeo-Gentile relations, and had a marked impact also on Jewish communal and cultural life. Their effects have been felt all through the modern period, and still underlie many of the crucial difficulties confronting Jewish life today.

ESTRANGEMENT FROM THE SOIL

Agriculture was the mainstay of all medieval economic systems in the East and still more in the West, but the Jewish share therein was constantly declining. Even in ancient Palestine and Babylonia, Jewish landownership had been exposed to heavy taxes and chicaneries by the powerful Roman and Persian bureaucracies. The talmudic sages, though favorably disposed toward farming, coined such pithy epigrams as "there is no occupation inferior to agriculture," or "land has only been given to strong-armed men." During the numerous wars between the Eastern Roman Empire and Sassanian Persia all farming in the Babylonian borderlands must have suffered severely, Jewish farming doubly so, since Jews also had to contend with the aroused religious fanaticism of the combatants on both sides. At the same time, Palestine's economic recovery in the fifth and sixth centuries, which had also accrued to the benefit of Jewish landowners and tillers of the soil, was largely nullified in the stormy years of Heraclius' reign, which culminated in the Persian conquest of 614, the Byzantine reconquest of 628, and the ensuing severe reprisals against the Jewish population. Outside the Palestino-Babylonian center, the dispersed and isolated Jewish farmers must have had an even harder struggle for survival against the accumulated hatreds of neighbors and the heavy hand of tax collectors.[1]

Islam's rapid expansion brought little relief to Jewish farmers. On the contrary, the new forces set in motion by this upheaval tended to eliminate altogether many rural Jewish settlements. In its early stages the Muslim administration had to contend against a severe landflight of the overburdened peasantry in Palestine. Under Harun ar-Rashid it was forced to issue appeals, backed by tax relief, to farmers to return to their abandoned lands. Very likely only a fraction of Jewish farmers heeded that call. Jewish and Christian farmers, moreover, not only carried the additional burdens of capitation taxes but also suffered from the governmental policy of setting far below the market value the prices for produce delivered in payment of taxes. As Claude Cahen has pointed out, these artificial prices sometimes represented an increase of the fiscal burden by one half or more. Less important in the case of land taxes which usually consisted of a portion of the taxable crop, these oppressive price policies rested most heavily on the shoulders of the poll-tax paying *dhimmis,* who often saw themselves forced to pay in kind for a tax computed in monetary terms. Ultimately, despairing of the effectiveness of such palliatives, the state increasingly tried to attach the peasants to the soil, thus strengthening the forces of regimentation which led to the establishment of a semifeudal order in the Near East. In addition to being subject to taxes individually collected from his produce, many a farmer also suffered from the collective responsibility resting upon entire villages in certain areas. From an unsigned geonic responsum, apparently written in early tenth-century Muslim Spain, we learn of inhabitants of such villages who were supposed to contribute not only to the collective taxes in ratio of their landholdings, but also to "the bribery fund, wherewith they bribed [the officials] to forestall forcible abuses." This pressure of discriminatory land taxes soon combined with the new economic expansion and growing differentiation of the Great Caliphate to stimulate the urbanization of Jewish masses. Although the original scheme of relieving Muslims from land taxes could not be upheld after the conversion of the majority of farmers to Islam, the "unbelievers" remained at a permanent competitive disadvantage. The equivalent trade taxes, on the other hand, were neither so universal nor so clearly discriminatory nor, for that matter, so easily collectible, as to constitute an equal handicap.[2]

Jews may also have caught some of the spirit of the Arab disdain for agriculture, translated from its original Bedouin motivations into a more "civilized" feeling of superiority of the city dwellers over the nearly illiterate peasants. If Muslim teachers advised residence in a city with a central mosque and other religious institutions, where alone a man could live up to all the requirements of organized religion, how much more did this apply to Jews whose faith was seriously jeopardized in small, isolated villages! The lure of a more abundant life in the growing metropolitan centers must also have proved irresistible to many Jews whose majority may already have become urbanized in the

Graeco-Roman dispersion. From the twelfth century on, finally, western Asiatic and Egyptian Jewry faced a growingly "feudal" order which, though it greatly differed from the contemporary European system, was basically antagonistic to Jewish farming.

Apart from such man-made difficulties, the farmers had to overcome a great many natural hazards, including earthquakes. From a contemporary liturgical poem, *Yoṣer ra'ash shebi'i* (The Seventh Earthquake), we learn of the great loss of life and property among Jewish farmers in the Palestinian Shefelah and the Valley of Sharon occasioned by such an elemental catastrophe (possibly in 1033). Where the agricultural economy possesses great vitality, or else where man has no alternatives, a catastrophe of this kind usually has only temporary effects. But, since Jewish participation in agricultural exploits had been declining for other reasons as well, sudden destruction of accumulated reserves must have permanently displaced many additional Jewish farmers.[3]

No apparent tax disadvantages affected Jewish farming in the Christian world. In Byzantium the very existence of a special Jewish tax is debatable. It certainly did not affect specifically Jewish landholdings or agricultural produce. That is why Benjamin of Tudela could find in the Balkans a whole community of 200 Jews (possibly families) in Crissa who "sow and reap on their own land." Probably many more Jews, like their non-Jewish compatriots among the landowning gentry, cultivated their lands with the aid of agricultural laborers, including *coloni*.[4]

In fact, here, as well as in the West, the Jews may actually have enjoyed a slight advantage, in so far as they did not have to pay the Church tithes. This issue seemed quite unimportant in the West during the earlier Middle Ages. But with the expansion of the Church's power and its ever more insistent quest for control over many secular aspects of life, this important source of revenue could not readily be overlooked; the less so as, together with the great increase in Jewish population and its wider geographic distribution, Jewish landholdings, too, assumed greater economic significance. Hence came also the more and more powerful drive on the part of Church leadership, beginning with Alexander III, to utilize this impost for the benefit of Catholic parishes.

Only after a protracted struggle against Jews and their royal backers, interested in safeguarding all taxable Jewish resources for their own treasuries, did some provinces of the Church succeed in imposing the ecclesiastical tithes upon Jews, at least with respect to properties previously held by Christians. The Fourth Lateran Council of 1215, finally, tried to establish that impost on a permanent and universal basis. To a resolution directed against the "heavy and immoderate usury" exacted by Jewish lenders from Christians, it appended a paragraph reading:

> We decree that by means of the same punishment [the sanction of a general boycott] the Jews shall be compelled to offer satisfaction to the churches for the tithes and offerings due them and which these churches were wont to receive from the houses and possessions of Christians before these properties had under some title or other passed into Jewish hands. Thus shall this property be conserved to the Church without any loss.

Obviously pyramided on top of a heavy and complex structure of Jewish fiscal contributions to state, baronial, and city treasuries, as well as toward defraying the costs of their own communal services, this additional tithe had all the earmarks of double taxation. To avoid practical complications in collecting that impost from an unwilling population which could not be made amenable by ecclesiastical censures, some churches managed to coerce the Jews to pay a certain stipulated amount per family to the local parishes. For example, the provincial Council of Narbonne, meeting in 1227, demanded that each Jewish family, even if it owned no land, contribute annually the sizable amount of six denarii. Since such an additional tax could but rarely be maintained for any length of time, many churchmen realized that the collection of ecclesiastical tithes could most effectively be attained only if Jewish landholdings were altogether suppressed by law.[5]

Considerations of this kind must have added much zest to the Church's insistence upon the elimination of Jewish ownership of Christian slaves. Originally conceived as a matter of prestige, lest infidels exercise mastery over the faithful, and as a protective measure against the conversion of Christians to Judaism, this outlawry could now be utilized for making Jewish landholdings economically unattractive. According to the then prevailing system, most lands were cultivated by lords employing large numbers of slaves and later villeins. The progressive Christianization of eastern Europe was drying up the supply of pagan slaves. Churchmen now readily forgot Gregory the Great's distinction between Christian slaves, whom no Jew was to own, and *coloni* whom Jewish landowners could readily employ as sharecroppers in a semidependent state. The agitation was extended to the outlawry of free contractual employment of Christian servants by Jews at home or on the farm. Finally, Peter the Venerable of Cluny denounced Jews for living as parasites from the field labors of others, and suggested that they be made to till the soil in person. He certainly did not feel that the same standard ought to be applied to the vast landholdings of his own order of Cluny, or for that matter of other monasteries, churches, or nobles, whose "parasitary" existence from villein labor was the very foundation of the entire feudal system.[6]

In fact some petty Jewish farmers cultivated, with the aid of their families, urban or suburban vineyards and orchards. Otherwise, northern Jews depended almost entirely on non-Jewish agricultural labor. While, owing to their general concentration on talmudic learning, French rabbis continued to expound talmudic labor laws relating to agriculture in all their ramifications, their casual remarks betray their awareness of the largely theoretical nature of such debates for their own time and country. Referring to the talmudic observation that synagogue attendance on weekdays suffered from the absence of workers, Jacob Tam observed succinctly, "Today we are not engaged in manual labor, and hence there is no difference between Sabbath and weekday attendance." Clearly, in areas of Jewish mass settlement like Spain and the Muslim Near East, many Jews derived a living from intensive manual labor. But even there most workers were engaged in crafts and transportation, rather than in agricultural labor.[7]

With the growing insecurity of Jewish life in both East and West agriculture lost its greatest economic advantage, namely its basic stability and its capacity to provide farmers with a minimum of food and shelter in emergency periods. Already the harsh Visigothic legislation of the seventh century had demonstrated the uncertainties of land tenure for Jews. At that time Sisebut's enforced conversion by the stroke of a pen potentially deprived all professing Jews of their landholdings. Later Egica "nationalized" Jewish landholdings which had at any time belonged to Christians. How was a Jewish owner to prove that his land had never before been Christian property? The promised compensation, if paid, could not be reinvested in land, unless it was acquired from fellow Jews. In England any misdemeanor sufficed to prevent the Jewish landowner from transmitting his estate to his heirs, unless these made special arrangements with the treasury for the "repurchase" of that property. Apart from such legal expropriations, grievous losses were inflicted on Jews indirectly by massacres and expulsions. Whenever Jews had to leave in a hurry—and they often had to do so under the threat of mobsters or legal compulsion—they had to dispose of their immovable property at any price. In some cases, as during Philip Augustus' expulsion of Jews from the royal sections of France in 1182, such withdrawal of toleration was overtly combined with outright confiscation. Certainly, movable property, and particularly objects made from precious metals and stones, lent themselves to far more effective concealment and removal.[8]

Nor must we minimize the impact of the Jewish religion also on this phase of social life. True, the edge of the severe biblical and talmudic agricultural laws had largely been blunted by their rabbinic treatment as "commandments attached to the soil" of Palestine, with no binding force elsewhere. Nevertheless there remained in Jewish law and observance sufficient obstacles to Jewish farming to make it less competitive in a Muslim or Christian environment. The Jewish Sabbath, for example, imposed much more rigid abstention from work than did the Muslim or Christian weekly days of rest. According to contemporary geonic interpretations, Jews were to force their slaves to observe strictly the Sabbath rest commandments. While Sherira or Hai Gaon absolved the master from responsibility for his slave's private transgressions, the latter insisted on another occasion that "if one found his slave consuming ritualistically forbidden food or violating the Sabbath, one should punish him once or twice, admonish and threaten him with dire consequences. But if the slave refuses to mend his ways, the master is allowed to sell him to Gentiles." Beginning with the councils of Orléans (Third) in

538 and of Narbonne in 589, moreover, the Church demanded that Jews and their employees refrain from working their fields on Sundays. Jewish farmers must often have seen their crops ruined by inclement weather during such a two-day interruption, while their Christian neighbors had safely stored away the produce in their barns. The Jewish holidays, well suited to the climate and seasonal changes in Palestine and neighboring lands, likewise often proved a serious handicap to farmers working in the northern climes. The exigencies of Jewish religious observance, finally, made living in close Jewish communities extremely desirable. Only occasionally could full-fledged rural settlements of Jews as in Byzantine Crissa, or in those western villages which still retained such names as Judendorf or Żydaczów, even Aliud (from *al-yahudi* in the province of Soria), if these stemmed from settlers, and not from mere owners, provide regular synagogue services, schools, and other facilities for rich Jewish living. In most Christian countries, however, isolated Jewish farmers had to limit their synagogue attendance to Sabbaths and holidays, as did perhaps the villagers around Venosa, incidentally recorded in the Chronicle of Aḥimaaz in connection with a local quarrel. Thus the Jewish faith—in a sense true to its own spirit—combined with outward circumstances to deprive medieval Jewry of its modicum of territorial moorings in non-Palestinian soil.[9]

All these legal and social difficulties should not convey the idea that Jewish religious leadership consciously tried to discourage Jewish farming. Rashi merely rationalized the existing situation when he explained the obviously utopian rejection of agricultural labors, indeed of all worldly pursuits, attributed by the Talmud to the great second-century sage R. Simon ben Yoḥai. Work of this kind, Rashi declared, "may be performed by Gentiles, whereas the Holy One, blessed be He, distributes nourishment and profit to those who carry out His will." Yet in practice, he himself helped cultivate his vineyard in Troyes, from which he derived his living. Jewish communities at times granted tax exemptions to farmers and landowners, and Rashi's predecessor, Joseph Bonfils (Tob 'Elem), as we shall see, regarded it as praiseworthy to encourage agricultural pursuits. Ritualistic requirements related to the consumption of meat, wine, and dairy products actually presupposed special Jewish supervision, and hence preferably also Jewish production. In contrast to some serious differences of opinion with respect to dairy products, there was considerable unanimity regarding the necessity of avoiding Gentiles handling wine for Jewish consumption. Although many scholars living in Muslim lands recognized that Islam did not require wine of libation in its worship, they rather strictly adhered to the ancient prohibition. Eliezer bar Nathan took pains to explain why the ancient Palestinian postulate, forbidding Jews to dispose of their land to non-Jews even in the dispersion did not apply to his time, "since the lands are not really owned by us, but are merely set aside for us by the Gentiles for purposes of taxation." Similarly, he contended, the talmudic prohibition of renting houses to Gentiles did not apply in western lands "because the Gentiles there are not idolaters and there is no fear of their introducing idols into their dwellings. . . . But in Russia and Greece they are fanatics and place [icons] on the gates, doors and all over their houses." These purely academic debates certainly were a far cry from the increasingly frequent governmental prohibitions directed against Jewish acquisition of Christian land.[10]

REGIONAL VARIATIONS

In the Muslim world Jewish agricultural endeavors were not hampered by sudden wholesale expulsions. Even the exceptional decrees of Al-Ḥakim or the Almohades probably induced only few Jewish landowners and farmers immediately to abandon their lands. Most of them probably took their time about disposing of their property and leaving for more hospitable countries. A remarkable story of the vicissitudes affecting Jewish owners of a fig grove near Granada before and after the Almoravid invasion is told in an inquiry addressed to Isaac Alfasi (Resp., fol. 19 No. 131). But whatever were that inquiry's legal implications, and the effects of the intervening appropriation by a greedy governor, the grove apparently reverted to Jewish possession. There was a remarkable continuity in Jewish participation in Spain's agricultural endeavor also after her transition from Muslim to Christian rule.

Spain was in many ways extraordinary, however. Her great fertility, the character and density of her population, which made the suburban type of farming highly remunerative, and the prolonged friendly relations with both the Muslim and Christian regimes, encouraged more Jews there than probably in any other country of the world to own and cultivate land. Many a Jew undoubtedly would have echoed the praises sung by a patriotic Spanish Muslim, Aḥmad ar-Razi: "Spain surpasses all other countries through the ingenuity of its inhabitants, their audacity and courage in combat, their propensity and vigor in work, their loyalty to their overlords, their zest for study, their vivacious speech and accomplished manners. No country in the world can compare with her in regard to these advantages, just as none equals her with respect to the solidity of its fortresses" (ed. by E. Lévi-Provençal in *Al-Andalus*, XVIII, 63). We shall see that some such sentiments were also expressed by Jewish writers and poets (not only such customary glorifiers of the past as the forced expatriate Moses ibn Ezra), in relation to Spain's magnificent social and intellectual attainments.

Not surprisingly, therefore, most of the early records pertaining to the Jews of Barcelona deal with one aspect or another of Jewish landownership. The following are some of the more interesting examples: In 1000, the count disposed of lands left behind by Jews who had lost their lives during the city's occupation by the Saracens fifteen years before. In 1022 he similarly took over the property of a Jew who had committed adultery with a Christian woman. On two other occasions the Commodore of the Templars granted some Jews extensive lands in the vicinity of Lerida for hereditary possession against the payment of a stipulated annual rent (1157–58). In 1176 Alphonso II transferred considerable acreage to Perfet, nephew of Saltel (probably identical with the poet Sheshet bar Isaac Beneveniste) of the well-known family of landowners and financiers, for free disposal and permanent possession, and stipulated that, after Perfet's death, the land be taken over by any Jew (*omnis Judaeus*) designated by the latter. Evidently, the king feared that the land might fall into the hands of a Christian lord, and thus be permanently withdrawn from under royal control. It is doubly remarkable, there-

fore, that much later (in 1293), Sancho IV of Castile, yielding to
the demands of the Cortes of Valladolid, agreed to outlaw acquisitions of Christian lands by either Jews or Moors, under the
excuse that "through that [such acquisitions] a very large portion
of our possessions is being withdrawn and we lose our rights
therein." Obviously the king incorporated here bodily the complaints voiced by the landowning gentry at the Cortes rather than
expressed his own apprehensions. Somewhat analogous conditions
seemed to prevail only in Sicily, where intensive cultivation of
fruit occurred even within the confines of the largest cities. Certainly those North African Jews to whom Frederick II was later
to entrust the cultivation of a palm grove and the raising of henna
and indigo in the city of Palermo were no exceptions.[11]

Many such crosscurrents in the socioeconomic life of the countries of Jewish settlement affected Jewish participation in their
agricultural systems. On the whole, in the older and more advanced countries, Jewish farming was in constant decline. To be
sure, in perusing the vast material accumulated in the legal decisions of the Babylonian and, to a lesser extent of Palestinian,
Jewish authorities, one still finds much stress laid on the ownership of land. But, apart from the frequent difficulty of distin-
guishing here between rural property under cultivation and urban
real estate, this emphasis largely stems from the geonic adapta-
tion of talmudic law to contemporary realities. At times, an entire
responsum is devoted to a mere exegetical elucidation of a talmudic passage. For this reason the rabbinic responsa of that and
the later age often reflect the talmudic outlook, an outgrowth of
the ancient, preponderantly agricultural economy, rather than
that of the medieval communities. This theoretical slant is particularly noticeable in the writings of Maimonides. On the one
hand, the sage of Fusṭaṭ waxed eloquent in extolling the merits of
the biblical Jubilee year which had prevented the permanent
alienation of the soil from its owners. Writing as if the matter
still had practical possibilities, he even advised Palestinian farmers
not to rely on the Jubilee law of restitution, but to hold on to their
land, except in extreme emergencies. Yet in his responsa, more
directly dealing with contemporary affairs, he tacitly assumed that
most of his coreligionists lived in cities, and that "land" for them

usually had the meaning of urban property. Without saying so clearly, he obviously believed with Farabi that "the villages exist only for the service of the city." In a characteristic geonic responsum of 787, the distinction is already drawn between Babylonia, the Caliphate's commercial center, where the majority of Jews no longer owned land, and "other" places, where one could still speak of a farming majority.[12]

In newer countries of Jewish settlement, on the other hand, especially in western Europe, Jews were often attracted to agriculture because of the opportunities opened here for their pioneering efforts. As a rule coming from more advanced countries, Jews could employ more refined techniques in the cultivation of old, and introduce new crops, to their own and society's advantage. Reference has already been made to such pioneering services rendered on the Arabian Peninsula by Jewish immigrants and, through them, by the Judaized local tribes. Together they converted large stretches of that arid land into a flowering garden. As soon as Jews vanished from large parts of the Peninsula, the country returned to its former backwardness. Similarly, through its cultivation of rice, the agricultural economy of the Khazar empire excelled those which preceded or followed it in the southern steppes of Russia. Some such pioneering services were also rendered by Jews in western Europe at the time of its emergence from the "dark ages." Spanish Jews, in particular, actively participating in the task of "repopulating" the deserted northern regions, concentrated many of their energies on redeeming vast acreages of fertile soil from centuries of neglect. That is obviously why the nascent states of Leon and Castile, of Aragon and Catalonia, as well as those of neighboring Provence, so lovingly fostered Jewish landownership, and why even the Church raised few objections there. Many churches and monasteries themselves are recorded as active collaborators with Jews in developing the newly recovered lands. F. de Bofarull y Sans could claim, though with much exaggeration, that between the tenth and the twelfth centuries Jews owned one third of all the land around Barcelona. On their part, Jews, whose ownership of entire villages is attested by the frequency of such designations as *allodium Judaicum* or *mons Judaicus*, or those derived from *al-yahud* or *yahudi*, soon developed that attachment to the soil characteristic of persons born and bred on it. A French Jewish landowner's exclamation, reported by Rashi "I do not want the patrimony of my forefathers to fall into the hands of strangers," well illustrates that pride of ownership. In the Frankish Empire, too, Gaudiocus and his son complained to Louis the Pious' officials, in 839, of the loss of an earlier privilege assuring them quiet possession of estates called Valerianis or Bagnilis which had belonged to them "by virtue of legal succession from their forefathers." [13]

Understandably, these more advanced farmers concentrated primarily on areas of intensive exploitation. While rabbinic sources mention Jews raising grain through the then customary extensive rotation of crops, most Jewish farmers seem to have devoted themselves to viticulture, the cultivation of orchards, or dairy and truck farming, all of which required an initial investment of more capital and labor, but later yielded higher returns on limited areas. In the Arab countries, and especially in Muslim Spain, vineyards and orchards dotted the countryside and provided large sections of the population with daily food and much produce for exchange. It was easy for Jews immigrating from Muslim lands to transplant the same methods especially to countries of comparable climatic conditions such as northern Spain, Provence, and parts of Italy.

For Jews these branches of agriculture appeared doubly attractive, as they could be cultivated in the immediate vicinity, or even within the confines, of many medieval towns. After the initial plantings, orchards and vineyards required more intelligent supervision than constant labor. Hence, even scholars like Rashi could grow grapes for a living, while devoting their main attention to research and teaching. Rashi's grandson, Jacob Tam, though a prosperous moneylender and possibly tax farmer, also engaged in the cultivation and the production of wine. This practical experience taught him to be less stringent with respect to the laws of the "wine of libation." On one occasion he justified his liberal interpretation by saying: "Wherever a considerable financial loss is involved, the Torah always evinces concern for Israel's money. Should I not evince such concern, and refuse to decide that the matter is permitted?" Near Eastern rabbis likewise tried to facilitate intensive cultivation by elaborating the talmudic innovation of promiscuously sowing wheat or barley in a vineyard. "This is the law and custom," declared succinctly Naṭronai Gaon, later echoed by Abraham ben David of Posquières. Directly or indirectly, Jews also stimulated the production of certain raw materials needed for industrial output. The three Jews of Arles, for example, who in 1138 contracted with Abbot Pontius of Montmajour for the entire output of the *kermes* dye in the district of Miramar, certainly gave further impetus to the farmers of that district to breed the insects producing that dye. Similarly, the French term *bousache* for watermelon makes it likely that Jews were the first to cultivate it in France.[14]

As usual, such services were highly appreciated for a time, but were speedily forgotten when the local population acquired the new techniques. Sooner or later the Jews were bound to lose out because of the basic incompatibility of their pursuits with the forces of feudalism. Land became not only the mainstay of the economy, but also the ultimate source of political power. He who owned land controlled so and so many villeins, and even noble vassals had to swear to him an oath of fealty. Jews fit badly into this hierarchical system. They neither could take the oath, which after the Carolingian era was increasingly standardized and was couched in overtly Christological terms, nor was it considered desirable that they should exercise mastery over Christian peons, and still less over dependent nobles. Economic forces, to be sure, sometimes prevailed over these political and religious objections. Near Narbonne there was a *Terra hebraeorum*, where Jewish feudal lords held sway over Christian as well as Jewish vassals. In Angevin England Jews owned entire villages. In his privilege for Isaac son of Rabbi Joce and his sons, of 1190, Richard Lion-Heart specifically renewed their right

to reside in our land freely and honorably, and to hold all those things from us which the aforesaid Isaac and his sons held in the time of Henry the King, our father, in lands, and fiefs, and pledges, and gifts, and purchases, viz., Hame, which Henry, our father, gave them for their service, and Thurroc, which the said Isaac bought from the Count of Ferrars, and all the houses, and messuages, and pledges which the said Isaac and his sons had in our land in the time of King Henry, our father.

In his renewal of the still older privilege by Henry I in 1201, John confirmed the Jews' possession of "all that they now rightfully hold in lands, fees [*feodis*], gages, and purchases." Under Henry III Jews entered even more fully the tenurial system, assuming "baronial state, claiming for themselves wardships, escheats, and even advowsons." In 1227, the Jewish contribution to the marriage of the king's sister, Johanna, was called *auxilium*, a term usually reserved for feudal dues. Yet these exceptions merely proved the rule that wherever the feudal system prevailed Jews were sooner or later ousted from most of their landholdings. Even where the law did not specifically prohibit them from owning land (such prohibitions were to multiply only after the twelfth century) they played less and less of a role in both landownership and the tilling of the soil. To a lesser extent this was also true in the Near East after the establishment of the Latin Kingdom of Jerusalem and, more generally, after the Mongol conquests, when feudalism, though of a special variety, had begun to shape the life of the entire farming population.[15]

INTENSIFICATION OF INDUSTRY

Connected with agricultural output were numerous processing industries, such as flour mills, winepresses, spinning and weaving establishments. In the more backward Western countries much of that work was still performed at home, but in Byzantium, and still more in the Muslim world, production was large enough to maintain substantial groups of professional workers, sometimes organized in guilds of their own. Jews were found in all these occupations as both entrepreneurs and workers.

The Jewish share in viticulture and its allied industries, already large in antiquity, increased further under Islam on account of the Muslim prohibition of wine drinking. Since Muslims consumed grapes, grape-juice, and raisins, vineyards were common in all Muslim countries with suitable climatic conditions. But because of the temptation they offered to imbibe the forbidden beverage, some Muslim pietists demanded their complete outlawry. Nobody objected, however, to Jews and Christians cultivating and processing wine for their own consumption. There was no need of "bootlegging," therefore, for the *dhimmis* to maintain wine presses. Nor were there any sharp controls over the distribution, and any Muslim desirous of drink could acquire as much wine as he wished. The caliphs themselves, both in East and West, often broke that prohibition which, as the ecclesiastical heads of Islam, they were supposed to enforce. Nevertheless its mere existence increased the competitive advantages of Jews and Christians over Muslim producers, and also added impetus to Jewish innkeeping. Jews, too, had to contend with some orthodox wings trying rigidly to enforce the old laws governing the "wine of libation." But some rabbis taught that, since Muslims did not use wine for sacramental purposes, their mere contact with a bottle of wine did not disqualify it for Jewish consumption. Western Jewries, on the other hand, looked askance at the possible ritualistic uses of sacramental wine by their Christian neighbors. With supervision facilitated by the presence of numerous Jewish vintners, the Western rabbis often discussed the implication of that ancient prohibition in a fairly rigid vein. Here even Tam suggested only a somewhat more liberal treatment of wine touched by Christian servants in Jewish households. Of less importance was the geonic warning to Jewish innkeepers against accommodating Gentile customers, lest the latter "ogle" their wives. From the few extant sources it appears that innkeeping became a prominent trade among Eastern Jews.[16]

Under Islam, industry concentrated more and more on satisfying the ever growing hunger for textiles. Understandably, we hear less about the coarse products used for clothing by the masses than about the costly garments and rugs purchased by the rich and mighty. In western Europe almost all industrial production outside the home was devoted to such luxury articles. Most precious materials had to be imported from abroad, but their ultimate utilization largely depended on local artisans. Jews, who played a great role in that import trade, seem also to have taken an active part in converting the oriental goods into clothing or home furnishings to satisfy the needs of their highly placed customers. All these matters were taken for granted and alluded to rarely in contemporary sources. The Eastern writers are somewhat more outspoken. According to Al-Jahiz, Jews predominated in the dyeing and tanning industries in Egypt, Syria, and Babylonia, and formed the majority among the Persian and Babylonian barbers, cobblers, and butchers. The latter trade had, of course, a bearing on their ritual law. Describing conditions in Syria and Palestine, Muqaddasi, too, emphasized that "for the most part, the assayers of corn, dyers, bankers and tanners, are Jews; while it is usual for the physicians and the scribes to be Christians." [17]

Most remarkable are the references to numerous Jewish tanners. In Byzantium, too, some Jews turned to this malodorous trade, which did not increase their popularity with their Christian neighbors. An admiring biographer of Archbishop Nicetas of Chonai (about 1150) graphically described that churchman's abhorrence of Jews, "wherefore they were ejected from their residences, and like hungry, leather-gnawing dogs they prowled about the towns, as tanners and dyers of old clothes." Soon thereafter Benjamin observed the widespread hatred of Jews among the Greeks of Constantinople which, he believed, was "fostered by the tanners who throw out their dirty water in the streets before the doors of the Jewish houses and defile the Jews' quarter." One Azac Tannador is mentioned also in Huesca among the Jews to whom Queen Sancha of Aragon, in cooperation with the nuns of Sigena, assigned a garden in which they could build their houses (1190). Obviously, neither the owners nor the Jews were disturbed over the prospect of harboring a tanner in their midst. This was a noteworthy deviation from the old talmudic banishment of this trade outside the confines of cities. An unnamed gaon offered an interesting explanation for the tannaitic exemption of tanners, as well as dung collectors and copper smelters, from the obligatory three annual pilgrimages to Jerusalem. He denied that anything could remove their objectionable odor, for, he believed, that odor penetrated the very flesh of workers. For this reason people used to segregate them "so that they had synagogues of their own, and there still exist [such separate synagogues] in many places." The exemption from the pilgrimage, the gaon added, came from the rabbis' fear that forced separation from other pilgrims might have an adverse psychological effect on these craftsmen and lead to sin. But he failed to give any reason why forced permanent separation should be less prejudicial to their morality. Nonetheless the economic pressures were so powerful that many Jewish workers disregarded not only this low prestige factor, but also the risk that their wives might sue them for divorce with full payment of the marriage settlement. Rabbinic law allowed wives to do so if they found the smell unbearable.[18]

Low esteem by one's compatriots was not limited to odoriferous trades. Despite their great economic importance, weavers were little appreciated throughout the Arab world. Farabi expressed the prevailing sentiments when he contrasted the high-class trade in spices and cambric with the "proletarian" occupations of weavers and street cleaners. Poets sometimes even called weaving an "unclean" occupation. When Yaqut's informant claimed that "if you investigate the genealogy of the noblest families of Isfahan, it is impossible not to find that they originate either from weavers or from Jews," he thought that he hurled a superlative insult. He could have gone a step further and claimed that they were descendants of Jewish weavers, of whom there was a large number in the city. We do not find these views so bluntly expressed in Hebrew letters. Nonetheless, social prejudices animated also many Jewish intellectuals who looked down on the whole class of more or less illiterate artisans as falling within the category of *'amme ha-areṣ,* so sharply disparaged in the Talmud. The Karaite Sahl ben Maṣliaḥ accused Rabbanite judges of outright miscarriage of justice whenever members of lower classes appeared in court. Hai Gaon himself had to warn ruthless disciples not to take too literally the irate utterances of the Talmud concerning the *'amme ha-areṣ,* and treat lightly property rights of the unlearned. To counteract such trends, Maimonides, writing almost in the style of a modern apologist, emphasized that many ancient sages themselves had derived their livelihood from such lowly trades as wood chopping and water carrying.[19]

On the other hand, skilled crafts, like silk weaving, dyeing, and silver- and goldsmithery, not only yielded greater returns, but also enjoyed higher social acceptance. Even before the rise of Islam, Near Eastern Jews were admired or envied as a people endowed by grace divine with special gifts for handicrafts. Cosmas Indicopleustes, referring to the biblical story of the construction of the Tabernacle, added that in most arts Jews still played a dominant role in his own time (early sixth century). In the West, particularly, Jews long pioneered in introducing more refined methods of production. As early as the seventh century Greek glassblowers in France boasted of their ability to produce glass of a quality known as Jewish glass. Five centuries later Benjamin still extolled the art of Jewish glassblowers in Tyre. Jews also practiced the highly skilled art of gold embroidery. Some precious garments of the time contained more gold than linen or silk threads and, for instance, the so-called *badanahs* manufactured for the caliphs in Egypt cost as much as 1,000 dinars or $4,000 apiece. Extraordinary skill was also required for weaving into the cloth the names of the monarch and, less frequently, of other men of power or wealth; specimens of such cloth may still be seen in the world's museums. The famous silk robe, for instance, interlaced with gold, manufactured in 933 for Roger II of Sicily and subsequently used in the coronation of Habsburg emperors, had possibly been made by Jewish artisans working for the royal factory (*ṭiraz al-malik*) in Palermo. The equally advanced process of dyeing through a complicated chemical process had even more Jewish devotees. In fact, the latter was an ancient Jewish industrial art, which the Jews may have further refined during the Babylonian Exile. Now we hear more and more frequently of Jews transplanting that skilled craft to the Western countries. The extraordinary durability of the dyes then used, whether natural or chemically compounded, is attested by the numerous tapestries and vases still extant in museums and palaces. In 1129 a Jewish dyeing establishment is recorded in Gaeta. Four decades later Benjamin found ten Jewish dyers in Brindisi, just as he was impressed by the presence of Jewish dyers in the Latin Kingdom of Jerusalem. Although they enjoyed there a formal monopoly, some itinerant Jewish craftsmen visited even remote Druze villages in quest of new markets. Not surprisingly, therefore, Frederick II arranged with Jewish artisans for the establishment in Sicily and Naples of regular government monopolies of dyeing and silk manufacture. While Frederick's measures really fall into the thirteenth century, they were anticipated as early as 1147, when Roger I attacked Byzantine Thebes, the center of silk industry in the Balkans, and evacuated "all" Jews and many Christians to southern Italy. Jews apparently played a certain role also on the famous silk routes connecting western Asia and Europe with China.[20]

It is difficult, in fact, to find a trade from which Jews were completely absent. Even in such newly introduced industrial branches as the manufacture of paper, which after its importation from China to Samarkand began spreading throughout the Muslim and Christian countries, Jews seem to have played a certain role. It is not accidental that the main center of paper manufacturing in the eastern Mediterranean was for a time the city of Tiberias. This city, an old center of Scriptural learning, probably was the first in Palestine and Syria to sense the advantages of this cheaper supply of writing materials to replace the ever scarcer and more expensive Egyptian papyrus or the equally expensive parchment. Jews must also have participated in the Spanish paper manufacture, extolled by Muqaddasi, and especially in the production of the fine *shaṭbi* paper still extant in many beautiful medieval manuscripts. Frequently mentioned in the Christian period, the Jewish community of Jativa in the province of Valencia, the main center of that manufacture, appears to have been both prosperous and learned already under the Muslims. We can readily envisage how much this industrial progress affected also the literary output of Arabs, Jews, and Eastern as well as Western Christians. There was more than mere chronological coincidence between this new industrial output and the literary revolution of the tenth to twelfth centuries.[21]

Lack of interest of contemporary Hebrew writers, other than Benjamin, in Jewish occupations, and the merely incidental and vague references to one or another tradesman in connection with a legal question in the geonic and postgeonic responsa, deprive much of what has been said here of any substantial documentation. The same holds true for other industrial occupations. However, if there could be a Jewish salt mine in far-off central Germany (near Halle) in the days of Ibrahim ibn Ya'qub's visit to Emperor Otto I, there is certainly no reason for assuming that Jews did not help exploit similar mines, as well as those producing precious and other metals, on a much larger scale in the Muslim countries. Jews must also have been found on the managerial or labor side of the numerous stone quarries, including those which yielded precious stones so extensively used in the Jewish jewelry trade. We actually hear little even about Jewish jewelers, or gold- and silversmiths (except when, for instance, King John granted, in 1199, a sweeping privilege to "Leo the Jew, our goldsmith"). Most craftsmen were simultaneously merchants in this branch in which Jewish businessmen and minters must have had a deep and lasting interest. Nor do we get much information about Jewish carpenters, masons, and other workers in the extensive building and furniture trades, which even at that time supplied employment to many skilled and unskilled workers. The aforementioned report of Masha'allah advising Caliph Al-Manṣur about building plans for the new capital of Baghdad shows that many of them must have been trained in higher, as well as lower, branches of construction work. In the North African city of Segelmessa, we are told by the Arab geographer Al-Bakri, the occupation of masons was an exclusively Jewish preserve. The large, often palatial, Jewish stone houses in England, which, as we recollect, gave rise to unfavorable comments by invidious contemporaries, must also have been built under Jewish direction.[22]

In addition to entrepreneurs there also were numerous Jewish employees, other than slaves. Legal problems of contract labor are frequently enough aired in the contemporary letters, although these are rarely specific with respect to the type of work a particular laborer was expected to perform. Nor do they indicate in any detail the conditions of labor, or the prevailing wages. We may merely guess that the wages of Jewish workers did not materially differ from those received by non-Jews in similar occupations. While Jewish labor laws were somewhat more favorable to the workers than were the comparable Muslim or Christian provisions, as summarized for instance in the famous "Book of the Prefect" in ninth-century Constantinople, they did not erect insurmountable competitive barriers for Jews seeking employment.[23]

In all these activities Jews were not yet hampered by guild restrictions. The Western guilds, which in the later Middle Ages were sharply to discriminate against Jewish members and ultimately greatly to reduce Jewish craftsmanship in many countries, still were in their infancy. Neither the Muslim nor the

Byzantine guilds seem to have pursued equally discriminatory policies. Jews may have encountered some difficulty by virtue of the prevailing concentration of certain crafts in streets of their own. Most Jews, including artisans, preferred to live in their own quarters. But they apparently could freely display their wares in the cities' central bazaars, even if these were located, as was frequently the case, in the vicinity of the main mosques. Where Jews lived in large and closely knit settlements, they formed associations of their own, which under the general supervision of their communal organs regulated tariffs, zones, and conditions of labor. Much of this activity was but a carry-over from Roman Palestine and Sassanian Babylonia, and, in perusing the sources, it is not always easy to distinguish records of existing practice from purely historical-halakhic reminiscences. However, a measure of continuity seems to have existed between these ancient associations and the Jewish guilds which were to flourish particularly in later medieval Spain and early modern Poland.[24]

Available data concerning the ratio of handicrafts to other occupations among the Jews of our period are no more conclusive. Three small Genizah lists, examined by Eli Strauss, show percentages ranging from 38.4 to 52.1 for industrial occupations, as against only 17.3–37.5 percent for commerce and banking. But the total number here recorded covers only ninety-three persons. Hence the sample is much too small to allow for far-reaching conclusions. All three documents come from Egypt which, with its age-old state-capitalistic structure, was by no means typical even of the other Near Eastern countries. Yet some such general ratio must be postulated also for other countries with a relatively dense Jewish population, which certainly could not have lived from commerce and banking alone.[25]

ENTRY INTO WORLD TRADE

In contrast to its steadily declining share in agriculture the Jewish people's commercial evolution outstripped that of its neighbors. Even in the last centuries of antiquity the proportion of Jews in the merchant class outside Palestine and Babylonia may already have exceeded their general ratio in the population.

But now a new stimulus was given to Jewish commerce by the rigid separation between East and West. Although still dominated by semibarbarians, the West European countries revealed a growing demand for cultural and economic amenities. Their upper classes, particularly, developed an unquenchable thirst for luxury articles obtainable only in the Orient. On the other hand, despite their extraordinary increase in population, the Eastern countries soon had a shortage of labor and were forced to import hands for agriculture, industry, and domestic service, as well as women for the numerous harems. They brought slaves from India, Turkestan, Central Africa, and especially from Europe, since white slaves were in the greatest demand, and commanded the highest prices. The Slavonic countries supplied the bulk of these white slaves (*saklab—sclavus—sclavonus*), but the West as a whole may be said to have engaged in this exchange of human cargo for Eastern luxuries.

A class mediating between these two worlds, hostile in the economic even more than in the political and cultural spheres, was bound to arise. The Muslims were great travelers, both for mercantile and intellectual purposes, but their journeys rarely brought them into the hostile Christian countries. "Towards Christians," rightly observed J. H. Kramers, "Mohammedan navigators were often nothing but pirates, but . . . the same thing is true of Christian navigators." Travel on the Mediterranean Sea became so perilous that most Muslim traders preferred to ply the long and arduous caravan route from Egypt to Kairowan, and thence to Morocco and Spain. Describing the perils of that route taken by "western" (Moroccan and Spanish) travelers to Egypt, an inquiry to Sherira Gaon emphasized that "the road is extremely long and most of its stations are in the desert. Some travelers know the route and can foretell the place where they would spend the Sabbath. Others do not know it." The ancient division of the Mediterranean trade routes between the southern Phoenician and the northern Greek spheres of influence was now revived in the separation between the Semitic North African mainland, with its more or less temporary bridgeheads in Crete, Sicily, and Spain, and the northern heirs of the Graeco-Roman civilizations in Europe and Asia Minor. After the First Crusade, when the Western world went over to the offensive, Islam was doubly grateful that the Isthmus of Suez sharply separated the Mediterranean Sea from the Indian Ocean. Remembering the Qur'anic verses, "He has let loose the two seas that meet together, between them is a barrier they cannot pass!" Muslims now considered this separation as a god-send. The Eastern Muslims evinced far less concern for those western lands, which had, in any case, long pursued vastly different economic and political courses. Had not already Ibn Ḥauqal, in his description of the vast extent of the world of Islam (about 975), "omitted the frontier of the Maghrib and Andalus, because it is like the sleeve of a garment"? [26]

Serious linguistic obstacles further complicated the commercial contacts between the two worlds. Few, if any, Arabs knew Latin, the *lingua franca* of the West, while very few Europeans could converse in Arabic, the international medium of the Islamic empires. The Syrian merchant, now largely converted to Islam, soon lost that dominant position in Mediterranean commerce which had been his during the fifth and sixth centuries. His place was now taken by the Jew. Living under the full protection of public law in both the Muslim and Western lands, Jews were able to communicate with one another in Hebrew, which for that very reason came to be widely used in the West for practical purposes. Solomon ibn Parḥon contrasted the linguistic uniformity of the Arabian world with the variety of languages used in Christendom in his day (twelfth century), and observed that "when travelers arrive in Christian lands, they do not understand the native Jews. That is why the latter are forced to converse in the holy tongue which explains their greater fluency in its use." True, among the merchant travelers there were individuals endowed with extraordinary knowledge of languages. One of them, Sallam, apparently a Jew from Spain or Khazaria, who about 845 reached the "wall of Gog and Magog" in China, served as an interpreter, because he allegedly conversed in thirty languages. Some multilingual documents have, indeed, turned up in the Cairo Genizah. Yet for Jews the easiest medium of exchange of both ideas and deeds was the Hebrew language, which in the ninth century became the main international language used in commercial transactions between Paris or Aix-la-Chapelle on the one hand, and Baghdad,

Cairo, or Fez on the other hand. The aforementioned journeys of the Jewish interpreter Isaac, the sole survivor of Charlemagne's embassy to Harun ar-Rashid, and of Ibrahim ibn Ya'qub, the Spanish-Jewish ambassador to Otto the Great, are but political illustrations of much further reaching mercantile relations.[27]

Perhaps even more important was the basic uniformity of Jewish law and of the Jewish administration of justice throughout the world. It gave an easy advantage to the Jewish international trader over his Gentile competitor, whose business transactions often had to be adapted to legal systems radically differing from one another. To a lesser extent, these linguistic and legal advantages also favored the Jewish businessman in the eastern periphery of the Islamic world. The Jewish communities in India or East Africa, beyond the area of Arabian culture, likewise extended a more brotherly reception to their coreligionists arriving from Egypt or Iraq than was offered to non-Jewish merchants by the local pagan majorities.

For this reason Jewish traders achieved increasing prominence even in the eastern parts of the Caliphate.

The Jewry of Isfahan [states A. Mez, summarizing contemporary Arabian sources] was the business quarter of this Persian capital; of Tustar, the headquarters of the Persian carpet industry, it is expressly attested that the greatest dealers there were Jews. A Jew controlled the whole of the pearl fishery in the Persian Gulf. Kashmir was closed against all foreigners; only a few such traders had access, especially Jews. . . . In the 5/11th century Nasir Khosrau was told about a rich Cairene Jew, Abu Sa'id, on the roof of whose house 300 trees stood in silver tubs.

Such cases as that of Abu Imram, the Egyptian Jew who gave the power of attorney to one surnamed "the candle maker" to look after all his business affairs in Morocco, Sicily, and other places, as well as to manage his houses in Sicily and Spain (about 1115–17), revealed the vast expanse of business dealings of a single firm. Another merchant, Halfon ben Nethanel, who in the spring of 1134 had returned from a lengthy stay in India to Aden, soon thereafter proceeded to Cairo. Before the end of 1135 he had already visited Morocco and Spain, and was returning home. Occasionally we even learn of members of the same family living as far apart as Cairo, Aden, and India.[28]

A number of interesting documents recently uncovered by S. D. Goitein have opened new vistas on the crucially important Indian trade of the period. Because of its provenance from the Cairo Genizah, this material is largely limited to Jewish merchants from Egypt and Tunis. But the Jewish traders of Iraq must have had at least as intensive a share in this lucrative branch of commerce. In contrast, little information is available about Jewish trade with China and beyond. Even Chinese sources, which often refer to traders from the Muslim countries, are quite inarticulate in differentiating the faiths of these foreigners. Yet the chances are that Jews actively developed that phase of their international trade, too.[29]

Similarly, in the Carolingian Empire that Jewish trader whose frequent visits to Palestine were mentioned as a matter of course in connection with a practical joke played on the archbishop of Mayence, or those others who seem to have been instrumental in importing Ascalon wine to France, encountered no difficulty in moving across long distances. From the beginning Jewish settlements in Western cities were strung out along the old Roman trade routes, and apparently Jewish merchants never had to travel very far before encountering fellow Jews. They also helped develop many regional and local fairs; for instance, in the Champagne cities or at Cologne. Two Jewish merchants coming to Cologne from as far apart as Carentan, France, and Vladimir, Ukraine, were involved in 1171 in a denunciation by a local money changer, together with one of their Christian customers. The community of Cologne made strenuous efforts to secure their release. They were ultimately acquitted for the payment of 105 silver pieces (*zequqim*), to which the Cologne and several neighboring communities contributed fully 75 pieces. Jews took a conspicuous part not only in international, but also in more regular local fairs. According to Agobard, the imperial messengers arriving in Lyons postponed the local fairs from Saturday to any day, including Sunday, which the Jews might prefer. So important did they consider the presence of Jews at these weekly markets.[30]

From Germany, as well as from the Byzantine Empire and Khazaria, Jews also pioneered in trading with Slavonic eastern Europe. Next to Hungary and Czechoslovakia, Ratisbon served as a major emporium of that trade centered especially in Kiev. Frederick Barbarossa doubtless had this role of Ratisbon Jews in international trade in mind when in 1182 he renewed their old privilege, specifically stressing that "they be allowed to sell gold, silver, and any other kinds of metals and merchandise of any sort, as well as to buy them according to their ancient custom. They may also exchange their property and their merchandise, and provide for their own requirements in their accustomed way." [31]

All this could not have been accomplished without the security extended by the uniform Jewish law. On one occasion the Jewish court of Cairo, under the chairmanship of the Nagid Samuel, felt entitled to instruct the authorities of Aden how to dispose of merchandise salvaged after the shipwreck of an Egyptian Jew. The writers unquestioningly assumed that their decision would be accepted without demurrer by the Jewish court of Aden. A slave accused of libel before the local governor of the Sudanese port of Aidhab thought that he could escape punishment by shouting "I am the slave of the Chief, the Head of the Academy," probably Joshua ben Dosa, a well-known Jewish leader in Cairo. He succeeded in enlisting the sympathies of the local Jewish community and the active intervention of a Jewish visitor from Maghrib. Indeed, a Jew from Baghdad could easily draw up a contract with a coreligionist of Marseilles using exactly the same legal terminology, and knowing that, by bringing the contracting party before the Jewish court of either city, he could obtain full justice.[32]

Advantages of legal uniformity, to be sure, were somewhat diminished by the Jewish judges' customary reluctance to apply the full rigor of law in civil affairs, and their preference to settle litigations by way of compromise. In the case of business dealings, particularly with distant lands, they were doubly guided by existing mercantile usages and the general sense of equity—a procedure facilitated by the frequency with which they, as well as their Muslim and eastern Christian confreres, engaged in business on their own. In this way there began to arise a type of law merchant, which often transcended denominational bounds. Only through such community of commercial practices was it possible to develop those intimate business relations, sometimes actual partnerships, between Jews, Christians, Muslims, and Hindus, as are reflected in the documents relating to the India trade reviewed by Goitein. Yet denominational separation permeated so deeply all walks of life that Jews had their own "trustees of merchants" and generally applied to their business dealings, too, the principles of their own law and ethics. At the beginning of a litigation, moreover, or when no voluntary settlement was secured, either party could invoke the existing formal law. It was particularly applicable to formal contracts, and to situations in which the testimony of witnesses was required by law.[33]

Jewish merchant-travelers also felt much safer under the protection of their own communal leaders. Letters of introduction were found in that inexhaustible archive, the Cairo-Fusṭāṭ Genizah, which assured a foreign Jew, pilgrim, merchant, or rabbi a brotherly reception in a far-distant locality. A Spanish community, for example, recommended a French Jew, who had lost his considerable fortune as a result of persecutions in his native country, to the benevolence of Fusṭāṭ Jewry. On another occasion, the Jewish leaders of Salonica wrote in favor of a Jew speaking only "the language of Canaan" (Slavonic). A Jewish merchant adventurer also derived great comfort from his coreligionists' hospitality in the case of shipwreck almost anywhere in the Mediterranean, Red, Black, or Caspian Seas, and parts of the Indian Ocean. More, his law gave him considerable assurance that, if he happened to fall into the hands of pirates, a frequent contingency at times, he would be ransomed by one of the near-by communities. The latter were ever mindful of such injunctions as that voiced by Maimonides, that "there is no commandment so great as that of ransoming captives, for the captive is among the hungry, thirsty and naked, and lives in constant danger." Egyptian Jewry frequently strained its resources in order to release Byzantine Jews captured by Arab pirates. Of course, relatives at home were even more helpful. In an interesting twelfth-century letter, a Byzantine Jewess Maliḥah complained to her two brothers in Egypt about their reluctance to come and fetch her back together with her daughter. "By Heaven, you have seen that when men from Byzantine communities are captured, their relatives travel to redeem them." (Maliḥah herself was not a captive, however.) How involved some of these redemptions became is well illustrated by the following inquiry addressed to Isaac Alfasi:

A was taken captive, and *B* ransomed him from his own funds, receiving from *A* a note for that amount. When he came to Valencia he found there *A*'s father, who paid him back half the amount and issued a note on the other half. *A* returned home and after a time passed away. Thereupon *B* sent his plenipotentiary to collect from *A*'s father the pledged sum. The latter paid half the balance, remaining in debt for the residual quarter [of the original ransom money]. Subsequently *A*'s father went to Denmark [?] and found there *B*'s heirs [*B* had interveningly died]. Since they were in need, *A*'s father paid them that balance, and returned home. There he was approached by the aforementioned plenipotentiary with the demand for payment of the note.

He escaped paying for the second time that final quarter, which must have been quite sizable to have occasioned such protracted dealings, only on the purely formal ground that with *B*'s death the power of attorney had automatically expired.[34]

How well Arab corsairs knew that Jews would ransom their captive coreligionists is seen in the price they demanded. It averaged 33⅓ dinars, while the average price of a slave, at least about the year 750, had been no more than 200 dirhams or half that sum. Exceptionally, as in 1180, Jews paid 100 dinars (some $400) for a single captive, but in periods of war and temporary oversupply of prisoners, as after the conquest of Palestine by the Crusaders, prices dropped sharply.

UPSURGE AND DECLINE

Emergence of the Jew as a chief figure in international trade was much more conspicuous in the West, where he was often admitted with the explicit or tacit understanding that he would maintain commercial relations with the Eastern lands. The masses of Jews in western Asia, North Africa, and even Spain, undoubtedly retained their more diversified occupations. Among the peoples under the caliphs' rule were other highly mercantile nations, such as the Syrians, Babylonians, Persians (including the commercially gifted Sogdians), and Arabs themselves; and there is no reason to assume that Jews played a particularly conspicuous role in the internal trade of the Muslim world.[35]

Of course, there were innumerable Jewish shopkeepers in both East and West who were rarely mentioned in the sources, and then only in connection with some exceptional occurrence or intriguing legal problem. If Petaḥiah described his encounter in Tiberias with a physician, R. Nehorai, who was selling spices in the market, he did it only because of Nehorai's possession of a genealogical record tracing the family's descent all the way from Judah the Patriarch. Our traveler was also impressed by that physician's excess zeal in placing his children in front of him in the shop, but covering their faces "so that they may not look hither and yonder." On occasions such a humble shopkeeper could lift himself, so to say, by his own bootstraps, and reach a position of eminence and power. Samuel ibn Nagrela's startling career illustrates the possibilities inherent in a small vendor's contacts with different customers. On the whole, however, there was nothing peculiarly Jewish in either that branch of commerce or the methods of its exercise. In fact, in many Near Eastern, as well as Spanish, communities Jewish traders were displaying their wares in public bazaars, alongside Muslim and Christian merchants. They were subject to the same general supervision by the *muhtasib,* although in their dealings with Jewish customers they were also affected by Jewish law and the market supervision of Jewish authorities.[36]

Bazaars or central marketing halls existed also in some Christian countries, especially Spain. That is why Jewish merchants sought to secure privileges, like that enacted in 1131 by Alphonso I of Aragon for the city of Calatayud, which specifically provided that "Christians, Moors, and Jews may buy from one another wherever they wish and are able to." At times the government or a church reserved to itself the right of ownership of the shops, with the merchants occupying the premises only as leaseholders. In such cases Jews were sometimes discriminated against. In his privilege of 1141 for Calatalifa, Alphonso VII of Castile encouraged the growth of a Christian merchant class by allowing each Christian trader erecting a shop on royal land to retain hereditary ownership, whereas Jewish or Muslim shopkeepers were to remain mere tenants. Elsewhere, however, enterprising Jews built their shops on Church property, or even erected regular shopping centers for an entire locality. Wherever the number of Jewish shopkeepers was large enough they could also form bazaars of their own. Such a "Jewish market" is recorded, for instance, in Jerusalem, although the Holy City was but a minor commercial center (except in so far as it catered to numerous tourists, pilgrims, and purchasers of books and religious articles), and its merchants completely depended on the officials and businessmen of Ramleh.[37]

The Jewish petty merchant class included at all times a substantial number of peddlers who brought their wares directly to the customers in cities and countryside. Even in the Near East, and still more in the backward European countries, they often had to accept from the farmers agricultural produce in barter for their merchandise. A geonic responsum speaks of "traders who circulate in small towns and villages, and sell utensils, linen, wool, and spices, and collect in return wheat, barley, wax, and other articles. They then get money from businessmen on their wax, wheat, and barley . . . which these [in turn] sell for profit." That such trips were not without danger even in Muslim Spain is evident from one of Alfasi's responsa referring to legal problems arising from rumors about two peddlers perishing on the road. Apart from many clerks and other business employees, agents of all kinds did business for the account of others. Dependent on the degree in which they assumed personal responsibility for the risks involved, the agents stipulated in the various *commenda* (*'isqa*) contracts for a share in the profits ranging from one quarter to two thirds. Many legal problems were aired in the geonic and postgeonic letters relating especially to the respective areas of responsibility of agent and his principal in the cases of loss or damage.[38]

It was primarily the growing foreign commerce, especially with the West, which lent Jewish merchants a certain preeminence and permitted them proportionately to outnumber Gentile businessmen even under Islam. In his *Book of Routes*, Ibn Khurdadhbah, the Caliphate's postmaster-general, described the four principal trade routes used by Jewish merchants, to whom he gives the curious designation of *Radhanites,* in their mercantile journeys linking the extreme West to India, Turkestan, and China.

These merchants [he declared] speak Arabic, Persian, Roman [Greek and Latin], the Frank, Spanish, and Slav languages. They journey from West to East, from East to West, partly on land, partly by sea. They transport from the West eunuchs, female slaves, boys, brocade, castor, marten and other furs, and swords. They take ship from Firanja (France) on the Western Sea, and make for Farama (Pelusium). . . . On their return from China they carry back musk, aloes, camphor, cinnamon, and other products of the Eastern countries. . . . Some make sail for Constantinople to sell their goods to the Romans; others go to the palace of the King of the Franks to place their goods. . . . These different journeys can also be made by land.

In this much-quoted work, written in 846 and rewritten some forty years later, Ibn Khurdadhbah also mentioned Russo-Norman traders professing Christianity who brought to Baghdad beaver skins and hides of black foxes. Passing through Khazaria, they had to pay a tithe to the Khazar rulers. On the other hand, the Khazars themselves, who had to import nearly all their clothing as well as the coins for their limited local circulation, exported or reexported to the East isinglass, wax, honey, skins, and particularly lumber. According to Ibn al-Ḥusayn, the latter constituted "their greatest wealth." Some Jewish and Arab merchants apparently reached even Korea and Japan.[39]

Although on the whole encouraged by the governments to carry on that trade (in his treaty with the Nubians 'Abdallah ibn Sa'd had already secured a pledge of protection for "Muslims and *dhimmis* traveling in Nubia"), the Jewish merchants often had to contend with a variety of legal, fiscal, and administrative obstacles. In Muslim countries they often had to pay higher custom duties than their Muslim competitors: 5 percent rather than the usual rate of 2½ percent. According to Abu Yusuf, foreigners (inhabitants of the "world of the sword") had to defray fully 10 percent, which probably somewhat favored the Jewish foreigner, who could arrange with a local coreligionist to serve as his importing agent. But even 5 percent was a high surcharge in the time of greatest unity and affluence of the Caliphate. It could become ruinous in the period of the Caliphate's dissolution, when at each of the numerous frontiers Jews had to pay a double duty, apart from many other imposts on trade devised by the fiscal ingenuity of collectors. When "Iṣḥaq the Jew's son" returned from India after a thirty-year absence, in a ship laden with merchandise, he had to pay in Oman the enormous duty of 1,000,000 dirhems (some $280,000). Madmun, head of the Jewish merchants in Aden, sent a large consignment of 60 camel loads of lac to Cairo, but added 100 Qasi robes and 8 camel loads of pepper for the payment of duties and tolls at the various ports and for the cost of transportation up the Nile to Cairo. Here as in the West, pepper often served as the international medium of payment (in French Nîmes Jews were even expected to pay a pound of pepper, or two solidi, for each burial). Understandably, therefore, when the foreign merchants gained the upper hand in the empire of Saladin, they secured the reduction of that duty to the customary one fortieth of the value of the imported merchandise. On the other hand, since Jews under Spanish Islam were among the main traders, and hence also the main clients of custom houses, it is not surprising to find the caliphal administration making use of talented Jewish officials in this fiscal service. At least Ḥisdai ibn Shaprut, along with his other duties at the court of 'Abd ar-Raḥman III, apparently also served as head of the Bureau of Customs.[40]

In the West, on the other hand, Jews often secured privileges allowing them free travel and transportation of goods without surcharges. This is indeed the tenor of the main privileges granted them by Louis the Pious in France, Henry IV and Frederick Barbarossa in Germany, and the Angevin kings of England. With much effort some local rulers secured the right to collect the customary revenues from all traders, including Jews. Exceptionally, the Christian merchants obtained more favorable treatment, as in Charles the Bald's ordinance of 877, which obliged Jews to pay one tenth of the value of their goods (or of their profits?), while Christian traders paid only one eleventh. In addition to regular duties, moreover, there were innumerable local tolls on bridges and roads. For example, Jewish visitors to the fairs in Angers were obliged to pay one denier for every horse or any other merchandise they brought over the bridge, according to Henry II's charter of 1162. In many cases, on the contrary, local rulers tried to attract Jews to their fairs by fiscal concessions. For this reason Countess Blanche of Champagne specifically pledged herself not to raise the Jewish taxes in the future.[41]

More serious were certain legal and extralegal difficulties placed in the way of Jewish merchants. In his "Book of the Prefect" Emperor Leo VI specifically provided that "the guild of dealers in raw silk must not sell any raw silk to Hebrews or to merchants who intend to dispose of it outside the city [of Constantinople]. Violators will be flogged and shorn." Even more drastic was, as we recall, the Venetian attempt a few decades earlier not only to prevent Jews from traveling on Venetian vessels, but also from handling articles of clothing or metal work provided with the sign of a cross. The latter request was rejected by the emperor, while the former prohibition was the less damaging as Jews themselves were often in possession of ships. The tradition of the Jewish *navicularrii* of Alexandria was maintained in such important centers of Mediterranean trade as Marseilles. According to the somewhat unreliable account of a monk of St. Gallen, Norman ships once approached a harbor in Gallia Narbonnensis, but the spectators were uncertain at first whether these were boats of Jewish, African, or British merchants (about 810). Apparently Jewish shipowners did not travel nor transport goods on Sabbaths and holidays, not even with the aid of Gentile personnel. The author of the early German legal compilation, *Ma'aseh ha-geonim*, echoed by Eleazar of Worms, insisted on the prohibition of thus employing Gentile workers, but both clearly took it for granted that there were many Jewish owners of ships and carriages. Among the early decrees relating to Jews of Barcelona, that of 1104 established the temporary monopoly of four local Jews in transporting Saracens for ransom. Even more remarkably, the count provided that "no Jew or Christian shall travel on their [the four Jews'] ship for business without their consent and their cooperation." Jewish shipowners seem to have played an even greater role on the Indian Ocean. In his interesting letter of 1145, Mahruz ben Jacob of Mangalore, India, offered a friend a trip home on his ship, because "it is better than that you travel in the ships of foreign people." Nevertheless Jewish merchants must often have traveled and transported merchandise in non-Jewish vessels, but we hear of little friction between Jewish passengers or shippers and Gentile crews or fellow-passengers. Were it not for the frequent piratical raids, not only in the Mediterranean Basin but also on the Indian Ocean, the Persian Gulf, and the other eastern seas (the extended coastline of the Arabian Peninsula harbored many corsairs' nests), sea travel might generally have been preferred to the arduous landlocked caravans.[42]

Whatever means of transportation he used, the merchant-adventurer's occupation at that time was always risky. In the West, especially, there were deep-rooted suspicions among the masses against the very methods and outlook of the mercantile classes, even if they consisted entirely of Christians. F. Barlow's observation concerning the situation in Angevin England applied with equal vigor to all other feudal countries north of the Alps and the Loire. "The bourgeoisie," he emphasized, "developed its own ethics different alike from those of the peasantry and from those of the aristocracy. The merchant was only less suspect than the Jew . . . and the ghetto was merely a cell within another ghetto —the town itself." Ordinary peddlers ran the gamut of both highway robbery and local hostility. For this reason a peddler in the district of Acco, mentioned in one of the Maimonidean responsa, left most of his merchandise with a friend in the city and took along only what he needed for immediate sale. In another case, recorded in a responsum by Gershom bar Yehudah, a Jewish trader aroused much animosity because he accepted cattle in payment for his costly goods and resold them at a much higher price in his home town. Since many of his clients had stolen the cattle from their neighbors, the Jew was accused of actively promoting thefts. Business trips, particularly over long distances, were considered sufficiently perilous for many travelers to leave behind conditional writs of divorce for their wives, so that if they failed to return by a certain date these "divorcees" might remarry. Otherwise their death would have to be proved through difficult, often altogether unobtainable evidence, and most wives would have remained 'agunot (tied to their marital bonds)—a fate often viewed as worse than death.[43]

Sprouting of mercantile guilds in Western lands likewise boded ill for the future of Jewish commerce. In 1183, the guild of clothing merchants in Magdeburg secured from the archbishop the exclusive privilege of selling or cutting cloth. But, on the whole, Jews did not feel the detrimental effects of these monopolies until after 1200. In the Muslim world, especially, the mercantile guilds were no more exclusive than their industrial counterparts. In fact, governments at times opposed the formation of artisan and merchant guilds, not so much because of their denominational bias, as because of their partial withdrawal from under the governmental *ḥisba* (the caliph's canonical right to regulate market morality). In Egypt they were sharply repressed by Saladin, under whose regime Jewish businessmen seem to have enjoyed much equality of opportunity.[44]

On their part, Jews also tried to control business, and especially to reduce ruinous competition among their own coreligionists. They sought to achieve this aim by a judicious control over the admission of foreign Jews to trade in each locality. Their so-called *ḥerem ha-yishub* (residential ban, or rather permit), although based on talmudic antecedents, now became a major instrument of Jewish communal control, especially in the West, which was progressively more feudal from the tenth century. In this respect it became in many ways "the medieval Jewish counterpart to the gild merchant," as described by L. Rabinowitz. A related institution also developed in western Europe as early as the tenth century. Through the so-called *ma'arufiah* (a term of uncertain origin) merchants and moneylenders were protected against competition with respect to certain customers who were treated as their special preserve. This protective institution was used especially by Gershom bar Yehudah to promote the interests of scholarly merchants. In larger communities Jews often had their own business associations, more or less loosely organized, with recognized, though largely self-appointed, "trustees of merchants."[45]

Occasionally Jews also freely engaged in joint enterprises with members of other faiths. Thus Madmun, the trustee in Aden (until 1151), had as business associates many Muslims, including the famous vizier of southern Yemen, Bilal ben Jabir, Christians (one of them named 'Abd al-Masiḥ, servant of Christ), and Hindus. Another Jewish merchant, Mahruz ben Jacob from Mangalore, wrote about a Hindu associate, Tinbu, "between him and me there exists an inseparable friendship and brotherhood." All that despite the prohibitions in both Muslim and Jewish law against interdenominational partnerships. But everywhere increasing regimentation, an integral part of the growing feudal controls, cast its long shadows over the continued prosperity of Jewish merchants as well.[46]

Much more far-reaching were the adverse affects of the new power constellations in the world. With the progressive dissolution of the Great Caliphate and the simultaneous rise of great trading emporia in Christian Europe, the Jewish role in international commerce was gravely jeopardized. Arab-Christian hostility, to be sure, which had previously fostered Jewish mercantile expansion, continued undiminished; indeed, it reached a new height of intensity in the era of Crusades. Only thus can we understand a prayer composed in the geonic period which was unheard of in any other period of Jewish history in the dispersion: "Be it Thy will, O Lord, that the kings should wage war on one another!" But now the increasing weakness of the divided Arab kingdoms merely stimulated the predatory appetites of the rising Italian republics. Instead of awaiting the peaceful arrival of oriental Jewish traders, the Genoese, Pisan, or Venetian merchant princes now preferred to proceed to the Eastern countries and, under the pressure of superior armaments, to impose upon the natives an "exchange of goods." Even before the Crusades, the commercial relations between East and West were thus transformed into half-mercantile, half-military exploits. After 1099 the Italian republics secured many vital concessions from the Latin rulers of Jerusalem and Antioch, as well as from Byzantium, and even established in the Near East regular merchant colonies of their own, which traded with their homelands under the effective naval protection of their mother countries. A similar preponderance of heavily armed merchants was established along the northern routes by the formation of the Hanseatic League, although for a time Jewish traders were still hospitably received in the League's southwestern outpost, Cologne. Jews obviously could no longer compete with these heavily armed Italian and Hanseatic merchant marines.[47]

SLAVERY AND SLAVE TRADE

One major branch of international Jewish commerce gradually diminished in importance for other than competitive reasons. The Jewish slave trade, from its inception seriously hampered by a maze of Christian, Muslim, and Jewish laws, began completely drying up, as Slavonic eastern Europe became Christianized. The progress of feudalism, too, converted most peasants in both Europe and the Near East into half-free villeins, who largely replaced unfree labor in agriculture and, to a lesser extent, in industry and domestic service. Only residual areas around the Black Sea and central Africa still remained sources of supply for the declining number of slaves in the Muslim world, but the role of Jewish traders there had always been quite limited.

During the era of Islamic expansion, however, from the seventh to the tenth centuries Jews may have played a somewhat more important role as exporters of slaves from eastern Europe. Imports from foreign countries became the main sources of supply of slaves, since the cessation of large military conquests after the first century of Islam. Jewish slaveholders had to overcome the ancient legal prohibitions of owning Christian slaves in Christian countries and Muslim slaves in Muslim countries. Clearly, even the handling of pagan slaves was precarious in so far as each slave could determine for himself whether he preferred to secure freedom, or at least a change of masters, by the mere act of conversion. Jews often ran afoul of their own law, too, which required them immediately upon acquisition to circumcise the slave, submit him to ritualistic ablution, and introduce him into the observance of Jewish religious laws. If the slave resisted circumcision, the master was allowed to retain possession for twelve months, after which time, he had to dispose of him to a non-Jew. Amram Gaon qualified this talmudic law by ruling that only circumcision could thus be delayed, but that a slave's refusal to accept Judaism altogether enforced immediate sale to a Gentile master. If circumcised, however, a slave was considered sufficiently Jewish for the rabbis to discourage his subsequent sale to non-Jews. According to Sar Shalom Gaon, a female slave submitting to ablution, even against her will, was to be treated as a Jewish member of the household, and food, including wine, handled by her was permissible for consumption.[48]

Circumcision of Christian slaves was extremely perilous, since it was reiteratedly outlawed in Christian countries; in Byzantium under the threat of capital punishment. Here Christian slaves of Jews, even if not circumcised, were to be instantaneously liberated and their masters punished by the severe fine of 30 pounds. Western Europe, far more dependent on slave trade for the payment of goods imported from the Orient, was somewhat less exacting in legal theory, and in practice often winked at infractions of existing laws. In Visigothic Spain the very clergy sometimes sold slaves to Jews, evoking a sharp prohibition, combined with a lengthy sermon, by the Tenth Council of Toledo (656). Yet Western Christendom, too, could not permanently condone a practice sharply condemned by its own secular, as well as ecclesiastical, laws and made the target of sharp attacks by rabble-rousing churchmen.[49]

Western Jewish slaveholders derived little comfort from the stated indemnity for each slave freed by conversion to Christianity. The generally anti-Jewish First Council of Mâcon of 583, established 12 solidi as an appropriate compensation. This rule, probably derived from the then prevailing average prices, must have affected adversely owners of more highly skilled slaves or more beautiful girls, that is, precisely those groups which were most likely to benefit from freedom. Once incorporated into the official canonical collections, the amount remained "frozen," later canonists taking little cognizance of changes in market prices. On the other hand, abetted by their royal protectors viewing all Jewish property as their own, Jews often succeeded in exacting even from local churches an indemnity more closely approximating the particular slave's market value. In his bitter letter of complaint, addressed to Alphonso VIII of Castile on May 5, 1205, about the alleged favoritism shown to Castilian Jewry by the royal administration, Innocent III asserted that Jewish slaveholders were allowed to collect high indemnities there by merely swearing how much a particular slave was worth to them. "Whence recently you ordered that 200 *aurei* be paid by our Venerable Brother the

Bishop of Burgos for a certain Saracen woman the servant of some Jew, though the Bishop says she was worth hardly ten solidi." One can readily imagine how greatly such indemnities, further increased by the cost of maintaining liberated slaves until they could earn a living, deterred impecunious or avaricious bishops from propagating large-scale conversions of this type. Yet Jewish slaveowners could hardly rely on this victory of economic over religious motivations.[50]

In this dilemma between observing Jewish law and running counter to stringent governmental prohibitions, Jewish slave traders would have had no chance of survival, were it not for a loophole in rabbinic law. According to the Talmud, a slave did not have to be circumcised if his former master had specifically made non-circumcision a condition of the sale. Now rabbis could interpret the existing stringent governmental prohibitions as blanket conditions of that kind. Although first recorded in the thirteenth century (by Mordecai bar Hillel ha-Kohen), this sweeping evasion must have originated in the earlier period of more intensive slave trade. With all such compromises Jewish slaveholdings in Christian countries were precarious enough to offer a great temptation for Jewish dealers to convert themselves, or their children, to Christianity. We recall how in the days of Gregory the Great, one Basil had escaped punishment by claiming that the Christian slaves belonged to his converted children. Undoubtedly, after each decree of forced conversion in Byzantium, Visigothic Spain, and elsewhere, there remained behind a certain number of insincere converts who failed to return to Judaism after the revocation of the original decree. They found it advantageous economically to remain overt adherents of the Christian faith, even if, in the secrecy of their homes, they continued to observe Jewish customs—a practice to which they had become involuntarily inured during the period of persecution. It was against such insincere converts that the Second Council of Nicaea of 787 legislated that they not be admitted to the Christian communion, but be made to live openly as Hebrews, "neither baptizing their children, nor purchasing slaves, nor possessing them." As a rule, however, such converts were made to adhere to their new faith even against their will.[51]

Jewish law itself gave a maltreated slave many opportunities to force the master's hand. Because the ancient rabbis had wished to encourage immigration to the Holy Land, they allowed a slave to demand from his master transfer to Palestine. Theoretically this law remained valid also in the Middle Ages, and Maimonides expressly stated that it "is to be enforced at any time, even today when the country is in Gentile hands." More, a slave escaping to Palestine from abroad was to be treated as a full-fledged proselyte; he was to pay an indemnity to his master only if he could afford it later. This opinion was shared by the majority of rabbis, including Jacob Tam, despite the obvious objection, raised by another Tosafist Joseph bar Yom Tob, that "all slaves could get rid of their masters by fleeing to Palestine." Nor was the recapture of fugitive slaves even in the Diaspora altogether simple, in view of the outright Deuteronomic prohibition, however qualified by later rabbinic law. Many runaway slaves were always roaming through the Muslim world. In answer to all these perplexities, Jewish slaveholders had to treat their slaves more humanely and thus stifle their desire to change masters. But one need not doubt that the availability of these numerous escape clauses in Jewish law strengthened the rabbis' determination, nurtured by the general fear of informing so characteristic of embattled minorities, to withhold the resources of Jewish learning from slaves even more than from other Gentiles. Masters were to impart to slaves the fundamentals of Judaism, and particularly ritualistic laws relating to their services at home, but not to teach them the Torah.[52]

Other legal difficulties beset the trader engaged in supplying the ever present Muslim market for slave girls and eunuchs for the numerous Near Eastern harems. Nor was concubinage with slaves absent from Christian countries. In his correspondence with the Baghdad Caliph Muthi of 964, Emperor Nicephoros Phokas gloated over the effects of his conquest of Crete. "We have made prisoners," he wrote, "of the inhabitants of that island. Their women with their long floating coiffures have been carried away to our harems." In Aleppo, too, many "noble and illustrious virgins" have been made concubines of the conquerors. To which the Caliph rightly answered, "We possess a million slaves and servants taken from among your women." While the ruling classes of all countries were thus interested in maintaining this branch of international trade, they imposed special restraints on the traders who often had to guard their higher-priced virgins during lengthy journeys and frequent resales. At the same time, as we shall see, the rabbis maintained their rigid opposition to free sexual relations between Jewish masters and slave girls. Not because they wished to safeguard the slaves' chastity. Slaves were proverbially promiscuous and, according to legal theory, did not even have any recognized family relations. Masters were entitled to give slave girls in marriage to two male slaves simultaneously, and even marry off a slave to his own mother. But masters suspected of cohabitation with their slaves were at least made to liberate them and marry them in due form.[53]

Jewish trade in eunuchs likewise encountered serious legal obstacles. In periods of Muslim affluence, to be sure, the demand must have been very great and the profits enormous. Certainly Caliph Muqtadir must have paid handsomely for the 11,000 Greek and Sudanese eunuchs allegedly serving at his palace. But Jewish traders must have known that castration of eunuchs ran counter not only to the ancient prohibition of castrating even animals, but also to that of mutilating slaves in any form. While the Bible had mentioned only the loss of an eye or a tooth, the Talmud added twenty-four other categories of mutilation which entitled the slave to immediate emancipation. Among these was castration, as agreed upon also by such medieval interpreters as Rashi and Alfasi. True, Maimonides, perhaps mindful of the economic realities in his own community of Fusṭaṭ-Cairo, the locale of one of the world's leading slave markets, tried to exclude castration from that list by a legal technicality. A eunuch, moreover, trying to secure freedom from a Jewish court, faced staggering difficulties in proceedings. But the very existence of that stringent legal prohibition, which even Maimonides did not deny, must have exerted a restraining influence on religiously conscientious, or commercially prudent, Jewish traders. These were advised, therefore to use non-Jews for the performance of that operation before the slave's transfer into their possession. Muslims, on their part, were equally reluctant to perform castration, and tried to delegate that responsibility to Christians or Jews. Byzantine legislators from Justinian on likewise forbade that operation and tried to force dealers to bring in eunuchs already castrated abroad—all of which did not prevent the very emperors who issued those laws from employing many eunuchs at their courts. Obviously, here too Jewish dealers ran into innumerable difficulties with local prohibitions and the force of public opinion.[54]

Quite apart from these legal difficulties, merchants, dealing with a merchandise endowed with its own will, had to overcome peculiar business risks. Although the alternatives offered by freedom were not always inviting, many slaves succeeded in escaping. There also existed the great hazards of transporting slaves across perilous deserts or seas. Slaves were doubly exposed to piratical raids, and their mortality on the road must have been extremely high. We need not take literally the miracle tale of a Christian saint, Eustratios, concerning his experience as a prisoner in Kherson; he was allegedly mishandled by his Jewish master, who wished to make him eat Passover food (about 1100). Certainly, the story of the saint surviving fifteen days on the cross, but being instantaneously killed by a spear, does not inspire much confidence. Yet his report that he was the only one of fifty prisoners to survive the ordeals of the journey because he had been "a habitual faster from his youth," does illustrate these great hazards. On the slave markets in civilized countries, on the other hand, one had to beware of a lot of fraudulent sales. Slave traders were proverbially dishonest. According to a story told with relish in Malaga, a Muslim lady, working hand in hand with a dealer, pretended to be a captive. After her sale she tried to induce her master to marry her. If she liked the arrangement she stayed on, otherwise she went to court and secured liberation by proving her original free status. By another trick the purchaser was also cheated out of whatever redress he might have had against the merchant. More than in the case of animals the buyer also had to beware of hidden faults, not all of which invalidated the sale. Special "experts in blemishes" of slaves are mentioned in a geonic responsum. Character defects, especially, were not considered such technical blemishes by Jewish law. If a slave is found to be, Maimonides summarized the existing law, "a thief, robber, kidnaper, constant fugitive, glutton, or the like, he cannot be returned [to the seller], because all slaves are expected to possess all these bad traits." In short, echoing views expressed by philosophers from Plato to his Arab contemporaries, Maimonides declared the slave to be "the lowest among men." [55]

Notwithstanding these harsh words, there developed then, as under all slave civilizations, many human relationships in the homes, where slaves often became affectionate members of the family. In fact, the rabbis' verbal rigidity was perhaps mainly intended to counteract excessive friendships. When humanity demanded it the rabbis themselves made significant concessions. In the case of R. Isaac bar Abraham of Sens' Slavonic (?) slave, who had died on a Sabbath, the rabbi permitted the breaking of the Sabbath rest, so that the slave's wife might be brought from Worms to attend his funeral.[56]

Economic necessity overcame all social and legal difficulties. In the East, obviously only a small minority of Jewish merchants traded in slaves. That is why relatively so few geonic and postgeonic responsa from eastern areas deal with slaves as objects of commerce. In the Christian West, on the other hand, where the total Jewish population was long exceedingly small, a larger proportion of traders seems to have entered for a time this risky but lucrative branch. It was primarily for their benefit that the rabbis now restricted to slaves already circumcised the old talmudic prohibition of the sale of slaves to non-Jews. Formerly such a transfer had involved, as rule, the loss of a permanent member of a Jewish household and, in a sense, also of the Jewish community, but now temporary slaveholdings, with the aim of early reselling, became a branch of Jewish commerce.

Asked by an unnamed community, where slaves were exceedingly cheap and the demand great ("there is no merchandise like it") and only one of a hundred slaves observed Jewish law, Naḥshon Gaon ruled that because they refused to abide by Jewish commandments they might freely be sold to Gentiles. The Carolingian privileges were aimed primarily at increasing the domestic supply of slaves. That is why Louis the Pious specifically allowed Jews to import slaves and to sell them only *within* the Empire. Louis' restriction was based on earlier decisions by both

Church and state which generally forbade the exportation of slaves abroad, principally to Muslim Spain. Through this prohibition the Frankish Empire wished to prevent the alienation of prospective new members of the Christian faith, as well as the direct increase in the manpower of its hereditary enemy. Later rulers, however, acquiesced in this exchange which alone made possible the continued importation of luxury products from the Iberian Peninsula. That Jews were active in exporting slaves across the Pyrenees already in the Carolingian period was repeatedly asserted at least by their enemy, Agobard, who even accused them of stealing Christian children and selling them across the border. If at all true, this accusation was probably based upon the archbishop's exaggeration of some individual incidents. Otherwise, the main sources of slavery remained the Slavonic countries, as attested by Ibrahim ibn Ya'qub and still mentioned, perhaps as a mere historical reminiscence, by Benjamin. It is possible, though not necessarily true, that when the apostle Methodius's work collapsed in Moravia, his followers were sold to Jews and brought to Venice, where they were ransomed by the Byzantine ambassador. The Raffelstetten toll ordinance, which specifically referred to Jewish importers of slaves, obviously had in mind such imports from the neighboring Slavonic lands. That this was no one-way traffic, however, is well illustrated by the story of one Sa'adun ibn Fatḥ al-Sarumbaqi, a Christian convert to Islam, who was captured by Normans from the Portuguese coast in 858–61 and sold to Jews. His story was recorded mainly because, after obligating himself to repay the ransom money, he paid the interest but defaulted on the capital.[57]

Before long emancipated Slavs and their descendants injected a significant new ethnic element into the cosmopolitan population of the Caliphate of Cordova. Some of these Slavonic Spaniards, professing Islam, played a considerable role in the army, administration, and political intrigues on the Peninsula in the tenth century and after. Prosperous Spanish Jewry, too, appeared among the customers of slave dealers, acquiring numerous slaves for its own households. More frequently than anywhere else, we even find Spanish-Jewish moralists, especially after 1200, complaining of widespread Jewish concubinage with slave girls.

In this respect, Spain seems not to have been representative of other Muslim countries. While our information in the obscure realm of sex relations is necessarily very limited, doubly so wherever they were placed under severe legal sanctions, it appears that most Jews under Islam, to the amazement of their Arab neighbors, obeyed the stringent talmudic prohibitions and abstained from sexual intercourse with slaves. Just as under Sassanian rule the Jewish leaders had insisted on the preservation of family purity, as they understood it, by stressing the prohibition of incest, so did they now, confronted by a civilization in which many of the very caliphs were sons of slave-girls, reiterate and sharpen the old talmudic regulations against such sex relations. To facilitate concubinage Muslim law had early drawn the distinction between pagan and Zoroastrian slaves who had to be converted before serving as concubines, and Jewish or Christian women who could thus be used even if they refused conversion. In contrast thereto, Simon Qayyara, the eighth-century compiler of the law code, *Halakhot gedolot,* declared intercourse with a slave girl (even after she had undergone the partial conversion via ablutions and observance of Jewish law required of all slaves) to be a cumulative violation of fourteen different prohibitions. A century later Naṭronai Gaon decreed that "if a son of Israel is caught with his slave . . . she is to be removed from him, sold, and the purchase price distributed among Israel's poor. We also flog him, shave his hair, and excommunicate him for thirty days." Unless an unfree mother was freed and married by her master, other geonic responsa insisted, her child was to be considered a regular slave, with no rights of inheritance (unlike other illegitimate children). He could be sold as a slave by his father or the latter's heirs. Women were not allowed to acquire male slaves. The rabbis only debated the point as to whether they could purchase boys aged nine or less in view of the more remote danger of sexual licentiousness. In order to safeguard themselves against possible rivals, brides often brought into their household slave girls of their own choice, and disposed of them at the first sign of their husbands' flirtation. They often took the additional precaution of having their grooms insert into their marriage contracts a clause providing for the immediate sale of any female slave found objectionable by the mistress of the household. Such contracts, also used by brides to guard themselves against more legitimate rivals under the then prevailing polygamy in the Near East, became quite common in Egypt and other North African lands. A number of specimens, especially from a somewhat later period, have been found in the Cairo Genizah.[58]

For this reason the very employment of slaves in Jewish households required a rationale. Hai Gaon supplied it by stressing the dangers to the morals of Jewish women if they had to fetch water from the wells and mingle there with licentious Gentile slaves. More consistently, Maimonides and others urged their coreligionists to employ in their houses Jewish servants, rather than Gentile slaves, on both nationalistic and charitable grounds. The philosopher of Fusṭāṭ waxed eloquent when he wrote,

The sages have enjoined us to keep as one's domestics poor Jews and orphans rather than slaves; it is better to employ the former so that the descendants of Abraham, Isaac, and Jacob should derive the benefit of one's fortune, and not the descendants of Ham. He who increases the number of his slaves increases sin and iniquity in the world from day to day, whereas the man who employs poor Jews in his household increases merits and religious acts from hour to hour.

However widely such moral exhortations may have been disobeyed, particularly by those wealthy Jews who needed a large retinue of slaves for conspicuous display, they must have greatly reduced the number of unfree servants in Jewish domestic employ. The ever increasing prices of slaves, on the other hand, made their large-scale employment in agriculture and industry the less remunerative to Jews, as the latter could invest the funds at high rates of interest and hire free labor at prevailing low wages. Only where permanence was important, as in the employment of slaves as business agents (for instance, by Joshua ben Dosa), did such investment pay off. But the number of unfree business executives must always have been rather small. Neither slave trade, therefore, nor slaveholding seem ever to have been so important a factor in Jewish economic life as it long appeared to students familiar only with the fulminations of churchmen against them. As a commercial branch, in particular, it doubtless was always insignificant and dwindled to very minor proportions after the Christianization of the Slavonic peoples in the tenth century.[59]

MONEYLENDING

Another significant transformation in Jewish economic life resulted in the large-scale entry of Jews into banking and liberal
professions. There were some Jewish money-changers and dealers
in bullion as well as physicians and scribes, in the Roman and
Sassanian Empires. But now, owing to their rapid urbanization,
widespread popular education, and intellectual alertness, they,
as well as the Christians, far outnumbered the Muslims in all these
professions. The conditions in tenth-century Palestine and Syria
(we recall Muqaddasi's statement that most assayers of corn, dyers,
bankers, and tanners were Jewish, while Christians predominated
in the professions of physicians and scribes) may have changed
rapidly under the disintegrating Caliphate. But the relative preponderance of Jews in banking and dyeing, even after that date,
appears indubitable. At the same time, many more Jews entered
the medical and scribal professions all over the Muslim world and,
to a lesser extent, in Christian countries. We shall see that medical science, in particular, played a great role in Jewish intellectual
life from the tenth century on.

Apart from the vital contributions of tenth-century financiers
in Baghdad, Islamic banking felt the cumulative effects of Jewish
transactions in Egypt, Kairuwan, and Spain. Toward the end of
the ninth century the Coptic Patriarch of Alexandria, Anba Michael, raised a heavy contribution to the government by selling
a church and other estates to Jews. Certain Judeo-Arabic business
expressions (for instance, *Muballit* instead of *Mufallis* for bank-
rupt, similar to the German *Pleite*) came into general mercantile
usage. Everywhere the Islamic prohibition of usury, as in western
Europe the similar canon laws of the medieval Church, fostered
the concentration of moneylending in the hands of "infidels." The
Muslim jurists, to be sure, like their European confreres, detected
various means of circumventing the laws of *ribbah* which, by including any unlawful gain (for instance, through misrepresentation of a sold object), went much further than anything Jews or
Christians called "usury." The *'ullama* particularly found numerous loopholes, as did the rabbis, to justify interdenomina-

tional moneylending on interest. Yet, by virtue of their lesser numbers alone, Jews were able to extend many more loans to Muslims and Christians than vice versa. Their constant dependence on the favoritism of leading statesmen and their inability overtly to compete for high office also made them more pliable tools of both fiscal exploitation and the concealing of those "secret profits," through which administrators tried to accumulate fortunes during their brief and uncertain tenures of office.[60]

Despite the large literature on the subject, often written with more heat than discernment, the full story of the Jewish entry into large-scale banking is yet to be told. But it appears that in antiquity and, in its continuation, under Byzantine domination Jews never constituted an important segment of the banking profession. By legalizing a modest rate of interest, the later Roman and Byzantine Empires obviated the necessity of legal evasions and prevented the creation of special ethnic or religious groups dedicated to this commercial branch. True, Church Fathers like Saints Basil and Ambrose argued vehemently against Christians charging "usury" to fellow Christians. But the government paid no heed to these warnings, or at least took off their edge by defining usury as referring only to excessive profit over and above the legally permissible rate of interest. Even Justinian, pious Christian though he was, only set maximum rates ranging from 4 to 8 percent, dependent on the class of lenders. Jews apparently belonged to the majority allowed to charge 6 percent. On loans connected with exceptional risks, like those secured by ships' cargoes, the permissible rate was 12 percent. The government itself often entered the banking business, extending loans at 6 percent or more. Ultimately, Nicephoros I (802–11) outlawed moneylending on interest by private citizens, but continued governmental banking as a royal monopoly, and raised the rate to 16.66 percent. For these reasons Jews never played any role in the credit system of the Empire. Even after its transition to Muslim rule Palestine, where the Byzantine patterns of administration and economic life persisted longer than elsewhere, has preserved no records of professional Jewish moneylenders.[61]

Palestine was not typical, however, of other countries of Islam. In Iraq or Egypt the rapidly expanding economy demanded a speedier turnover of capital resources, and offered greater facilities for productive credit. These growing needs opened up new opportunities for enterprising *dhimmis* to enter what was quickly becoming a very lucrative trade. Surely, there were many legal obstacles to overcome in their own and the country's general laws. But these could in no way be compared with the legal handicaps of slave traders.

Since all these laws were ultimately derived from the biblical prohibition of usury, they followed the Old Testament's lead in allowing interest to be charged to "strangers." The Hebrew phrase, *la-nokhri tashshikh* (unto a foreigner [or stranger] thou mayest lend upon interest; Deut. 23:21) could be interpreted as an imperative, and some ancient zealots, followed by Maimonides but not by the majority of rabbis, considered it a commandment to charge interest. True, in their general segregationist endeavor, talmudic sages tried to reduce all commercial transactions with non-Jews to a minimum, and hence proscribed extending loans to Gentiles except in cases of dire necessity. But such a policy, perhaps remotely practical in ancient Palestine and Babylonia with their dense and economically differentiated Jewish populations, became utterly untenable in countries where Jewish minorities increasingly lived from trade or industrial exchanges with their non-Jewish neighbors. An unnamed gaon (Saadiah?) specifically urged his inquirers to refrain from excommunicating lenders of money on interest to Gentiles. Although Amram Gaon still tried to dissuade scholars from pursuing this line of business, other teachers favored scholarly creditors as the least likely to succumb to missionary blandishments of Gentile clients. In Cairo there even seems to have existed in 973 a regular guild of Jewish bankers.[62]

Once credit had lost its primary function of helping neighbors in temporary need, and had significantly accelerated the stream of production, the ancient prohibition of charging interest to fellow Jews, too, became meaningless. Theoretically, Jewish religious leaders, like those of the other faiths, adhered to this ancient taboo. But they accepted the talmudic distinction between biblically outlawed usury and only rabbinically forbidden "shades of usury." The latter constituted what Roman law called an *obligatio na-*

turalis, that is, they were not forcibly collectible from debtors but, once paid, could not be reclaimed with the aid of courts. Only Sar Shalom Gaon suggested that a creditor who had secured such an unlawful gain be forewarned that, in case of repetition, he would be fined and made to return his profit. To what lengths ancient and medieval rabbis went in outlawing even verbal usury, may be seen from their insistence that, unless the debtor used to do so before receiving the loan, he must not teach the creditor Bible or Talmud, praise him before others, or greet him. Knowing of the borrower's inability to repay the loan, the lender "must not appear before, or even pass by, his debtor. . . . He may frighten him, or shame him, even if he does not ask for repayment." If anything, such excesses must have led precisely to that "shutting of gates before debtors" which had induced Hillel to assure creditors of the return of their loans after the Sabbatical moratorium with the aid of a *prosbol.* This instrument was still included in the standard Books of Deeds by Hai and Yehudah bar Barzillai. It was increasingly taken for granted to such an extent that the usual rules of evidence had to be relaxed in its favor.[63]

Western churches progressively sharpened their opposition to Christian moneylending. But they thus merely created an ever larger vacuum which Jews were invited to fill. Invariably, when high-principled laws ran counter to basic economic needs, legal subterfuges of one kind or another were easily detected by ingenious businessmen and their juristic advisers. The technicalities of the ramified Jewish laws governing loans necessitated certain peculiar adaptations; Jews could make use of modified versions of the *contractus mohatrae* or the *contractus trinus,* the "purchase of rents" or the acquisition of deeds with a discount. The latter was a most facile evasion based upon the assumption of Jewish jurists that only direct relations between lender and borrower could be usurious. But there was no objection to a merchant selling some commodity on credit at a high profit, and then discounting the bill with a banker at less than its face value. Similarly, an agent could readily pay a gratuity to the banker for a loan extended to his client, the latter of course bearing the brunt. Perhaps the most significant method of evasion was the use of the regular commercial *commenda* contract. Here the lender appeared as the debtor's silent partner and hence as participant in profits. While the rabbis insisted that the "partner" performing the actual service had to be separately remunerated for it, the remuneration and shares in profits or losses were left to the parties' discretion. In time, the capitalist partner's profit could be fixed in advance and his losses minimized. Such an *'isqa* contract became, therefore, but a regular loan contract on interest. By writing the clause *'al ṣad hetter 'isqa* (on the basis of the permissibility of the *commenda*), many a pious Jew even in the twentieth century salved his conscience while charging or paying whatever rate of interest had been stipulated.[64]

Notwithstanding the ready availability of such numerous alternatives, moneylending as such never became a major independent occupation among the Jews under Islam. It was usually combined with money changing and other aspects of banking. Many bankers were simultaneously merchants dealing with various commodities on their own account. Some also performed the semipublic services of taxgatherers or tax farmers, since tax collectors often had to advance funds to needy administrators in expectation of later reimbursements from fiscal revenues. 'Ali ibn 'Isa's letter to his two Jewish bankers well illustrates that combination of banking and tax farming:

Do you want to avoid [the vizier threatened] my inflicting penalties on you that may affect you and your heirs for ever? I shall only refrain from it in consideration of a matter that will cause you no damage whatever. At the beginning of each month I need an amount of 30,000 dinars, which must be paid within the first six days to the infantry troops. However, I am usually not in possession of such a sum, neither on the first nor on the second day of the month. I want you, therefore, to advance on the first of each month a loan of 150,000 dirhems, an amount that you, as you know, will get back in the course of the month from the Aḥwaz revenue. For the administration of the Aḥwaz revenue belongs to you, and these moneys are a permanent advance of money to you, to which I am going to add (as security) the amount of 20,000 dinars that are payable every month by Ḥamid ben 'Abbas [a dismissed vizier].

Only under the threat of dire punishments were the two bankers induced to obligate themselves to the monthly advance of some $40,000, or about a third of the wages of the imperial infantry. Certainly neither the revenue from Aḥwaz, nor the repayments agreed upon by the treasury and the deposed vizier could be considered first-rate security. But the bankers had to yield to these ever increasing pressures. They went out of business in the following decades of imperial anarchy.[65]

Prominent bankers, indeed the entire Jewish population, were exposed not only to extortions by public officials, but also to popular riots and individual vendettas. When in 996 Abu 'Ali ibn Fadhlan of Baghdad refused to lend the desired amount to Emir Baha ad-Daula, the result was an attack on the entire Jewish community. Ibn 'Allan al-Yahudi, a wealthy Jewish tax farmer of Baṣra, who among other clients provided Nizam al-Mulk with a large loan of 100,000 dinars (some $400,000), was assassinated in 1079. At that time the sultan himself, likewise Ibn 'Allan's debtor in the same amount, had to persuade Nizam to cease mourning the Jewish banker after three days. The latter's popularity was also attested by the previous funeral of his wife, attended, we are told, by the entire population of Baṣra, except the qadhi.[66]

Under Western Christendom, on the other hand, powerful forces increasingly drove Jews into moneylending as their major occupation. In the earlier Middle Ages they had continued there, too, along the paths of their ancient economic differentiation. The various church councils meeting in Toledo or in Merovingian cities would undoubtedly have attacked Jewish moneylending, had it occupied a significant place in the Jewish occupational structure. In fact, we hear of only a single Jewish creditor, Armentarius, who was assassinated at Tours by two Christians (584); he shared that fate with a Jewish and two Christian associates. After the expulsions of the seventh century, however, Jews, now largely despoiled of their landholdings and welcomed mainly as traders, found the money trade a minor but profitable side line. So did many Christians, including churches and monasteries. When, in her *Liber manualis,* written in 841–44, Countess Dodona of Toulouse enjoined her son William to repay her debts, she mentioned both Christians and Jews as her creditors. In a capitulary of somewhat dubious authenticity, attributed to Charlemagne and Louis the Pious (before 814), Jews were merely prohibited to accept as pledges church objects, or to hold Christians in prison as security for debts owed to other Jews or Christians.[67]

In time this trade proved more and more attractive. From the outset, Jews arriving from more advanced lands possessed more cash than their Christian competitors. Many of them must also have realized considerable amounts from the sale, even enforced liquidation, of their landholdings. The Church's increasing stress on the canonical prohibition of usury, likewise ultimately bore fruit. Although as late as the twelfth century the clergy still belonged to the most important groups of moneylenders and even later many Christians succeeded in evading the prohibition by various subterfuges, the Jews, being able to engage in this business openly and under legal protection, had an enormous competitive advantage. Often Christian lords entrusted cash to Jews for profitable investment. Even Jewish debtors now often borrowed money on interest from other Jews by using their Christian servants as intermediaries. Since most petty credit was extended on the security of pledges, it was easy enough for a Jew to send his servant with a valuable object to the banker, the loan formally appearing as extended to that Christian servant. The rabbis, realizing that otherwise Jews would be unable to secure any loans at all, winked at such practices, even if they did not themselves indulge in them.[68]

Most importantly, the kings soon became vitally interested in the Jewish money trade. In the sixteenth century, the Hessian clergy applied to these proceedings the apt simile of a sponge. The medieval state, often unable directly to collect taxes from the wealthiest classes in the population, the nobility and the clergy, used Jewish usury as an indirect way of sucking up some of the latter's wealth and then squeezing the sponge dry for its own benefit. This could be accomplished either by regular high taxation, or by the sudden expropriation of Jewish fortunes. With the growth of the medieval theory of Jewish serfdom, the kings, first in England and then elsewhere, arrogated to themselves the right freely to dispose of Jewish property. After the death of a Jew, especially, the king could take over his estate, or else strike a compromise with his heirs. In any case, the more riches a moneylender had accumulated through the prevailing high rates of interest, averaging some 33–60 percent, the more did the Crown benefit directly. We recall the large amounts left behind by Aaron of Lincoln, and the revenue derived from his estate by the *scaccarium*

Aronis. It was probably this sizable revenue, together with the popular reaction during the riots of 1190, which induced the Crown in 1194 to put Jewish moneylending on a firm basis by placing it under full governmental supervision in the six or seven chirograph offices. Implementing his memorable "extradition" treaty with Count Thibaut of Champagne, Philip Augustus in 1198 ordered all his bailiffs and prefects to see to it that the count should receive within two years full payment for debts owed the Champagne Jews now being returned to the king.[69]

How these "Ordinances of the Jews" were administered mainly for the king's benefit came clearly to the fore a few years later during John Lackland's arbitrary rule.

Although the royal charters to the Jews [observes Sidney Painter] promised free inheritance of property, in practice heirs had to buy their inheritance at any price the king asked. He usually took a third as his share, and left the rest to the heirs as working capital. A Jew had practically no chance of collecting a debt from a Christian without the king's aid, and he had to pay for that assistance. While the fee for this service varied, it was usually two shillings on the pound, or 10 per cent. It seems probable that John meant to establish this as a standard fee, but his greed often led him to demand more. When the king needed the friendship of a baron, he often forgave him his debt to the Jews. On several occasions John freed men from their debts to the Jews in return for armed service in his host.

At times the king as well as monasteries (for instance, the Abbey of Meaux about 1197) took over land of impecunious barons mortgaged to Jews by paying off the loans, thus increasing the royal and especially the ever growing Church domains. Some abbots or their underlings, on the other hand, were extremely careless in their financial administration, and allowed initially small debts to pyramid in the course of years to unmanageable heights. According to Jocelin of Brakelond, 40 marks (26.66 pounds) secretly borrowed from Benedict of Norwich by William the Sacristan of the Abbey of St. Edmund's for the restoration of a hall, grew in a short time to 400 pounds, which together with another loan of 100 pounds, rapidly increased to a total of 880 pounds. Together with "smaller" debts the Abbey owed Benedict 1,200 pounds, "not counting the accumulated interest." The Abbey was indebted, moreover, to another Jew, Isaac son of Rabbi Joce, to the tune of

400 pounds, and to a Christian, William fitz Isabel, to the amount of 1,040 pounds, "and I have never known the why or the wherefore." Conditions were to go from bad to worse in the thirteenth century.[70]

Undoubtedly many pious Jews and Christians had pangs of conscience for charging interest to coreligionists, but the economic pressures proved irresistible. In drawing the distinction between "open" and "concealed" usury, in his *Dialogus de Scaccario*, Richard son of Nigel defined the former as "receiving, like the Jews, more than we have lent of the same substance by virtue of a contract." The author admitted that Christians, too, although as a rule preferring more "concealed" forms of usury, often signed such contracts. But he threatened them with the prospect of confiscation after the creditor's death when such a "disgraceful charter comes to the knowledge of the king or of his chief justiciar." Richard could not deny, however, that the king, "with his usual liberality" as a rule abated the principal. In practice, heirs of a Christian moneylender merely had to compromise with the treasury more or less in the same way as did the heirs of Jewish creditors, despite the greater legality of the latter's contracts. In his charter of 1204, Philip Augustus overtly promised the burghers of Caen that none would be arrested for usury, unless he charged 100 percent or more. Recognizing the economic necessity which forced both Christians and Jews to sign such contracts, even with members of their own faiths, Jacob of Orléans, one of the greatest of English rabbis and ultimately a martyr of the London riots of 1189, actually prepared a regular formula for a deed to be used on such occasions.[71]

On the Continent, too, the constant deterioration of Jewish status pointed in the same general direction, although it was not until the thirteenth century that moneylending became the preeminent occupation of Jews in France, and still later in Germany. In his privilege of 1084, for the Jews of Spires, Bishop Rüdiger-Huozmann mentioned only their freedom to transact business, including the exchange of gold and silver. Mercantile freedom is also the keynote of the privileges later enacted by Henry IV and Frederick I. True, occasional credit operations by German Jews are recorded before that time. For instance, before his death in

1075 Archbishop Anno of Cologne enjoined his administrators impartially to pay off his debts to Jewish and Christian creditors alike. Moneylending increased in frequency and volume in the course of the twelfth century, but it had not yet become a major target for Continental Jew-baiters, as it was during the York massacres in England. Not even Peter of Cluny, who sharply denounced Jews for all sorts of dishonest dealings, singled out Jewish "usury" —that standard refrain in the later antisemitic literature—for special attack. On the other hand, St. Bernard of Clairvaux, though writing in the defense of Jews, coined that unfortunate term, *judaizare* for Jewish moneylending and merely expostulated that Christian lenders charged even worse "usuries." [72]

Only after the expulsion and despoliation of the Jews by Philip Augustus in 1182, and their subsequent return, did many of them specialize in moneylending. They were encouraged both by the obvious precariousness of their other occupations, and by the royal wish to profit from Jewish "serfs" in the same way as did the English kings, his archrivals. That is why Philip Augustus so closely emulated, in 1206 and 1218, the English Ordinances of 1194 and, improving on them, concluded his treaties of extradition with the counts of Champagne and Nevers, who had interveningly derived great economic and fiscal benefits from their Jewish bankers. This new liberality evoked the censure of Innocent III who, in his letter to the king in 1205, complained that "in the French kingdom the Jews have become so insolent that by means of their vicious usury, through which they extort not only usury but even usury on usury, they appropriate ecclesiastical goods and Christian possessions. Thus seems to be fulfilled among the Christians that which the prophet bewailed in the case of Jews, saying, 'Our heritage is turned unto strangers, our houses unto aliens.' " [73]

In Spain, too, Jewish moneylending was gradually gaining ground, although it never was to assume the preponderant character it had in England, France, and even Germany after 1200. Here, too, the thirteenth century witnessed a rapid increase in credit transactions. Of the 1,131 Arabic documents from Toledo published by C. A. González Palencia, 54 refer to Jewish creditors, and only 3 to Jewish debtors. None seems to date from the twelfth century. Otherwise, we are largely limited to such legal sources as Alphonso VI of Castile's decree of 1091 regulating procedural questions in litigations between Jews and Christians concerning debts, or the formularies for deeds of indebtedness included in Yehudah bar Barzillai's collection. Only occasionally do we get a glimpse of actual loans, as when Count Ramon Berengar IV complained, in 1132, about his vicar recapturing a pledge from one of his Jews without paying the debt. Such records, too, begin to multiply in the thirteenth century, but become truly numerous and illuminating only during the last two centuries of Jewish life on the Iberian Peninsula.[74]

We must bear in mind, however, that Jews never became the sole, and frequently were not even the main, suppliers of credit. The Church may have been increasingly successful in eliminating moneylending by the clergy, but it never seriously hampered such transactions among merchants. Foreigners, in particular, were generally less subject to the pressures of public opinion and threats of anathemas and, often enjoying the protection of kings and nobles, extended credit on interest not only to their mercantile customers, but also to outsiders. Before Aaron of Lincoln achieved his preeminence in the English money market, his older Flemish contemporary, William Cade, had financial dealings there on an even grander scale. Afterwards, foreigners from Mediterranean countries who were frequently called by such names as Lombards and Cahorsins (often, like the term "Jews" these designations were used in a generally pejorative vein) took over a major share in English and French banking. Even if employed in the service of the Papacy, particularly in the shipping of funds collected by local churches for the papal treasury, they were no more popular with their debtors. Ultimately they, like their Jewish competitors, suffered from street attacks and formal expulsions. In fact, they were usually expelled before the Jews. But, outside Italy, these developments came to a focus mainly in the thirteenth century.[75]

BANKING RAMIFICATIONS

Neither Jewish nor general banking was limited to moneylending. Money increased in circulation and gradually displaced barter even in the more backward Western countries. From the outset it played an enormous role in the more prosperous economies of the Caliphate and Byzantium. Hence experts in the handling of currency found many avenues for the application of their talents and experience.

Among the new branches of banking, in part developed by Jews under medieval Islam, was a fairly extensive business in deposits. Unlike the Graeco-Roman temples and Christian churches, neither the mosques nor the synagogues served as large-scale depositories of funds and valuables. While many persons used the old-fashioned methods of hiding their treasures in cellars, attics, or burying them in the ground, others found it more convenient to entrust them to the safekeeping of prominent bankers. True, such deposits were not absolutely safe. Occasionally a greedy governor, like Al-Baridi of Ahwaz, raided the offices of bankers and confiscated their own and their clients' property. Yet in many cases high officials themselves utilized the bankers' services for the deposit of "secret profits," which though unlawful were fully countenanced by public opinion, the bankers being instructed not to enter them into their regular ledgers. The high-ranking depositors could the more readily entrust the management of these accounts to their private bankers, especially Jews and Christians, as the latter were utterly dependent on their good-will. The relatively honest Vizier 'Ali ibn 'Isa, asked during his trial, in 923, how much he could pay back to the state from his secret profits, offered the modest sum of 3,000 dinars (some $12,000). When it was pointed out to him that his banker, Ibn abi 'Isa, had on deposit from him 17,000 dinars, 'Ali's reply was that these were in part public funds, and in part belonged to the banker personally. 'Ali's rival, Ibn al-Furat, made extensive use of the services of two Jewish bankers, Aaron ben Amram and Joseph ben Phineas. But there also were a great many private clients who appreciated the ready availability of "call money" in the hands of trustworthy bankers.[76]

With the increase in deposits, their nature changed radically, forcing the rabbis to make the necessary legal adjustments. Instead of receiving the funds for pure safekeeping, as he had done in ancient times, the banker was now allowed to use them in his own business. Because of the ensuing profits, he could dispense with service charges. On the other hand, he was now considered responsible for losses sustained beyond his control, as in the afore-mentioned Al-Baridi raid. He was generally treated on a par with a debtor, who had to return the full amount of the deposit. Of course, the owner could stipulate that the funds be treated as mere deposits, thus withholding the banker's right to invest them, but also sharply reducing his responsibility. This branch of banking seems to have sufficiently increased by the early tenth century for Saadiah Gaon to compile a special halakhic monograph dealing with deposits and pledges.[77]

No such function seems to have been performed by the medieval Jewish bankers in Europe. The general insecurity of Jewish life in the West offered little inducement for clients to entrust their deposits to Jews. They rather went to a church or monastery, with its special religious safeguards, or to one of the new Italian banks like the famous Banco di San Giorgio, founded in Genoa in 1148. Even "deposits" held for coreligionists played such a minor commercial role that they are rarely mentioned in the responsa of Franco-German and Spanish rabbis before 1200. The deposit, for example, left by a convert to Christianity with his Jewish relative, recorded in one of Rashi's responsa (No. 174), has none of the earmarks of a business deal.

More important in both parts of the Mediterranean world were dealings in bullion and the minting of it into coins, exchange of currencies, and the transfer of funds to distant localities through newly developed commercial instruments anticipatory of our checks and drafts. Jewish bankers and money experts (the Arabic term *jahbadh* connotes both) participated prominently in all these activities. Even in antiquity, it had been difficult under talmudic law to reconcile the prevailing gold standard of the Roman Empire, including Palestine, with the silver standard of Sassanian Persia, which included Babylonia. Perhaps for that very reason Jews were doubly well prepared to handle transactions in both standards inherited by the Caliphate, and to help synthesize them for practical use. By declaring, somewhat at variance with the Babylonian Talmud, gold coins as mere "merchandise," Hai Gaon released this currency from the shackles of talmudic law relating to monetary transfers. The law of "misrepresentation," which invalidated any sale of objects over- or undervalued by more than one sixth of their market price, would still apply to that metal, but not the harsher "protective" laws for the purchaser of currency. In practice, it seems, even opponents of that liberalization, like Alfasi and Maimonides, did not seriously interfere with the profitable exchange of gold for silver coins at a time when the diminution of their precious metallic content required expert appraisal, at least outside the area of each currency's official circulation. Such expert familiarity was of growing importance in the anarchical period of the Caliphate's dissolution in the East, and from the tenth century also in Byzantium, where after half a millennium of undisputed stability the value of the gold bezant itself underwent serious deterioration. It was doubly important in Europe, where in France alone during the twelfth century eighty-odd feudal lords had unrestricted minting powers.[78]

Because of their considerable expertness in the money trade, Jews played a great role already during the transition from Byzantine to Muslim rule. A Jewish minter, Sumeir, is recorded to have performed a major function in the monetary reform of 'Abd al-Malik (695–96). This reform, which finally displaced the age-old Byzantine currency in Palestine, made such an impression on Jewry that it appeared among the signs of the approaching messianic age in the apocalyptic chapter of the eighth-century *Pirqe de-R. Eliezer*. According to Mas'udi, some Jewish financiers opposed the tyrannical governor Hajjaj ibn Yusuf in Iraq when he wished to depreciate the metallic content of coins. On the other hand, a Jewish mathematician Masha'allah was the first to write a special treatise on prices. Though no longer extant, it presumably took up the problem of prices in relation to various coins in circulation. We also have scattered records of Jewish minters as far apart as medieval Egypt, Milan (Gideon, 923), Barcelona (David, 1066), the Carolingian Empire, and later in Vienna (Schlom, about 1200) and in Poland (twelfth century or earlier). Less certain is the collaboration of Jewish minters in the manufacture of the early Arabic coins in Spain, although those artisans' frequent inaccuracies with respect to the correlation of the Christian and Muslim eras makes their Jewishness quite likely. Only in Byzantium where the governmental minting monopoly and currency control proved quite effective even in the inflationary period after Nicephoros I, Jews seem to have played no role in this branch of production. But elsewhere they drew considerable profits from minting and such by-products as the residual gold dust, which was put to various industrial uses. Human labor being very inexpensive, one could easily convert precious metals into useful or decorative, even artistic, objects without much additional cost. Hence the frequent interlocking of money trade with both minting and gold- or silversmithery, in which, too, Jews played a great role in many countries and periods.[79]

For many years a stimulating, though largely futile, debate was carried on among scholars as to how European Jews had accumulated the relatively large capital necessary for their ramified monetary transactions. Some economists came forth with the suggestion, necessarily undocumented, that Jews had succeeded in hiding stores of precious metals during the barbarian invasions, and after the return of more normal conditions brought them back into circulation. The only shred of evidence adduced came from the discovery of numerous treasure troves in the Middle Ages, but this evidence comes more from Muslim than Christian countries, and even there many concealed treasures were of recent vintage. It was just as likely for a rich collector to put away his cash and jewels in a place inaccessible to a rapacious governor, as to hide them before an approaching enemy. Nor did Jews necessarily excel in this hide-and-seek game, although, being politically less influential, they probably had more frequent occasion to fear official raids. On the other hand, we recall the canard about Jews and Christians inventing stories of treasures allegedly buried under the foundations of mosques, in order to induce greedy officials to destroy these buildings.

We may look for a far simpler explanation from the constant increase in the exploitation of gold and silver mines throughout the countries of Islam and in neighboring central Africa. The Muslim world could afford to lose some precious metals through its unfavorable trade balance with both Europe and India, and yet accumulate in time substantial surpluses. The exportation of Muslim gold to both East and West, looming large in the eyes of both contemporaries and modern scholars, has proved exaggerated, but it indubitably played a certain role in the balance of payments, especially with the West. Had not the tenth-century Spanish Arab traveler, Ibrahim aṭ-Ṭartushi, expressed amazement at the numerous Samarqand dirhems, as well as the products of the Far East, which he had observed in Mayence? Jewish participants in that international exchange imported a great many gold and silver luxury objects for the benefit of European nobles and churchmen in exchange for the staples they took back to the East. Arabian gold and silver coins, including the much-debated *mancosi* (probably from Arabic *manqush*), also found their way into the European economy as far north as the Scandinavian countries. Many eastern Jewish immigrants must also have brought along most of their possessions in the form of precious movables.[80]

Precisely the hazards of shipping movables, and particularly cash, opened up new possibilities for Jewish and non-Jewish businessmen. In rudimentary form, such transfers of money were accomplished in ancient times through messengers. By giving special signs, orally or in writing, the messenger conveyed to the holder of funds in a distant city the owner's wish that the latter pay a specified amount to that messenger or some other recipient. However, in their general conservatism, the talmudic sages long resisted such a transfer of funds through a *dioqni,* a deed containing such "signs" (possibly a seal) and issued in favor of a particular person. Generally opposed to impersonal business dealings, they also tried to discourage the use of "letters of authorization" for the transfer of funds—all to little avail. The various limitations imposed by them on these letters, such as their revocability, their invalidation by the writer's death, and also the inability of a defendant or borrower to transfer to a messenger what was considered a nonexistent right, were largely disregarded in commercial practice. In an inquiry addressed to Hai Gaon, a Kairuwan rabbi contended that "it has been a custom among the inhabitants of Kairuwan from the days of their forefathers until today to issue letters of authorization permitting the recipient to receive money in countries across the sea." Such writs of authorization became so common even in Babylonia that Hai's father-in-law, Samuel ben Ḥofni Gaon, felt prompted to compose a monograph on the subject. Originally the rabbis had even less use for outright bearer instruments, in which the recipient was not named. But it was precisely such a draft, called in Arabic *suftaja* and a proto-type of our "check" (this word is of medieval Persian origin), which now became extremely popular with merchants wishing to secure funds in distant localities.[81]

Jewish merchants and bankers, making extensive use of these more advanced instrumentalities, forced the rabbis to reconsider their opposition. These legalistic discussions revealed that there was enough pliability in the rabbinic regulations concerning au-thorizations for bankers to adjust them to the newly expanded needs of large-scale transfers of funds through bearer instruments. Jews may, therefore, have been among the early users, if not the co-inventors of the *suftaja*. In an interesting geonic responsum we are told that "there exists nothing in the fundamentals of our law to permit the dispatch of a *suftaja*. . . . But since we have seen people making use of it, we have begun accepting it as a basis for our judgments, lest the commercial transactions of the people be nullified." The gaon insisted merely that one should strictly adhere in this practice to "mercantile usage." Isaac Alfasi likewise legalized this "contemporary practice among merchants" in eleventh-century Morocco and Spain. By making such drafts valid even if the name of recipient or messenger was not mentioned, the rabbis helped convert them essentially into bearer instruments.[82]

Informal transfers of this kind became important not only in private transactions, but also in moving huge amounts of tax revenue from the provinces to the imperial treasury. Considering that the total imperial revenue in the ninth and tenth centuries was often in excess of 300–400 million dirhems (some $100–150 million) and that, at Muktafi's death, Treasury accumulations were valued at 100 million dinars (some $400 million), one can realize the importance of that aspect of banking, including Jewish banking, for the entire imperial administration. In the West, on the other hand, money transfers became particularly vital in con-nection with attendance at fairs. Here they were often combined with advances of funds to traders. Already Gershom bar Yehudah had to legalize, as we recollect, higher returns for such advances to merchants traveling to a Cologne fair, provided the creditors assumed part of the risk.[83]

None of these Jewish financiers appear to have amassed the

extraordinary fortune of an Ibn al-Jaṣṣaṣ, the Muslim jeweler of Baghdad who, early in the tenth century, allegedly paid a fine of 4,000,000 dinars ($16 million) and yet remained very wealthy. The Baghdad bankers and tax farmers of the family of Madaraʻi compromised with Ibn al-Furat by promising to pay the Treasury 2,300,000 dinars ($9,200,000) for their debts in *kharaj* arrears from their estates in Egypt and Syria. After paying 500,000 dinars, they were freed from the residue by the vizier's successor, ʻAli ibn ʻIsa. In contrast to these vast sums, Abraham ibn Daud thought that the Kairuwan scholar, R. Ḥananel, was very rich because he owned 10,000 dinars. But it is almost certain that the big Baghdad and Cairo Jewish bankers were much wealthier. Otherwise Ibn al-Furat would hardly have entrusted to them his enormous deposits, which at one time, according to his own confession, amounted to 160,000 dinars. Other sources indicate that his account had reached, in fact, 700,000 dinars, or $2,800,000. Nor did the 200,000 dinars lent by Ibn ʻAllan to the sultan and Nizam al-Mulk represent that banker's total holdings. In the far more backward economy of Angevin England, Aaron of Lincoln must have stood out as a financial magnate of the first order. Fifteen years after his death, despite the loss of a large part of his fortune during transport over the Channel and the intervening liquidation, his claims were still estimated at £15,000. There also were Jews famed for their wealth in Bari and elsewhere.[84]

Obviously the high rate of interest (often exceeding 30 percent under Islam, and reaching 86⅔ percent in Angevin England) and the quick turnover of capital, made possible speedy multiplication of these bankers' original resources, if they stayed in business long enough and got away with moderate "presents" to their superiors. In the jewelry trade, too, which often went hand in hand with pawnbrokerage, profits were often commensurate with the generally great demand for precious stones for purposes of both display and investment. Such luxury articles rarely had a regular market price, the law taking cognizance of the desire of many purchasers to acquire a particular gem at any price. Discussing the reason why in barter trade the usual provisions against overcharge were abolished, Maimonides stressed the fact that either party might consciously wish to exchange a coat of mail for a needle or a horse for a lamb. Profits are well illustrated by the story of a Khorasan Jew's purchase of a precious ruby. Having secured it for 30,000 dirhams, he informed the seller that he would willingly have paid 50,000. Although to pacify the disappointed owner he voluntarily added 100 dinars (about 1500 dirhams), he doubtless could resell the ruby with a profit of 100 percent or more. Although poetically embellished, the story has an authentic ring.[85]

LIBERAL PROFESSIONS

Besides the large army of employees of these wealthy bankers and merchants, there existed a substantial "white-collar" class in most Jewish communities. There was, in the first place, a large and influential communal bureaucracy. Long before the rabbinate became a salaried profession, there were many professional judges in the East. Communities or individual congregations also maintained a large number of professional readers, sextons, and other salaried "sacred vessels." A multitude of scribes, both in communal employ and working for private clients, supplied educational and liturgical compilations, reproduced a growing number of literary works, and prepared letters and documents for business or private use. The teaching profession was predominantly private, but the great academies of learning maintained fairly large teaching staffs and, as a rule, supplied also room and board to their students. This system could continue only so long as the communities or individuals supplied the necessary funds; at times the personnel of the academies suffered severely from shortages. But in the long run the Jewish people was able to maintain a large, and probably growing, body of scholars and students.

Lawyers did not constitute an independent professional class. The rabbis tried to discourage the use of intermediaries in court proceedings, which they wished to keep as informal as possible. They demanded, therefore, personal appearance of the parties, and their submission to the judges of all the necessary evidence through direct oral exchanges. Nevertheless, rabbinic learning stood one in good stead in the preparation of deeds, and it helped to avoid running afoul the numerous rabbinic provisions in commercial and private life. Despite reiterated objections by idealists like Maimonides, the professionalization of rabbinic learning proceeded apace, and its devotees were able to secure direct financial benefits from their scholarship. In the fairly large coterie of attendants at the mansions of the mighty, there also were quite a few poets living off their wealthy patrons. This economic dependence of the Jewish poets, particularly in Spain, greatly contributed to the rise of the court poetry of the period. The medical profession, too, furnished, as we shall see, a good livelihood to an increasing number of practitioners, as well as druggists and drug merchants. A weird story of a Jewish merchant from Kairuwan, who, after his arrival in Egypt, got involved with an alchemist and first lost and then regained his merchandise, is one of numerous illustrations of the professional by-paths to which Jewish businessmen might resort. In short, every major community included a larger or smaller class of "professionals," whose economic and intellectual importance far exceeded their ratio in the population.[86]

THEORETICAL ADJUSTMENTS

Despite the far-reaching importance of these economic transformations affecting the whole structure of Jewish life, few Jewish thinkers of the age paid more than passing attention to their theoretical implications. There arose no economic literature at all among the Jews, not even of the kind produced by Aristotle and "Bryson" among the ancients, Al-Dimashqi and later Ibn Khaldun among the Arabs, and Thomas Aquinas among the Christian scholastics. Even the Hebrew translation of Bryson was not available until the fourteenth century. Thus a people which, more than any other of that time, pioneered in various phases of economic endeavor and to whom high economic achievement was a prerequisite for group survival, got along without rendering to itself full theoretical account of the propelling forces behind the various human occupations and the economic "laws" governing the ever more complex interrelations among groups and individuals.

Not that the rabbinic leaders of the period—and almost all Jewish leadership was rabbinic in learning if not by profession—

underestimated the power of money and of the human drives for its acquisition. Saadiah, one of the earliest and most articulate and level-headed thinkers among them, succinctly but dramatically described that power, at least as alleged by the champions of its accumulation.

Food and drink and sexual intercourse, which are the basis of physical existence, are made possible by it and it alone. Similarly commerce and marriage and all transactions among men are executed by means of it. Even the investiture of kings with their duties of government and the homage paid to them requires money. Armies are collected and fortresses conquered because of the monetary advantages they afford. Mines and concealed treasures are dug up for the purpose of extracting the wealth they contain. And whither do men repair and where do they meet and visit if not at the gates of those who are financially successful? And who else can be liberal and charitable and philanthropic, and who else is the recipient of greetings and thanks except such persons?

Abraham Maimonides could go so far as to attribute to economic motivations diverse attitudes toward religion. He believed that farmers and hunters, whose callings make them entirely dependent on fortuitous circumstances, are likely to place their main trust in God and belong to the firmest believers. On the other hand, persons dependent on other human beings, for instance office holders subject to royal appointment and recall, usually are weak in their faith. In between one will usually find traders, merchants, and artisans.[87]

Practical leaders of the people and its jurists likewise recognized the enormous importance of economic endeavor. One of the six sections of Mishnah and Talmud had already for the most part been devoted to laws governing economic relations. Some discussions of economically relevant problems were also scattered through the other sections. Hence the medieval jurists could not escape constantly referring to these laws, even if they themselves had not come face to face with their own and their fellow man's problems of earning a living. We shall see that many of the juristic monographs written in the geonic age, which were to lay the foundations for a recodification of the entire Jewish law, were devoted to such economic matters as Saadiah's and Samuel ben Ḥofni's aforementioned treatises on "Pledges" and "Letters of

Authorization." In the Maimonidean Code three entire sections (XI–XIII) are principally devoted to economic matters, while much economic material is scattered through the rest of the work. In his *Guide for the Perplexed,* too, the sage of Fusṭaṭ arranged the entire biblical-talmudic legislation under fourteen headings, somewhat dissimilar from those of his Code. Here (in III. 39–42) the fourth group deals exclusively with charities, loans, and gifts, the fifth discusses responsibility for various types of damage, the sixth speaks of crimes including infractions of property rights, while the seventh group is entirely dedicated to civil law (*dine memonot*).

Precisely this serious consideration of economic affairs by jurists seemed to obviate any further concern on the part of philosophers. The latter knew from Aristotle, Farabi, and other Greek and Muslim thinkers of the existence of an economic science. Taking the Greek term *oikonomia* in its narrower sense, they mentioned the *hanhagat ha-bayit* (management of the household) as a fit object for study. They also included many aspects of national economy under the heading of political science. After generally defining the goal of practical philosophy as consisting in the attainment of happiness, Abraham ibn Daud added, "This goal can be attained first, by ethics; secondly, through domestic economy; thirdly, through political laws." Maimonides, too, included the "management of the household" among the four subdivisions of practical philosophy. True, in his youthful classification of sciences, he defined the range of that discipline very narrowly as "the science by which one knows how the members are to help one another and how they are to be provided for in the best possible way in accordance with the requirements of a given time and place." But he realized that broader aspects of national economy constituted parts of other subdivisions of practical philosophy, which he sometimes altogether identified with political science. He also knew of the existence of a ramified ancient literature on these subjects. "On all these matters," he averred, "philosophers have written many books which have been translated into Arabic, and perhaps those that have not been translated are even more numerous." [88]

In this context Maimonides and his predecessor, Ibn Daud,

explained why they did not consider it necessary to deal extensively with economic problems as such. Ibn Daud made it perfectly clear that the three goals of practical philosophy which he had defined were "all found in our Law to the fullest possible extent." On his part, Maimonides, apparently speaking in behalf of Islam as well as Judaism, claimed that "nowadays we no longer require all this, namely the statutes and laws [governing economics and politics], since man's conduct is [determined] by the divine regulations." In other words, because the practical aspects of human behavior were fully regulated by Jewish (or Muslim) law, there was no need for their independent reexamination in the light of reason, such as was required for the more metaphysical aspects of religion, which were less fully and clearly spelled out in the traditional sources. Of course, no one at that time submitted the economic life itself to careful observation and derived from such scrutiny valid generalizations. The first important steps toward a sociological, rather than economic, empiricism were to be taken in the fourteenth century by Ibn Khaldun. Most Jews, as well as Muslims and Christians, were prepared to argue even in strictly scientific fields on the basis of book learning and the citation of established authorities. In economic matters, moreover, the traditional law itself had been far more empirical, since it had been based upon the observation of frequent conflicts of interest arising among human beings in connection with contracts, inheritances, and the like. Certainly, Jewish law never could become so unworldly and abstract, as could purely metaphysical or even ethical speculations.[89]

As a matter of fact, Jewish law was extremely pliable in taking care of changing economic needs. Without probing deeply into the underlying economic factors, the rabbis were able to modify the existing laws by using the long-recognized methods of juristic reinterpretation. Many such adjustments have been mentioned in this and other chapters. Another telling example may be adduced here from western Europe, where theoretical discussions on economics were even less appreciated than in the countries of Islam. The ancient tannaitic law, forbidding Jews to trade with Gentiles three days before the latter's holidays, had already caused difficulties in Babylonia, and induced Mar Samuel to restrict it to the holidays themselves. Adhering to the talmudic discussion, Maimonides forbade expressly trading with Christians in Palestine from Thursday through Sunday. We have no evidence that this rigid interpretation, perhaps also betraying Maimonides' personal anti-Christian bias, was ever observed by the few Jewish traders under the Latin Kingdom of Jerusalem. In western Europe, even Mar Samuel's limitation proved unsatisfactory. As we recall, Agobard had complained that the weekly market of Lyons had been switched from Saturday to Sunday to accommodate Jews. It would have been of little comfort to Jewish merchants in Lyons, if Sunday had been a day forbidden by their own law to trade with non-Jews. Evidently, long before the rabbis had any chance to consider the matter, life itself had made the necessary adjustment, and Jews traded at fairs and other places with Christians on Sundays and Christian holidays. Rabbinic theory speedily followed suit. While Samuel bar Meir, followed by many other rabbis, argued that Christians were not in the same class with ancient idolaters, and that it was impossible to suppress such an essential trade without damaging the economic interest of traders and exposing all Jews to the ill-will of their Christian neighbors, his brother Jacob Tam simply limited the original talmudic prohibition to trading in objects used directly for idolatrous worship. In practice, they all agreed on the permissibility of Sunday trade, and only a few rabbis (including Rashi and Samuel bar Meir) tried to salvage the ancient prohibition by reducing it to the Christmas holiday.[90]

Behind the neglect of economic theory also loomed the thinkers' general idealism and the ensuing ambivalence of their attitudes to economic pursuits as such. On the one hand, they all echoed the old rabbinic insistence on the duty of earning a living, if need be through hard, even humiliating labor. Jurists and moralists united in singing the praises of such self-reliance. On the other hand, they observed the negative effects of concentration on gainful employment. Maimonides voiced the general opinion that "most of the damage done to people in the various states arises from the lust for money and its accumulation, and the excessive desire to increase possessions and honors." Those philosophers who were not preaching the "golden mean" and moderation in all human affairs, leaned to asceticism and self-abnegation. There were no medieval Jewish enthusiasts for the idea of "poverty" as such. All thinkers agreed that riches accumulated honestly were signs of divine grace which may be enjoyed in moderation and utilized for good works toward less fortunate neighbors. Nonetheless, moralists viewed with considerable diffidence all human behavior dictated by purely economic motivations. Baḥya, for example, tried to discourage emigration in search of gain or employment not only from Palestine, which had good tannaitic precedents, but also from any other country. He viewed such departures as betraying lack of trust in divine Providence. In Baḥya's opinion, a person with faith will grieve "little if his wares remain on his shelves, or a business transaction is delayed, or he cannot collect an account due him, or if he falls sick; since he is conscious that the Creator, blessed be He, arranges his affairs better than he himself would be able to do." Others, more realistically, tried to stave off at least the professionalization of learning, long recognized as a major evil, and preached the obligation to teach and pronounce judgments free of charge. At the same time they disparaged learned men looking forward to charitable support. They merely demanded that fellow Jews promote a scholar's business by giving him preference in his competition with non-scholars, by taking him as a silent partner into their businesses, and particularly by granting him full tax exemption. With their excessive idealism these doctrinaires could advise ordinary workers, as did Maimonides, to devote, whenever possible, only three hours a day to earning a living and the rest of the day to the study of Torah.[91]

In all these debates we find no questioning of the legitimacy of private property. Christian scholastics, starting with a tradition of early Christian communism in consumption, if not in production, and facing the monastic glorification of poverty, had to look for a moral and philosophic justification of property. But Jewish and Muslim thinkers could simply accept it as part of the divinely instituted order. Their main concern was to balance the rights of individual owners with those of neighbors and society at large. Certainly, as a minority, Jews could not favor any undue increase in the public domain and its administration by a generally rapacious and extortionist bureaucracy. They also knew from experience that, on the whole, they prospered best in areas of free enterprise and fared least well in countries and occupations hampered by state regulations. Yet from ancient times, Jewish law had retained many features of social control. In searching, therefore, for a balance between individual rights and public welfare, the medieval rabbis fully recognized private property rights, but subjected them to severe limitations in favor of the public at large. Land, especially, was not considered a simple commodity, and its ownership entailed many responsibilities. Extensively defined in the ancient biblical-rabbinic legislation reflecting the then predominantly agricultural economy, these responsibilities were nevertheless retained, with but slight modifications, in the later period of a predominantly urbanized Jewry. Movable property, too, was hedged around with ramified provisions in favor of neighbors, relatives, and orphans, and generally subjected to the superior interest of society at large. Maimonides voiced the regnant opinion when he emphasized the community's rights to take over any individual's possessions. "A judge," the great jurist declared sweepingly, "may always expropriate money belonging to whomsoever, destroy it and give it away, if in his judgment, this would serve to prevent the breaking down of the fences of the law, to strengthen its structure, or to punish a mighty offender." Of course, the judge, too, operated *under* the law, and was subject to the strong controls of public opinion.[92]

A similar balance between the interests of the individual and society at large was sought in the "just" price. Here, too, the medieval Jewish thinkers failed to come to grips with the theoretical underpinnings of this economic doctrine. We shall search in vain for a discussion of either the more objective criteria like costs of production or the element of work from the standpoint of the producer, or the more subjective needs and an object's utility for the consumer. Such discussions, though in a rather rudimentary form, were found already in Aristotle's works, and were elaborated by Christian thinkers from Augustine to Thomas Aquinas and Duns Scotus. Jewish philosophers and jurists handled this problem, too, merely from the standpoint of traditional law and ethics, with their emphasis on equity and justice. Summarizing the ramified rabbinic teachings concerning the price structure, as reflected in the Maimonidean Code and other medieval works, one finds that

(1) every community, if necessary with the cooperation of a great leader, may in its discretion fix the prices of all articles; (2) every community should fix the prices of necessaries, allowing for a total profit of but one-sixth; (3) wherever there are no communally fixed prices, the seller is wholly free to set his own price on land, slaves, free labor, and commercial paper; (4) a merchant may do the same with respect to movables, if he gives complete and candid information to the other party; (5) however, in case of failure to do so, he runs the risk that the injured party may choose to demand restitution of the balance of precisely one-sixth, or complete annulment of the contract if the difference exceeds one-sixth of the market price; (6) an error in weight or measure merely calls for the restitution of the difference; (7) the merchant is entitled freely to sell below the prevailing market price and employ other "fair" methods of competition.

In short, honesty and full disclosure of the facts appeared more significant than the purely economic considerations of supply and demand, or even the more subjective factors of need or ability to pay. Certainly, under the relatively uncontrolled Near Eastern economy (outside Egypt), Jews had even less reason to favor governmental price fixing than did their Muslim neighbors. Approached with the suggestion to set maximum prices, Caliph 'Umar II had allegedly replied, "This is not our business; God fixes prices." In the more regimented Western lands, too, Jewish merchants represented the relatively freest and most competitive segment of the economy.[93]

In so far as the idealistic postulates of devoting as much time as possible to study could be practically applied at all, they stimulated further Jewish concentration on commerce and especially on moneylending. All other occupations, especially in agriculture and industry, were extremely time consuming. With the prevalent long hours of labor it was undoubtedly very difficult for artisans and day laborers to set aside even an hour daily for study, which later rabbis had set up as a minimum requirement. Most businesses, on the other hand, even if they involved extensive travel, could much more readily be reconciled with such a program.

Although the thought was not formulated until the fifteenth

century, it must have been present in many a rabbinic mind before that time. "The reason," stated Shalom bar Isaac Sekel, as quoted with approval by one of Israel Isserlein's pupils, "why the Torah holds a higher place in Germany than in other countries is that Jews here charge interest to Gentiles and need not engage in a [time-consuming] occupation. . . . He who does not study uses his profits to support the students of the Torah." Of course, such an argument sounded more convincing to Jews than to Gentiles. In answer to numerous Christian attacks on Jewish "usury," a Narbonne Jew felt prompted to probe more deeply into the economic aspects of moneylending. Citing an imaginary dialogue between a nobleman and a Jew, Meir bar Simon, author of *Milḥemet miṣvah* (War in Fulfillment of a Commandment, an apologetic treatise) written in 1245, argued that

divine law prohibited usury, not interest. From the standpoint of society, it is necessary for the peasant to secure a loan, which he could not obtain without interest, even by turning to your wealthiest men. Not only the peasant must borrow money, but also the lords, and even the Great King of France. The rulers have, in fact, not stopped contracting large loans for two years in succession. The King would have lost many fortified places, if his faithful agent, a Jew of our city, had not secured for him money at a high price.

However, even Jewish apologetic literature, especially before 1200 when these debates were still rather sporadic, contained but few such theoretical rationales for the great economic transformations which had taken place in the preceding seven centuries.[94]

JEWISH "ECONOMIC MAN"

Under the impact of Islam's memorable expansion, the Oriental communities thus reemerged from the oppressive nightmare of Byzantine and late Sassanian intolerance into the free, broad daylight of history. Their rise and decline, or rather ultimate stabilization on a lower level of life, closely paralleled the patterns of the surrounding civilizations. Once they had weathered Mohammed's reversal from the role of a grateful pupil to that of a ruthless mentor and had proved their mettle and usefulness as a constructive and cementing force in the ever expanding structure of the new empire, they availed themselves with increasing zest of the new opportunities opened to their spirit of intellectual and economic pioneering. Before long every one of the vast metropolitan and many lesser cities, now revitalized or newly founded from India to the Pyrenees, embraced a substantial Jewish group. Distinguished by their religious mores and often also by their attire, if not by their speech or names, Jews added a peculiar hue to the colorful motley of ethnic and sectarian groups inhabiting these large urban centers. From the outset they became, and remained ever after, an integral but distinct element in that far-flung heterogeneous society which went under the name of the "world of Islam."

Integral, but distinct, were particularly the productive, distributive, mediating, and fiscal functions of Jews within the ramified economy of the Great Caliphate and its successor states. Even more distinct was the role played by the nascent or renascent Jewish communities in the Carolingian Empire, its successor states, and its emulators in England and Christian Spain. In fact, for the first time in their history Jews became a principal object of economic and fiscal concern to their neighbors. Since Vespasian and Sassanian Persia, to be sure, Jews had been paying special taxes of one kind or another. But the sum total of such special imposts was but a small fraction of their general fiscal contributions to the state treasuries which they shared with their non-Jewish neighbors. It certainly was but an insignificant item in the total imperial revenue. Now, however, owing in part to precedents set by the treaties between Mohammed and the Arabian Jewish (and Christian) communities, as well as the needs of the early Muslim armies dedicated to world conquest, the *dhimmis* were assigned the specific task of upholding the imperial economy and fiscal structure. Although hidden behind religious verbiage, the role of the Jew, perhaps even more than that of other "unbelievers," from the standpoint of Muslim legislation was that of the "economic man" and taxpayer. In western Europe there was not even an attempt at concealment. Here Jews were avowedly admitted to serve as royal allies or "serfs" in helping provide the sinews of war and administration by their fiscal contributions, made possible by their ever expanding trade and banking.

This new emphasis upon the Jew's "usefulness" to state and

society had far-reaching social and religious implications. For the first time the state unwittingly became the silent partner in the totality of Jewish economic enterprise—a trend which was to reach its climax in later medieval Europe. Occasional outbursts of religious fanaticism, to be sure, or personal whims of rulers and statesmen, often interfered with the peaceful pursuit of Jewish careers. By permitting temporary need or greed to ruin many a flourishing Jewish business venture, the state itself sometimes came close to killing the goose which was laying its golden eggs. But, on principle, it always reverted to its policy of encouraging Jewish economic enterprise within and without its borders. It must have appreciated, particularly, the Jews' function in international trade and their ability—in the case of the renascent West often preponderant ability—to keep the gates open for the mutually advantageous exchange of goods.

For this reason the Great Caliphate and its successor states often had to compromise with the perennial principle of Muslim legislation concerning the nonadmission of "infidels" to public office. Religiously and politically desirable and the logical consequence of that original division of functions between Muslims and unbelievers, this principle frequently proved impracticable. The growing complexity of the fiscal administration alone must have persuaded many rulers of the soundness of Ziyad ibn Abihi's advice that "treasury officials should be recruited from among the chiefs of the conquered peoples who well understand this matter" (Al-Ya'qubi's *Tariḥ*, ed. by Houtsma, II, 279). As treasury transactions grew into a multimillion-dollar business and the state often required very large loans, it had to have recourse to the great banking experience of its Jewish subjects to whom Muslim intransigeance in regard to "usurious" gains had delegated great (at times almost monopolistic) controls over the credit system. This conflict between legal principle and practical needs was seriously aggravated by the arbitrary rule of caliph or vizier, the maladministration of a rapacious bureaucracy, the ensuing resentment of the exploited masses, and the easily inflamed religious passions. Together they accounted for the recurrence of those meteoric careers of Jewish "court bankers" and statesmen, whose speedy rise and fall deeply affected the destinies of their community.

To a lesser extent the same factors operated also in the West, although the problem of Jewish fiscal advisers to the Crown did not become a major issue here until the later Middle Ages. But there were sufficient departures from, even overt violations of, the long-accepted canonical teachings for many a pope, and particularly the power-hungry Innocent III, to issue fulminating letters to various Christian rulers for their excessive leniency toward Jewish trade and moneylending.

Despite these unceasing tensions and frequent disturbances, a *modus vivendi* was thus established between the Muslim and Christian majorities and the Jewish minority. These varying, but essentially similar, systems of legal and extralegal checks and balances proved more or less workable over vast stretches of western Asia, North Africa, and Europe almost to the eve of the French Revolution in the West and the First World War in the East. With all their imperfections they made possible the permanent survival and, at times, great flowering of the Jewish communities. They also deeply affected the flow and ebb of economic progress throughout the divided worlds of Islam and Christendom.

NOTES

ABBREVIATIONS

AHDE	Anuario de historia del derecho español
AHDL	Archives d'histoire doctrinale et littéraire du moyen âge
AHR	American Historical Review
'A.Z.	'Abodah Zarah (talmudic tractate)
BAH	Boletín of the R. Academia de la Historia, Madrid
BJPES	Bulletin (*Yediot*) of the Jewish Palestine Exploration Society
BJRL	Bulletin of the John Rylands Library, Manchester
B.M.	Baba Meṣiah (talmudic tractate)
B.Q.	Baba Qammah (talmudic tractate)
BSOAS	Bulletin of the School of Oriental and African Studies (University of London)
BZ	Byzantinische Zeitschrift
CHE	Cuadernos de historia de España
CRAI	Comptes rendus de l'Académie des Inscriptions et belles-lettres
CSOC	Corpus Scriptorum orientalium christianorum
Dubnow Festschrift	Festschrift zu Simon Dubnows siebzigstem Geburtstag. Berlin, 1930
EHR	English Historical Review
EI	Encyclopaedia of Islam
HJ	Historia Judaica
HTR	Harvard Theological Review
HUCA	Hebrew Union College Annual
HZ	Historische Zeitschrift
IC	Islamic Culture
JA	Journal asiatique
JAOS	Journal of the American Oriental Society
JBL	Journal of Biblical Literature and Exegesis
JGJCR	Jahrbuch der Gesellschaft für die Geschichte der Juden in der Čechoslowakischen Republik
JJLG	Jahrbuch der Jüdisch-Literarischen Gesellschaft, Frankfurt a. M.
JJS	Journal of Jewish Studies

JQR	Jewish Quarterly Review (new series, unless otherwise stated)
JRAS	Journal of the Royal Asiatic Society
JSS	Jewish Social Studies
Kohut Mem. Vol.	Jewish Studies in Memory of George A. Kohut. New York, 1935
Marx Jub. Vol.	Alexander Marx Jubilee Volume. 2 vols. New York, 1950. A volume each of English and Hebrew essays
M.	Mishnah
MGH	Monumenta Germaniae Historica
MGWJ	Monatsschrift für Geschichte und Wissenschaft des Judentums
MIOG	Mitteilungen des Instituts für osterreichische Geschichtsforschung, Vienna
Miscellanies JHSE	Jewish Historical Society of England, Miscellanies
MJC	Medieval Jewish Chronicles, ed. by A. Neubauer
M.T.	Moses ben Maimon's Mishneh Torah (Code)
MWJ	Magazin für die Wissenschaft des Judentums
O.Ḥ.	Oraḥ ḥayyim (section of Jacob ben Asher's Ṭurim and Joseph Karo's Shulḥan 'Arukh)
OLZ	Orientalistische Literaturzeitung
PAAJR	Proceedings of the American Academy for Jewish Research
Philippson Festschrift	Beiträge zur Geschichte der deutschen Juden. Festschrift . . . Martin Philippson. Leipzig, 1916
PL	Patrologiae cursus completus, series Latina
PO	Patrologia orientalis
Rashi Anniv. Vol.	American Academy for Jewish Research, Rashi Anniversary Volume, New York, 1941
RBPH	Revue belge de philologie et d'histoire
REJ	Revue des études juives
Resp.	Responsa (Teshubot or She'elot u-teshubot)
RH	Revue historique
RHC	Recueil des historiens des croisades
RHDF	Revue historique de droit français et étranger
RMAL	Revue du moyen âge latin
RMI	Rassegna mensile di Israel
RSO	Rivista di studi orientali
RSR	Revue de science religieuse
SB	Sitzungsberichte der Akademie der Wissenschaften (identified by city: e.g., SB Berlin, Heidelberg, Vienna)
SH	Sefer ha-Shanah li-Yehude Amerika
SRIHP	Studies of the Research Institute for Medieval Hebrew Poetry
Starr Mem. Vol.	The Joshua Starr Memorial Volume: Studies in History and Philology, New York, 1953. Jewish Social Studies, Vol. V

T.	Tosefta. Ed. by M. S. Zuckermandl
Transactions JHSE	Jewish Historical Society of England, Transactions
VSW	Vierteljahrsschrift für Sozial- und Wirtschaftsgeschichte
Y.D.	Yoreh de'ah (section of Jacob ben Asher's *Ṭurim* and Joseph Karo's *Shulḥan 'Arukh*)
ZDMG	Zeitschrift der Deutschen Morgenländischen Gesellschaft
ZDPV	Zeitschrift des Deutschen Palästina Vereins. Some vols. are entitled Beiträge zur biblischen Landes- und Altertumskunde
ZGJD	Zeitschrift für die Geschichte der Juden in Deutschland (new series, unless otherwise stated)

NOTES

CHAPTER XX: WESTERN CHRISTENDOM

1. The phonetic explanation, suggested already in 1852 by S. J. L. Rapoport in his *'Erekh millin* (Opus encyclopaedicum), I, 156 ff., was elaborated by M. Mieses and others. (Incidentally, in a MS note, probably from Rapoport's own hand in a presentation copy of the book in the writer's possession, the talmudic designation of "Cortova" is identified with Corduena or Kurdistan.) This and numerous other explanations were discussed by S. Krauss in "The Names Ashkenaz and Sefarad" (Hebrew), *Tarbiz*, III, 423–35, with comments by J. N. Epstein. Krauss's own "historical" explanation looked for the original transfer of these names to the region around the Bosporus, as intimated in the case of Sefarad by Jerome. But he failed to offer a satisfactory reason for their further extension to western Europe. His equation, especially, of Ashkenaz with Khazaria, has rightly been rejected by J. Mann in his "Are the 'Ashkenazim' the Khazars?" (Hebrew), *Tarbiz*, IV, 391–94. Mann's arguments have by no means been invalidated by Krauss's reply in "Die hebräischen Benennungen moderner Völker," *Kohut Mem. Vol.*, pp. 387 ff., 402 ff. Cf. *supra*, Chap. XIX, n. 53. The most plausible explanation was offered by L. I. Wallach in his "Zur Etymologie Aschkenaz-Deutschland," *MGWJ*, LXXXIII, 302–4. Pointing out that the first use of this term occurs in Jewish writings under Islam, Wallach argued that it originated from the mistaken identification of Ashkenaz with As-Skandz, the Arabic designation of the Scandinavian and, more generally, all North-European countries. On the use of the name Sefarad for Crimean localities, see also the data assembled by Poliak in his *Khazariyyah*, pp. 166 ff.

2. Leo VII, *Epistolae et privilegia*, xiv, in *PL*, CXXXII, 1084 f.; P. Jaffé, *Monumenta Moguntina*, pp. 336 ff. (more briefly in his *Regesta pontificum romanorum . . . ad annum MCXCVIII*, 2d ed. by W. Wattenbach, I, 457 No. 3613). Cf. also M. Elias's succinct review of "Die römische Kirche, besonders Innozenz III, und die Juden," *JJLG*, XII, 37–82; W. Holtzmann's "Zur päpstlichen Gesetzgebung über die Juden im 12. Jahrhundert," *Festschrift Guido Kisch*, pp. 217–35; and the literature listed *supra*, Chap. XVI, n. 32. See *infra*, n. 18.

3. The oldest extant text of this significant decree is that enacted by Alexander III and reproduced in the Introduction to the canons of the Third Lateran Council, over which he presided. See Mansi, *Collectio*, XXII, 355 f. (Hefele, *Histoire*, V, Part 2, p. 1111). Because of the absence of the original proclamation we cannot be certain about its date, nor do we know to whom it was addressed or whether it contained the important formula, *in perpetuum*, characteristic of most of Calixtus' privileges as contrasted with his letters. Cf. U. Robert, *Etude sur les actes du pape Calixte II*, pp. 17 ff. Yet the most likely occasion seems to have been the meeting of the First Lateran Council of March, 1123, which, perhaps

in connection with its call for renewed crusading efforts in the direction of both Jerusalem and Spain, also endeavored to reinforce the *treuga Dei,* such as had been enacted in Germany in favor of Jews, too, in 1103. See the canons of that council, reproduced in Hefele's *Histoire,* V, Part 1, pp. 634 ff., 637. The inclusion of Alexander III's renewal of Calixtus' bull in the Acts of the Third Council thus seems to go back to the original record, heightening the likelihood that the bull was first enacted (and subsequently renewed) in connection with the Jews' fears that the First Lateran Council of 1123 might adopt resolutions hostile to them. See *infra,* nn. 9, 15. This nexus may in turn explain the reasons for Calixtus II's original enactment and Eugenius III's renewal, as suggested here. Apart from Alexander's text we possess only an archival reference to Clement III's privilege of 1188; the renewal by Innocent III (with the additional preamble), is reproduced with an English translation in S. Grayzel's documentary collection, *The Church and the Jews in the XIIIth Century,* pp. 92 ff. Cf. also Grayzel's Introduction, pp. 76 ff.; Aronius's comments in his *Regesten,* pp. 132 No. 310, 136 f. No. 313a, 150 No. 334, 155 No. 346; and those by W. Holtzmann in *Festschrift Guido Kisch,* p. 221 n. 3.

4. During Rome's years of anarchy and civil strife from the tenth to the twelfth centuries, sepulchral vandalism was quite common. Cf. the data cited by F. Gregorovius in his *History of the City of Rome in the Middle Ages,* III, 537 ff. A contemporary Hebrew scholar-poet, Nathan ben Yeḥiel of Rome, took cognizance of these barbaric incidents in his poem, *Neder nadarti* (I Have Made a Vow), printed at the conclusion of his *Sefer 'Arukh ha-shalem* (Aruch completum sive Lexicon), ed. by A. Kohut, VIII, 300. Cf. also the literature on this poem listed in I. Davidson's *Thesaurus of Medieval Hebrew Poetry,* III, 204 No. 149; and Vogelstein and Rieger's *Geschichte der Juden in Rom,* I, 220 f. On the related protective laws against excessive governmental exactions at the time of Jewish burials, see *infra,* n. 103. Because of the provision against the disturbance of Jewish festivals, G. Caro assumed that Calixtus II, himself a Frenchman, had issued his bull under the influence of southern French communities, where such disturbances are indeed recorded. See his *Sozial- und Wirtschaftsgeschichte der Juden im Mittelalter und der Neuzeit,* I, 288 f., 496. However, there is no evidence that his decree, or any of its successors, was addressed to foreign Jews. In any case, the overriding positive principle of outlawry of forced conversions applied to all countries, and it was frequently upheld by popes against overzealous local rulers. In 1065 Alexander II severely reprimanded the lord of Benevento for attempting forcibly to convert his Jewish subjects. The efficacy of that papal censure is evidenced by the presence there of a substantial and prosperous Jewish community of some 200 Jewish souls, or more likely families, during Benjamin's visit a century later. Cf. his *Massa'ot,* pp. 10 (Hebrew), 9 (English).

5. Cf. the illustrations cited by L. I. Newman in his *Jewish Influence on Christian Reform Movements,* pp. 1 ff.; and *supra,* Chap. XVI, n. 1. The slow progress of the Christianization of the peasant masses north of the Alps until the Carolingian era is rightly stressed by L. Génicot in *Les Lignes de faîte du moyen âge,* 2d ed., pp. 83 f., 102 f. The heated sectarian controversies of the period, the Jewish influences thereon, alleged and real, and the occasional conversions to Judaism will be discussed *infra,* Chap. XXIV.

6. Mansi, *Collectio*, XII, 384 f. (canon 10); XX, 507 (Intro.); Hefele, *Histoire*, III, Part 2, p. 852; Gregory VII's Epistle to Alphonso VI of August 25, 1081, in P. Jaffé, *Monumenta Gregoriana*, pp. 331, 472. The canons themselves, adopted by the Council of Rome, did not further elaborate the general principle of not entrusting Jews with positions of power over Christians.

7. A. Ciaconius (Chacon), *Vitae et res gestae pontificum romanorum et S. R. E. cardinalium . . . ad Clementem IX*, I, 977. Cf. Vogelstein's remarks in his and Rieger's *Geschichte*, I, 222. To be sure, Ciaconius quotes Innocent's reply from the Book of Church Rituals, rather than from a contemporary source. He also implies that this ceremony had already been habitual before Innocent II, and states that the Jews of Paris had previously offered the Pope a scroll of law in homage. However, his seems to be the first recorded mention of this practice.

8. J. B. Villars in *Les Normands en Méditerranée*, p. 224. Anacletus II's family background, personal characteristics, and disputed election were the subject of heated partisan controversies during his pontificate, and they have often intrigued modern scholars as well. Relatively the fullest review of the contemporary polemics may be found in E. Mühlbacher's older monograph, *Die streitige Papstwahl des Jahres 1130*, and in the more recent literature well summarized in H. Bloch's searching investigation of "The Schism of Anacletus II and the Glanfeuil Forgeries of Peter the Deacon of Monte Cassino," *Traditio*, VIII, 159–264 (stressing especially the major issues involved). Cf. also Gregorovius, *History*, IV, 412 ff.; L. Erler's comprehensive, if incomplete, "Die Juden des Mittelalters," *Archiv für katholisches Kirchenrecht*, XLVIII, 386 ff.; and other works listed by A. Fliche *et al.*, in *Du premier Concile du Latran à l'avènement d'Innocent III* (Fliche and Martin, *Histoire de l'Eglise*, Vol. IX), pp. 50 ff. On the family Pierleoni, see also P. Fedele's detailed study of "Le Famiglie di Anacleto II e di Gelasio II," *Archivio della R. Società Romana di storia patria*, XXVII, 399–433. The briefer genealogical observations of R. Silbergleit and A. Czelliczer on "Die Familie des Papstes Anaklet II" and "Die angebliche jüdische Stammutter der Hohenstaufen und der Habsburger," *Jüdische Familienforschung*, II, 291–93, have shown how, by wrongly identifying Roger II's wife Alberica, *filia regis Castiliae et Leonis*, with Alberica Pierleoni, the thirteenth-century chronicler Ordericus Vitalis started a chain reaction which not only made Roger II a brother-in-law of Anacletus II, but also turned the Pierleonis into ancestors of Frederick II, the last Hohenstaufen emperor, and of Rudolf I, the founder of the Habsburg dynasty. Similarly mistaken is the assumption that the mighty Pope Gregory VII was, on his mother's side, related to Anacletus. Defended by Fedele (pp. 409, 437), this assumption was rejected, though not on wholly conclusive grounds, by M. Tangl in his "Gregor VII jüdischer Herkunft?" *Neues Archiv der Gesellschaft für ältere deutsche Geschichtskunde*, XXXI, 161–79; and by P. Browe in *Die Judenmission*, pp. 211 f. On the possible impact of that controversy on the spread of contemporary Christian heresies, see L. I. Newman's somewhat overstated remarks in *Jewish Influence*, p. 254. Understandably, European Jewry was no less impressed with the pope's Jewish origin. On various legends connected with "Jewish" popes, see *infra*, Chap. XXXII. Not at all surprisingly, a modern novel, *Der Papst aus dem Ghetto* by Baronesse G. Le Fort, has enjoyed considerable vogue in Germany in recent years.

9. P. Jaffé and W. Wattenbach, *Regesta pontificum romanorum*, I, 850 (I) No. 7487; Shem-Tob Sonzolo, cited in the continuation of Solomon ibn Verga's *Shebet Yehudah* (Judah's Rod; a Chronicle), ed. by M. Wiener, p. 112; also in Wiener's German translation, p. 231; ed. by A. Shohet, p. 147. This continuation was compiled by the author's son, Joseph ibn Verga, from Jewish and non-Jewish records utilized by Sonzolo. The extant texts of the chronicle refer to the date of [1]139. Because of the chronological difficulties arising from other dates furnished in that paragraph with its mixture of Jewish and Christian eras, Zunz and Graetz suggested that our chronicler had in mind the year 1179 and referred to the Third Lateran Council. See Graetz, *Geschichte der Juden*, VI (4th ed.), 340 f. (Note I, 6), still followed by 'Azriel Shohet in his new ed. of Ibn Verga's chronicle, pp. 146, 221. No plausible explanation has as yet been offered, however, as to why the Jewish communities should have been so greatly agitated by the convocation of a council by Alexander III, who was on the whole known for his moderation in Jewish policies. Nor did that council speak "kindly words" about the Jews; rather it adopted, as we shall see, a fairly sharply worded canon against them. Cf. also Vogelstein and Rieger, *Geschichte der Juden in Rom*, I, 212, 224 ff.; and *infra*, n. 15. These difficulties disappear if we assume that the original date "139" referred to 1139 C.E. and not, like some other dates in that calendar, to the Jewish era, which in this case would have been the equivalent of 1379(!). The chronological confusion may have arisen from Joseph ibn Verga's juxtaposition of Sonzolo's Christian and Jewish sources. In the sixteenth century the Second Lateran Council must have been forgotten among Jews. On the general paucity of records concerning its deliberations, see Hefele, *Histoire*, V, 721 ff.; and A. Fliche *et al.*, *Du premier Concile du Latran*, pp. 70 f., 137 f. The chronicler, or his source, may also have confused the "kindly words" spoken at the First Lateran Council of 1123, namely the provisions in favor of the truce, and the ensuing privilege of Calixtus II (see *supra*, n. 3), with the resolutions of the Second Council—a confusion facilitated by Eugenius III's renewal of Calixtus' bull a few years after the Second Council.

10. Cf. the illustrations furnished by E. Rodocanachi in *Le Saint-Siège et les Juifs*, pp. 128 ff., 145 ff.; and by Erler in "Die Juden des Mittelalters," *Archiv für katholisches Kirchenrecht*, XLVIII, 369 ff. The ceremony of greeting emperors as well as popes with Hebrew chants had been sufficiently standardized in the days of Otto III (983–1002) for the book of ceremonies issued under his auspices (somewhat akin to the earlier and more elaborate work of Constantine Porphyrogenitus for the court etiquette at Constantinople) to include a special provision relating to such Hebrew, as well as Greek and Latin, "acclamations" during the emperor's ascent to the Golden Capitol. See Gregorovius, *History*, III, 471. Since these occasions occurred quite frequently, they undoubtedly stimulated many Roman Hebrew poets to compose appropriate odes. Unfortunately, not having become part of the regular Jewish liturgy, these poems offered little inducement for copyists to reproduce them for later generations. But they must have preserved a measure of poetic creativity among the Jews of Rome, which may help to explain some peculiarities of the Italian Hebrew poetry which, differing in many ways from both Spanish and Franco-German modes of versification, soon was to reach its heights in the works of Immanuel of Rome. Cf. also *infra*, n. 27; and Chap. XXXII.

11. J. Régné's careful "Etude sur la condition des Juifs de Narbonne du Ve au XIVe siècle," *REJ*, LV, 221 ff. (analyzing pertinent documents and arguing for their substantial authenticity); *Los Fueros de Aragon*, 1.5, ed. by G. Tilander, p. 11; Fourth Lateran Council, canon 67, in Mansi, *Collectio*, XXII, 1054 f. (Hefele, *Histoire*, V, Part 2, pp. 1385 f.); Grayzel, *The Church and the Jews*, pp. 134 No. 22; 308 No. ix. On the stipulations of the monastery of St. Edmundsbury, see *The Kalendar of Abbot Samson of Bury St. Edmunds and Related Documents*, ed. by R. C. H. Davis, pp. 81 No. 11, 144 f. No. 117, 151 No. 130, 160 f. Nos. 145, 147, and 166 No. 156. In its constant repetition this must have become a fairly standardized formula. At times the ecclesiastical tithe itself seems to have aroused the cupidity of superior churchmen. At least the bestowal by Charles the Simple on the Archbishop of Narbonne in 899 of Jewish property, "on which formerly God's churches had customarily collected the tithe in whatever fashion the Jews may have acquired" it, seems to have in essence ceded this Jewish impost to the archbishop, at the expense of the local churches which had collected that revenue before the Jews acquired the land. Cf. the second privilege cited by Régné, p. 223 n. 6; and the interpretation thereof in Caro's *Sozial- und Wirtschaftsgeschichte*, I, 145. According to the existing version, Charles included in his transfer houses owned by Jews. This would seem to indicate that the Church already had sought successfully to collect the tithe from rents as well. Although not in the nature of either "praedial" or "mixed" tithes (those imposed upon crops and such land-supported revenues as those from cattle) such imposts could be classified among the "personal" tithes. Régné (pp. 229 f.) may be right, however, that the word *domos* was substituted for the original *salinas* (salt mines) by a later copyist, in whose day the tax had been extended to dwellings. The Jewish tax on urban real estate had been fully established in the twelfth century. A complaint by the clergy of Rouen that Jews "had taken over the major part of the parish of St. Lo," evoked Celestine III's sharply worded reply demanding full payment by Jews of tithes and other imposts. Cf. the text published by W. Holtzmann in *Festschrift Guido Kisch*, pp. 224, 234 f. Cf. also C. E. Boyd's *Tithes and Parishes in Medieval Italy*; J. San Martin's dissertation, *El Diezmo eclesiastico en España hasta al siglo XII*; and other literature listed in A. C. Jemolo's article "Decima" in the *Enciclopedia italiana*, XII, 460–61. On some occasions Jews arranged for paying an annual lump sum in lieu of the variable tithe. For example, when the Jewish community of Cologne acquired in 1174 some seven acres of ground for a cemetery, the contract provided for the regular payment of four denarii annually. See Aronius, *Regesten*, pp. 131 f. No. 308. The interplay of Jewish moneylending and landownership, and the latter's relationship to the Church's self-interest in the preservation of the tithe, will be more fully elucidated in Chap. XXII.

12. Benjamin, *Massa'ot*, pp. 6 (Hebrew), 5 f. (English); Solomon the Babylonian's poem in J. Schirmann's *Anthologie der hebräischen Dichtung in Italien*, pp. 21 ff., cited in the English excerpt by C. Roth in *The History of the Jews of Italy*, p. 72. Complaints of fiscal pressure are frequently voiced by Solomon in his other poems, as well as by other authors. Cf. the two poems published by D. Goldschmidt in "Some Religious Poems by Solomon the Babylonian" (Hebrew), *Tarbiz*, XXIII, 203–9; and L. Zunz, *Synagogale Poesie des Mittelalters*, pp. 9 ff. As elsewhere, it is uncertain whether Benjamin's figure referred to persons or families. See *supra*, Chap. XVII, n.

48. However, in view of the relative importance of Rome's Jewish community, to which some legal inquiries were addressed even from France (see *infra*, Chap. XXIII, n. 83), an estimate of some 1,000 Jews, or 3 percent of the population, is hardly exaggerated. Of course, nearly all population figures for the earlier Middle Ages are largely conjectural. We do not even have reliable estimates for the general population of such cities as Rome, which had sustained tremendous losses during the barbarian and subsequent invasions. In ancient times probably exceeding 1,000,000, Rome's inhabitants seem to have declined to less than 35,000 during the tenth to the twelfth centuries. Cf. A. M. Ghisalberti, "Roma: Vita economica e sviluppo demografico," *Enciclopedia italiana*, XXIX, 767–68. In any case, C. J. Bail's undocumented estimate of some 4,000 Jews in Rome, out of 28,000 in all of Italy about 800 c.e., is but one of the numerous demographic exaggerations characteristic of that early nineteenth-century author. See his *Etat des Juifs en France, en Espagne et en Italie*, p. 49.

13. Mansi, *Collectio*, XXII, 231 (Hefele, *Histoire*, V, Part 2, pp. 1105 f.); Grayzel, *The Church and the Jews*, pp. 296 f. Unfortunately, neither the date nor the recipient of Alexander III's epistle is indicated in the extant manuscripts. It is only available in the copy included in the appendix to the decisions of the council. See *infra*, n. 14.

14. Benjamin, *Massa'ot*, pp. 6 (Hebrew), 5 f. (English); Grayzel, *The Church and the Jews*, pp. 27 ff.; and *infra*, n. 19. On Yehiel's family, Dei Mansi, one of the four Italian-Jewish families claiming direct descent from captives brought to Rome by Titus, see the genealogical tree reconstructed by E. Rodocanachi in *Le Saint-Siège et les Juifs*, pp. 134 f.

15. Mansi, *loc. cit.*, Hefele, *loc. cit.*; Grayzel, *The Church and the Jews*, pp. 296 f. By being incorporated in the Decretals of Gregory IX, these canons became part of the *Corpus juris canonici* (E. Friedberg's 2d ed., pp. 322, 773). Through a similar process Alexander III's epistle achieved permanent validity. First included in the appendix to the resolutions of the Lateran Council, it, together with the pope's renewal of the protective constitution *Sicut Judaeis*, found its way into Gregory's Decretals and thus into the *Corpus*. Cf. also Aronius's observations in the notes to *Regesten*, pp. 132 No. 310, 136 ff. Nos. 313a and 313b.

16. Innocent's letter, extensively discussed in Jewish historical literature, is readily available in both Latin and English in Grayzel, *The Church and the Jews*, pp. 104 f. Cf. also other data cited *ibid.*, pp. 18 ff., 46 n. 24, and in Caro, *Sozial- und Wirtschaftsgeschichte*, pp. 294 ff., 366 f., 497, 506; J. Parkes's review of the political and economic situation of *The Jew in the Medieval Community*, pp. 128 ff., 141 ff.; and *infra*, n. 60. These conflicts, too, reached a climax in the thirteenth and fourteenth centuries.

17. Jacob bar Yequtiel's mission, to be discussed *infra*, n. 74. J. Müller's ed. of *Teshubot hakhme Sarefat ve-Lotar* (Responsa of French and Lotharingian Rabbis), fols. 20b f. No. 34; Vogelstein and Rieger, *Geschichte*, I, 212, 224 ff. In his "Apiphior, nom hébreux du pape," *REJ*, XXXIV, 238, S. Krauss argues that, because of the use of the term *niphiora* in the responsum ed. by Müller, the latter must be dated

in the eleventh century, before the equation of *apiphior* with pope was fully established. This dating, in itself quite likely, remains unimpaired by T. Reinach's criticisms of Krauss's interpretation of the first occurrence of *piphiora, niphiora,* and their variants (in 'A.Z. 11a), *ibid.,* pp. 239–40. Cf. also Krauss's *Griechische und lateinische Lehnwörter im Talmud, Midrasch und Targum,* p. 363 (with Löw's note thereon). These diplomatic journeys diminished in number in the later Middle Ages, doubtless owing to the growing jealousies for national sovereignty in the European countries. They were nevertheless to reappear sporadically even in early modern times.

18. *Collectio veterum canonum ecclesiae hispanae,* attributed to St. Isidore of Seville, in *PL,* LXXXIV; Agobard's *Epistola de judaicis superstitionibus, ibid.,* CIV, 77 ff.; Amulo's *Epistola (seu Liber) contra Judaeos ad Carolum regem,* XLV, *ibid.,* CXVI, 172 f.; Aronius, *Regesten,* pp. 38 No. 71, 48 No. 110; Mansi, *Collectio,* XIV, 836 ff., canon 73 (Hefele, *Histoire,* IV, Part 1, pp. 120 ff., and Part 2, pp. 1298 ff.). Cf. Parkes, *Jews in the Medieval Community,* pp. 26 f., and *infra,* n. 67. The aforementioned anti-Jewish Archbishop Frederick of Mayence (937–54), apart from asking the pope for advice, commissioned a cleric, Gerhard, to prepare for him a selection of existing canon laws governing the status of Jews in Christian countries. This small compilation included only one conciliar canon from Meaux, and several passages from Gregory I's epistles. Cf. Jaffé, *Monumenta moguntina,* pp. 338 ff.; and Aronius, *Regesten,* p. 55 No. 128. In Gerhard's opinion these few passages "ought to suffice" to regulate the Jewish status. Unfortunately, none of the larger codes here mentioned, except the *Hispana,* are extant. There is no way of telling, therefore, whether Agobard, Amulo, and the churchmen of Meaux collected only more or less authentic texts, or also included spurious records. One or another editor may even have resorted to outright forgeries *ad majorem Dei gloriam,* such as were lavishly included about that time by the Gallic compiler of the famous "Pseudo-Isidorian Decretals." Cf. P. Hinschius's ed. of the *Decretales pseudo-Isidorianae et capitula Angilramni.* Since until the fifteenth century practically everybody was convinced of their authenticity, these Decretals and, to a lesser extent, the other contemporary compilations, exercised a profound influence on the evolution of canon law. A careful scholarly analysis, therefore, of their provisions, both spurious and authentic, concerning Jews is long overdue. See also *supra,* n. 2. On the anti-Jewish compilation by Florus of Lyons, see *infra,* nn. 67 and 71.

19. *Decretum Gratiani,* I, dist. LIV, c. 13–18, in Friedberg's 2d ed. of the *Corpus juris canonici,* I, 211 f. The Toledan Council of 633 was cited by Gratian also in connection with the prohibition for Jewish converts to relapse to their former faith, the separation of Jewish husbands from Christian wives, the obligatory profession of Christianity by offspring of mixed marriages, and the rights of converted children versus their aroused Jewish parents. *Ibid.,* I, dist. XLV, c. 5; II, causa 1, qu. IV, c. 7, and causa 28, qu. I, c. 10–12; III, dist. IV, c. 94, in Friedberg ed., I, 161 f., 419, 1086 f., 1392. Gratian also quoted the sharper resolution of the Council of Agde and the Sixth Toledan Council concerning the rigid segregation of Christians and Jews (II, causa 28, qu. I, c. 13–14). Otherwise he limited himself to the inclusion of a provision against accepting Jewish testimony against Christians (II, causa 2, qu. VII, c. 25; causa 4, qu. I, c. 1), and the requirement of a preparatory period of eight months for prospective Jewish converts (III, dist. IV, c. 93), all in

Friedberg's ed., I, 489, 536 f., 1087 f., 1392. Cf. also the brief summary in J. Jacobs's source collection in English translation, *The Jews of Angevin England*, pp. 15 ff. We must bear in mind, however, that the Friedberg edition no longer satisfies contemporary requirements; a new edition, sponsored by the new Institute of Research and Study in Medieval Canon Law, is now being prepared. Cf. its Bulletin for 1955, appended to *Traditio*, XI, 429–48, and esp. S. Kuttner's "Notes," pp. 433 ff. Cf. also J. Rambaud-Buhot's pertinent suggestions in "Plan et méthode du travail pour la redaction d'un catalogue de mss. du décret du Gratien," *Revue d'histoire ecclésiastique*, XLVIII, 211–23; and the essays included in the *Studia Gratiana*, Vols. I–II. The later papal decretals and canonistic literature, of course, had much more to say about the position of Jews in the Catholic world. On the antecedents of the *Decretum*, cf. P. Fournier and G. Le Bras, *Histoire des collections canoniques en Occident*, esp. I, 127 ff., 313, 364 ff.; and, more generally, J. de Guellink's analysis of *Le Mouvement théologique du XIIe siècle*, 2d ed., pp. 52 ff., 203 ff., 416 ff. Cf. also W. Holtzmann's detailed compilation in *Festschrift Guido Kisch*, pp. 218 ff.; M. Stern, *Urkundliche Beiträge über die Stellung der Päpste zu den Juden* (a collection of 170 texts ranging from 1272 to 1773); L. Erler, "Historisch-kritische Uebersicht der national-ökonomischen und sozial-politischen Literatur. Die Judenverfolgungen des Mittelalters," *Archiv für katholisches Kirchenrecht*, XLI, 3–96; XLII, 3–80; XLIII, 361–408; XLIV, 353–416; XLVII, 3–52 (continued in his aforementioned essay, *ibid.*, XLVIII, L, LIII) and more generally P. Browe, *Die Judenmission, passim;* and K. W. Deutsch's suggestive review of "Anti-Semitic Ideas in the Middle Ages," *Journal of the History of Ideas*, VI, 239–51.

20. G. I. Ascoli, *Iscrizioni inedite o mal note greche, latine, ebraiche di antichi sepolcri giudaici del Napolitano*, pp. 10 ff., 92 ff., 117 ff., and H. P. Chajes's comments thereon in *Centenario della nascita di Michele Amari*, I, 232–40; N. Ferorelli's comprehensive review of *Gli Ebrei nell' Italia meridionale dell' età romana al secolo XVIII*, pp. 25 ff.; *Consuetudini di Palermo*, xxxvi, ed. by L. S. Villanueva in *Raccolta delle consuetudini siciliane*, I, 300 f. Cf. also R. Straus's excerpts in *Die Juden im Königreich Sizilien unter Normannen und Staufern*, p. 103; U. (M.D.) Cassuto's "Nuove iscrizioni ebraiche di Venosa," *Archivio storico per la Calabria*, IV, 1–9, V, 129–34; his comments thereon in "The Hebrew Inscriptions of the Ninth Century from Venosa" (Hebrew), *Kedem*, II, 99–120; his "Iscrizioni ebraiche a Bari," *RSO*, XV, 316–22; and other data mentioned *supra*, Chap. XVI; and in G. P. Bognetti's documentation of the suggested relation between Italy and the Near East through Jewish mediation in "Les Inscriptions juives de Venosa et le problème des rapports entre les Lombards et l'Orient," *CRAI*, 1954, pp. 193–203. The conditions of Jews under the earlier Byzantine and Muslim dominations in what was long called *Magna Graecia*, or in Hebrew *Italiah shel Yavan*, were briefly treated above together with the broader developments of these large civilizations. Under Norman domination, however, Sicily, Apulia, and Calabria were increasingly drawn into the orbit of Western Christendom. Unfortunately the records pertaining to Jewish status, both political and economic, flow more freely only from the later Middle Ages. Cf. the fine, though incomplete, documentary collection by B. Lagumina and G. Lagumina, *Codice diplomatico dei Giudei di Sicilia*. On the significant intellectual contributions of Jews to the great cultural renascence centered around the brilliant courts of Roger II and Frederick II, see *infra*, Chaps. XXXV and XXXVI.

21. *Annales Cavenses* (13th cent.), ed. by G. H. Pertz, in *MGH*, Scriptores, III, 192; Otto of Freising, *Gesta Friderici imperatoris*, ed. by R. Wilmans, 1.33, *ibid.* XX, 370; Straus, *Juden im . . . Sizilien*, pp. 98 f.; J. Starr, *Jews in the Byzantine Empire*, p. 223 No. 173. On the political and military issues involved in the Byzantine-Norman war, see P. Rassow, "Zum byzantinisch-normannischen Krieg 1147–1149," *MIOG*, LXII, 213–18 (showing its connection with the Crusader principality of Antioch). The Jewish role in the growing royal monopolies will be discussed *infra*, Chap. XXII, n. 20. Roger II attracted not only Jewish and Christian refugees from Muslim persecutions, but also such outstanding Muslims as Idrisi, whose great geographic work, *K. al-Rujari* (Book of Roger), was written at the Norman court with the king's personal cooperation.

22. Lagumina and Lagumina, *Codice*, I, 12 ff. Nos. 16–18; Straus, pp. 95 ff., 104. As early as 1089 Sicalgaita, Duke Robert's widow, had bequeathed her entire income from Palermitan Jewry to the archbishop and Church of that city. Lagumina, I, 9 f. No. 12. It is noteworthy that some of the legislators failed to distinguish clearly between Jews and Saracens, by then declassed into but another religious minority. When Roger I, for instance, transferred a large number of "Saracens" to the control of the Church of Palermo (about 1095) he included several persons bearing indubitably Hebraic names. Cf. Straus, p. 96. The growing struggle between the feudal powers and both the monarchy and the burghers, which affected also the position of Jews, is well documented in I. Peri's detailed enumeration of "Signorie feodali della Sicilia normanna," *Archivio storico italiano*, CX, 166–204.

23. *Consuetudini di Palermo*, xv, LXXVII, in Villanueva's *Raccolta*, I, 229 f., 542; *Chronicle of Ahimaaz*, ed. by Salzman, pp. 24 (Hebrew), 100 (English); ed. by Klar, p. 50. The much-debated Messina privilege of 1129, first published by S. Baluze in 1678, has long since been established as a pious fraud, but its modern critics admit that the text is based on an older, authentic version. See esp. M. Amari, *Storia dei Musulmani di Sicilia*, 2d ed., III, Part 1, pp. 57 ff. With all the reasons advanced for the subsequent forgeries and interpolations—a fairly common procedure in the Middle Ages—none was suggested as to why a sweeping provision for Jewish equality should have been inserted at a later time. Cf. also L. Erler's observations in *Archiv für katholisches Kirchenrecht*, XLVIII, 15 n. 2; and R. Straus's succinct analysis of the general legal status of Jews under Norman domination in *Juden im . . . Sizilien*, pp. 17 ff., 53 ff. Like almost all of his contemporaries, Straus attached undue significance to verbal assertions relating to Jewish "serfdom." This extremely complex legal institution, gradually evolving north of the Alps over the preceding several centuries and expanding in differing degrees and with substantial modifications to the Mediterranean countries as well, attained its full meaning and legal formulation only in the thirteenth century. Its comprehensive analysis must therefore be reserved for a later volume.

24. Benjamin, *Massa'ot*, pp. 9 ff. (Hebrew), 8 f. (English). Even at the end of the thirteenth century Naples' population amounted to no more than 30,000, according to estimates cited by Ferorelli in *Gli Ebrei*, p. 43. That author's deduction from the contemporary fiscal contributions for the number of Neapolitan Jews is far from conclusive, however. Cf. also E. Munkacsi's survey, mainly of later

monuments in *Der Jude von Neapel*. The estimate of 40,000 Jews in a total population of 8 or 9 million is given by A. Milano in *Gli Ebrei in Italia nei secoli
XI⁰ e XII⁰*, pp. 60 f. Although based almost exclusively on Benjamin's figures and
on even more questionable assumptions for cities and the countryside not mentioned by the traveler from Tudela, this estimate seems plausible. Benjamin
emphasized that the medical school of Salerno belonged to the "children of
Edom" (Christians), but this did not preclude Jewish influences on its formation. Cf. *infra*, Chap. XXXVI. Remarkably, in 1121, the Jews of that city (whose
quarter is recorded in 1012 and 1031 to have been precariously located on land
belonging to a local church) were entrusted with a monopoly for the slaughtering
of animals, the non-Jews being expressly prohibited from running another slaughterhouse. Cf. *Codex diplomaticus Cavensis*, ed. by M. Morcaldi *et al.*, IV, 196 f. No. 651;
V, 211 f. No. 841; G. Paesano's *Memorie per servire alla storia della chiesa salerni-
tana*, II, 72, cited by Straus, p. 30 n. 41. No such Jewish monopoly is recorded
elsewhere. Nor did slaughtering ever become a royal monopoly in the kingdom of
Sicily. One wonders, therefore, whether this exceptional treatment was not in
some way the result of either the extraordinarily large ratio of Jews in the population (Benjamin's 600 families may actually have constituted the majority of
the city's twelfth-century inhabitants) or of the role Jews played in connection
with the supply of meat or animal cadavers to the medical school.

25. Benjamin, *loc. cit.*; G. L. F. Tafel and G. M. Thomas, *Urkunden zur älteren
Handels- und Staatsgeschichte der Republik Venedig*, I, 38 (also in *PG*, CXVII,
616 f.). Cf. G. Caro, *Sozial- und Wirtschaftsgeschichte*, I, 193; Starr, *Jews in the
Byzantine Empire*, p. 169 No. 117. On the growingly competitive relations between
Jews and the "Lombards" in western Europe, cf. *infra*, Chap. XXII, n. 75.

26. Tafel and Thomas, *Urkunden*, I, 20; Aronius, *Regesten*, pp. 53 f. Nos. 123–24;
and *supra*, Chap. XIX, nn. 10–12. On the Giudecca, cf. S. Romanin, *Storia docu-
mentata di Venezia*, I, 46 No. 3, 245, 370 f. Although himself mentioning the
spelling *Judaica*, Romanin doubted the connection of Giudecca with Jews. Cf.
also C. Roth's history of the Jews in *Venice*, pp. 8 ff.; and other studies listed by
G. Gabrieli in his bibliographical guide to *Italia Judaica*, esp. pp. 56 f., 74; and by
A. Milano in his *Bibliotheca historica italo-judaica, passim*.

27. Louis II's decree, cited in *Conventus Ticinensis*, III.4, ed. by G. H. Pertz, in
MGH, Leges, I, 437 (under date of July, 855); Ratherius of Verona's *De qualitatis
conjectura*, xi, in *PL*, CXXXVI, 535 ff.; and *supra*, n. 2; and Chap. XVI, n. 39.
There is no evidence, however, for the contention of the generally well-informed
local biographers Peter and Jerome Ballerini that the Jews "are known to have
had great power [praepotentes] in Verona." Cf. their introduction in *PL*, col. 114.
At a loss to explain this sudden outburst of intolerance on the part of Louis II,
so sharply running counter to the long-established policies of the Carolingian
dynasty, L. Erler suggested that this decree may have been provoked by rumors
concerning Jewish aid to the invading Moors in Sicily and vicinity. See his remarks in *Archiv für katholisches Kirchenrecht*, XLVIII, 12. Although nowhere
expressly recorded, such rumors may indeed have circulated widely here as they had
in Spain and southern France in the preceding century. Yet it is less likely that
Louis II, who must have known something about his family's sustained efforts to

restore the Christian domination on both sides of the Pyrenees, should have been swayed by such uncontrolled generalizations. He must also have known of some patriotic Jews, like those poets who (according to the contemporary Scotsman Sedulius) composed Hebrew poems extolling his wife, Empress Irmingard, as well as his cousin, Charles the Bald, though none of these poems is extant today for reasons discussed *supra*, n. 10. Cf. Sedulius Scottus' *Carmina*, II, ed. by L. Traube, in *MGH*, Poetae latini, III, 186 No. xx, 193 f. No. xxviii.

28. Benjamin, *Massa'ot*, pp. 5 f. (Hebrew), 5 (English); Alcuin's *Epistolae*, No. 172 (dated April–May, 855), ed. by E. Dümmler, in *MGH*, Epistulae, IV, 285; Ratherius, *loc. cit.*; Mansi, *Collectio*, XIII, 852 (canon 13), and XIV, 937 (canon 20); Hefele, *Histoire*, III, 1093 ff. (also explaining why the date of 796, rather than 791, is correct), and IV, 186 ff. (canon 24). That Italian policies of the time were not primarily determined by religious considerations is well illustrated by "La Corrispondenza di Berta di Toscana col califfo Muktafi," republished with an Italian translation by G. L. della Vida in *Rivista storica italiana*, LXVI, 21–38. In this curious correspondence of 905-6 the Italian princess offered Islam's world leader an alliance against Byzantium. In good medieval fashion she allegedly also ordered the envoy to suggest orally that her marriage to the caliph would best seal that alliance. Yet even Lucca was not completely free of conversionist pressures. An admiring hagiographer described the missionary successes of an anchorite named Simeon, who upon his arrival in Lucca had been hospitably received in the house of a Jew (before 1016). With the aid of a miracle, Simeon allegedly succeeded in converting Lucca's entire Jewish community. Cf. *Vita Symeonis Eremitae*, vii f., in *Acta sanctorum ordinis S. Benedicti*, ed. by L. d'Achery, Saec. VI, Part I (Vol. VIII of the series), pp. 139 f. On Ibn Ezra's sojourn in Lucca, cf. especially J. L. Fleischer's "Abraham ibn Ezra and His Literary Creativity in Lucca, III" (Hebrew), *Ha-Soqer*, IV, 186–94; and *infra*, Chap. XXXV.

29. C. Ghirardacci's *Della historia di Bologna*, I, 91 (without mentioning a source), also cited by G. B. Depping in *Les Juifs dans le moyen âge*, p. 104; D. Romanelli's *Antichità nella regione Frentana*, II, 130 ff., cited by Ferorelli in *Gli Ebrei*, pp. 36 f. The reason given by Ghirardacci for the expulsion from Bologna, namely "the great damage they [the Jews] had done the city by their excessive usuries," is more in keeping with his own time than with the twelfth century. A considerable number of other Italian Jewish communities in our period are listed in Straus's *Juden im . . . Sizilien*, p. 11, and Roth's *Jews in Italy*, pp. 74 ff. Cf. also N. Ferorelli's well-documented monograph, *passim;* G. Sommo, *Gli Ebrei in Puglia dall' XI al XVI secolo;* M. Jacobone, *La più importante comunità ebraica del mezzogiorno d'Italia sui confini dell' Apulia;* G. Carano-Donvito, "Gli Ebrei nella storia economica di Puglia," *Rivista di politica economica*, XXIII, 836–43 (both more valuable for later periods); and A. Milano's aforementioned comprehensive survey, *Gli Ebrei in Italia nei secoli XI° e XII°*, supplemented by his recent *Vicende economiche degli Ebrei nell' Italia meridionale ed insulare durante il medioevo* (reprinted from *RMI*, Vol. XX); also other studies listed in G. Gabrieli's *Italia judaica* and in A. Milano's more recent *Bibliotheca historica italo-judaica*.

30. R. Menendez Pidal in *La España del Cid*, pp. 92 n. 2, 675 (*The Cid and His Spain*, English trans. by H. Sunderland, p. 456; the former note is omitted

here), and in *El imperio hispanico y los cincos reinos*, pp. 155 ff.; E. Lévi-Provençal, "Toledo," *EI*, IV, 811. It is possible that Mar Abisai, whose death on May 15, 1135, is recorded on an epitaph in Leon, came to that city in anticipation of that great celebration. Cf. Fidel Fita, "Nuevas inscripciones romanas y hebreas," *BAH*, XLVII, 143 ff. Cf. also H. J. Hüffer's well-documented analysis of "Die mittelalterliche spanische Kaiseridee und ihre Probleme," *Saeculum*, III, 425–43; and M. Defourneaux's data on *Les Français en Espagne aux XIᵉ et XIIᵉ siècles*. The various influences on medieval Spanish law are well analyzed, with some reference also to its Jewish and Arab ingredients, by L. Manuel Torres in his *Lecciones de historia del derecho español*, I, 45 ff., 51 f. Cf. E. Wohlhaupter's observations on "Das germanische Element im altspanischen Recht und die Rezeption des römischen Rechtes in Spanien," *Zeitschrift für Rechtsgeschichte*, LXVI, 135–264, esp. pp. 183 ff. (showing the perseverance of that element despite the replacement of the old personal principle by the newer territorial divisions; this change infringed but little on Jewish autonomy); and *supra* Chap. XVI, n. 53.

The history of the Jews of Spain, understandably, has long attracted considerable attention of Spanish, Jewish, and other scholars. Of the prodigious literature on the subject we need but refer to the older, but far from superseded, works by J. Amador de los Rios, *Historia social, politica y religiosa de los Judios de España y Portugal;* and M. Kayserling, *Die Juden in Navarra, den Baskenländern und auf den Balearen*. The extensive and widely scattered sources have been authoritatively reviewed and commented on by F. Baer in his "regesta" concerning *Die Juden im christlichen Spanien*, of which a third part relating to the Judeo-Christian controversial literature is yet to appear. Baer subsequently synthesized his findings in his *Toledot ha-Yehudim bi-Sefarad ha-noṣrit* (History of the Jews in Christian Spain). Only the underlying philosophical preconceptions of this standard work have been criticized by I. Sonne in his review article, "On Baer and His Philosophy of Jewish History," *JSS*, IX, 61–80. An English translation of this work has not yet appeared, but some readers unfamiliar with Hebrew may find J. M. Millás Vallicrosa's summary quite helpful. See his review, "Historia de los Judios españoles," *Sefarad*, V, 417–40; VI, 163–88. On the other hand, A. A. Neuman's study of *The Jews in Spain: Their Social, Political and Cultural Life during the Middle Ages*, has contributed more to the knowledge of the internal life of the Jews in the later Middle Ages than to the period before 1200. Cf. also M. Vallecillo Ávila's more recent survey of "Los Judíos de Castilla en la alta edad media," *CHE*, XIV, 17–110; and many monographs mentioned in Chap. XVI. nn. 41 and 45, as well as in the forthcoming notes.

31. *Poem of the Cid*, vv. 78 ff., ed. with an English translation by A. M. Huntington, I, 4 ff. (Spanish); II, 4ff. (English); F. Baer's excerpt and note in *Die Juden im christlichen Spanien*, I, Part 1, 4 f. No. 7, and the sources listed in his *Toledot*, I, 310 n. 4. Cf. also the reference, in 982, to a Judicas or Judaiques in the district of Besalù and to a Villa judaica or Villajuiga in the district of Peralada in R. d'Abadal i de Vinyal's *Catalunya carolingia*, II, 168 f., 173, 241. 243. While Baer (*Toledot*, p. 44) senses in the passage of the *Cid* (the poem was written about 1140) decided anti-Jewish overtones, E. Garcia Gomez sees in it but a reflection of contemporary popular misconceptions. Cf. his "Esos dos Judios de Burgos," *Al-Andalus*, XVI, 224–27. Cf. also *infra*, Chap. XXII, n. 74.

32. Baer's *Juden im christlichen Spanien*, I, Part 1, pp. 15 ff. Nos. 27–28, 919 ff. Nos. 569–70. Nothing in the text of the decree of 1115 bears out the suggestion by Moret (repeated by Kayserling and Neuman) that the Jews of Tudela had left the city in protest against the royal promises to the Moors, and returned only after they had exacted that decree. Cf. Kayserling's *Juden in Navarra*. pp. 12, 16; Neuman's *Jews in Spain*, I, 4 f. It is more likely that the king merely wished to encourage the return of Jews who had departed before the siege. Nor did the Toledo regulation of 1118 that recent converts, as well as professing Jews, should exercise no jurisdiction over Moors (Baer, I, Part 2, pp. 9 f. No. 18) pursue any racialist aims. On the location and growth of the Jewish quarter in Toledo, cf. L. Torres Balbás's remarks in "Los Adarves de las ciudades hispanomusulmanas," *Al-Andalus*, XII, 164–93. Cf. also his "Mozarabias y juderias de las ciudades hispanomusulmanas," *ibid.*, XIX, 189 ff.; and *infra*, nn. 39 and 42. The interesting Tortosa document, first published in full by J. Miret y Sans in "La Carta de franquicias otorgada por el Conde de Barcelona a los Judíos de Tortosa," *Homenaje a Francisco Codera*, ed. by E. Saavedra, pp. 199–205, was reedited, with minor corrections by Baer on the basis of a MS collation. We must understand these developments against the background of the city's conquest by ardent Crusaders as a part of the Second Crusade and with the aid of a Genoese fleet. Cf. the treaty republished in the *Codice diplomatico della Repubblica di Genova*, ed. by C. Imperiale di Sant' Angelo, I (*Fonti per la storia d'Italia*, Vol. LXXVII), pp. 166 f., 204 ff. Cf. also J. M. Font Rius's remarks in "La Comarca de Tortosa á raíz de la reconquista cristiana (1148)," *CHE*, XIX, 124 f.

These treaty provisions seem to have been largely followed also in other communities, such as Lerida, even where special compacts with Jews are not recorded. That the number of Jews residing, for instance, in Lerida in 1150 may have warranted some such special consideration, is evident from the numerous transactions affecting Jews in the following decades and the existence there, in 1169–73, of a former synagogue and a slaughterhouse "of Saracens and Jews." Perhaps Ramon Berenger felt less free to legislate here because he had conquered the city jointly with the count of Urgel. Cf. P. Loscertales de Valdeavallano's ed. of the *Costumbres de Lérida;* J. M. Font y Rius's well documented monograph on *La Reconquista de Lérida y su proyección en el orden jurídico* (significant also for the juridical analysis of similar stipulations in the treaty with Tortosa); and Baer's *Juden*, I, Part 1, pp. 15 No. 26, 20 ff. No. 31. In any case one ought not to exaggerate the failure of some treaties to mention Jews. Certainly at the surrender of Toledo in 1085 the Jewish community was of sufficient importance to warrant special legislation, if Alphonso VI had considered it necessary. On that event, significant also in Spanish-Jewish history, see E. Lévi-Provençal's "Alphonse VI et la prise de Tolède (1085)," reprinted in his *Islam d' Occident*, pp. 109–35; on the hitherto unpublished documents in the Municipal Archives of that city, in part relating to "las aljamas de moros y judíos," see M. Vallecillo Ávila's brief observations in "Los Judíos de Castilla," *CHE*, XIV, 48.

33. Ibn al-Qama's "Eloquent Evidence of the Great Calamity," cited by R. Menéndez Pidal in *The Cid and His Spain*, Sunderland trans., pp. 3 f. Cf. also Menéndez Pidal's review article, "La Politica y la reconquista en el siglo XI," *Revista de estudios politicos*, XIX, 1–35.

34. Moses ibn Ezra's poem '*Ad an be-galut* (How Far . . . over Exile's Path) in *Shire ha-ḥol* (Secular Poems), ed. by H. Brody, I, 66 f. No. 67, and in S. Solis-Cohen's English translation of his *Selected Poems*, pp. 2 ff.; his *K. al-Muhadhara w'al-Mudhakara* (Book of Discussion and Remembrance; on poetic arts) in the Hebrew translation by B. Z. Halper, entitled *Shirat Yisrael*, p. 34; Yehudah Halevi's poem, *Ekh aharekha* (How Shall I Find Rest After Thee) in his *Diwan*, ed. by H. Brody, I, 92 f. No. 66 (ed. by I. Zemorah, III, 11). Cf. the biographical data, largely culled from these poems, in Brody's "Moses ibn Ezra—Incidents in His Life," *JQR*, XXIV, 309–20; his Introduction to the *Selected Poems;* A. Díez Macho's *Moše ibn 'Ezra como poeta y preceptista*, pp. 38 ff.; and other literature listed *infra*, Chap. XXXII. On Yehudah Halevi's brief sojourns in Christian Spain, both in his youth and middle years, and his relations with Moses ibn Ezra, cf. H. Schirmann's comprehensive Hebrew biography, "The Life of Yehudah Halevi" in *Tarbiz*, IX, 36 ff., 219 ff. In his supplementary note, "Where Was Yehudah Halevi Born?" (Hebrew), *ibid.*, X, 237–39, Schirmann argued in favor of Tudela, rather than Toledo, as a birthplace of both Halevi and Abraham ibn Ezra. The evidence relating to Halevi, however, is supported mainly by an unclear reading in a Bodleian MS (the corresponding passage in a Leningrad MS could not be consulted by Schirmann). It is far from sufficient to overcome the difficulties mentioned in Schirmann's note. Certainly one might expect Moses ibn Ezra to hail the younger poet as coming from *Se'ir* (Christian Spain), if the latter's native city had been conquered by the Christians when Halevi was approximately ten years old (Toledo in 1085), rather than if he had come from Tudela, which had remained Muslim for thirty years longer. Moreover, Tudela was incorporated in 1115 in Navarre and not Castile, and we would be hard put to explain, on the basis of his brief residence in Toledo in later years, the designation "Castilian" given to Halevi by later German authors. Cf. also *infra*, Chap. XXXII.

35. Galo Sanchez's ed. of the *Fueros castellanos de Soria y Alcala de Henáres*, p. 305 No. 171; and Baer's *Juden*, I, Part 2, p. 11 No. 20. On the scientifically-minded archbishop of Toledo and the circle of scholars around him, see esp. M. Alonso Alonso's various studies, referred to in his "Traducciones del árabe al latín por Juan Hispano (Ibn Dāwúd)," *Al-Andalus*, XVII, 129–51. Cf. also *infra*, Chaps. XXXV–XXXVI.

36. Cf. I. Loeb's "Notes sur l'histoire et les antiquités juives," *REJ*, II, 135–38 (based on communications by Fidel Fita). Much new epigraphic material has come to light since 1907 when M. Schwab published his "Rapport sur les inscriptions hébraïques de l'Espagne," *Nouvelles archives des missions scientifiques et littéraires*, XIV, 229–421. In recent years F. Cantera Burgos and J. M. Millás Vallicrosa, especially, have added a number of new inscriptions and shed new light on those previously known. Cf. Cantera's "De epigrafia hebraico-española," *Sefarad*, II, 99–112; "Lápidas hebraicas del Museo de Toledo," and "Nuevas inscripciones hebraicas leonesas," *ibid.*, III, 107–14, 329–58; his "Inscripciones hebraicas de Toledo, Nuevo hallazgo epigrafico," *ibid.*, IV, 45–72; his "Nuevo hallazgo epigráfico en León," *ibid.*, XIV, 119–21 (the Hebrew characters seem to indicate an eleventh-century date); and his "Epigrafia hebraica en el Museo arqueologico de Madrid," *ibid.*, XI, 105–11 (a new interpretation of three Hebrew and one bilingual inscription, with additional comments by Millás, *ibid.*, pp. 389–92); and his "Nuevas inscrip-

ciones hebraicas," *ibid.*, XIV, 389–91. Millás himself published several studies in this field, including "Epigrafia hebraicoespañola," *ibid.*, V, 285–302 (with C. Roth's comments on "The Judaeo-Latin Inscription of Merida," *ibid.*, VIII, 391–96); "Nuevos epigrafes hebraicos," *ibid.*, XIII, 337–43; "Una Lápida hebraica sepulcral en Besalù," *ibid.*, XIV, 117–18; "Lápidas hebraicas de Tarragona," *Boletín arqueologico,* XLV, 92–97; and "Una nueva lápida hebraica de Tarragona," *ibid.*, XLIX, 188–90. These and many other essays, including those cited in the forthcoming notes have but partially been superseded by Cantera and Millás's recent comprehensive edition of *Inscripciones hebraicas de España.* On the ancient religious symbolism see E. R. Goodenough's *Jewish Symbols in the Greco-Roman Period;* and my review of the first three volumes in *JBL,* LXXIV, 196–99.

37. Cf. A. Duran Sanpere and J. M. Millás Vallicrosa's description of "Una necrópolis judaica en el Montjuich de Barcelona," *Sefarad,* VII, 231–59; Antonio Prevosti's "Estudio tipólogico de los restos humanos hallados en la necrópolis judaica de Montjuich (Barcelona)," *ibid.*, XI, 75–90; his and Maria Prevosti's fuller analysis in *Trabajos del Instituto Bernardino de Sahagun de Antropologia y Etnologia,* 1951.

Most of the other Jewish cemeteries thus far unearthed seem to date from the thirteenth century and later. See e.g., the initial description of the excavations in Teruel in A. G. Floriano Cumbreño's "Hallazgo de la necrópolis judaica de la ciudad de Teruel," *BAH,* LXXXVIII, 845–51; and his more comprehensive study of *La Aljama de los Judios de Teruel y el hallazgo de su necrópolis.* Cf. also F. Cantera's brief review of "Cementerios hebreos de España," *Sefarad,* XIII, 362–67 (discusses Cordova, Calatayud, Teruel, and announces further excavations).

38. Baer, *Juden,* I, Part 1, pp. 1 f. No. 1, 5 f. No. 9; R. d'Abadal i de Vinyals, *Catalunya carolingia,* II, 434 f. No. viii (mentioning earlier debates and arguing for 877 as the date of this significant communication extant in the original); Yehudah bar Barzillai al-Barceloni, *Sefer ha-Sheṭarot* (Book of Deeds), ed. by S. Z. H. (J.) Halberstam; Ibn ʿAbd al-Munʿim al-Ḥimyari, *K. ar-Rawd,* No. 42, ed. by E. Lévi-Provençal in *La Peninsule ibérique,* pp. 42 (Arabic), 54 (French). The literary connections between Spain and Babylonia are reviewed by S. Eppenstein and J. Mann. Although pertaining largely to Muslim Spain, the sources cited by them include data on northern communities as well. Cf. *supra,* Chap. XVII, n. 42, and *infra,* Chap. XXIII, nn. 13 and 19.

Of great historical as well as juristic significance have been the discoveries of contemporary Hebrew deeds, as well as those written in other languages with Hebrew annotations or signatures. An initial, searching study, "Zum Urkunden-wesen und Privatrecht der Juden in Spanien," was included by Baer in Appendix II to his *Juden,* I, Part 1, pp. 1044 ff. C. A. González Palencia's comprehensive documentary collection in *Los Mozárabes de Toledo en los siglos XII y XIII* includes many deeds relating to Jews. See Baer's comments thereon in his Hebrew review of this book in *Tarbiz,* V, 228–36, and those of Millás in his *Escrituras mozárabes de Hebreos toledanos.* See also Vallecillo Ávila, "Los Judíos de Castilla," *CHE,* XIV, 98 ff., and J. Bosch Vila's survey of "Los Documentos árabes y hebreos de Aragón y Navarra," *Estudios de Edad Media de la Corona de Aragón,* Sección de Zaragoza, V, 407–16. We shall see that Yehudah bar Barzillai's *Sefer ha-Sheṭarot* was not the first work of its kind, but the author had at his disposal ample documentation emanating from the various notarial offices in Spain and other European countries. A thorough juristic and historical analysis of these materials in the light of both the evolution of Jewish law and the notarial practices in the West is a prime scholarly desideratum. Cf. *infra*, Chap. XXVII, n. 74.

39. Baer, *Juden*, I, Part 1, p. 2 No. 2; Ibn 'Abd al-Mun'im al-Ḥimyari, No. 42, in E. Lévi-Provençal, *Peninsule ibérique*, pp. 42 ff. (Arabic), 54 ff. (French); J. Sanchez Real's twin studies, "Los Judíos de Tarragona," *Boletin arqueológico de Tarragona*, XLIX, 15–39; and "La Juderia de Tarragona," *Sefarad*, XI, 339–48; Idrisi (Edrisi), *Description de l'Afrique et de l'Espagne*, ed. with a French trans. and notes by R. Dozy and M. J. de Goeje, pp. 191 (Arabic), 231 (French). See also *supra*, n. 36. Of considerable importance was also the Jewry of Burgos, already mentioned in the well-known episode of the Cid and his Jewish moneylenders. In fact, one of the city's two sections was predominantly Jewish, according to Ibn 'Abd al-Mun'im al-Ḥimyari (No. 43). Cf. Lévi-Provençal, *Peninsule ibérique*, pp. 44 (Arabic), 55 f. (French), disproving Baer's contention that the Jews did not occupy the quarter around the castle until the twelfth century. Cf. Baer's interpretation of Didacus Gelmirez' *Historia Compostellana*, I, c. 85 (ed. by H. Florez in *España sagrada*, XX, 157) in his *Juden*, I, Part 1, p. 39; M. Suarez's Spanish trans. of Gelmirez' work with J. Campelo's notes thereon; and, more generally, T. López Mata's "Moreria y Juderia [burgalesas en la edad media]," *BAH*, CXXIX, 335–84 (dealing mainly with the fourteenth and fifteenth centuries); F. Cantera's detailed analysis of "La Juderia de Burgos," *Sefarad*, XII, 59–104; and Torres Balbás's essays cited *supra*, n. 32.

40. Baer, *Juden*, I, Part 2, p. 1 No. 1, and J. Rodriguez Fernandez, "Juderías de León," *Archivos Leoneses*, I, 33–72; II, 3–113; IV, 11–52 (including documents from 905 on); his "Juderia de Cea," *ibid.*, IX, 5–46; and his essay mentioned *infra*, n. 49. Mainly of historiographic interest are the "Notizie concernenti la storia degli Ebrei in Portogallo estratte per ubra di Attilio Zuccagni-Orlandini [1784–1872] dai manoscritti del sign. Antonio Ribeiro Dos Santos," *RMI*, XVI, 32–40, 79–87 (from a Lisbon MS). Cf. also J. González's "Repoblación de la 'Extremadura' leonesa," *Hispania*, XI, 195–273 (the references to Jews in Salamanca begin flowing more freely after 1225, pp. 244 f., 270 ff.); J. M. Lacarra's study of *La Repoblación de Zaragoza por Alfonso el Batallador* (claiming that Jewish settlers were more important from the economic than from the numerical standpoint); his comprehensive publication of *Documentos para el estudio de la reconquista y repoblación del valle de Ebro* (includes document of 1143 showing two Jewish signatures on the bishop's privilege exempting one Abolhazam from the tithe; 3d ser., pp. 572 f. No. 351); and R. del Arco's data, chiefly later medieval, on "Las Juderías de Jaca y Zaragoza," *Sefarad*, XIV, 79–98. Undoubtedly the great period of growth of the Saragossan and other northern communities was to come in the thirteenth and fourteenth centuries. Nevertheless, in view of the small size of most Spanish cities immediately after their reconquest by the Christians, Jews constituted a far from negligible quantity. Certainly only a sizable Jewish population could have impressed outsiders like Al-Ḥimyari and Idrisi sufficiently for them to exaggerate the way they did.

41. T. Muñoz y Romero, *Collección de fueros municipales y cartas pueblas*, I, 37 ff.; Baer, *Juden*, I, Part 2, p. 1 No. 2. In his *Toledot*, I, 33, Baer interprets these

passages as a concession of the count to the burghers in 974 so that the fine for the murder of a Jew might not exceed that of a villein (whatever that term meant in the tenth century). He also believes that in 1035 the burghers removed the Christian population from Mercatello. Neither explanation is borne out by the simple meaning of the text. In fact, after Alphonso VI's death the inhabitants of Castrojeriz staged another anti-Jewish disturbance in 1109, and, while they secured forgiveness from Queen Urraca, they had to pay for every Jewish victim *sicut per christianum.* Cf. Muñoz's *Collección,* p. 41; Baer, *Juden,* I, Part 2, p. 9 No. 18; and, on the events of 1109, *infra,* n. 49. Cf. also L. Huidobro y Serna's succinct survey, "La Juderia de Castrojeriz," *Sefarad,* VII, 137–45.

42. Amador de los Rios, *Historia social,* I, 185 f., 189, and 331 n. 1; Vallecillo Ávila, "Los Judíos de Castilla," *CHE,* XIV, 107 (both listing a number of *castra judaeorum*); R. del Arco, "Las Juderías de Jaca y Zaragoza," *Sefarad,* XIV, 79 f.; Solomon ibn Adret, *Responsa,* IV, 84 f. No. 268, with I. Epstein's comments thereon in *The Responsa of R. Solomon ben Adreth of Barcelona (1235–1310) as a Source of the History of Spain,* p. 92; Baer, *Juden,* I, Pt. 2, p. 934 No. 578. This provision was repeated verbatim in Sancho's privilege for the Jews of Funes, *ibid.,* p. 934 No. 579.

43. J. A. Condé, *Historia de la dominación de los Arabes,* Vol. III, Chaps. XVI–XVII (Madrid ed., 1874, pp. 185 ff.); Isaac bar Moses Or Zaru'a, *Sefer Or zaru'a* (Halakhic Treatise), I, 194 No. 693 (based on Eliezer ben Joel ha-Levi's *Sefer Rabiah,* ed. by A. [V.] Aptowitzer; cf. the latter's *Mabo le-Sefer Rabiah,* pp. 447 ff.). The story of the battle of Zalaqa, embroidered by popular legend with such fictional features as the king's suggestion to the Arab commander to abstain from battle on Friday, Saturday, and Sunday out of respect for the days of rest of the three major segments of their armies, was repeated with much delight by later Arab chroniclers. It has been analyzed especially by R. Dozy in his *Histoire,* III, 127; and by A. Huici Miranda in "La Invasion de los Almoravides y la batalla de Zalaca," *Hespéris,* XL, 17–76 (for exaggerated figures of participating combatants, see pp. 57 and 69); E. Lévi-Provençal, E. García Gómez, and J. Oliver Asín, "Novedades sobre la batalla llamada de Zallaqa (1086)," *Al-Andalus,* XV, 111–55. Cf. also Baer's note in *Juden,* I, Part 2, pp. 9 f. No. 18. Armed intervention of Jews is recorded also in such civil strife as that between Alphonso VII "the Emperor" and one of his high officials in Carrion and Burgos (1126). Cf. the *Chronica de Alfonso VII,* ed. by H. Florez in *España sagrada,* XXI, 322 ff. (since the official refused to surrender the castle of Burgos, "a Judaeis et Christianis expugnatum est"). This important chronicle, also available in a recent critical edition by L. Sanchez Belda, entitled *Chronica Adefonsi imperatoris,* was written by a near-contemporary. Cf. the latter editor's introduction, pp. xx f. and text, p. 11; and B. Sanchez Alonso's *Historia de la historiografia española,* 2d ed., I, 122 ff.

44. Baer, *Juden,* I, Part 2, pp. 4 No. 29, 552 n. 1; his *Toledot,* pp. 39, 49 ff. Baer's suggestion that Joseph ibn Ferrizuel, rather than the famous halakhist Ibn Megas, was addressed by Yehudah Halevi in his poem, *Rashe 'am* (Heads of the People; in *Diwan,* ed. by Brody, I, 157 f. No. 102; ed. by Zemorah, III, 324 f.) was borne out by the superscription on the poem, specifically mentioning "Cidela." Cf. Schirmann's biography of Halevi in *Tarbiz,* IX, 219 f. It seems that on his visit to Guadalajara, conquered by Alphonso VI in 1086, Joseph was able to intervene suc-

cessfully in behalf of the Jewish community there, although its first recorded action does not antedate the local *fuero* of 1133. Cf. Amador de los Rios, *Historia*, I, 194 (giving the date of 1139); and Baer, *Juden*, I, Part 2, p. 80 No. 95. Of course, we need not take such glorification of an influential leader by a contemporary poet at its face value. According to the literary fashion of the age such praises were sung not only by direct beneficiaries of a leader's largesse, but also by outsiders. Cf. also Baer's interesting analysis of "The Political Status of Spanish Jewry in Ye-hudah Halevi's Generation" (Hebrew), *Zion*, I, 6–23; *infra*, n. 47; and Chap. XXXII, *passim*.

45. Ibn Tibbon's "Will" in I. Abrahams's edition of *Hebrew Ethical Wills*, I, 59; Baer, *Juden*, I, Part 1, pp. 8 f. No. 15, 20 ff. Nos. 31–40, 87 No. 87, 1011 No. 612, 1020 f. No. 627. The title *saḥib ash-shurta*, whose tenth-century connotations are fully documented in E. Lévi-Provençal's *Espagne musulmane*, pp. 88 ff., may have undergone some change in the following century or two. In any case, Abraham bar Ḥiyya probably was engaged in land surveying—concern for correct land measurements prompted him to write his main treatise on geometry, see *infra*, Chap. XXXV—rather than in functions of a police chief or prosecutor. The story of Fermosa-Raquel, her hold over the great conqueror-statesman, and her tragic end at the hand of aroused courtiers, has often intrigued scholars and fiction writers alike. First narrated by Alphonso the Wise in 1260, less than half a century after the decease of his grand-uncle, this romantic tale found many critics, but was defended by Amador de los Rios in his *Historia*, I, 334 ff. Cf. also Marques de Mondexar's *Memorias historicas de la vida y acciones del rey D. Alfonso el Noble, Octavo del nombre*, pp. 67 ff.; M. Vallecillo Ávila's more recent summary in "Los Judíos de Castilla," *CHE*, XIV, 81 ff.; B. Portnoy's more fanciful description of "Raquel, la reina hebrea de Castilla," *Heredad* (Buenos Aires), I–II, 9–18; and Lion Feucht-wanger's latest novel, *Raquel, the Jewess of Toledo*. Of considerable interest also is a document of 1162 showing Abraham Alfaqim and Saltiel Profet as co-signers with three bishops, two abbots, and four knights on Ramon Berenger IV's writ of indebtedness for the substantial amount of 6,000 maravedis. Cf. Baer, *Juden*, I, Part 1, p. 24 No. 35. On other Jewish advisers to princes, including members of the Ibn Ezra family, cf. Baer, *Toledot*, pp. 41 ff., 64 ff., with the notes thereon; Al-Maqqari, *K. Nafḥ aṭ-ṭib* (Smell of Perfumes), in *Analectes*, ed. by R. Dozy *et al.*, I, 126 f.; H. Pérès, *Poesie andalouse*, p. 266 n. 3; and *supra*, Chap XVIII.

46. Cf. the sources cited *supra*, n. 44. The purpose of Solomon Ferrizuel's journey to the "son of Ramir," that is Alphonso I el Batallador of Aragon, and the reason for his assassination on his return in 1108 are nowhere noted. The event can be but partially reconstructed from three poems, *Ba'alat Keshafim* (The Witch), *Ahah lo yom* (Alas This Is Not a Day of Good Tidings), and *Zot ha-tela'ah* (That Misfortune) by Yehudah Halevi, and the superscriptions on them inserted by later hands. Cf. his *Diwan*, ed. by Brody, I, 14 f. No. 13; II, 92 f. Nos. 11–12 (ed. by Zemorah, III, 341 f.; IV, 69 ff.); and Schirmann's comments thereon in "Life of Yehudah Halevi," *Tarbiz*, IX, 220. It may not be too venturesome to suggest, how-ever, that Solomon's fateful journey and his uncle's loss of status related to the same episode. Through the maze of contradictory reports one may still perceive how deeply aroused the influential circles of Castile were at the death in 1107 of Count Raymond of Burgundy, the husband of Doña Urraca, Alphonso VI's presumptive

heiress. It appears that a faction at court advocated her betrothal to Don Gomez Gonzalez, count of Candespina. Joseph seems to have allowed himself to propose that match to the king, but drew the stinging rebuke, "I do not blame you for presuming to speak thus to me, but rather myself whose familiarity encouraged your boldness." Thus censured, Joseph seems to have gone over to the party favoring Urraca's marriage to Alphonso I of Aragon. Solomon Ferruziel was sent to Aragon to negotiate that compact, which could open the way for the unification of the two most powerful Christian principalities on the Iberian Peninsula. On his return Solomon was murdered by the opposing faction, but when Alphonso VI died in 1109, Doña Urraca married the Aragonese king. As a queen she restored Joseph to his former position. On these complex intrigues and disputes, which gave rise to a variety of biased narratives, cf. *Chronica Adefonsi imperatoris,* ed. by Sanchez Belda, pp. 68 ff. Nos. 90 ff.; A. Ballesteros y Beretta's *Historia de España,* II, 247 ff.; and J. M. Ramos y Loscertales's comprehensive data (not referring to Joseph, however) in "La Sucesión del Rey Alfonso VI," *AHDE,* XIII, 36–99.

47. According to Abraham Ibn Daud, Cidellus had expelled the Karaites "from all the castles of Castile, with the exception of one small castle, for he did not wish to exterminate them." Cf. his *Sefer ha-Qabbalah* (Book of Tradition) in *MJC,* I, 79 ff. These efforts were continued under Alphonso VII and VIII. See *infra,* Chap. XXVI, n. 72. Although Ibn Daud is far from an unbiased chronicler (in fact, he wrote his chronicle primarily for anti-Karaite reasons; see *infra,* Chap. XXVIII, n. 69, we need not doubt these governmental persecutions instigated by influential Rabbanite leaders which help explain the weakness of that sectarian movement on the Iberian Peninsula.

48. Baer, *Juden,* I, Part 1, pp. 12 f. No. 21, 70 ff. No. 78. Cf. R. del Arco's brief survey, "La Aljama judaica de Huesca," *Sefarad,* VII, 271–301. The privilege issued for the benefit of Alaçar embraced his family and that of his son-in-law, and exempted them also from the jurisdiction of any, except the royal, court, running counter to the very fundamentals of Jewish autonomy and communal control. A similar concession was granted in 1178 by Sancho VII of Navarre to his court physician, Solomon, son of his alfaquim, Avenardus, for "numerous and good services." In 1202 Sancho VIII conferred upon two Jewish favorites the right of contributing no more than 1.5 percent of the total amount in royal imposts payable by the community of Tudela. This privilege was to last *per infinita secula seculorum,* and any Jew attempting to subvert it was threatened with royal wrath and a fine of 50 maravedis. Baer, *Juden,* Part 1, pp. 937 ff. Nos. 580, 582.

49. E. Sanchez, ed., *Los Fueros de Sepulveda,* pp. 73 ff. Art. 37–40; Baer, *Juden,* I, Part 2, pp. 9 f. No. 18; Part 1, pp. 48 f. No. 60. The Sepulveda custumal, which also contained different regulations concerning crimes committed by or against Moors (Art. 40–43), clearly reflected later usages. These provisions are absent from the original Latin compilation, confirmed by Alphonso VI in 1076, and are given only in the Romance version. Among the most noteworthy regulations with respect to Jewish *wergeld* in Leon and Castile one may mention the following: Castrojeriz, 974 (equality with Christians); Najera, 1076 (equality with nobles and clerics; this decree was renewed in 1136 and often served as a model elsewhere); Miranda, 1099 (Jews and Moors have general equality of rights with Christians); Toledo Mozarabs,

1101 (pay only one fifth of all fines, except for the slaying or robbing of a Jew or Moor, when they must pay the full amount, "so that the whole town may know the evident truth that he had killed him unjustly"); Belorado, 1116 (equal *wergeld* for Jew and Christian); Alcala de Henares, after 1126 (equal treatment); Escalona, 1130 (equal fine for assault and 300 solidi for the slaying of a Jew); and Avia de Torres, 1130 (equal rights). Cf. Baer, *Juden*, I, Part 2, pp. 1 No. 2, 4 f. No. 11, 8 Nos. 15–17, 11 Nos. 20–22; and *supra*, nn. 32, 35. Cf. also F. Cantera Burgos's ed. and trans. of the *Fuero de Miranda de Ebro*, pp. 75 Art. 36, 137 n. 163, referring also to that of Logroño; his "La Judería de Miranda de Ebro (1099–1350)," *Sefarad*, I, 89–140; R. Ureña y Smenjaud's critical edition of, and detailed commentary on the remarkable *Fuero de Cuenca*, enacted by Alphonso VIII in 1189–90 (on the latter's provision, p. 80, reserving the public baths for Jewish use on Fridays and Sundays, cf. A. Ruiz-Moreño's comments in "Los Baños públicos en los fueros municipales españoles," *CHE*, III, 155 f.; the more general review of Jewish baths in Spain by L. Torres Balbás in "La Judería de Zaragoza y su baño," *Al-Andalus*, XXI, 188 ff.; and *supra*, Chap. XVIII, n. 24); and the few comparative data offered by R. Gilbert in his juridical analysis of the *Fueros de Sepulveda*, in Sanchez's ed., pp. 421 ff. Apparently there were fewer regulations of this type in later years in Castile, and still fewer in Navarre and Aragon, but those which are extant for the most part reveal the same attitude of fair play. Cf. e.g., Baer, *Juden*, I, Part 1, pp. 13 No. 22 (Daroca, 1142), 921 f. Nos. 571 (Carcastillo, 1129?) and 572 (Caseda, 1129). Since there is no evidence of any disparity among these countries in the number of violent crimes, one may only conjecture that the Castilian rulers pursued a more consistent colonizing policy, and hence sought more vigorously to attract Jewish settlers. Among the earlier Castilian *fueros* it was especially that of Sepulveda which sharply discriminated between a Christian murderer of a Jew, who paid only 100 maravedis, and a Jewish murderer of a Christian, who was subject to capital punishment and confiscation of property. Cf. E. Sanchez's ed.; and Baer, *Juden*, I, Part 2, pp. 114 ff. No. 125. However, extant only in its confirmation of 1309, this law seems to reflect the usage of the fourteenth century, rather than that under Alphonso VI. Similar alterations have also been noted in the *fuero* of Alba de Tormes, originally issued in 1140 and published in *Fueros leoneses de Zamora, Salamanca, Ledesma y Alba de Tormes*, ed. by A. Castro and F. de Onís, pp. 287 ff., 297 Art. xii; Baer, *Juden*, I, Part 2, pp. 32 ff. No. 59. Cf. also J. Rodriguez's "Judería de Sahagún," *Archivos Leoneses*, VII, 5–77; and Vallecillo Ávila's pertinent observations in *CHE*, XIV, 39 f., 60 f., 72 ff.

50. E. A. O'Malley's dissertation *Tello and Theotonio, the Twelfth-Century Founders of the Monastery of Coimbra; supra*, Chap. XVIII, n. 45; and *infra*, Chap. XXI, n. 4. Cf. especially the important privilege granted in 1091 by Alphonso VI to the bishop, the count, and the population of Leon in return for a special tax for the prosecution of his war against the Almoravids, in Baer, *Juden*, I, Part 2, pp. 6 ff. No. 14. One must bear in mind, however, the exceptional nature of this decree and its underlying motivations. Otherwise Alphonso VI, like Alphonso VIII, and to a lesser extent Alphonso VII, pursued a far more egalitarian policy. This is indeed the burden of Vallecillo Ávila's reconstruction of the Jewish status in Castile under the three monarchs in *CHE*, Vol. XIV, although his analysis presupposes greater consistency than was customary with rulers subjected to the enormous pull of varying local traditions and temporary exigencies. On the Jewish

attitude toward ordeals, cf. *infra*, n. 63. Cf. also the occasional references to Jews in P. Merêa, *Estudos de direito hispânico medieval*, esp. I, 32 n. 64; II, 207 (referring also to the so-called "Hehlerrecht" of the custumals of Evora and Ledesma); and, more generally, I. de las Cagigas's comprehensive study of the *Minorias etnico-religiosas de la Edad media española* (the first four volumes deal only with the Mozarabs and Mudejares, that is Muslims under Christian domination); and his illuminating general observations on "Problemas de minoría y el caso de nuestro medievo," *Hispania* (Madrid), X, 506–38.

51. *Fuero* of Teruel of 1176, in the passages relating to Jews, reprinted with variants and an introduction in Baer's *Juden*, I, Part 1, pp. 1037 ff., 1043. This law exercised considerable influence on the Jewish status in Castile during the thirteenth century, although its impact can be fully assessed only by comparison with other legislative enactments and records of actual life of that period. On the local background, cf. especially J. Caruana Gomez de Barreda's twin essays, "Alfonso II y la reconquista de Teruel," *Teruel*, VII, 97–141; and "Organización de Teruel en los primeros años suguentes a su reconquista," *ibid.*, X, 9–108 (referring also to his earlier publications in that journal); E. Bayerri y Bertoméu's comprehensive *Historia de Tortosa y su comarca*, Vol. VI (covering the period from 415 to 1148); and *supra*, n. 37. The meaning of Jewish "serfdom" is tentatively discussed *supra*, Chap. XVI, n. 53; and *infra*, nn. 91–92.

52. Cf. the text of the *Usatges*, with a French translation in C. Poumarède's Toulouse dissertation, *Les Usages de Barcelone*, pp. 28 f., 74 f., 118 f., 152 ff.; and the editor's comments, pp. 208 ff., 238, 241, 391 f., 432 ff.; Baer, *Juden*, I, Part 1, p. 3 No. 5. To be sure the *fueros* of Aragon likewise contain a very long formula of Jewish oath (*Los Fueros de Aragon*, II.138–39, ed. by Tilander, pp. 66 ff.). But this text, too, doubtless represents the thirteenth-century expansion, rather than the original form. The evident contradiction between Articles 51 and 129 of the *Usatges*, has long been explained as the difference between criminal prosecution, in which the Jews were not allowed to demand an oath from a Christian, and civil litigations when such an oath was in order. As to the former, the *Usatges* tried to introduce a general class distinction relieving the nobility from all oaths in criminal cases involving ordinary Christians. Cf. Amador de los Rios, *Historia*, I, 253 ff. The interesting provision in the *Usatges de Barcelona*, Art. 75, cited by that author, which imposed a severe fine of twenty gold ounces for a mere verbal reminder of his former status to a converted Jew or Muslim, was another later insertion.

53. Muñoz, *Collección*, p. 537; Baer, *Juden*, I, Part 1, p. 13 No. 22; Pope Stephen's epistle cited *infra*, n. 60; Grayzel, *The Church and the Jews*, pp. 90 f. No. 4, and 112 ff. No. 17. In his letter to the clergy of Barcelona of 1206 (*ibid.*, pp. 118 f. No. 19), Innocent admitted that Christian slave owners were equally guilty of obstructing the path of would-be converts to Christianity, because evidently the official fees for the redemption of such slaves lagged far behind their market price. See *infra*, Chap. XXII. See also, more generally, D. Mansilla's "Innocencio III y los reinos hispanos," *Anthologia Annua*, II, 9–49. Of interest also was the inquiry, addressed by the bishop of Segovia to Clement III (1187–91), about the rights of converts from Judaism or Islam to remarry, if their wives refused to join them in their

new faith. Cf. the pope's affirmative reply in Jaffé and Wattenbach, *Regesta pontificum*, II, 569 No. 16595.

54. Baer, *Juden*, I, Part 1, p. 5 No. 8; Part 2, p. 4 No. 8; Jaffé and Wattenbach, *Regesta pontificum*, I, 572 No. 4582; *supra*, n. 11; and *infra*, Chap. XXI, n. 4. Cf. A. Garcia Gallo's careful juridical analysis of "El Concilio de Coyanza," in *AHDE*, XX, 275–633, also showing the significance of its canons for the development of canon law in Spain; and M. A. Orté Belmonte's recent observations on "El Fuero de Cordoba y las clases sociales en la ciudad. Mudejares y judíos en la Edad Media," *Boletin de la R. Academia de Ciencias . . . de Cordoba*, 1954, pp. 5–94. Through pious donations of rulers, churches and monasteries often acquired control over all or part of the fiscal revenues from Jews. Cf. Baer, *Juden*, I, Part 1, pp. 7 Nos. 11–12, 9 No. 16, 12 No. 20, etc. On the other hand, Ramon Berenger IV specifically exempted the revenue from Jews and Saracens from the gift he made to the bishop of Tortosa in 1151, while the bishop of Saragossa himself in 1175 freed the Jews from all tithes and "first fruit" taxes in return for an annual lump sum (*ibid.*, pp. 18 f. No. 30, 33 f. No. 44). Similar provisions, exemptions therefrom, as well as special immunities for individual Jews, can also be documented from Navarre and Castile.

55. H. Pirenne's well-known theses, best summarized in his *Mohammed and Charlemagne* (English trans., 2d impression, p. 284 ff.), have been effectively controverted by R. S. Lopez (in "Mohammed and Charlemagne," *Speculum*, XVIII, 14–38), D. D. Dennett (in "Pirenne and Muhammad," *ibid.*, XXIII, 165–90), M. Lombard (in "Mahomet et Charlemagne," *Annales*, III, 188–99), and others. They have considerable bearing also on Jewish economic history of that period. See *infra*, Chap. XXII, n. 26. Allowing for all the necessary qualifications, however, they have helped place into bolder relief the growth of the northern territories and the new mediating role of Jews between the two hostile worlds of Islam and Christendom. Cf. also, from another angle, J. Ebersolt's twin studies, *Orient et Occident: Recherches sur les influences byzantines et orientales en France avant les Croisades*, and . . . *pendant les Croisades* (chiefly concerned with artistic influences, they also shed light on other cultural exchanges).

56. Raban Maur's letter to King Ludwig in his *Epistolae*, xviii, in *MGH*, Epistulae, V, 432 (cf. also his letter xiv, p. 403); Alcuin, *Epistolae* lxxvii, *ibid.*, IV, 118 f.; E. S. Duckett's *Alcuin, Friend of Charlemagne; His World and His Works*, pp. 260 ff.; and more specifically "A Preliminary Study of Alcuin's Bible" by E. K. Rand in *HTR*, XXIV, 323–96. On Donnolo see *infra*, Chap. XXXVI. Cf. also P. Rieger's "Wer war der Hebräer dessen Werke Hrabanus Maurus benützt hat?", *MGWJ*, LXVIII, 66–68. Rieger's contention that the archbishop of Mayence only consulted Jewish writings cited in Christian letters is controverted especially by Raban's *Commentary* on Matt. 5:22 (*PL*, CVII, 806). Any Jewish trader, learned in the law, could have shown the Christian author a pertinent passage in a Hebrew book without necessarily being a scholar of note remembered in later Jewish tradition. Such contemporary advice certainly fits Raban's reference to *modernis temporibus* much better than do such writings as Pseudo-Jerome's *Quaestiones*, suggested by M. L. W. Laistner in his "Some Early Medieval Commentaries on the Old Testament," *HTR*, XLVI, 27–46.

It also stands to reason that when Remigius of Auxerre and Theodulf of Orléans made incipient efforts to compare the current Latin versions with the Hebrew text of the Bible, they, too, enlisted the assistance of learned Jews. So did the contemporary author of the *Quaestiones hebraicae in libros Regum et Paralipomenon,* modeled after St. Jerome's *Quaestiones hebraicae in Genesin.* Cf. the latter text in *PL,* XXIII, 983–1062; A. Vaccari's ed. of "Il Genuino commento ai Salmi de Remigio di Auxerre," *Biblica,* XXVI, 52–99; L. Delisle's comments on "Les Bibles de Thédulfe," *Bibliothèque de l'Ecole de Chartres,* XL, 42 f.; L. Ginzberg's observations in *Die Haggada bei den Kirchenvätern,* I (Die Haggada in den pseudo-hieronymianischen Quaestiones), esp. pp. 105 ff.; and B. Smalley's comprehensive analysis of *The Study of the Bible in the Middle Ages,* pp. 37 ff. Precisely such personal contacts with Jewish scholars may have induced Remigius, at sharp variance with his namesake of Lyons, to counsel moderation in condemning Jews for the crucifixion of Christ. In his fifth sermon on Matthew he preached to his listeners that Christian sinners were even more guilty than Jews, for the latter still had a chance to repent for their misdeeds until the second coming of Christ. Cf. his *Sermones* in *PL,* CXXXI, 892 ff. All the Bible commentators here mentioned belong to the second part of the ninth century. But intellectual contacts of this sort doubtless antedated the Peace Treaty of Verdun, although a thinker like Alcuin remained remarkably silent on Jews and Judaism. He merely repeated some stereotype views, such as that contemporary Jews no longer deserved that designation since they adhered too literally to their tradition. The real Jews in spirit were the Christians. Cf. his *Commentary* on Rev. 2:9 in *PL,* C, 1111 f. Cf. also *infra,* Chaps. XXIV and XXIX.

57. The story of Isaac is given in the semi-official *Annales,* attributed to Eginhard (Einhard), under the years 801 and 802. Cf. the text ed. by G. H. Pertz in *MGH,* Scriptores, I, 190 (summarized in Aronius, *Regesten,* p. 26 No. 71). Although Eginhard's work is generally the mainstay for the reconstruction of Charlemagne's period (cf. the judicious weighing of evidence and the literature cited in L. Halphen, *Études critiques sur l'histoire de Charlemagne,* pp. 60 ff.), some scholars have cast doubts on the historicity of these diplomatic exchanges between the two powers and particularly of Isaac's part therein. However, the plausibility of this account is heightened not only by Eginhard's report concerning a new embassy sent by Charlemagne to Baghdad (it returned in 806 accompanied by two monks from Jerusalem and an Arab delegation headed by 'Abdallah; *Annales Eginhardi ad* 802 and 807, in *MGH,* I, 190, 194), but also by his comments thereon in his *Vita Caroli,* XVI (*MGH,* II, 451 f.; in L. Halphen's edition with a French translation, pp. 46 ff.). Writing some thirty years after the event (about 830), this chronicler remarked that the Frankish envoys "had obtained from him [the caliph] what they had asked in behalf of their master." True, he and other ecclesiastical chroniclers were particularly interested in the keys to the Church of the Holy Sepulcher, which had allegedly been brought back by the envoys. Before long this simple donation, whether or not given with the caliph's authorization, was magnified into a conferral, by Harun upon Charlemagne and his successors, of a regular protectorate over the Holy Land. Of more immediate relevance is the chronicler's intimation of the vigilance of Charlemagne's envoys in evading Byzantine outposts in the Adriatic Sea, which clearly betrays the anti-Byzantine background of that friendship pact between the two empires. Cf. the debate between E. Joranson (in

"The Alleged Frankish Protectorate in Palestine," *AHR*, XXXII, 241–61) and L. Bréhier (in "Charlemagne et la Palestine," *RH*, CLVII, 276–91) arguing in the affirmative; F. W. Buckler's somewhat overdrawn picture of the relations between *Harunu'l-Rashid and Charles the Great* ("the action implied the suzerainty of Harun over Charles," pp. 30 f.); W. Björkman's critique thereof in *OLZ*, XXXVI, 693–95; as well as G. Neyron's more general observations on "Charlemagne, les papes et l'Orient," *Orientalia christiana periodica*, XIII, 251–63; and *infra*, Chap. XXII, n. 27.

58. *Gesta Caroli Magni ad Carcassonam et Narbonam*, attributed to "Philomena" and ed. by F. E. Schneegans, pp. 176 ff. The passage pertaining to Jews was reproduced and carefully analyzed by I. Lévi in "Le Roi juif de Narbonne et le Philomène," *REJ*, XLVIII, 197–207, XLIX, 147–50; and again by J. Regné in his aforementioned study of the conditions of Jews in Narbonne, *ibid.*, LV, 13 ff. Important additional data, though of questionable historical value, have been derived from the manuscript of an apologetic treatise, *Milḥemet miṣvah* (Holy War) by the Narbonnese homilist, Meir bar Simon, and from a local Narbonnese extension of Ibn Daud's chronicle, both published by A. Neubauer in his "Documents inédits, XVI: Documents sur Narbonne," *REJ*, X, 98–105. Meir, writing about 1245, exhorted the French authorities to keep their ancient pledges to the Jews. He asserted that King Charles and all his successors "had conquered many lands with the aid of Israelites who served their masters so faithfully with their persons and funds that they entered the thick of battle and sacrificed their lives for kings and commanders. This matter is well known, and is written in many documents in our possession and in that of the *maison d'obédience* [monastery]." Cf. also J. Aronius's interpretation of these data in his "Karl der Grosse und Kalonymos aus Lucca," *ZGJD*, [o.s.] II, 82–87. Curiously, during the last four decades nothing of significance has appeared in either new documentary information or historical interpretation to resolve the riddles posed by these records, which more frequently converge with, than diverge from, one another. On the general background of the "Incursions of the Muslims into France, Piedmont and Switzerland," cf. especially the data culled from Arabic sources in Haroon Khan Sherwani's pertinent essay in *IC*, IV, 397–422, 588–624; V, 71–112, 472–95 (was to be continued); and B. Luppi's summary, *I Saraceni in Provenza, in Liguria e nelle Alpi Occidentali*. A description of the two Jewish quarters in Narbonne (also in Béziers, Nîmes and Uzès) is given by A. Dupont in *Les Cités de la Narbonnaise première*, pp. 432, 527 f. (incidentally mentioning also the local legend about the reign of a Jewish and an Arab king in Narbonne before Pepin, p. 287 n. 2).

59. *Gesta Caroli*, Schneegans's ed., pp. 178 f. In any case, the presence of a large Jewish community in Narbonne in the 750's controverts Julian of Toledo's assertion that after suppressing a revolt, King Wamba had expelled the Jews from Narbonne. Cf. *supra*, Chap. XVI, n. 56. Aronius, Lévi, Régné and other scholars, Jewish and non-Jewish, have taken part in the protracted discussions which tried to segregate the historic kernel of truth from the legendary accretions of this story. But they seem to have overlooked the vital connection between the arrival of Makhir and its parallel to Harun's alleged sacred gifts to the Christian world, and the real appearance in the West of exilarch Naṭronai, generally recognized as a true scion of the house of David. Cf. Sherira Gaon's *Iggeret* (Epistle), ed. by B. M.

Lewin, p. 104; and Yehudah bar Barzillai's *Sefer ha-'Ittim*, ed. by J. Schor, p. 267. From the latter account, especially, we learn that Naṭronai had communicated the knowledge of the Babylonian Talmud to his Western coreligionists. Cf. *infra*, Chap. XXVII, n. 21. His arrival about 772, between Pepin's occupation of Narbonne and Isaac's return from Baghdad, readily lent color to that later historical combination. Moreover, the facts that, following medieval custom, Jews secured confirmation of Pepin's privilege from his sons Carloman and Charlemagne, that the latter repelled a Saracen onslaught on the city in 793 and soon thereafter established the Spanish March, easily led to the substitution of Pepin's name by that of his more famous son. That is why Ibn Daud could refer to Charlemagne as the originator of the favorable privilege for the Jews of Narbonne, "as it is written in a Christian [Latin] charter, confirmed by Charles' seal, which they still possess today." Cf. his *Sefer ha-Qabbalah* in *MJC*, I, 82. A document still extant before 1789 in the abbey of La Grasse, some of whose monks served in prominent positions in Narbonne, contained an alleged confirmation by Charlemagne in 791 of the Jewish "king's" control over a third of the city. Cf. M. Du Mège's "Mémoire sur quelques inscriptions hébräiques découvertes à Narbonne," *Mémoires de la Société Royale des Antiquaires de France*, VIII, 340 n. Cf. also B. Gaillard's ed. of "Une Charte inédite du XIIIᵉ siècle (1269) en faveur des Juifs de Narbonne," *Mémoires de la Société archéologique de Montpellier*, 1920. These difficulties of the documentary tradition are by no means surprising. Even under Charlemagne and Louis the Pious much business was conducted orally, and there are major obscurities in such basic documents as the *capitularia missorum*. Cf. F. L. Ganshof's "Charlemagne et l'usage de l'écrit en matière administrative," *Moyen Age*, LVII, 1–25. The basic authenticity of the original privilege, though not necessarily of the division of the city into three independent sections, has been upheld by a special investigation in a hitherto unpublished paper by my pupil Arthur Zuckerman. On the background, see also R. de Abadal y de Vinyals's observations on "El Paso de Septimania del dominio godo al franco a través de la invasión sarracena, 720–768," *CHE*, XIX, 5–54.

60. Stephen III's (IV) Epistolae, II, in *PL*, CXXIX, 857 (in Jaffé and Wattenbach, *Regesta pontificum*, I, 288 No. 2389); and in Régné's French trans. in *REJ*, LV, 28 f. On the meaning of *"Allodium dans les textes latins du moyen-âge,"* representing as a rule free property, see H. Dubled's pertinent essay in *Moyen Age*, LVII, 241–46. It has long been assumed that the letter was written by Stephen III in 768–69 before Aribert's replacement by Daniel in the bishopric of Narbonne. Cf. Régné's observations, p. 27 n. 3. However, its vigorous denunciations are somewhat out of character with Stephen, a typical "ecclesiastical bureaucrat" who, after his election in August of 768, sought to ingratiate himself to the Frankish rulers. Other objections to its authenticity have been raised by Caro in his *Sozial- und Wirtschaftsgeschichte*, I, 473. These difficulties are removed if we assume that the initiative had been taken by the Narbonne bishop himself, especially during his attendance at the Lateran Council of April, 769, and that the papal epistle was addressed to Daniel. Cf. E. Amann's data in Fliche and Martin, *Histoire de l'Eglise*, VI (L'Epoque carolingienne), pp. 38 ff.; Mansi, *Collectio*, XVIII, 177 f. (Hefele, *Histoire*, III, Part 2, pp. 730 ff.; and more briefly in his *History*, trans. by Clark, V, 331 ff.). From this French ecclesiastical source undoubtedly stemmed also the curious assertion in the letter that the Jewish privileges had been "conceded at a

monetary price by enactments of Frankish kings," the latter phrase apparently taking in both Pepin, who had died in September of 768, and his sons. It is not impossible, however, that this letter was wrongly attributed to Stephen III, having been written instead by some later pope, perhaps Stephen V (885–91), elected to office against the emperor's will, or Stephen VI (896–97) at the time of the empire's final dissolution. Assuming the latter date, E. Camau suggested that as a result of this papal intervention Charles the Simple conferred upon the archbishop in 899 all the lands, houses, and other possessions of Jews in the surrounding county. Cf. Camau's chapter, "Les Juifs en Provence" in *La Provence à travers les siècles*, IV, 268, against Devic and Vaissete's *Histoire générale du Languedoc*, rev. ed., II, Part 1, 340 f.; Part 2, cols. 211 f. No. liv; III, 62 ff. No. lxvi. In 977 certain Jews (four sons of one Abraham) are said to have voluntarily sold a mill from their *allodia* to the Church. Cf. D. de Sainte-Marthe *et al.*, *Gallia christiana*, VI, 142. Cf. also, more generally, A. Dupont's careful review of *Les Cités de la Narbonnaise première*, section iv.

61. Benjamin, *Massa'ot*, pp. 3 f. (Hebrew), 2 ff. (English); Jacob ben Meir Tam, *Sefer ha-Yashar* (Halakhic Treatise), Vienna ed., 1811, fol. 64a No. 579; L. Finkelstein, *Jewish Self-Government in the Middle Ages*, pp. 43, 163 ff. On the commercial importance of these Jewish communities, cf. *infra*, Chap. XXII, n. 30. Like the city as a whole the Marseilles community exerted considerable influence on all of France. Cf. R. Bouquet's pertinent discussion of the pros and cons of the query, "Marseille a-t-elle ou n'a-t-elle civilisé la Gaule?" *RH*, CCXI, 1–10. Of some interest also are the few Jewish epigraphic sources from that region which have come down to us. Cf., for instance, the two Provençal inscriptions republished and analyzed by N. Slouschz in his "Jewish Antiquities in Europe" (Hebrew), *Mabbua*, I, 123–31; and *infra*, n. 79.

62. *Formulae Merovingi et Carolini aevi*, Nos. 30, 31, 52, ed. by K. Zeumer in *MGH*, Legum sectio V: *Formulae*, pp. 309 ff., 314 f., 325 (summarized and commented on in Aronius, *Regesten*, pp. 30 ff. Nos. 81–83). These formulas were in part repeated in a privilege granted Christian (probably Frisian) merchants in 828. Here Louis promised the recipients immunity from seizure of their ships for governmental transportation, freedom from military service, and other rights, provided they would "faithfully serve our palace like the Jews." *Formulae*, No. 37, *MGH*, p. 314 (Aronius, p. 41 No. 98). To be sure, in his "Zum Judenschutzrecht unter den Karolingern," *Neues Archiv für ältere deutsche Geschichtskunde*, XXXIII, 197–200, M. Tangl has plausibly argued for the replacement of the crucial concluding clause, *sicut Judaeis*, by the nondescript *sicut diximus* (as we have said). There also were substantial differences in the respective rights of these merchants and their Jewish confreres. Cf. Caro's comments in his *Sozial- und Wirtschaftsgeschichte*, I, 130 ff., 470. Nevertheless, the striking similarities could not be accidental. It stands to reason that Jews, long accustomed to living under self-governmental institutions, pioneered here in securing autonomy for themselves and, indirectly, also for other foreign merchants. Cf. also F. Rörig's observations on Tangl's emendation in his "Magdeburgs Entstehung und die ältere Handelsgeschichte," *Miscellanea Academica Berolinensia*, published by the Berlin Academy, II, 108 n. 1. Before their standardization these privileges must have borne an individual character. But none of their prototypes issued by Charlemagne himself

has come down to us. His only enactments relating to Jews which the Church-oriented chroniclers and jurists cared to preserve were procedural regulations for litigations among Jews and Christians, and protective regulations for Church property, which some worldly priests had often turned into cash with Jewish assistance. Cf. Aronius, pp. 26 ff. Nos. 72–73, 76–78.

Since most aspects of Carolingian history and administration have long been in the focus of historical scholarship, it is not surprising that only little new information on the status of the Carolingian communities has been forthcoming in either source publications or secondary literature of recent years. A few interesting details and insights, however, may be gleaned from the more recent studies by L. Halphen, *Charlemagne et l'empire carolingien*, rev. ed.; and H. Fichtenau, *Das karolingische Imperium. Soziale und geistige Problematik eines Grossreiches*. Cf. also W. Zuncke's dissertation, *Die Judenpolitik der fränkish-deutschen Könige und Kaiser bis zum Interregnum* (with a strong Nazi coloring). On the problem of relative paucity of charters issued by Charlemagne himself, cf. also F. L. Ganshof's pertinent observations in "Charlemagne et l'usage de l'écrit," *Moyen Age*, LVII, 1 ff. Though stressing the general increase in written documentation, Ganshof admits its great deficiencies.

63. The problem of Jewish flogging has often puzzled scholars familiar with the disappearance from Jewish practice of the regular *malqot* of the talmudic age. However, a substitute form of *makkat mardut* had long been developed in the Eastern communities, and apparently was adopted also in the Frankish Empire. If we may take a clue from the privilege given to David and his associates in Lyons (*Formulae*, No. 31) Louis had previously issued a capitulary stating, among other matters, "for which transgressions they should be coerced through flagellation." No such decree is extant, but Louis had doubtless followed the provisions of Jewish law, as communicated to him by some of his Jewish advisers. In view of the absence of Western rabbinic sources in that period and the considerable uncertainties about the frequency and specific character of corporal punishments in the later rabbinic law, this loss is doubly regrettable. On that problem and that of Jewish oaths, cf. *infra*, n. 78; Chaps. XXIII, n. 14, and XXVII, n. 77; G. Kisch's "Studien zur Geschichte des Judeneides im Mittelalter" and other pertinent essays reprinted in his *Forschungen*, pp. 137 ff.; and F. Bujanda and F. Cantera's "De como han de jurar los Judíos," *Sefarad*, VII, 145–47 (both based mainly on later medieval texts).

64. No *magister Judaeorum* is mentioned in the three charters. The presence of such an official and his intervention in behalf of Jews placed under his protection is evident from the complaints on this score voiced by Agobard (see next note). The aforementioned charter in favor of other merchants (*Formulae*, No. 37) likewise speaks of the appointment of a *magister* (if we accept Zeumer's emendation for *missus*) in charge of merchants. By underestimating the number of non-Jewish merchants in the Carolingian Empire, Aronius (*Regesten*, p. 41 No. 98) advanced the hypothesis that the *magister Judaeorum* also served as protector of all merchants. This seems to be too far-fetched a conclusion from a dubious passage, especially since non-Jewish traders may have enjoyed the protection of their respective tribal laws under the general supervision of such higher authorities, as the *missi dominici*. Despite the awkward formulation, one might even defend the original reading of *missus* as referring to one of these high officials, rather than to the subaltern

magister. On the autonomy, even regular guilds of Frisian merchants, see D. Jellema's recent "Frisian Trade in the Dark Ages." *Speculum*, XXX, 15 ff., 33 f.

65. The term *fideliter* here and in other charters clearly reflected the high standing of their Jewish recipients, treated as the king's *fideles*, or vassals. Cf. C. E. Odegaard's analysis of the terms *Vassi and Fideles in the Carolingian Empire*, esp. pp. 54 ff. Odegaard also emphasizes that the oath of fealty had not yet become universal (p. 78). The Lyons charter's limitation of the right of Jewish owners freely to dispose of their landed property seems to have been exceptional. Donatus and his nephew were specifically authorized to sell their possessions, as well as to exchange them with whomever they wished. When in 839 Louis found himself obliged to restore to the Jew Gaudiocus and his sons two estates of which they had been deprived by some "malevolent" persons, he specifically provided that they and their descendants should have free disposition over these lands and be allowed to sell, exchange, or give them away. Cf. the text in the *Diplomata Ludovici Pii Imperatoris*, No. 232, in M. Bouquet's *Recueil des historiens des Gaules et de la France*, new ed. by L. Delisle, VI, 624 (Aronius, *Regesten*, pp. 42 f. No. 102). This enactment was both liberal and outspoken and contrasts favorably, with for instance, with the emperor's conferral on Count Oliba of the free right of disposition over two villages in the same region (834). Cf. "Un Diplome inconnu de Louis le Pieux pour le Comte Oliba de Carcassonne," ed. and commented upon by R. d'Abadal in *Annales de Midi*, LXI, 345–57. The very fact, however, that such rights depended on the king's more or less arbitrary decision underscored the peculiar nexus between Jewish status and royal protection.

66. These similarities are so far-reaching that they gave rise to the theory of the "alien law" (*Fremdenrecht*) origins of medieval Jewish "serfdom." The main expounder of this much-debated theory was J. E. Scherer in his still very useful study of *Die Rechtsverhältnisse der Juden in den deutsch-österreichischen Ländern*, which includes a comprehensive introduction of more than a hundred pages devoted to the analysis of the general principles of medieval European legislation concerning Jews. Although Scherer's theory has in part been controverted by subsequent legal research (especially such works by G. Kisch as *The Jews in Medieval Germany: a Study of Their Legal and Social Status*, including an extensive bibliography), there remained enough parallels between the two groups to create the impression of their interlocking in the minds of medieval men even more than in those of modern scholars. Whatever their actual historic origins, therefore, these interrelations explain many regnant ideas in medieval jurisprudence and their impact on the realities of Jewish status. A fuller analysis of these aspects must be postponed, however, to our treatment of the later period and its more clearly articulate sources.

67. Agobard of Lyons, *De judaicis superstitionibus*, in *PL*, CIV, 77 ff. (*MGH*, Epistulae V, 185 ff.); and the reference thereto in his *De insolentia Judaeorum*, v. *ibid.*, col. 75 (*MGH*, pp. 182 f.). On the use of canonical collections as a means of stemming undesirable innovations also in Jewish affairs, see *supra*, n. 18. On the Old Testament legacy in the imperial evolution under Charlemagne and his successors cf. the studies by M. David, "Le Serment du sacre du IXe au XVe siècle," *Revue du moyen-âge latin*, VI, 5–272 (was to be continued; includes discussion of "Le precédent biblique," pp. 24 ff.); and E. Rieber, "Die Bedeutung alttestament-

licher Vorstellungen für das Herrscherbild Karls des Grossen und seines Hofkreises" (unpublished diss. Tübingen).

Neither the precise date nor even the sequence of the five anti-Jewish writings by Agobard are definitely known, although they all seem to date from the first half of Louis' reign; more specifically from 822 to 828. If these dates are correct, Agobard's reference in *De insolentia Judaeorum* (*PL*, CIV, 76; *MGH*, Epistulae, V, 185) to consultations with brother priests could refer to the Council of Lyons of 821, as is suggested in *PL*, note *e*. These writings are most conveniently available in *PL*, CIV; and *MGH*, Epistulae, V. This complicated question has recently been reopened by B. Blumenkranz in a searching reexamination of "Deux compilations canoniques de Florus de Lyon et l'action antijuive d'Agobard," *RHDF*, 4th ser. XXXI, 227–54, 560–82. Concentrating on the so-called excerpt "Ex epistola episcopi . . . de baptizatis hebreis" (see *infra*, n. 71), of which he republishes an improved version in the context of a general legal compilation from a Troyes MS, Blumenkranz has made a strong case for placing the letter in the early period of Agobard's career between 816 and 825. This would, then, be the archbishop's first anti-Jewish epistle. Blumenkranz's most telling argument is that after 840 no single ruler could have been asked to order local authorities from Mâcon to Arles, since these provinces had been divided between Lothar and Charles the Bald. However, the bishop was really interested only in forcing the hand of the Arles authorities and an appeal to Lothar should have sufficed. Such an early date would raise other difficulties which cannot be elaborated here. Our treatment follows, therefore, for the time being, the accepted sequence of the anti-Jewish activities of the three archbishops Agobard, Amulo and Remigius. Their main juridical adviser was, in any case, the same Florus, deacon of Lyons. Cf. esp. the literature listed *infra*, n. 71. Although frequently cited by modern vulgar antisemites, Agobard himself was too honest a person to be placed in the same category. In many ways he was merely the most effective spokesman of the canonical tradition which, he felt, was being undermined by the new feudal "anarchy." For this reason he bent every effort on securing legal unification through some combination of canon and Salic laws. Cf. his interesting letter to the emperor of 817, in *PL*, CIV, 113 ff. (*MGH*, Epistulae, V, 158 ff.). His anti-Jewish agitation must be understood, therefore, against this background of his total outlook and activity. Cf. the older but still very useful study by R. Foss, *Leben und Schriften Agobards Erzbischofs von Lyon* (on p. 106 explaining the designation *Saint* Agobard used by Baluze and others); and the more recent biographies by Brussolles, *Saint Agobard*, and J. A. Cabaniss, *Agobard of Lyons: Churchman and Critic*. His anti-Jewish polemics were comprehensively reviewed half a century ago by F. Wiegand in his "Agobard von Lyon und die Judenfrage," *Festschrift . . . Luitpold von Bayern*, I, 221–50. Cf. also A. L. Williams's "Haman-Agobard or St. Agobard?" *Church Quarterly Review*, CXV, 67–78; and the English excerpts from Agobard's writings in his *Adversus Judaeos*, pp. 348 ff.

68. Agobard's *De insolentia Judaeorum* II, III, V, in *PL*, CIV, 69 ff. (*MGH*, Epistulae, V, 182 ff.); and other passages excerpted and commented upon by Aronius in his *Regesten*, pp. 33 ff. Nos. 84–96. Agobard was particularly aroused by the prohibition to convert pagan slaves of Jews, the preferential treatment often accorded to Jews at court, and the overt promotion of their trade through the transfer of fairs from Saturday to other days including Sunday. Cf. *infra*, Chap.

XXII, n. 30. We may believe him that he had found himself facing the dilemma: "If we observe that order [to abstain from converting slaves against the will of their Jewish owners], we run counter to the ecclesiastical rules and offend God. If we follow the latter we fear the emperor's indignation, especially since the *magister* of the infidel Jews threatens us constantly that he would call in the *missi* from the palace who will hold judgment over us and restrain us from such acts" (*De baptismo judaicorum mancipiorum*, in *PL*, CIV, 176; *MGH*, Epistulae, V, 181). Evidently the *missi* intervened, but could not restrain the outspoken critic.

69. Cf. Prudentius' Trecensis in *Annales Bertiniani*, in *MGH*, Scriptores, I, 433; Amulo's *Contra Judaeos*, XLII, in *PL*, CXVI, 171; Eleazar-Bodo's correspondence with Alvarus published by H. Florez in his *España sagrada*, XI, 171 ff.; and J. Madoz's critical ed. of *Epistolario de Alvaro de Cordoba*, *passim*. Both editions contain only Alvarus' letters. Florez was unable to reproduce more than a mere beginning of Eleazar's reply because the remaining 14 lines of that page in the old Cordovan MS had been erased and several pages removed by the previous owner, "lest the transgressor's delirious outpourings be read" (pp. 177 f.). The inadequacy of the existing texts of our main record is stressed by F. L. Ganshof in his "Notes critiques sur les 'Annales Bertiniani,'" *Mélanges dediés à la mémoire de Felix Grat*, II, 159–74. Cf. M. Kayserling's "Eleasar und Alvaro: ein Fragment," *MGWJ*, IX, 241–51; and A. Cabaniss's more recent essays on "Bodo-Eleazar: a Famous Jewish Convert," *JQR*, XLIII, 313–28; and "Paulus Albarus of Muslim Cordova," *Church History*, XXII, 99–112 (on pp. 104 f. he expresses doubts about Alvarus's Jewish origin). On the general aspects of conversion to Judaism, including further details of the Alvarus-Bodo controversy, cf. B. Blumenkranz, "Les Auteurs chrétiens latins du moyen âge sur les Juifs et le Judaïsme," *REJ*, CXIV, 377 ff.; and *infra*, Chap. XXIV, nn. 40 and 56.

70. R. Anchel in *Les Juifs de France*, p. 97. On feudalism's impact on Jewish economic life, cf. *infra*, Chap. XXII, n. 15. The broad implications of the Church's propaganda for an ever expanding *treuga Dei* are briefly discussed by R. Bonnaud-Delamare in "Fondement des institutions de paix au XIe siècle," *Mélanges Louis Halphen*, pp. 19–26. Cf. also *infra*, n. 90.

71. "Ex epistola episcopi ad imperatorem de baptizatis Hebraeis," appended to Deacon Florus' *Opera* in *PL*, CXIX, 422; and Blumenkranz's edition, cited *supra*, n. 67. As pointed out by Aronius (*Regesten*, pp. 40 f. No. 112), the heading ascribes this compilation to Florus, probably the deacon of Lyons. On this important apologist and poet, cf. the data summarized by P. Godet in "Florus," *Dictionnaire de théologie catholique*, VI, 53–55; and by C. Chartier in "Une Oeuvre inconnue de Florus de Lyon: la collection *De Fide* de Montpellier," *Traditio*, VIII, 81–109 (he believes that this compilation dates from 825–30). Since Florus, however, served under Remigius, as well as under Amulo and Agobard, the attribution to any of these archbishops still remains open. On the general difficulty of keeping apart these authors of contemporary epistles, see E. Amann's remarks in Fliche and Martin, *Histoire de l'église*, VI, 332 f. On the administrative difficulties of the period, cf. E. Fournal, "Recherches sur les comtes de Lyon aux IXe et Xe siècle," *Moyen Age*, LVIII, 221–52. Cf. also *infra*, Chap. XXIV.

72. *Annales Bertiniani* to 848, in *MGH*, Scriptores, I, 443 (see *supra* n. 69); other chronicles reproduced in Bouquet, *Recueil*, IX, 115 ff.; X, 154 f.; and I. Lévi's analysis of these and other data in "Les Juifs de France du milieu du IXᵉ siècle aux croisades," *REJ*, LII, 161–68 (was to be continued). On Toulouse, cf. also G. Saige, "De la condition des Juifs dans la comté de Toulouse avant le XIVᵉ siècle," *Bibliothèque de l'Ecole de Chartres*, XXXIX, 255–322, 432–80; XL, 424–56; and R. Limouzin-Lamothe's more recent study of *La Commune de Toulouse et les sources de son histoire, 1120–1249*. The Jewish quarter in Béziers is described by G. Galtier in his "Béziers, étude de géographie urbaine," *Bulletin* of the Société languedocienne de géographie, 2d ser. XIX, 3–125. Cf. also, more generally, the data assembled by C. Roth in "The Eastertide Stoning of the Jews and Its Liturgical Echoes," *JQR*, XXXV, 361–70.

73. Benjamin, *Massa'ot*, pp. 5 (Hebrew), 4 (English); Camau, *Provence*, pp. 276 ff.; and Albanès, *Gallia christiana novissima*, III, 247 No. 635. Curiously, the Jewish community of Arles, already accused of disloyalty by the sixth-century bishop Caesarius (see *supra*, Vol. II, p. 398 n. 10) seemed to suffer no permanent ill effects from the tensions generated by the Saracen incursions of the eighth and ninth centuries. This generally friendlier local attitude to Jews also helps to explain the persistence of the Jewish community there to the end of the fifteenth century, long after the expulsions from other French territories. Cf. also *infra*, nn. 76, 78; H. Gross, *Gallia judaica, Dictionnaire géographique de la France d'après les sources rabbiniques*, pp. 73 ff.

74. Odorannus, *Chronicon*, in *PL*, CXLII, 771; Raoul Glaber's and Adhémar de Chabannes' chronicles in Bouquet, *Recueil*, X, 34 f., 152; A. Berliner's ed. of an excerpt from a Hebrew Parma MS (which he called "A Horrible Story") in *MWJ*, III, 220, and its Hebrew section (*Oṣar tob*), pp. 46–48, reprinted in A. M. Habermann's *Sefer Gezerot Ashkenaz ve-Ṣarefat* (Records of Anti-Jewish Persecutions in Germany and France), pp. 19 ff., and translated into French by S. Schwarzfuchs in his "Chroniques hébraïques du XIᵉ siècle," *Evidences*, VI, No. 41, pp. 33–37; Lévi in "Les Juifs de France," *REJ*, LII, 164 ff.; and Gross, *Gallia judaica*, pp. 32, 71 ff. Cf. also *supra*, n. 17. On the enforced attendance at missionary sermons, see G. P. Browe, *Die Judenmission*, pp. 13 ff.

If we are to accept also the rather confused conclusion of the Parma fragment, we may have here the first testimony to Jewish settlers in Flanders. Count Baldwin IV, we are told, invited Jacob and thirty associates to settle in that province some twelve years after Jacob's return to Lotharingia (about 1024). Jacob died here (in Arras?), but had to be buried in distant Reims. Cf. Gross, *Gallia judaica*, p. 72. J. Stengers's skepticism on this score seems unjustified. Cf. his otherwise admirably documented study, *Les Juifs dans les Pays-Bas au Moyen Age*, pp. 85 f. Perhaps the intensification of relations between Flanders and the German Empire, shown by the conferrals of imperial estates as fiefs on Baldwin IV and other Flemish counts, stimulated Jewish traders to settle in the country and the counts to attract them there. Cf. F. L. Ganshof's study of "Les Origines de la Flandre impériale," *Annales de la Société r. d'archéologie de Bruxelles*, XLVI, 99–173 (includes four appendixes by F. Hofmans *et al.*). On the Jews of Reims, which was the ecclesiastical center of the dioceses of Tournai, Arras and other parts of Flanders, cf. the older and undocumented, and yet useful, summary by E. Cahen, *Les Juifs à Reims au moyen âge (Xe siècle) et la fondation de la nouvelle communauté et sa synagogue (1879)*.

75. Mann, *The Jews in Egypt*, I, 32 ff.; A. Büchler, "Relation d' Isaac b. Dorbelo sur une consultation envoyée par les Juifs du Rhin en l'an 960 aux communautés de Palestine," *REJ*, XLIV, 238; and the extensive comments thereon listed in A. Freimann's "Verbindungen von Juden in Deutschland mit denen in Babylonien und Palästina während des Mittelalters bis zum ersten Kreuzzuge," *ZGJD*, I, 166 n. 8. We must disregard many overtly legendary accretions in both these accounts. L. Musset's remark on another story by Glaber that "neither his first-hand informa-tion, nor his literary reference is derived from respectable sources," applies to our portion of his narrative as well. Cf. Musset's "Raoul Glaber et la baleine," *RMAL*, IV, 172. Whatever we think, however, of his factual dependability, Glaber certainly reflected the opinions and prejudices of his generation. Cf. P. Rousset's "Raoul Glaber, interprète de la pensée commune au XIe siècle," *Revue d'his-toire de l'église de France*, XXXVI, 5–24. We may decidedly accept the historicity of the initial hostility of many bishops toward the Jews (Glaber and Adhémar) and of Jacob's appeal to the supreme pontiff (Parma MS). In any case, the con-nection of the Egyptian disturbances with the Byzantine campaign of 999 is evident from the description by the Christian chronicler Yaḥya ibn Sa'id of Antioch. See his *Histoire*, ed. by J. Kratchkovsky and A. Vasiliev in *PO*, XXIII, 459 ff. Cf. also *supra*, Chap. XVIII, nn. 3–5; *infra*, n. 85; and Chaps. XXI, nn. 2–3; XXIV, n. 40.

76. Albanès, *Gallia christiana*, Aix, col. 57; Arles, I, 97; A. Luchaire, *Louis VI le Gros*, pp. clvi ff., 74 No. 140; J. L. A. Huillard-Bréholles, *Historia diplomatica Friderici Secundi*, II, Part 1, pp. 473 ff. (in Frederick II's confirmation of 1225); Gross, *Gallia judaica*, p. 77; Camau, *Provence*, pp. 272, 278 ff.; *Papsturkunden in Frankreich*, ed. by H. Meinert and J. Ramacker, II, 116 No. 45. Cf. also J. de Font Réaulx, "Diplomes de Conrad III et Frédéric Barbarousse pour le Royaume d'Arles," *Bibliothèque de l'Ecole des Chartres*, CVIII, 124–26 (together with U. Brumon defending the authenticity of most of these decrees, impugned by H. Hirsch); and P. Kehr's ed. of *Die Urkunden der deutschen Karolinger*, II, 227 f. No. 242 (Charles III confirms in 886 the transfer of a "village called Judaeis" in the vicinity of Chartres). The churches' jurisdiction over Jews was frequently facilitated by the physical proximity of the Jewish quarter to the cathedral. Despite objections by Gregory the Great and other churchmen because Christian worshipers were some-times disturbed by voices penetrating from a neighboring synagogue, this top-ographical closeness existed in many localities. Apart from the Jewish quest for greater security by living in the immediate vicinity of a cathedral or baronial castle, the common origin of many Jewish quarters and these central buildings from ancient historic sites accounted for their location in the heart of town. We have seen (*supra*, Chap. XVI, n. 60) that the Jewish quarter in Paris was located at the crossroads of early trade routes existing in Roman times. Confluence of settlers along neighboring trade routes was also responsible for "Le Peuple-ment de Toulouse aux XIIe siècle," according to C. Higounet in *Annales de Midi*, LV, 489–98. For the same reason the main church of Poitiers was located close to the synagogue, and the Jewish quarter occupied the central position as one of

two thoroughfares dividing the Gallo-Roman city, although we have no definite evidence of the presence of Jews there before the tenth century. Cf. [J.B.] Vincent's data in "Les Juifs de Poitou, au bas moyen âge," *Revue d'histoire économique et sociale*, XVIII, 267 f. (also reprint). In some cases, the Jews themselves outgrew the bounds of their original quarters, and had to move elsewhere. This may have been the main reason for the existence of two Jewish quarters each in Narbonne and Marseilles, although the division of sovereignty between viscount and archbishop may have been a contributory cause. On the vacillating status of these "sovereigns" themselves, cf. M. Zarb's pertinent remarks in her "Du statut juridique des vicomtes de Marseille aux XIe et XIIe siècles," *RHDF*, 4th ser. XXVII, 239–55. Certainly, no such political reasons can be advanced, for instance, for the existence of two Jewish quarters in the important city of Troyes, Champagne. Cf. my remarks in "Rashi and the Community of Troyes," *Rashi Anniv. Vol.*, pp. 51 f.

77. Devic and Vaissete, *Histoire générale de Languedoc*, V, 734 ff. No. cccx (on col. 899 document reproduced in the first ed., II, 418 No. ccclxxxviii has been omitted); Baer, *Juden*, I, Part 1, p. 15 No. 26; Benjamin, *Massa'ot*, pp. 73 (Hebrew), 81 (English); U. T. Holmes, Jr., *Daily Living in the Twelfth Century*, pp. 65 f., 277 nn. 63–65. Very frequent were the prohibitions, such as that enacted by William V of Montpellier in 1121 and repeated by his successors in the following years, to employ Jews as bailiffs. This prohibition did not prevent these very rulers from employing a Jew Saltiel as a fiscal agent. Cf. S. Kahn's "Documents inédits sur les Juifs de Montpellier au moyen âge," *REJ*, XIX, 259. Incidentally the Hebrew name of that city, *Har ga'ash* (Mountain of Trembling) seems to offer as good an explanation of that unusual name, as any of those suggested by modern French scholars. Cf., e.g., M. Grammont's equation with "strong mountain" in "Une Etymologie de 'Montpellier'," *Revue des langues romanes*, LXX, 39–40. Cf. also the data culled from scattered sources in Caro, *Sozial- und Wirtschaftsgeschichte*, I, 354 f., 502 ff.; H. Gasnos, *Etude historique sur la condition des Juifs dans l'ancien droit français*; and E. H. Perreau's succinct review of "Condition des Juifs dans notre ancienne France," *Mémoires de l'Académie des Sciences de Toulouse*, 13th ser., IV, 281–97; as well as the local histories by G. Saige, *Les Juifs au Languedoc antérieurement au XIVe siècle;* his monograph on Toulouse in *Bibliothèque de l'Ecole des Chartres*, XXXIX, 255–322, 432–80; XL, 424–56; E. Azémard, *Etude sur les Israélites de Montpellier au moyen âge*, especially pp. 35 ff.; Léon Kahn, *Les Juifs à Paris depuis le VIe siècle*, Chap. I; S. Kahn, "Les Juifs de Posquières et de Saint-Gilles au moyen-âge," *Mémoires de l'Académie de Nimes*, 7th ser. XXXV, Part 3, 1–21; M. Ginzburger, "La Première communauté israélite de Strasbourg (des environs de 1150 à 1349)," *Publications de la Faculté des Lettres de l'Université de Strasbourg*, CIV, 65–92 (discusses also possible earlier origins); and other monographs listed by R. Anchel in the selected bibliography appended to *Les Juifs en France*, pp. 281 ff.; as well as many documentary studies published in *REJ*, titles of which can readily be ascertained with the aid of the full index to the first fifty volumes and the list of articles in Vols. LI–C. A good reference work, despite its partial obsoleteness and exclusive orientation on rabbinic sources, still is H. Gross's *Gallia judaica*, emphasizing the intellectual developments in various communities. More socially oriented are the monographs *La Vie privée en France au XIe siècle d'après les commentaires de Rachi* by P. Klein (thesis at the Ecole des Chartres, typescript); and *The Social Life of the Jews in Northern France in*

the XII–XIV Centuries as Reflected in the Rabbinical Literature of the Period, by
L. I. Rabinowitz. A more up-to-date study of the legal position of Jews under the
later Carolingian and early Capetian kings still is a major desideratum. The
pertinent chapters in H. Gaillard's juridical thesis, *La Condition des Juifs dans
l'ancienne France,* largely based on stray items in secondary literature, have added
little to our knowledge of this subject. The age-old controversy on the meaning
of feudalism and its impact on European history likewise still is far from concluded.
Cf. C. Stephenson's review of these debates on "The Origin and Significance of
Feudalism" (1941), reprinted in his *Mediaeval Institutions: Selected Essays,* pp.
205–33; and F. L. Ganshof's concise study of *Feudalism* (English trans. by Grierson), with special reference to the region between the Loire and the Rhine before
the thirteenth century.

78. Cf. the text in C. Giraud, *Essai sur l'histoire du droit français au moyen
âge,* II, 203, 234, 244 f. (Leges municipales Arelatis, Nos. 42, 146, 193), and his
general observations *ibid.,* I, 328 ff.; Camau, *Provence,* pp. 280 f. As pointed out by
Giraud, the text of the oath reveals similarities with that of the *Usatges of
Barcelona* which, however, is much longer. See *supra,* n. 52. There is no comprehensive study of the Jewish content of the French custumals and other local
statutes, and of their impact upon Jewish status. For the most part compiled in
the thirteenth century or later, they include some indubitably older provisions.
These local records may be supplemented, here as elsewhere, by archaeological
data such as were assembled half a century ago by S. Fassin in "Le Viel Arles. Le
Montjuif et les cimetières israélites," *Bulletin de la Société des Amis du Viel-Arles,*
1903–4; and, more generally, in M. Schwab's *Rapport sur les inscriptions hébraïques
de la France.* More recently D. Sidersky has briefly commented on "L'Inscription
hébraïque de Saint-Gabriel à Tarascon," *REJ,* XCIX, 123–26, suggesting the date
of 1193, as against the more widely held date of 1196. The general effect, political
and economic, of the rise of the medieval city on the Jewish communities will
be discussed further *infra,* Chap. XXII, n. 2. Cf. also *supra,* n. 61.

79. A. Luchaire, *Etudes sur les actes de Louis VII,* p. 143 No. 136; and *supra,*
n. 74. On the problem of relapsed converts, whose number always increased after
temporary mass conversions resulting from decrees of expulsion or massacres, cf.
supra, Chaps. XVI, nn. 13, 47 and 51; XIX, n. 14; and *infra,* Chap. XXI, nn. 21
and 38.

80. Alexander III's letter to Wido, archbishop of Sens, 1179, in Bouquet, *Recueil,*
XV, 968 No. 408; Robert Altissiodorensis, *Chronologia, ibid.* XVIII, 248; Rigord, *Gesta
Philippi Augusti,* I, *ibid.,* XVII, 5 ff.; and other sources conveniently listed in Caro,
Sozial- und Wirtschaftsgeschichte, I, 504 f. The mainly economic motivations are by
no means controverted by the youthful king's occasional generosity toward converts.
One of these, named Philip (perhaps because the king served as his godfather) was
freed, in 1180, from all imposts, together "with all his heirs." Cf. *Chartres et diplômes
relatifs à l'histoire de France,* published by the Académie des Inscriptions et
Belles Lettres, VI, 22 f. No. 16. While the text of the decree of expulsion is not
extant, we have a confirmation of a sort in Rigord's narrative of the king's receipt,
issued before April 17, 1183, for 45 livres from Abbot Hugo of Chateau-Landon
as a quit-claim for the abbot's debts to Jews. *Ibid.,* p. 83 No. 62. According

to Rigord himself, several archbishops soon joined many worldly lords in object-
ing to the royal move. They certainly helped defeat Philip II's evident plans
to secure the expulsion of Jews from all of France. Caro's reconstruction of the
events (pp. 360 ff.), often at variance with Rigord's report, merely follows the traditional view of blaming most outbreaks of medieval intolerance on clerical
propaganda. But, according to all extant sources, the hierarchy was nowhere im-
plicated in either the initiation of Philip II's decree or its execution. Its suddenness
is well illustrated by the developments in the important community of Etamps.
A short time before (1179–80), Louis VII had specifically forbidden the Jewish
elder to arrest Jewish and non-Jewish visitors at fairs of that city, or to seize their
merchandise on account of unpaid debts (Art. 25). Now Jews were expelled and
their synagogue converted into a church. Cf. *Ordonnances des rois de France*, XI,
211 ff.; and, on the date, Luchaire's *Etudes*, pp. 336 f. No. 759. Of course, individual
monks like Bernard, whom the youthful king held in great veneration, may have
instilled in the latter's receptive mind enough antagonism to Jews to account in
part for the decree of expulsion. The king's uncle, Willelmus, Archbishop of Reims,
may also have given the decree at least his tacit approval. Cf. also Anchel's reference
to a Paris MS in *Juifs de France*, p. 102; A. Temko's nostalgic description of
"The Dark Age of Medieval Jewry: Persecution, Expulsion, the End of the Paris
Synagogue," *Commentary*, XX, 228–39; and *infra*, Chap. XXI, n. 60.

Curiously, the controversy over Christian servants of Jews continued for many
years. As late as 1205 Innocent III still tried in vain to impress on Philip the
necessity of adhering to that canonical prohibition. Unable to secure compliance
from the king, the pope appealed to the French episcopate to threaten all offenders
with excommunication. Cf. his letters of January 16, and July 15, 1205, reproduced
in Grayzel, *The Church and the Jews*, pp. 104 ff., 114 ff. In his second letter the
pope mentioned similarly futile intercessions with Duke Odo III of Burgundy
and Countess Blanche of Champagne. This lack of success is doubly noteworthy if,
as Caro suggested (p. 366), these papal letters had been written in conjunction
with the concordat concluded by Philip with the Church of Normandy, upon
that province's return to French control in 1204. Here the clergy was specifically
authorized to excommunicate the Christian concubines (*meretrices;* the more
correct reading probably is *nutrices* or nurses) of Jews. Cf. Grayzel, p. 46 n. 24.
It is small wonder, then, that in 1244 Innocent IV had once again to appeal to
the Crown of France to stem such employment.

81. Cf. Rigord's *Gesta*, in Bouquet, *Recueil*, XVII, 6, 10, 36, 48 f.; Guillaume
Brita (Amoricus), *Gesta Philippi Augusti, ibid.*, pp. 66, 71, 73; XX, 740, 748, 760;
Saige, *Juifs au Languedoc*, p. 39; E. Azémard, *Etudes sur les Israélites de Montpellier
au moyen âge*, pp. 508 f.; L. Delisle, *Catalogue des Actes de Philippe-Auguste*, pp.
203, Nos. 890, 890A; 230 f., No. 1003; *Chartres et diplômes* of the Académie des
Inscriptions, VI, 129 ff. Nos. 581–83, 549 f. No. 955. On the English chirograph
offices see *infra*, n. 109; and Chap. XXII, n. 69. The rather dubious events of 1191
in Bray are discussed *infra*, Chap. XXI, n. 44. The treaty of 1198 seems to have
been connected with a general treaty between the king and Count Theobald of
Champagne. In this context Caro (p. 505) also enumerates numerous renewals of
the treaty aimed at extraditing Jews, and similar ones concluded by the king
with other feudal lords and between these lords themselves. By 1204 another
document of Philipp Augustus already enumerates 41 Jewish heads of households

residing in the royal possessions (26 in Ile de France, 15 in Normandy). Cf. Delisle's *Catalogue*, pp. 508 f. (omitted in *Chartres et diplômes*, VI); L. Kahn, *Juifs à Paris*, pp. 10 ff. Ultimately, Philip II was even prepared to pay a substantial price for additional Jews. He acquired all those belonging to his brother, Count of Alençon, for the large sum of 20,000 small Tourraine pounds, while Countess Blanche of Champagne, with whom he had renewed the earlier treaty in 1210, "purchased" the Jewish subjects of the Lord of Ervy. Cf. N. Brussel, *Nouvelle examen de l'usage des fiefs en France*, I, 579 f., 604; and U. Robert, "Catalogue d'actes relatifs aux Juifs pendant le moyen-âge," *REJ*, III, 211 f. This valuable summary covers only the period of 1183–1300. On the clergy's unfavorable reaction to such deals, cf. Anchel, *Juifs de France*, p. 102.

82. *Tosafot* on B. Q. 58a *s.v. Inammi*, also quoted with approval by Naḥmanides in his *Resp.* No. 46, in S. Assaf's ed. of *Sifran shel rishonim* (Book of Ancients), p. 88. According to an unnamed Tosafist (on B. Q. fol. 113a *s.v. Noderin*), some masters forced their Jewish subjects to swear that they would not leave their lands. Because of the enforced nature of that oath, the rabbi permitted mental reservations nullifying it, although generally Jewish law was opposed to such subterfuges. These discussions in the medieval juristic literature reveal the frequent embarrassment of rabbis torn between their loyalty to the state, abetted by the old talmudic principle of the respect due to "the law of the kingdom," and the harsh reality of these lords' often insufferable demands. On the general problems of that talmudic principle and its medieval modifications and elaborations, cf. *infra*, Chaps. XXI, n. 60; and XXIII, n. 93.

83. Cf. R. Folz's data in *Le Souvenir et la légende de Charlemagne dans l'Empire germanique médiéval;* supplemented by his *Etudes sur le culte liturgique de Charlemagne dans les églises de l'Empire;* Aronius, *Regesten*, pp. 51 f. Nos. 119, 121. The early history of Jews in Germany has been the subject of careful scrutiny for the last century. Research in this field received a special stimulus from the organization, in 1885, of the Historische Commission für die Geschichte der Juden in Deutschland, which published five vols. of *ZGJD* [o.s.], and several basic collections of texts. Apart from many communal histories, a host of articles appeared in that journal (revived in a new series in 1929–37), the *MGWJ*, various yearbooks, as well as in the general historical and literary periodicals. Not surprisingly, Nazi historiography evinced considerable interest only in later phases of German-Jewish history which, because of frequent tensions, had produced numerous antisemitic manifestations in both life and letters. But it was practically silent with respect to the more moderate historic evolution before the First Crusade, and had little to say about the fairly tolerant policies of the first emperors, including the otherwise much-exalted Charlemagne (often disparaged, however, in comparison with his Saxon opponent, Widukind) and Frederick I. One will look in vain, for example, for any substantial contribution to that period in the eight volumes of *Forschungen zur Judenfrage* which allotted more space to antiquity. Such Nazi "specialists" in Jewish history as G. Kittel and W. Grau paid exclusive attention to either ancient times or the later Middle Ages and the modern period. Cf. *supra*, Vols. I, p. 370 n. 6; II, p. 406 n. 42. Despite their bias, Kittel's researches, cited there, produced some additional evidence for the presence of Jews in Roman Treves, a subject which had been debated by A. Altmann (see *ibid.*), by A. Kober

in his and K. Galling's reviews of Altmann's study in *ZGJD*, IV, 210–13; and in Kober's article "Trier" in *Germania Judaica: von den ältesten Zeiten bis 1238*, ed. by M. Brann *et al.*, pp. 376 ff., 380 n. 13. The numerous legends current in various parts of medieval Europe concerning the great antiquity of the local Jewish settlement will be discussed *infra*, Chap. XXIII. Of considerable interest are the older bibliographical surveys by Kober, "Die Geschichte der deutschen Juden in der historischen Forschung der letzten 35 Jahre," *ZGJD*, I, 13–23; and Z. (H.) Lichtenstein, "Recent Literature on the History of the Jews in Germany" (Hebrew), *Tarbiz*, II, 218–34. Many later bibliographical entries were listed by G. Kisch in *The Jews in Medieval Germany*; and his more recent *Forschungen zur Rechts- und Sozialgeschichte der Juden in Deutschland während des Mittelalters*. Although mainly concerned with the legal developments, these volumes mention studies in many related fields as well. Remarkably, however, we do not possess a comprehensive scholarly history of German Jewry. I. Elbogen's *Geschichte der Juden in Deutschland*; and M. Lowenthal's independent publication, *The Jews of Germany: a Story of Sixteen Centuries*, pursue overtly popularizing aims, while the *Germania Judaica* is merely a good reference work to historic sources shedding light on individual communities up to 1238. Some of the numerous monographs on the latter will be quoted here and in other chapters.

84. Aronius, *Regesten*, pp. 52 No. 122, 56 f. Nos. 132–34, 59 No. 140; and the sources listed there; *MGH*, Diplomata, I, 415 f. No. 300; II, 38 f. No. 29, 225 No. 198; III, 78 No. 64; Thietmar's *Chronicon*, III.1, VI.12, ed. by M. Lappenberg, *MGH*, Scriptores, III, 758, 809 (ed. by R. Holtzmann under the title *Die Chronik des Bischofs Thietmar von Merseburg und ihre Korveier Ueberarbeitung*, pp. 98, 295); Bondy and Dworsky, *Zur Geschichte der Juden in Böhmen*, p. 1 No. 1. As bishop of Merseburg in the eleventh century, Thietmar possessed almost first-hand information. Cf. Lappenberg's and Holtzmann's introductions to their editions. The expression *Judeos Apellas*, used by Thietmar (VI.12), seems to be a mere classical allusion, as is his earlier phrase, *Judeis recutitis* (VI.10, pp. 809 and 290, respectively). Both phrases, however, may have entered the stream of Latin literary usage long before Thietmar's time, and the Merseburg divine may merely have referred to their current use. C. G. Landauer's note on "Judaeus Apella," *ZGJD*, II, 78–79; and, more generally, A. H. Thompson's "Classical Echoes in Medieval Authors," *History*, XXXIII, 29–48. On the Raffelstetten toll ordinance, cf. also *infra*, Chap. XXII, n. 42.

85. *Annales Quedlinburgenses*, in *MGH*, Scriptores, III, 81 (Aronius, *Regesten*, pp. 61 f. No. 144); and *supra*, n. 69. In "Die Verfolgung der Juden in Mainz im Jahre 1012," *Philippson Festschrift*, pp. 1–5, H. Tykocinski has analyzed these data and compared them with some questionable references in Hebrew sources. He effectively controverted especially the alleged nexus between Vecelin's conversion and the decree of expulsion. But he failed to offer an alternative hypothesis. No one, however, has questioned the general assumption that Henry II's decree was aimed at the Jews of Mayence exclusively, whereas the phrasing in the *Annales* (*expulsio Judaeorum facta est a rege in Moguntia*) would admit the interpretation that, while in Mayence, the emperor instituted a more general persecution. The connection, here suggested, with Ḥakim's anti-Christian legislation and its repercussions in Europe would offer a far more plausible explanation for both the

initial persecution and its early cessation. See *supra*, nn. 74–75. Nor is it impossible that either the author of the *Annales* was mistaken about the date of Henry's decree, which may have been promulgated four or five years earlier, or that the awkward word *facta* erroneously replaced some such term as *revocata*, and that Henry, possibly prompted by the papal messenger, actually revoked an earlier anti-Jewish enactment during his sojourn in Mayence in 1012. In the latter case, Vecelin's defection in 1005–6 may have deepened the Christian public's suspicions concerning the alleged world-Jewish machinations. Cf. also the narrative in Alpertus, *De diversitate temporum*, II.22–24, in his *Opera*, ed. by G. H. Pertz in *MGH, Scriptores*, IV, 720 ff. The reconstruction of the events of 1007–12 here offered still leaves many questions unanswered, but it at least avoids the wholesale discounting of the credibility of extant sources to which modern scholarship has had to resort. Be this as it may, we sense in these events the first rumblings of the future Crusades and sharp popular outbreaks against Jews.

86. Most of the fundamental critical problems of the Spires and Worms privileges were aired in 1887 in the essays by R. Hoeniger, "Zur Geschichte der Juden Deutschlands im frühern Mittelalter," *ZGJD*, [o.s.] I, 65–97, 136–51 (reprinting the respective texts); H. Bresslau, "Diplomatische Erläuterungen zu den Judenprivilegien Heinrichs IV," *ibid.*, pp. 152–59, 294–95; and O. Stobbe, "Die Judenprivilegien Heinrichs IV für Speier und für Worms," *ibid.*, pp. 205–15. Cf. also D. von Gladiss's more recent edition of *Die Urkunden Heinrichs IV*, Part 2, pp. 543 ff. Nos. 411–12 (*MGH, Diplomata*, Vol. VI). In his "Urkundliche Beiträge zur Geschichte der Juden in Deutschland im Mittelalter," *Mitteilungen des Gesamtarchivs der deutschen Juden*, IV, 31 ff., E. Täubler has plausibly argued for the existence of a privilege granted to the Ratisbon Jews, too, by Henry IV. However, neither its text nor its date are certain. P. Scheffer-Boichorst, editor of Frederick I's confirming privilege in 1182 (in "Ein ungedrucktes Judenprivileg Friederichs I und II," *MIOG*, X, 459–62), followed by Täubler and others, simply assumed that its issuance coincided with Henry's stay in Ratisbon in 1097, and his permission then given to the Crusaders' Jewish victims to return to their former faith. Cf. *infra*, Chap. XXI, nn. 21 and 36. However, there is no record of Henry's similar general enactments in favor of other communities, though all of them were granted the same permission to retract. Henry even failed formally to reissue his decrees in favor of the Jewries of Spires and Worms. Cf. also Von Gladiss's doubts about the nexus between the three privileges, expressed in his ed., p. 545; and the scanty data assembled in S. Bromberger's Berlin dissertation, *Die Juden in Regensburg biz zur Mitte des 14. Jahrhunderts*. On the other hand, the intimate relationships between the Jewish communities of Spires, Worms, and Mayence, which found expression in their joint Hebrew abbreviation *Shum*, enhances the likelihood of their analogous treatment by emperors. Cf. S. Levi's concise data on "Die Verbundenheit zwischen den jüdischen Gemeinden Worms und Mainz im Mittelalter," *ZGJD*, V, 187–91.

An acute analysis of the extant texts and their historical background was more recently offered by S. Schiffmann in her Berlin dissertation, *Heinrich IV, und die Bischöfe in ihrem Verhalten zu den deutschen Juden zur Zeit des ersten Kreuzzuges*, esp. pp. 44 ff. Somewhat less significant were H. Fischer's observations on this subject in his otherwise very meritorious Breslau dissertation published about the same time, *Die verfassungsrechtliche Stellung der Juden in den deutschen Städten während des dreizehnten Jahrhunderts;* R. Straus's essay on "Die Speyerer Juden-privilegien von 1084 und 1090," *ZGJD*, VII, 234–39; and B. Altmann's "Studies in Medieval German History," *PAAJR*, X, 5–98. The latter's ideas are unfortunately obscured by linguistic ambiguities. Much substantive information may also be derived from the comprehensive older, but still very useful, works by O. Stobbe, *Die Juden in Deutschland während des Mittelalters in politischer, socialer und rechtlicher Beziehung;* and J. Scherer, *Die Rechtsverhältnisse;* as well as from the numerous more recent writings by G. Kisch. Cf. especially his *Jews in Medieval Germany* and *Forschungen.* The latter volume includes also revised reprints of Kisch's earlier monographs on "Die Rechtsstellung der Wormser Juden im Mit-telalter" (pp. 93 ff.); and on "Otto Stobbe und die Rechtsgeschichte der Juden" (pp. 199 ff.).

87. Aronius, *Regesten,* pp. 58 No. 136, 67 ff. Nos. 162, 168, 170–71. Although Bresslau's main argument for the Carolingian provenience of the Spires privilege of 1090, namely the mention therein of the Italian coin *mancosi,* was effectively controverted by Straus (in *ZGJD*, VII, 234 f.), the names of its recipients and some phrases in the text decidedly convey the impression that Henry's chancellery had directly followed Carolingian models. Cf., however, Von Gladiss's contrary observa-tions in his ed. of *Die Urkunden Heinrichs IV,* pp. 544 f., postulating the existence of intervening privileges, since lost. The chief negotiators in behalf of Spires Jewry, Judas (Yehudah) son of Kalonymos, David son of Masullam (Meshullam), and Moses son of Guthiel (Yequtiel), had apparently resided there only since 1084. They had come there, on the bishop's invitation, from Mayence, where the Jewish quarter had suffered severely from one of the recurrent conflagrations. Some, or all of these leaders, apparently belonged to the Kalonymide family originally transplanted from Lucca to Mayence because one of its members had saved Otto II's life during the battle against the Saracens at Cotrone, Calabria (982). Although found only in Thietmar's *Chronicle* (ed. by Lappenberg, III.12, in *MGH*, III, 765 f.; ed. by Holtzmann, III.21, pp. 124 f.), we have no reason to doubt the authenticity of Otto's escape with the aid of Kalonymos, since the Merseburg divine certainly did not invent that story for the benefit of Jews. Cf. also Aronius's essay cited *supra,* n. 58.

88. Aronius, *Regesten,* pp. 123 No. 280, 216 No. 496. Cf. J. Cohn's Hamburg dissertation, *Die Judenpolitik der Hohenstaufen;* and *infra,* n. 97. The indebted-ness of the later Austrian, Bohemian, Hungarian, and Polish-Lithuanian privileges to the decree of Frederick II and its antecedents has long become evident to scholars.

89. Cf. especially G. Kisch's analysis of the burghers' rights of Worms Jewry in his *Forschungen,* pp. 98 ff. Some of Kisch's conclusions are based upon the documentary materials assembled by J. Kohler in *Die Carolina und ihre Vor-gängerinnen,* Vol. IV: *Wormser Recht und Wormser Reformation;* and C. Köhne's "Uebersicht über die Geschichte der Wormser Stadtverfassung," included in that volume. These data, briefly mentioned also by Schiffmann, may help elucidate the Jewish status in other medieval cities as well. Like most of our sources, however, these records date from the thirteenth century or later. Hence their fuller con-sideration must be relegated here to a later volume.

90. The text of the *Landfrieden* of 1103 is not extant; we merely possess a reference to the oath taken on that occasion by the grandees of the Empire. Cf. *Constitutiones et acta publica imperatorum et regum*, ed. by L. Weiland in *MGH*, Legum Sectio IV, Part 1, pp. 125 f. No. 74; Aronius, *Regesten*, p. 97 No. 210; and Eleazar bar Yehudah of Worms, *Sefer Roqeaḥ* (Kabbalistic-Halakhic Treatise), No. 196. The date of Eleazar's enactment can be reconstructed from a poem, *Maṣor ba'atah ha-'ir* (The City Was Besieged) by Menaḥem bar Jacob of Worms (died in 1203), published from a Leipzig MS with a German translation by H. Fischer in *Die verfassungsrechtliche Stellung*, pp. 188 ff. Cf. Davidson's *Thesaurus*, III, 168 No. 2142; and Menaḥem's two related poems in A. M. Habermann's *Sefer Gezerot Ashkenaz ve-Ṣarefat*, pp. 147 ff., 239 f. The last named poem probably referred to the Crusaders' riots of 1196 during which Eleazar himself lost his wife and three children. See Graetz, *Geschichte der Juden*, VI, 233 f. This tragedy must have pointed up to the distinguished mystic the need for self-defense, and made him more amenable to permit the breach of the Sabbath observance five years later. Cf. also other sources cited by Kisch in his *Forschungen*, pp. 20 ff.; by Fischer in *Die verfassungsrechtliche Stellung*, pp. 98 ff.; and *infra*, Chap. XXI, n. 52.

91. Cf. L. Rabinowitz's study of *The Ḥerem Hayyishub;* my remarks in *Rashi Anniv. Vol.*, pp. 62 ff.; and *infra*, Chap. XXIII, n. 15. The relationship between the predominantly urban character of the Jewish population and the strictly limited nature of its "serfdom" has not yet been fully examined. On the general impact of city life on personal freedom and the widely recognized legal principle "Stadtluft macht frei" which, though formulated in modern times, well reflected the medieval realities, cf. H. Strahm, "Mittelalterliche Stadtfreiheit," *Schweizer Beiträge zur allgemeinen Geschichte*, V, 77–113.

92. Aronius, *Regesten*, pp. 123 No. 280, 139 ff. No. 314a; Täubler, "Urkundliche Beiträge," *Mitteilungen des Gesamtarchivs der deutschen Juden*, IV, 32 f., 44 f. Cf. also R. Straus, *Regensburg and Augsburg*, pp. 9 ff. The treaty of 1179, Art. 1 (in *Constitutiones*, ed. by Weiland in *MGH*, pp. 380 ff. No. 277), enumerated many more categories of persons than that of 1103, whose nondescript term, *laicis*, was entirely too vague. Because of this increase, Jews are not the last on the list. A similar preamble may have already been included in Henry IV's original text. But the absence of any such solemn declaration in Henry's other privileges, and the declamatory style so characteristic of Frederick Barbarossa, favor his authorship of the entire paragraph, which was subsequently retained also in the renewal of the privilege by Rudolph of Habsburg in 1274. We must once again bear in mind that such renewals in no way interfered with temporary transfers of control over Jews to other authorities. In 1233 Henry VII unconcernedly conferred the jurisdiction over, and the revenue from, the Jews of Ratisbon to Bishop Siegfried for life. Cf. Aronius, *Regesten*, pp. 201 f. No. 459.

93 Aronius, *Regesten*, pp. 127 f. No. 299 (although in many details and in its date of 1169 evidently a thirteenth-century forgery, this document reflects also twelfth-century practice); Bondy and Dworsky, *Zur Geschichte der Juden*, pp. 4 ff. Nos. 6 (1064), 15 (1174–78). Here the dukes of Bohemia are recorded to have issued independent regulations about the admission of Jews to Prague and the requirement of witnesses belonging to the ethnic and religious groups of both plaintiffs

and defendants. Although the former document is of dubious historic authenticity, it and other contemporary records show that the Bohemian dukes, though recognizing the overlordship of the German emperor and generally following German administrative patterns also in Jewish affairs, retained considerable freedom of action. Cf. also A. Kober, *Studien zur mittelalterlichen Geschichte der Juden in Köln am Rhein insbesondere ihres Grundbesitzes;* his *Cologne,* pp. 11 ff.; M. Grunwald, *Vienna,* pp. 1 ff.; I. Schwarz, *Geschichte der Juden in Wien bis zum Jahre 1625,* pp. 4 ff.; *Die Juden in Prag,* ed. by S. Steinherz, pp. 7 f.; and B. Bretholz's works, *Geschichte der Juden in Mähren im Mittelalter,* I (to 1350, and especially pp. 31 ff.), and *Quellen zur Geschichte der Juden in Mähren vom XI. bis zum XV. Jahrhundert (1067–1411),* the latter beginning with stray records of 1067, 1091, and 1140, but including really significant documents only from 1249 on. A comprehensive *Bibliographical Survey of Jewish Prague* has recently been compiled by O. Muneles.

94. Benjamin, *Massa'ot,* pp. 71 f. (Hebrew), 79 f. (English); the well-documented studies by S. Neufeld, *Die Juden im thüringisch-sächsischen Gebiet während des Mittelalters;* and M. Szulwas, *Die Juden in Würzburg;* and other local histories mentioned in the previous or the forthcoming notes. Cf. also E. Keyser's reference work, *Deutsches Städtebuch,* Vols. I–III. Arranged by geographic regions, this alphabetical description of cities in northeastern, central and northwestern Germany includes considerable data on their Jewish inhabitants, and it may be consulted profitably together with *Germania Judaica.* Cf. also *supra,* Chap. XIX, n. 57; and, on the legends concerning the early settlement of Jews in Austria and elsewhere, Chap. XXIV, n. 58.

95. Stobbe's *Juden in Deutschland,* pp. 46 f.; and *infra,* Chap. XXI *passim.* Of considerable interest also is the treaty of surrender by Archbishop Philipp of Cologne of 1188, in which this ecclesiastical leader promised Frederick I to take several oaths. One concerned the accusation that he had unlawfully mulcted the Jews of his diocese "to the emperor's shame." Cf. Aronius, *Regesten,* p. 147 No. 325; and A. Kober, *Cologne,* pp. 26 f. This treaty seems to controvert R. Koebner's contention that the Jews of Cologne had quite early been subjected to the preponderant control of the Church. Cf. his fine study of *Die Anfänge des Gemeinwesens der Stadt Köln,* pp. 117 n. 4, 141 f. Since the details of that controversy, however, are unrecorded, the emperor may merely have objected to a particular method or size of the assessment, rather than to the levy itself.

96. Aronius, *Regesten,* pp. 69 ff. No. 168. Although the text of this famous privilege seems to have undergone much alteration, largely designed to underscore the bishop's sovereign powers in the city, its essential authenticity has never been seriously impugned. Cf. especially the aforementioned detailed analyses by Hoeniger and Bresslau in *ZGJD,* [o.s.] Vol. I. On Rüdiger and his policies designed principally to enhance the position of his city, cf. E. Gugumus's study of "Die Speyerer Bischöfe im Investiturstreit," *Archiv für mittelrheinische Kirchengeschichte,* IV, 45–78. The changing topography of Spires, including its Jewish quarter, from the tenth to the thirteenth centuries is carefully reviewed in A. Doll's "Zur Frühgeschichte der Stadt Speyer," *Mitteilungen des Historischen Vereins der Pfalz,* LII, 133–200. The importance of this privilege for the evolution of the medieval ghetto will become clearer in connection with the developments after 1200.

97. Cf. especially the data assembled by H. Fischer in *Die verfassungsrechtliche Stellung,* pp. 7 ff. Despite a number of strictures made against this study by G. Kisch in his review, reprinted in his *Forschungen,* pp. 237–43, the author's analysis has elucidated many obscure phases in the relationships between the German cities and the Jews in the thirteenth century, and has also shed some light on the earlier period. In "Die Judenansiedlung der Staufer in Deutschland," *MGWJ,* LXXIX, 241–46, L. Wallach has shown how much the rise of German cities owed to the conscious promotion of Jewish settlement on the part of the famous Hohenstaufen emperors. Cf. also J. Cohn, *Die Judenpolitik der Hohenstaufen;* H. Dicker, *Die Geschichte der Juden in Ulm* (postulating their presence in the city at the first mention of its *civitas* in 1181 as a result of such colonizing efforts of the Hohenstaufen, pp. 8 f.); and *infra,* Chap. XXII, n. 31.

98. J. Jacobs in *The Jews of Angevin England,* p. iii. D. C. Douglas and G. W. Greenaway were not guilty of overstatement when, in their recent compilation of *English Historical Documents, 1042–1189* (p. 10), they contended that "from no other country in the world has there been preserved from this distant age a collection of historical evidence comparable to that which illustrates the history of England during these years." But even many of the (relatively less unmanageable) thirteenth-century sources of specific Jewish interest have not seen the light of day. Cf. H. Jenkinson's succinct discussion of "Medieval Sources for Anglo-Jewish History: The Problem of Publication," advance offprint from *Transactions JHSE,* XVIII. The old query, "Were There Jews in Roman Britain?" has been answered in the affirmative by S. Applebaum in his pertinent essay in *Transactions JHSE,* XVII, 189–205. Applebaum speaks, however, only of probabilities that some Jewish soldiers and traders "may have formed small communities in such places as Colchester, York, Corbridge and London. There is a stronger possibility of an early Jewish community at Exeter. . . . There is also the probability that a few Jews found their way to London (as slaves?) after the Bar Kosiba [Kocheba] rising, and that one or two Jews were officials in Britain in the fourth century" (p. 204). St. Jerome indulged in no mere rhetoric when he predicted that at the coming of the Messiah Jews, including persons of senatorial rank, would foregather from as far as Britain, Spain, and Gaul. Cf. his Commentary on Isa. 66:20 in *PL,* XXIV, 698. Other admittedly uncertain data, which in the aggregate seem to confirm the presence of Jews in England before 1066, are discussed by E. N. Adler in his *London,* pp. 1ff. More recently, B. Blumenkranz has argued for the presence of some Jews in tenth-century England and earlier on the basis of anti-Jewish canons, stemming indirectly from Theodore of Canterbury. He has also pointed out that the tenth-century *Altercatio Aeclesiae contra Synagogam,* edited by him, is extant only in English manuscripts and apparently uses only biblical quotations from texts current in pre-Norman England. Cf. the introduction to his edition in *RMAL,* X, 32 ff. These arguments are necessarily tenuous. Yet in the light of the general paucity of sources, particularly those pertaining to smaller groups living in England before 1066, one cannot dismiss lightly such evidence of a then existing ecclesiastical need to defend the masses against the infiltration of Jewish rituals and mores. Cf., on the other hand, C. Roth's generally skeptical remarks in *A History of the Jews in England,* pp. 1 ff., 269. In any case, the presence of Hebraic names is even less evidence of Jewish settlement on the British Isles than elsewhere. Cf., e.g., C. Selmer's "Israel, ein unbekannter Schotte des 10. Jahrhunderts," *Studien und Mitteilungen zur Geschichte des Benediktiner-Ordens,* LXII, 71 f.

99. Since Jacobs no one has attempted to ascertain the size of the Jewish population in twelfth-century England. His findings are largely based upon the number of recorded Jewish names, and especially upon the so-called Northampton *donum*, or the contributions to the ransom of Richard the Lion-Heart of 1194. Cf. his *Jews of Angevin England*, pp. 162 ff., 345 ff., 381 ff. A number of details have been revised and clarified by I. Abrahams in "The Northampton 'Donum' of 1194," *Miscellanies JHSE*, I, pp. lix–lxxiv. But Jacobs's general findings remained unaffected. His estimate of the Jewish population at some 2,000 in 1194, may have to be raised to 2,500 or more, however, if there were indeed 500 Jewish families. This figure probably represents the maximum attained by Jews in the twelfth century, since neither the number of victims nor that of Jewish refugees leaving England as a result of the massacres of 1189–90, was large enough to have substantially reduced the total Jewish population, which undoubtedly had gradually increased during the preceding decades. Cf. *infra*, n. 103; and Chap. XXI, n. 48. On the other hand, Jacobs's assumption that the total population of England at that time amounted to but a million and a half, is likewise an underestimate. Already in 1086 the Domesday Book indicated a population well in excess of 1,100,000, which doubtless increased greatly during the following hundred years to reach a total of more than 2,200,000 in 1377, according to J. C. Russell's estimates in his *British Medieval Population*, pp. 51 ff., 143 ff. In any case, a general Jewish ratio of one per thousand does not seem to be out of line.

100. William of Malmesbury, *De gestis regum Anglorum*, iv.317 in *PL*, CLXXIX, 1279 f. (ed. by W. Stubbs, II, 371, with minor MSS variants; Jacobs, *Angevin England*, p. 6). Cf. E. A. Freeman's observations on *The Reign of William Rufus*, I, 160 f. On the Judeo-Christian polemics, which grew in bitterness in England and elsewhere, cf. R. M. Ames, "The Debate between the Church and the Synagogue in the Literature of Anglo-Saxon and Medieval England" (unpublished Columbia Univ. diss.); and *infra*, Chap. XXIV, n. 42.

101. Anonymous chronicler (before 1177) in *Materials for the History of Thomas Beckett*, ed. by J. C. Robertson, IV, 148 (Jacobs, *Angevin England*, pp. 42 f.). Going even further than Jacobs, Roth believes that one could date Henry II's decree in favor of Jews (see next note) about 1164, "when the autonomy of the Jews was put forward as an argument in favor of the autonomy of the clergy." See his *History of the Jews in England*, p. 10 n. 1. The text of the argument in the case of Jews, however, does not refer to general jurisdictional autonomy, but rather to the rules of evidence, particularly to proof by oath rather than ordeal. This substitution had indeed been provided for in the original decree of Henry I relating to Jews, if we may take a clue from its renewal by John. All one can say, therefore, is that Henry's protracted controversy with Thomas Beckett may also have stimulated him to clarify further the position of his Jewish subjects. At the Council of Northampton in October, 1164, the king demanded from the archbishop full account for various items of revenue, including 500 marks "borrowed from a certain Jew on the king's security." Cf. William fitz Stephen's eye-witness account in Robertson, *Materials*, III, 49 ff., 52 f.; Douglas, *English Historical Documents*, II, 726; R. L. Poole's attempt to reconstruct "The Date of Henry II's Charters," *EHR*, XXIII, 79–83 (on the basis of L. Delisle's theory); and R. Foreville's comprehensive analysis, *L'Eglise et la royauté en Angleterre sous Henri II Plantagenet (1154–1189)*.

102. T. Rymer and R. Sanderson, *Foedera*, ed. by A. Clarke and F. Holbrooke, I, 51; Charter Rolls, 1201, p. 93 (Jacobs, *Angevin England*, pp. 134 ff., 212 ff.). As usual, there were also exceptions from the general freedom from customs. In his decree of 1162, addressed to the burghers and soldiers of Salmur, Normandy, Henry II expressed his joy over their completing a local bridge and ordered that Jews transporting merchandise over it should pay one denar for each passage. But, he added, "if a Jew is not given credence [as to whether particular objects were intended for sale], he shall swear by his Law, and thus cross [the bridge] immune." Cf. *Recueil des actes de Henri II . . . concernant les provinces françaises*, ed. by L. Delisle and E. Berger, I, 366 No. ccxxvi. Cf. J. Parkes, *Jews in the Medieval Community*, pp. 169 f. In the light of these laws and the widespread evidence of their application, F. I. Schechter's contention concerning "The Rightlessness of Mediaeval English Jewry," *JQR*, IV, 121–51, is hardly justified. This thesis is almost exclusively based on thirteenth-century documents, and requires considerable qualification even for that period. Cf. also H. S. Q. Henriques's analysis of *The Jews and the English Law*, pp. 52 ff., particularly significant for the Jewish status in later periods.

103. Roger Howden (Hovedene), *Chronica*, ed. by W. Stubbs, II, 218 ff., 231, 238; Pseudo-Edward the Confessor's *Leges ecclesiasticae*, XXI, in *PL*, CXLIX, 1195 f.; (Jacobs, *Angevin England*, p. 68); John's charter of 1201, Art. III in *Charter Rolls*, I, 93 (Jacobs, p. 212). On the similarities of status between Jews and knights (some Jews appear in a record antedating 1166 as "half a knight" or "three-parts of a knight"), cf. especially Jacobs, pp. 160 ff. When Jurnet of Norwich, however, married a Christian heiress, he had to pay a severe fine (with the community held responsible for its collection) and his wife lost her estates. Cf. Jacobs, pp. 90, 94 f. Scholars have long agreed that neither the passage relating to usury, nor that explaining Jewish serfdom, could have originated in the days of Edward the Confessor and that they both were interpolated in the chronicler's period (about 1180). Even during the turbulent years of civil strife when kings had to seek the support of individual barons, no formal transfers of control over Jewish revenue, so frequent on the Continent, are recorded in England. At times the Crown allowed a local churchman (see *infra*, n. 111) or later the burghers of certain cities to refuse toleration to Jews altogether—these concessions clearly adumbrated its ultimate surrender in the expulsion of 1290—but it never gave up its supreme mastery over the legal Jewish residents in favor of local grandees.

104. Jacobs, *Angevin England*, pp. 19 ff., 45 ff., 75; M. Adler, *Jews of Medieval England*, pp. 185 f. The story of Bristol is summarized here from a thirteenth-century MS which includes two pertinent drawings, one of which was reproduced by Jacobs, p. 152. On the origin and ramifications of the blood accusation, see *infra*, Chap. XXI, nn. 52 ff.

105. Howden, *Chronica*, II, 137; Gervase of Canterbury, *Chronicle of the Reigns of Stephen, Henry II, and Richard I* (to 1168), in *The Historical Works*, ed. by W. Stubbs, I, 205 (Jacobs, *Angevin England*, pp. 47, 62). Gervase's obscure reference to the effects of Frederick's embassy has been interpreted by Jacobs as relating to the dispatch to the Continent of some rich Jews as hostages. But neither this explanation nor that offered in the text, though considered by Roth (*History of*

the Jews in England, p. 12 n. 2) as the "most rational interpretation," is quite satisfactory. More likely, Henry's action had something to do with the rich presents brought by the German envoys. Perhaps forced to reciprocate, the king tried to raise the necessary funds by forcing the "richer Jews" out of England and confiscating their property, and by exacting 5,000 marks from the rest of the community. Whatever decline in the Jewish population may have been occasioned by this arbitrary act, however, was doubtless soon more than made up by Jewish immigration.

106. Gervase of Canterbury, *Chronica,* I, 422; C. Roth in *The Jews of Medieval Oxford,* pp. 2 f. (based on Wood's account); Jacobs, *Angevin England,* pp. 18, 93, 159 ff., 162 ff., 320 ff. Wood's reference to the confiscation of "all the goods of a [former] outlawed and apostate Jew" may actually relate to a Jew who had been excommunicated by his fellow Jews and has thereupon adopted Christianity, although the term *apostate* sounds strange when thus used by a thirteenth-century friar (Nigel, Wood's source). This may then be the first recorded application in England of the widely practiced regulation that the estates of converts to Christianity were escheat to the king. The methods of collection, it must be borne in mind, were Draconian even in the case of Christians. According to "Benedict of Peterborough," the king dealt harshly with the defaulters of the Saladin tithe. "If he found any rebellious, he at once had them imprisoned and kept in chains until they had paid the uttermost farthing. He dealt in a similar manner with the Jews of his land, from whom he acquired an enormous sum of money." Cf. his *De vita et gestis Henrici II et Ricardi I,* Oxford ed., 1733, II, 31; and S. M. Toynes's English translation in *The Angevins and the Charter (1154–1216),* p. 6. The tax of 1185, on the other hand, had been a mild impost intended to raise but some 50,000 marks from all royal possessions on both sides of the Channel, if we accept the computations of F. A. Cazel, Jr., in "The Tax of 1185 in Aid of the Holy Land," *Speculum,* XXX, 385–92. Although Jacobs's computation is based on many conjectures, it still offers the best estimate of the relative contributions of Jews to the royal Exchequer during the latter part of the twelfth century. By averaging data from various reigns it fails to take cognizance, however, of the indubitable constant rise of the Jewish population and its financial resources, which was but temporarily interrupted by the massacres of 1189–90. See *supra,* n. 99. For this reason the estimate of an average annual total of some £3,000 in Jewish taxes is quite arbitrary, just as is Jacobs's assumption that the royal revenue amounted on the average to only £35,000 annually. Cf. also S. Painter's concise summary of *The Reign of King John,* pp. 140 ff.; and, more generally, S. K. Mitchell's *Taxation in Medieval England.* One must also bear in mind the then emergent difference between the king's private "Chamber" and the governmental treasury, which to some extent affected also Jewish taxation. Cf. H. G. Richardson's pertinent remarks in "The Chamber under Henry II," *EHR,* LXIX, 596–611 which also shows the complications which could arise from the payment of a substantial sum to a Jew, in this case £479 paid to Isaac, the Jew (pp. 609 f.).

107. The story of Aaron of Lincoln, his ramified business transations, the confiscation of his estate, and the protracted operations of the *scaccarium Aaronis* are elucidated in J. Jacobs's essay, "Aaron of Lincoln," *Transactions JHSE,* III, 157–79 (includes Appendix on "Aaron's Debts" by S. Levy); with E. Haes's additional com-

ments on "Lincoln—1898," *ibid.*, pp. 180–86. Only a few details have been added since, largely in connection with the town and the Jewish community of Lincoln. Cf. the data included in *The Publications of the Pipe Roll Society*, LII, 19; and many other passages listed in the Index, *ibid.*, p. 344 *s.v.* Lincoln, Aaron Judeus de; and in J. W. F. Hill's *Medieval Lincoln*, pp. 217 ff. (on the "tradition" concerning Aaron's house, cf. *ibid.*, pp. 222 f.).

108. Jacobs, *Angevin England*, pp. 51 f. (from *Publications of the Pipe Roll Society*, XV, 78 = 16 Henry II, 1169–70); Alexander III's letter of 1172–73 concerning Beckett's debt published by Holtzmann in *Festschrift Guido Kisch*, pp. 226 f., 229 f. Cf. also *infra*, n. 110. Josce of Gloucester's action is doubly remarkable if, as William of Newburg informs us, Richard "Strongbow" had undertaken that expedition in part because he had been harassed by his creditors. Cf. his *Historia rerum anglicarum*, II, 26, in *Chronicles and Memorials of the Reigns of Stephen, Henry II and Richard I*, ed. by R. Howlett, I, 167 f.; and J. Stevenson's English translation in *Church Historians of England*, IV, Part 2, p. 482. Nevertheless Josce may well have been unaware of the royal order to Richard to desist from the expedition, or even of the royal claim to the control over Ireland, a claim fully supported by the papacy since 1155. Cf. Douglas and Greenaway, *English Historical Documents*, pp. 776 ff. The Jewish settlement in Ireland herself is not reliably recorded before 1232. Cf. B. Shillman's data in *A Short History of the Jews in Ireland*, p. 10. Shillman also discusses the various legends tracing the Jewish community in Ireland back to ancient times, and quotes the entry in the *Annals* of Innisfallen under 1062: "Five Jews came to Ireland from over the sea, bringing gifts to Tordelbach [Turlough] but were again expelled over the sea." These Jews may have come from England or the Continent.

109. Roger Howden, *Chronica*, III, 266 f. (Jacobs, *Angevin England*, pp. 156 ff.). The location of the first six or seven chirograph offices still is uncertain. Jacobs enumerated ten possible choices. Roth (*England*, pp. 29 f.) suggested London, Lincoln, Norwich, Winchester, Canterbury, and Oxford as the most likely places, while an additional office may have been established in either Northampton, Cambridge, Gloucester, Nottingham, or Bristol. In time this institution, important not only for Anglo-Jewish economic and political life but also for the operation of Jewish self-government, embraced twenty-seven local offices, headed by high Christian officials serving as Justices of the Jews. Cf. the older but still valuable studies by C. Gross, "The Exchequer of the Jews of England in the Middle Ages," *Papers Read at the Anglo-Jewish Historical Exhibition*, pp. 170–230; J. M. Rigg and H. Jenkinson's introduction to their basic source publication of the *Calendar of the Plea Rolls of the Exchequer of the Jews*, Vol. I; and, on the general governmental background, *An Introduction to the Administrative History of Mediaeval England* by S. B. Chrimes. Cf. also *infra*, Chap. XXII, n. 69.

110. Gervase of Canterbury, *Chronica*, ed. by Stubbs, I, 405; M. Adler, *Jews of Medieval England*, pp. 51 f.; and Jacobs's data in *Transactions JHSE*, III, 162 f. Alexander III's intervention and the internal feud between the two churches which often engaged the pope's attention (cf. the numerous documents reproduced in W. Holtzmann's *Papsturkunden in England*, especially II, 13 f., 388 ff. Nos. 190–91) must be viewed against the dramatic background of Archbishop Thomas Beckett's

murder and Henry II's submission and penance (1170–74). Curiously, Richard of Canterbury, Beckett's successor, complained that "if a Jew or a layman of the lowest grade be killed, justice is done, but this is not the case with a priest." Cited by Adler, p. 50. This grievance, reminiscent of the general demand of the clergy for equal treatment with Jews with respect to the rules of evidence (see *supra*, n. 101), is doubtless exaggerated. Yet it helps explain the relatively moderate and inactive policy of the English Church toward the Jews in the first century and a half of Norman rule.

111. Jocelin of Brakelond, *Cronica* (The Chronicle concerning the Acts of Samson Abbot of the Monastery of St. Edmunds), ed. and trans. by H. E. Butler, pp. 10, 21, 45 ff., 72 ff.; Jacobs, *Angevin England*, pp. 78 f., 141 ff. As Jacobs pointed out (p. 300) Jocelin was Samson's ardent admirer, and hence cannot be considered an unbiased reporter. The situation in Edmundsbury was exceptional, moreover, in so far as in 1173–80 William, as well as another official of the monastery, had borrowed money from Jews by using the monastery's seal without authorization. Cf. Jocelin, pp. 2 ff. (Jacobs, pp. 59 ff.). Such mismanagement must have deeply irked the able administrator Samson who readily placed the blame on the Jewish creditors. Cf. R. H. C. Davis's comments in his edition of *The Kalendar of Abbot Samson of Bury St. Edmunds*, pp. xi ff. On the growingly anti-Jewish animus permeating the apologetic literature of English churchmen, cf. *infra*, Chap. XXIV, nn. 42–43.

112. Ralph of Coggeshall, *Chronicon anglicanum*, ed. by J. Stevenson, p. 27. Cf. the photographs reproduced by Jacobs, *Angevin England*, pp. 91, 141; and *supra*, n. 107. As mentioned there, the identity of many medieval Jewish buildings (including Aaron's house) is uncertain. In general, the origin of the Jewish stone houses in England, though long debated, still awaits a more definitive solution. We know nothing about the architects or master masons who built them on their owners' orders. Many stone structures, especially of a military nature, dating from that period have also been discovered in recent years on the Continent, including Normandy. Rather than controverting the long-regnant view that Jews had introduced these buildings into the British Isles, such discoveries have merely removed the objection of why Jewish builders had not adopted similar architectural types in other areas of their settlement. Cf. the data assembled by F. Deshoulières in "Les Premiers donjons de pierre dans le départment du Cher," *Bulletin monumental de la Société française d'archéologie*, CVI, 49–61. Cf. also P. Héliot's "Sur les résidences princières bâties en France du Xe au XIIe siècle," *Moyen Age*, LXI, 291–317, showing the growing stress on the defensive nature of these structures. To be sure, neither the location of many Anglo-Jewish buildings, nor even of entire Jewish quarters is altogether certain. The story of the so-called "Jewry Wall" in Leicester, for example, although going back to Roman times, has not been cleared up even by recent archaeological excavations. Cf. S. Levy's "Notes on Leicester Jewry," *Transactions JHSE*, V, 34–42; and K. M. Kenyon's *Excavations at the Jewry Wall Site, Leicester* (chiefly concerned with pottery). The architectural character of the so-called "Jews' court" in Lincoln, which is frequently mentioned in the thirteenth century, and its identity with the local synagogue have likewise been subject to lengthy debates. Cf. H. Rosenau's "Note on the Relationship of 'Jews' Court' and the Lincoln Synagogue," *Archaeological Journal*, XCIII, 51–56

(in favor of such identity, but denying that "Moyses Hall" in Bury St. Edmunds had ever been a synagogue). Moreover, as against the few structures which survived, most others must have been poorly constructed and collapsed within a very short time. The former's survival, too, has often been "due to a solidity obtained by a most unscientific and uneconomic prodigality of building materials." Cf. L. F. Salzman's documentary history of *Building in England down to 1540*, p. 25 (deals for the most part with data posterior to 1200 and does not discuss Aaron's house).

113. The Anglo-Jewish scholars and writers, including visitors like Abraham ibn Ezra, will be mentioned in connection with their varied interests in later chapters. A good up-to-date survey is offered by C. Roth in *The Intellectual Activities of Medieval English Jewry*. On the so-called *Tosafot Gornish*, and their possible identity with such a collection made in Norwich, cf. E. N. Adler's data in *London*, p. 17. Cf., however, *infra*, Chap. XXVII, n. 63.

CHAPTER XXI: AGE OF CRUSADES

1. E. Barker, "Crusades," *Encyclopaedia Britannica*, 14th ed., VI, 772; Leo IV's letter to the French troops ("quisquis . . . in hoc bello certamine fideliter mortuus fuerit, regna illi coelestia minime negabuntur") in Mansi, *Collectio*, XIV, 888. The impact on Christendom of the Muslim idea of a Holy War is analyzed by J. L. LaMonte in his "Crusade and Jihad," in *The Arab Heritage*, ed. by N. A. Faris, pp. 159–98. Cf. also other data cited by S. Runciman in *A History of the Crusades*, I, 83 ff., 248. In his stimulating essay, "European Jewry in the Dark Ages: a Revised Picture," *HUCA*, XXIII, Part 2, pp. 151–69. C. Roth rightly points out that many of the difficulties which confronted later medieval Jewry antedated 1096. But he rather overdraws the allegedly accepted picture in Jewish historiography of Jewish well-being before the age of the Crusades, and also unduly minimizes the serious deterioration of status which took place after 1096. Nor does he pay enough heed to the tremendous psychological impact of the Crusades on both the Jews and the Christians.

The interrelations between Jewish and Christian pilgrimages to the Holy Land, their basic similarities, but also important divergences, such as the Christian quest for relics of saints absent from Jewish tradition, would deserve monographic treatment. Certainly Jewish pilgrims did not bring home such souvenirs as stones or oil from the Holy Sepulcher or some of the ninety-five relics catalogued by B. Bagatti in his "Eulogie Palestinesi," *Orientalia christiana periodica*, XV, 126–66. Even the story of Jewish 'aliyot to Palestine is yet to be told in full and illuminating detail. Considerable material is available in travelogues and letters, many of them collected in the aforementioned anthologies by Eisenstein and Adler, as well as in A. Yaari's collection of *Iggerot Ereṣ Yisrael* (Letters from Palestine); and in F. Kobler's *Letters of Jews through the Ages*. Cf. also *infra*, n. 25.

2. *Gesta Treverorum*, cont. prima, VIII, ed. by G. Waitz in *MGH*, Scriptores, VIII, 182 (Aronius, *Regesten*, p. 67 No. 160). According to the chronicler himself, the Treves Jews prevented the execution of the decree by burning the bishop's effigy and thus causing his death on the day set for their mass conversion. Of course, to the chronicler the bishop's sudden demise appeared as the effect of magic rather than divine intervention—that customary interpretation in the various acts of saints when such an event favored the Christian side. The Limoges story is dramatically told in an anonymous recital, published from a Parma MS by A. Berliner in *MWJ*, IV, Hebrew section *(Oṣar ṭob)*, pp. 49–52, and reprinted in A. M. Habermann's anthology, *Sefer Gezerot Ashkenaz ve-Ṣarefat*, pp. 11 ff., 246. The date usually given is 994. However, 992 is the real equivalent of "924 years from the destruction of the Second Temple," since the author doubtless followed the accepted medieval Jewish chronology which dated that destruction at 68 C.E. Cf. *supra*, Vol. II, pp. 116, 376 n. 33. On the Jewish as well as Christian belief in the sympathetic magic of killing a person by destroying the effigy, cf. J. Trachtenberg's *Jewish Magic and Superstition*, pp. 124 ff.; and *infra*, Chap. XXXIII. While miracle narratives of this kind, quite common among both Christians and Jews in the Middle Ages, generally deserve little credence, the

essential probability of some such anti-Jewish happenings is heightened by the fact that within less than two decades (in 1010) Bishop Alduin tried forcibly to convert all Limoges Jews, but succeeded in persuading only three or four to accept baptism. Cf. Adhémar of Chabanne's chronicle in Bouquet, *Recueil*, X, 152; H. Gross, *Gallia judaica*, p. 308; and *supra*, Chap. XX, nn. 74-75. Of course, the Hebrew record may have been but a romanticizing explanation of the bishop's enactment, in which case its date might have been 942 after the destruction, although in Hebrew this error could not have arisen from a mere transposition of two ciphers. The impact of the year 1000 on the millenarian expectations and the ensuing disillusionment have long been accepted by scholars, despite F. Lot's somewhat too sweeping denial in "Le Mythe des terreurs de l'an mille," *Mercure de France*, Dec. 1, 1947, pp. 639-55.

3. Gershom bar Yehudah's poem, *Elekha niqra* (To Thee We Call), stanzas 6-7, in his *Selihot u-pizmonim* (Penitential and Other Liturgical Poems), ed. by A. M. Habermann, pp. 12 ff. (also in Habermann's *Sefer Gezerot*, p. 17). Some of these complaints had by that time become stereotyped, and Gershom seems to have followed therein the lead of the Roman poet, R. Solomon the "Babylonian." Cf. D. Goldschmidt, "Some Religious Poems by R. Solomon the Babylonian" (Hebrew), *Tarbiz*, XXIII, 203-9. Cf. also Alexander Marx, "Rabbenu Gershom, Light of the Exile" in *Essays in Jewish Biography*, p. 43; S. Eidelberg, "R. Gershom the Light of the Exile, Reformer, Responsa Writer, and Poet" (Hebrew), *Sinai*, XVI, No. 214, pp. 57-66 (also more fully in his typescript dissertation on this subject at Yeshiva University); *supra*, Chap. XX, n. 12; and *infra*, Chap. XXXI.

4. Alexander II's letter of 1063 in Mansi, *Collectio*, XIX, 980; and Jaffé and Wattenbach, *Regesta pontificum*, pp. 572 f. Nos. 4528, 4532-33 (cf. *supra*, Chap. XX, n. 50). This protective step in favor of Jews is the more remarkable, as the pope was simultaneously trying to organize an all-European crusade against Spanish Islam. He not only promised an indulgence to all fighters for the cause, but stimulated the recruitment of troops in Italy and France. Cf. P. Rousset's data in *Les Origines et les caractères de la première Croisade*, pp. 31 ff. On the general background of that Crusade, its initial success and subsequent reverses, and the severe losses of the local civilian population, cf. P. Boissonade's "Cluny, la Papauté et la première grande croisade internationale contre les Sarracins d'Espagne —Barbastro (1064-1065)," *Revue des questions historiques*, CXVII, 257-301, which includes a vivid description of the valiant efforts of a Jewish merchant to ransom some Muslim girl captives (pp. 292 ff.).

5. Cf. Solomon ibn Verga's *Shebet Yehudah*, ed. by Wiener, p. 113 (in Wiener's German translation, p. 232); ed. by A. Shohet, pp. 147, 222 n. 19; and the data assembled by S. Krauss in "L'Emigration de 300 rabbins en Palestine en l'an 1211," *REJ*, LXXXII, 333-52; with an additional note by E. N. Adler, *ibid.*, LXXXV, 70-71; and H. J. Zimmels in "Erez Israel in der Responsenliteratur des späteren Mittelalters," *MGWJ*, LXXIV, 44-64. Typical of a great many other would-be pilgrims was the Jew, mentioned in a responsum by the Spaniard Joseph ibn Megas (No. 186, Warsaw ed., fol. 29a), who had "vowed never to eat meat or drink wine except on Sabbaths and holidays, until he would reach Palestine." So convinced were especially the pietist circles in Germany of the great merit of pil-

grimages to the Holy Land that they invented the legend of Hai Gaon's annual visits to the Holy City, whereas in fact that great leader of Babylonian Jewry, despite his longevity and deep attachment to the Palestine ideal, never came to the country of his yearnings. Cf. Yehudah he-Ḥasid (the Pious), *Sefer Ḥasidim* (Book of the Pious), ed. by Wistinetzky, p. 169 No. 630. Cf. also A. Epstein's comment thereon in "Die aharonidischen Geonim Palästinas und Meschullam b. Mose aus Mainz," *MGWJ*, XLVII, 340–45; J. Mann, *Jews in Egypt*, I, 115; and his *Texts and Studies*, I, 91 f. The uncertainty of travel in Palestine during the Seljuk conquest is well illustrated by such private letters as that addressed by 'Ali ben Yeḥezqel (Ezekiel) ha-Kohen to the later head of the Jerusalem academy, Abiathar. According to this writer it was impossible for a resident of Jerusalem even to visit Ramleh, because "all roads are considered dangerous." Cf. the text published by J. Mann in his *Texts and Studies*, I, 346 ff., 350; and another, edited by Goitein and cited *infra*, n. 25. Cf. also the sources listed by P. Alphandéry and A. Dupront in *La Chrétienté et l'idée de Croisade*, pp. 9 ff.; and *supra*, Chap. XVII, nn. 34–35.

On the main propelling forces behind the Crusades, see in addition to the aforementioned studies by Rousset and Runciman, C. Erdmann's searching analysis of *Die Entstehung des Kreuzzugsgedankens;* Adolf Waas's more recent observations on "Religion, Politik und Kultur in der Geschichte der Kreuzzüge," *Die Welt als Geschichte*, XI, 225–48; the comprehensive *Histoire des Croisades et du royaume franc de Jérusalem* by R. Grousset; and the even more ambitious collective enterprise, *A History of the Crusades*, being prepared under the general editorship of K. M. Setton, of which the first volume, dealing with "The First Hundred Years," was ed. by M. W. Baldwin.

6. Solomon bar Simson's chronicle, with reference to Ps. 113:9, in *Hebräische Berichte über die Judenverfolgungen während der Kreuzzüge*, ed. by A. Neubauer and M. Stern, with a German translation by S. Baer, pp. 10 (Hebrew), 102 (German); and in Habermann's *Sefer Gezerot*, p. 34. For the reader's convenience, Solomon's and the other Hebrew chronicles of the period will be quoted throughout this chapter from both these editions under the names of their editors. On the angelic hosts supporting the Maccabean warriors and the impact of the "Maccabean" martyrs on Judaism and Christianity, see *supra*, Vol. I, pp. 230 ff., 398 ff. nn. 25–29. As pointed out by Waas, four different Christian chroniclers reporting on the decisive battle before Antioch mention as an indubitable fact the sudden intervention of St. George at the head of a large contingent of white-clad knights on the side of the Crusaders. Cf. *Die Welt als Geschichte*, XI, 228. Among the rabbinic martyrs only 'Aqiba is mentioned by name in the Hebrew reports. See *infra*, n. 18. There is no reference to the so-called Ten Martyrs. This omission increases the likelihood that the list of Ten Martyrs and the detailed elaboration of their sufferings, first included in the special midrash, *Eleh Ezkerah*, resulted from the increased interest in these ancient witnesses generated by the sufferings of the Crusades. Cf. *supra*, Vol. I, p. 231; Vol. II, p. 370 n. 9; and *infra*, Chap. XXVIII, n. 44.

7. Solomon bar Simson's report, ed. by Neubauer and Stern, pp. 2, 4 (Hebrew), 84, 90 (German); ed. by Habermann, pp. 25, 28. The strange episode with the goose and the Crusaders' credulity in treating its behavior as an omen, is con-

firmed by the Christian chroniclers Albert of Aix (Aquensis) in his *Christianae expeditionis pro ereptione, emundatione et restitutione Sanctae Hierosolymitanae Ecclesiae libri* (in short *Historia Hierosolymitana*), 1.30, in *RHC,* Hist. occidentaux, IV, 295 (in H. Hefele's German translation, entitled *Geschichte des ersten Kreuzzugs,* I, 37 f.) and, with some reservations by Ekkehard Urangiensis (of Aura; or rather in this section by Frutolf of Michelsberg) in *Chronicon universale,* ed. by G. Waitz, in *MGH,* Scriptores, VI, 208.

The three sources here mentioned belong to the most informative and reliable guides for the history of the First Crusade in its early western phases. Like most of the other Hebrew and Latin sources they have been subjected to intensive scholarly scrutiny. Cf. especially the respective editors' introductions in the various volumes of the *Recueil (RHC)* which embraces also three additional series of *Documents arméniens,* 2 vols.; *Historiens Grecs,* 2 vols.; and *Historiens orientaux,* 5 vols. While most of these Christian writings are available in numerous manuscripts, two of the three Hebrew narratives relating to the First Crusade by Solomon bar Simson and the so-called Mayence (or Darmstadt) Anonymous, are available only in single MSS extant in London and Darmstadt respectively. Eliezer bar Nathan's report, perhaps owing to the author's halakhic reputation, is available in five MSS, but only one of them (now in Oxford) dates back to the fourteenth century. Cf. Stern's introduction, pp. vii ff. Nor was much new light shed on the textual transmission by the Yiddish translations of the first two reports. Cf. I. Sonne's "Nouvel examen des trois relations hébraïques sur les persécutions de 1096, suivi d'un fragment de version judéo-allemande inédite de la première relation," *REJ,* XCVI, 113–56 (includes excerpts from a sixteenth-century Yiddish MS now in Cincinnati); and Yuzpa Shammash (the Sexton) of Amsterdam's version in his *Ma'ase nissim* (Miraculous Deeds). It is small wonder then, that Neubauer and Stern's edition has given rise to many disagreements with respect to textual readings, as well as in regard to such substantive questions as the mutual relationships between the three sources and their historic priority. Among the main participants in this debate have been H. Bresslau in his introductory essay, "Zur Kritik der Kreuzzugsberichte," in Neubauer and Stern, pp. xiii–xxix; N. Porges in "Les Relations hébraïques des persécutions des Juifs pendant la première Croisade," *REJ,* XXV, 181–201; XXVI, 183–97; M. Brann in his sharply critical review of the Neubauer and Stern edition, *MGWJ,* XXXVII, 49–56, 103–4, 146–48, 197–200, 285–88, 342–44; I. Elbogen in "Zu den hebräischen Berichten über die Judenverfolgungen im Jahre 1096," *Philippson Festschrift,* pp. 6–24; H. Lichtenstein in "Zum Text des Berichts über die Judenverfolgungen von 1096," *ZGJD,* IV, 155–56 (offering corrections, often trivial, on the basis of a renewed collation of the London MS of Solomon bar Simson's narrative); S. Schiffmann in her *Heinrich IV,* especially pp. 5 ff.; and Sonne. All this confirms the feeling of long standing that a renewed scrutiny of all the available sources might justify a new truly critical edition of these chronicles. Such a project was indeed undertaken, in 1919–21, by a committee of experts headed by E. Täubler, under the sponsorship of the Academy for Jewish Studies in Berlin. Cf. the testimony of one of its main coworkers Y. (F.) Baer in his "Persecutions of 1096" (Hebrew), *Sefer Assaf,* pp. 126–40, where some additional literature is also quoted. These critical problems will crop up again and again in our discussion. See *infra,* n. 9.

Some additional information has long been available in the numerous penitential and other poems left behind by contemporaries or early successors, and reprinted in Habermann's *Sefer Gezerot*. By their very nature, however, these poems are not only repetitious, but also in general rather vague as to details. The same holds true for the *memor* books, that new branch of literature developed in medieval Germany to commemorate the death of leaders and martyrs. Usually limited to names and dates, they offer little factual elaboration. Cf. especially S. Salfeld's ed. of *Das Martyrologium des Nürnberger Memorbuches,* which includes also the so-called *memor* book of Mayence. Some further data may readily be culled also from the excerpts collected by S. Bernfeld in his *Sefer ha-Dema'ot* (Book of Tears; an anthology of Hebrew martyrologies); and B. Z. Dinaburg in his *Yisrael ba-golah,* especially II, 3 ff.

Events recorded in these sources have been told and retold in endless repetition. Perhaps the most lucid and convenient summaries may be found in G. Caro, *Sozial- und Wirtschaftsgeschichte der Juden,* I, 202 ff., 480 ff.; J. Parkes, *Jew in the Medieval Community,* pp. 59 ff.; and E. L. Dietrich's more recent study of "Das Judentum im Zeitalter der Kreuzzüge," *Saeculum,* III, 94–131.

8. Solomon bar Simson's and Eliezer bar Nathan's introductory paragraphs stress verbatim the same chronological setting. On the lunar cycles, which did not play such a conspicuous role in other messianic computations, cf. *infra,* Chap. XXXV. The messianic movement of 1096, which emanated from the Balkans (see *infra,* n. 24), will be discussed in connection with other similar movements of the period, *infra,* Chap. XXV, n. 64.

9. Neither Solomon bar Simson's date nor his other literary activity is known. The only basis for dating his chronicle at 1140 is a reference to that year in his report of the Jewish sufferings in Eller. Cf. Neubauer and Stern ed., pp. 21 (Hebrew), 123 (German; here incorrectly translated); Habermann ed., p. 48. If, however, as is frequently assumed, Solomon merely compiled written and oral traditions into a comprehensive narrative, somewhat modeled on Yosephon (see *infra,* Chap. XXVIII, n. 51), he may have taken over here, too, an existing fragment, which would not necessarily prove that the entire compilation dated from that period. Moreover, as has already been mentioned, his work is extant only in a single MS whose original or secondary copyist was evidently guilty of many sins of commission, and even more of omission. All conclusions drawn therefrom for the identity of this author is therefore doubly hazardous. Habermann's suggestion that he was identical with one of Rashi's colleagues by that name, known as R. Sason (p. 247), is unsupported by any further evidence.

Even less is known about the "Mayence Anonymous," except that he seems to be writing from more immediate observation, or from some independent local source. It is not altogether impossible, therefore, that he was himself a survivor of the Mayence massacre, perhaps because he had yielded to threats and accepted baptism, and that he wrote his chronicle early in the twelfth century, possibly in connection with the consecration of the new synagogue in Spires in 1104. But this suggestion by I. Sonne (in "Nouvel examen. . . ," *REJ,* XCVI, 137), as well as his concomitant doubt that Solomon bar Simson was the author of the first chronicle, is a matter of speculation. Cf. also his debate with Habermann in the latter's "Who Composed the Report No. 1 on the Persecutions of 1096?" (Hebrew), *Sinai,*

IX, No. 105, pp. 79–84 (includes a hitherto unpublished poem by Solomon); and Sonne's "Which is the Earlier Account of the Persecutions during the First Crusade?" (Hebrew), *Zion*, XII, 74–81. As a matter of fact, the Anonymus' historical interpretations for the most part reflect views held by later generations. The accusation, for instance, that the Mayence Jews had "boiled a Christian in water, which they threw into our wells in order to kill us" has a decidedly later medieval tinge (Neubauer and Stern ed., pp. 49, 172; Habermann ed., p. 95). This anachronism has already been pointed out by Bresslau (p. xiv) and remains such, Porges's efforts to the contrary ("Les Relations hébraïques," *REJ*, XXV, 199). On other indications of later reinterpretation see *infra*, nn. 13, 17. See also the literature listed *supra*, n. 7.

Only Eliezer bar Nathan is well known to us, especially through his distinguished legal work, the *Eben ha-'Ezer*. Unfortunately, although in his childhood he seems to have been an eyewitness of the Mayence massacre, his account is the least informative of the three. He seems to have intended to summarize the events as mere explanatory introductions to his elegies describing the downfall of the four communities of Spires, Worms, Mayence, and Cologne. On his life and work, cf. especially A. (V.) Aptowitzer's *Mabo le-Sefer Rabiah*, pp. 49 ff.; and E. Urbach's comprehensive recent study of the *Ba'ale ha-Tosafot* (The Tosafists: Their Lives, Works and Method), pp. 148 ff. In any case, I. Elbogen is right in saying (*Philippson Festschrift*, p. 20) that all the three extant texts "are so badly preserved that their present form does not allow for any definite conclusion concerning their mutual relationship." Perhaps the only generalization one might legitimately make is that, despite their frequent literal agreements, the authors of the three accounts had at their disposal also some more or less independent sources. This assumption remains the most probable despite Y. Baer's noteworthy reexamination of the underlying sources. In his penetrating essay in *Sefer Assaf*, pp. 126 ff., Baer has convincingly shown that all three chroniclers used a basic older narrative, compiled during the tragic events themselves on the basis of numerous letters exchanged by the threatened communities. This narrative was in part, however, victimized during the massacres, and reached the following generation in an incomplete and corrupted form. But it was the original chronicler who set the tone not only for the prose narratives, but also for the numerous penitential poems, partially incorporated into the Jewish liturgy. See *infra*, nn. 65–67. The availability of such a basic narrative in no way militates against the use, by our three chroniclers, of some underlying early sources, including the original letters or their transcripts which must have freely circulated in the surviving German communities. Cf. also *infra*, Chap. XXVIII, n. 82.

10. Solomon's report, ed. by Neubauer and Stern, pp. 25 (Hebrew), 131 (German); ed. by Habermann, p. 53; Jaffé and Wattenbach, *Regesta pontificum*, p. 654 No. 5336 (Aronius, *Regesten*, p. 94 No. 204). Some survivors of the catastrophe, to be sure, reported rumors that already the Council of Clermont had adopted anti-Jewish resolutions and had secretly circulated letters urging the Crusaders to do away with Jews. This seems to be the background of an obscure allusion to some such secret letters in Benjamin bar Ḥiyya's poem, *Berit kerutah* (Covenant Concluded), reprinted in Bernfeld's *Sefer ha-Dema'ot*, III, 310 ff. In explanation of this poem, L. Zunz quoted the statement of a thirteenth-century Hebrew exegete referring to an alleged letter brought by two monks from the Church of the Holy

Sepulcher in Jerusalem, appealing to the Christian world for the extermination of Jews. Cf. Zunz's *Literaturgeschichte der synagogalen Poesie*, p. 258. But all these unconfirmed rumors were obviously mere rationalizations after the event, trying to explain the overwhelming tragedy. As a matter of fact, French Jewry seems to have suffered relatively little from the great upheaval. The disturbances in Rouen were exceptional in so far as that city was under English suzerainty. It was administered by Robert, count of Normandy, eldest son of William the Conqueror, who soon thereafter (September, 1096) left for Italy on the way to the Near East. Cf. Guiberti of Novigento's somewhat dubious report in his *De vita sua*, II.5, in Bouquet, *Recueil*, XII, 240; and C. W. David, *Robert Curthose*, pp. 89 ff. Elsewhere in France we may detect only some faint echoes of relatively minor outbreaks in such later sources, as the *Notitiae duae lemovicenses de praedicatione crucis in Aquitania*, I.2, in *RHC* Hist. occidentaux, V, 351 (on the author, see the editors' preface, pp. lxxxiv ff.). On the other hand, Urban II himself voiced apprehensions about the menace of unleashed popular fury; for instance, in his letter to the Bolognese of September 19, 1096, in H. Hagenmeyer, ed., *Die Kreuzzugsbriefe aus den Jahren 1088–1100*, pp. 137 f. On his movements during 1096, and especially his sojourn in Toulouse during the crucial two months of May and June, see L. Paulot's data in *Un Pape français; Urbain II*. Cf. also A. Fliche, "Urbain II et la Croisade," in *Revue de l'histoire de l'Eglise de France*, Vol. XIII.

11. The three Hebrew chronicles *passim*, generally confirmed by such reports in non-Jewish accounts as that by Monk Bernold in his *Chronicon*, ed. by G. H. Pertz in *MGH*, Scriptores, V, 464 f. (this account stems from a later more anti-Jewish writer). Cf. S. Schiffmann's detailed analysis of the attitudes of the respective bishops to the Jews in her *Heinrich IV*, pp. 26 ff., and the literature listed *supra*, Chap. XX, n. 87.

12. *Annalista Saxo*, 1096, ed. by G. Waitz in *MGH*, Scriptores, VI, 729; and *Annales Patherburgenses*, ed. by P. Scheffer-Boichorst. In the highly abbreviated references to the persecutions in communities other than the four major ones in the Rhineland—fuller reports may have been included in portions of the Hebrew chronicles since lost—we hear little about the actions of the local bishops. Even the happenings in Treves are more fully described in the Latin *Gesta Treverorum* (*MGH*, Scriptores, VIII, 190 f.) than by the Mayence Anonymous. On the events in Prague, see the bishop's namesake and constant collaborator, Cosmas, *Chronicon Boemorum*, III.4–5, 21, 49, 57, ed. by R. Köpke in *MGH*, Scriptores, IX, 103 f., 112, 124 f., 128 f. (or in the revised text, edited with a detailed introduction by B. Bretholz in *MGH*, n.s. II, 164 ff., 188, 222, 231 f.); Bondy and Dworsky, *Juden in Böhmen*, I, 5 f.; and S. Steinherz's careful analysis of all pertinent data in his "Kreuzfahrer und Juden in Prag (1096)," *JGJCR*, I, 1–32. Cf. also *infra*, n. 38.

13. Hugo of Flavigny's *Chronicon*, ed. by G. H. Pertz, in *MGH*, Scriptores, VIII, 474; and the data analyzed by H. Fischer in *Die verfassungsrechtliche Stellung der Juden*, pp. 37 ff., 45 ff., 176 ff., and especially 183 ff. (note 7: "Die Schutzleistung der Wormser Bürger während der Judenverfolgung von 1096"). Obviously, neither the Hebrew nor the Latin chroniclers had any reason to play up the pro-Jewish activities of some burghers. We shall see that, in their grief over Jewish sufferings and their wrath over the unspeakable atrocities committed by the Crusaders, the

former were prone to view all Christians as sworn enemies, and to suspect even friendly acts as inspired by ulterior motives. This attitude is particularly pronounced in the case of the Mayence Anonymous, whose bitterness may be explained either by his personal experiences, if he happened to be an eyewitness to these events, or, what is more likely, by the growing mutual hostility in the course of the twelfth and thirteenth centuries, if he wrote at a much later date. Cf. *supra*, n. 9; and *infra*, n. 62. Injunctions to preserve order under the threat of excommunication may have been included in Archbishop Egilbert's sermon at the Church of St. Simeon of Treves, mentioned by Solomon bar Simson. Perhaps these very threats so incensed the large crowd of worshipers assembled there for the Pentecost services that they staged a riot and put the preacher to flight. See Neubauer and Stern ed., pp. 26 (Hebrew), 133 (German); Habermann ed., pp. 53 f.; and, on the location of the Church, S. Schiffmann, *Heinrich IV*, p. 37 n. 43.

14. Neubauer and Stern ed., pp. 5, 48 (Hebrew), 92 f., 172 (German); Habermann ed., pp. 29, 95. According to Solomon, Emicho received the substantial amount of 7 pounds gold, as against the 400 silver marks each paid to the archbishop and the burghers of Mayence. This difference may perhaps best be explained by the fact that Emicho, preparing for a long journey, wished to travel lightly. While traversing the territories of the Byzantine Empire, gold coins were also more likely to serve him in good stead.

15. Henry IV's order, addressed to "the princes, bishops, counts and Duke Godfrey," and enjoining them, "with respect to Jews to guard them lest anyone cause them bodily harm and to extend to them help and protection" is apparently quoted more or less exactly from the original decree. Cf. Neubauer and Stern ed., pp. 3 (Hebrew), 88 (German); Habermann ed., p. 27; and E. Täubler's comments thereon in *Mitteilungen des Gesamtarchivs*, V, 143 f. The main argument relating to Jews as infidels and Christ-killers is almost verbatim repeated by all three Hebrew chroniclers. Cf. Neubauer and Stern ed., pp. 1, 36, 47 (Hebrew), 82 f., 154, 169 (German); Habermann ed., pp. 24, 72, 93. Needless to say that these chroniclers, despite their nearly verbal agreement (only the Mayence Anonymous has important formal variants) and the substantial confirmation by such Christian chroniclers as Guiberti of Novigento (*De Vita sua*, 11.5, in Bouquet, *Recueil*, XII, 240), did not quote here literally the Crusaders' utterances. They merely applied the accepted technique of ancient and medieval historians to make heroes explain their motivations through imaginary speeches. That is why they could even put into the mouths of Crusaders technical terms derogatory to Jesus and the Church, which had long lost their original connotation in the daily usage of Jews, but which no professing Christians could possibly have employed. S. Baer was therefore right in replacing these offensive terms by more neutral designations (for instance, "house of shame" by church), a practice followed also in our quotation. Cf. H. Bresslau's introduction to the Neubauer and Stern edition, pp. xxvii ff. Similarly, the Gospel paraphrase need not have originated with the Crusaders, but probably was the form adopted by the Hebrew chronicler to convey the main argument of Jew-baiters.

16. Although reported only by the Mayence Anonymous, we need not doubt the historicity of either Dithmar's vow or the alleged reply of the Mayence community

to early letters of warning from France. The Mayence answer seems indeed to convey the state of mind among the Rhenish leaders. After informing the French Jews that they had instituted prayers in their behalf, the Mayence elders wrote, "As regards us, we have no grounds for apprehension. We have not even heard any rumors of a planned persecution and of the sword hanging over our heads." Neubauer and Stern ed., pp. 47 f. (Hebrew), 170 ff. (German); Habermann ed., pp. 94 f. This optimism is the less astonishing, as the great enthusiasm, generated, in both its positive and negative manifestations, by the call to the Crusade, was greatly to surprise its very originators. We shall also see that not even the tragic experiences of 1096 sufficed to teach the lesson to the Jewish communities half a century later. On the possible identity of Dithmar with the ringleader Volkmar in Saxony and Bohemia, cf. Aronius, *Regesten*, pp. 82 f. Nos. 179–81, 93 Nos. 201–2. The gradual adoption by the Christians of the basic concepts and methods of the Muslim Holy War is rightly stressed by J. L. LaMonte. See *supra*, n. 1; and J. Leclercq's "Gratien, Pierre de Troyes, et la seconde croisade," *Studia Gratiana*, II, 583–93 (analyzing the inquiry of the Latin patriarch of Jerusalem, addressed to Abbot Pierre Manducator of Troyes, 1147–67, and the latter's reply affirming that the blood of infidels may freely be shed in a war for the holy places).

17. Neubauer and Stern ed., pp. 6, 28 (Hebrew), 95, 137 f. (German); Habermann ed., pp. 30, 57; "Dalimil's" *Rýmovaná Kronika česka* (Czech Rhymed Chronicle), ed. by J. Jireček, in *Fontes rerum bohemicarum*, III, 182 f. (the pertinent passage is translated and analyzed by Steinherz in *JGJCR*, I, 18 f.). The identity of the city ŠLA in which the Jews offered that successful resistance, still is in doubt. In a note to his translation, Baer suggested a name like Zell or Celle; Porges ("Les Relations hébraïques," *REJ*, XXVI, 195 f.), recommended Vishehrad, near Prague; Salfeld (in *Das Martyrologium des Nürnberger Memorbuches*, p. 151) proposed another Bohemian city, Wessely. More recently, H. Tykocinski argued in favor of its identity with Halle on the Saale. Cf. his "Die Stadt ŠLA des ersten Kreuzzugs," *Dubnow Festschrift*, pp. 154–62; and his " 'Halle' und 'Prag'," in M. Brann *et al.*, *Germania judaica*, pp. 508 ff. Cf., however, the strictures by D. Herzog, who in turn suggested the identification with "Sachsenland." See Herzog's "Die Kreuzfahrer und die Juden in Prag (1096)," *Zeitschrift für Geschichte der Juden in der Tschechoslowakei*, I, 219–25; supplemented by his debate with B. Brilling, *ibid.*, II, 49–52. Porges's suggestion of a Bohemian city is the most likely in so far as a Jewish victory over Crusaders in some Bohemian locality is indeed reported by "Dalimil." Yet Steinherz's suggestion (in "Kreuzfahrer und Juden in Prag," *JGJCR*, I, 7 ff.) to read *u-be-khol* (and in all [Bohemia]) instead of ŠLA is too trenchant an emendation to be readily accepted. In any case, the number of 500 Jewish warriors in a single locality seems decidedly exaggerated. Not even Mayence could have marshaled such a force. See *infra*, n. 19.

There also occurred individual acts of retribution. A young Jew of Worms, Simḥah bar Isaac ha-Kohen, pretending to submit to baptism, was conducted to the church. There he knifed a relative of the bishop before he was torn to bits by the attendants. This story, told matter-of-factly by Eliezer bar Nathan, was greatly dramatized by the Mayence Anonymous, who added two more victims to Simḥah's fury and made him fall only after his knife was broken. Cf. Neubauer and Stern ed., pp. 38, 50 (Hebrew), 156, 175 (German); Habermann ed., pp. 74,

97. Elaborations of this type have indeed inspired diffidence in the Anonymous's account, and lent support to the view that it is the latest of the three chronicles. See *supra*, n. 9.

18. Neubauer and Stern ed., pp. 7, 44, 47, 52 (Hebrew), 96, 164 f., 169 f., 178 (German); Habermann ed., pp. 31, 51, 93, 98 f. On Shemaryahu, see also Salfeld's *Martyrologium*, pp. 106 n. 8, 139. Both the ghost congregation and the French letters urging the proclamation of fast days are mentioned only by the Mayence Anonymous. He may have given a pietistic turn to the aforementioned correspondence which dealt with such worldly means of staving off attacks as the supply of provisions to the Crusaders. He thus reflected the growing pietism of later generations, rather than the first reactions of the still intact Rhenish communities. But we need not doubt the fact itself that communal fasts were used already at that time as a means of propitiating the divine wrath. Solomon bar Simson, too, ascribed the failure of armed Jews to prevent Emicho's entry into Mayence in part to their weakness caused "by their numerous earlier sufferings and fast days." The unprecedented character of this wave of mass suicides did not escape the attention of chroniclers, and both Solomon and Eliezer pointed out how greatly the eleven hundred 'aqedot performed in Mayence in a single day overshadowed Abraham's celebrated attempt at sacrificing Isaac. See *infra*, n. 66.

19. Neubauer and Stern ed., pp. 2, 8, 23, 43 (Hebrew), 85, 98, 128, 163 f. (German); Habermann ed., pp. 25 f., 32, 50 f., 79; Gedaliah ibn Yaḥya's *Shalshelet ha-qabbalah* (Chain of Tradition; a history of the Jews), ed. Venice, 1587, fol. 110b. Eliezer bar Nathan gives the same number of 800 martyrs in Worms, but raises their figure from 1100 to more than 1300 in Mayence (Neubauer and Stern ed., pp. 38 f., 156 ff.; Habermann ed., pp. 74 f.). On the other hand, *Annalista Saxo* lowers it to 900 (*MGH*, Scriptores VI, 729). Cf. also Salfeld's *Martyrologium*, pp. 107 f., 118 f. From among the Cologne refugees this martyrology (p. 17) enumerates more than 60 persons who had lived in Xanten alone. Cf. J. Freimann, "Zur Geschichte der Juden in Xanten," *Dubnow Festschrift*, pp. 165 f. Despite his general unreliability, Gedaliah's testimony cannot be totally discounted, for he had at his disposal sources no longer extant. Certainly his figure is more reasonable than that of 12,000 victims, as is often asserted. All these "guestimates" are unfortunately quite arbitrary, because we cannot even say whether the recorded number of victims in Worms and Mayence is not exaggerated. The total Jewish population of either community had hardly exceeded the figures here given for the dead alone. Even the chroniclers themselves, though underplaying the betrayals to the cause, nevertheless clearly intimate that there were many Jews who saved themselves by conversion. Gedaliah himself contrasted the "more than 5,000" victims with "countless" apostates. See also *infra*, n. 22.

20. A. Marx's citation from a Parma MS in "The Expulsion of the Jews from Spain: Two New Accounts," *JQR*, [o.s.] XX, 241, 258 n. 4; Isaac ben Jacob Lattes's fourteenth-century chronicle, *Qiryat Sefer*, in *MJC*, II, 235; David Gans's *Ṣemaḥ David* (Scion of David; a world chronicle), Prague ed., 1592, fol. 53b. While one cannot deny the possibility that even some of the regular troops assembling in Italy for shipment across the Adriatic Sea to Byzantium may have committed acts of violence against individual Jews, such as Moses of Pavia, it would seem fool-

hardy to magnify such incidents into full-fledged persecutions without further evidence from more reliable sources. Certainly, Godfrey of Bouillon, blamed by Lattes, did not pass through Italy, but marched along the northern route through Hungary.

21. *Gesta Treverorum,* cont. prima, XVII, in *MGH,* Scriptores, VIII, 190 f.; Neubauer and Stern ed., pp. 29 (Hebrew), 138 (German); Habermann ed., p. 57; William II's decree of 1098 summarized in Eadmer's *Historia Novorum,* II, in *PL,* CLIX, 410 f. According to Eadmer, William II, prompted by a Jewish father's promise of sixty marks in silver, tried to force a Jewish youth, converted to Christianity out of conviction, to return to Judaism. Having been sharply rebuked by the young man, he nevertheless tried to collect the promised fee from the father. This story, very likely an ecclesiastical fabrication, was retold with relish by E. A. Freeman in *The Reign of William and the Accession of Henry the First,* I, 162 ff. See *supra,* n. 10; and Chap. XX, n. 100. Cf. also Henry IV's decree of June, 1197, briefly mentioned by Ekkehard of Aura in his *Chronicon universale,* ad 1097, ed. by G. Waitz, in *MGH,* Scriptores, VI, 208 (not included in Von Gladiss's ed. of *Die Urkunden Heinrichs IV*); Clement III's aforementioned letter to the Bishop of Bamberg in 1097–98 (both summarized in Aronius's *Regesten,* pp. 93 ff. Nos. 203, 204, 207); Rashi's *Teshubot* (Responsa), ed. by I. Elfenbein, pp. 188 ff. Nos. 168–70; other sources cited by Dinaburg in his *Yisrael ba-golah,* II, 30; and I. Elbogen's observations in *Der jüdische Gottesdienst in seiner geschichtlichen Entwicklung,* 3d ed., pp. 203, 231, 335 ff.

On another occasion Rashi spelled out the kind of behavior which was expected of forced converts during the period of their clandestine profession of Judaism. In order to be admitted later to testimony before a Jewish court, the sage of Troyes declared, "the court must be satisfied that during the period of their enforced submission they had lived secretly according to the law of Moses, and that they had not been suspected of sins committed in private without being forced to do so by Gentiles." Cf. his resp. in I. A. Agus's ed. of *Teshubot ba'ale ha-tosafot* (Responsa of the Tosafists), pp. 51 f. No. 9. Cf. also *supra,* n. 10. The author of the *Gesta Treverorum* himself admitted that, with the exception of Micheas, *all* Treves Jews reverted to Judaism in 1097. Perhaps such assertion is to be taken with a grain of salt, since some conversions to Christianity took place even in peaceful times. Probably some of the converts, particularly among the orphaned children who had been given away to Christian foster parents, must have remained faithful members of the Church. In any case, the period of severe persecution having been limited to the brief span of one year, Germany was spared the experience of large-scale Marranism, that permanent residue of sudden mass conversions.

22. Solomon bar Simson's report, ed. by Neubauer and Stern, pp. 30 (Hebrew), 140 f. (German); ed. by Habermann, p. 58. Cf. Runciman's description of "The First Crusaders Journey across the Balkan Peninsula," *Byzantion,* XIX, 207–21; and his *History of the Crusades,* I, 134 ff. (both mainly concerned with Byzantine territories). One cannot blame Solomon's Hebrew sources or personal informants for vastly exaggerating the number of Crusaders who lost their lives in the Balkans. Even such a generally reliable chronicler as Albert of Aix did not hesitate to attribute to Peter the Hermit's band a total of 40,000, of whom allegedly only 500 remained with Peter after their dispersal by the Bulgarians. Commenting on these

and other "pictorial figures" used in nearly all contemporary accounts, W. B. Stevenson objected even to the use of the term, "exaggerated." This description, in his opinion, "does not go far enough if it implies, or is understood to imply, that the numbers bear some proportion to reality and may be taken as a starting-point for an estimate of the actual numbers." Cf. "The First Crusade" in *The Cambridge Medieval History*, V, 278, 298. Cf. also Runciman's Appendix II on "The Numerical Strength of the Crusaders" in his *History*, I, 336 ff. These legitimate criticisms cast some doubt on, but do not completely invalidate, also the aforementioned numbers of victims of the massacres in Worms and Mayence. These were definitely not "pictorial figures," and contemporaries may well have retained the memory of the approximate size of losses sustained by their own communities. See *supra*, n. 19.

23. Baudri (Baldricus) of Bourgueil, *Historia Jerosolomitana*, 1.17, in *RHC*, Hist. occidentaux, IV, 23; J. Starr, *Jews in the Byzantine Empire*, p. 211 No. 157. The anonymous author of the *Gesta Francorum et aliorum Hierosolymitarum*, who had accompanied Bohemund and probably was an eye-witness of the event, mentioned only heretical victims. Cf. L. Bréhier's edition, with a French translation of *Histoire anonyme de la première Croisade*, pp. xiv, 22 (1.4). Even Baudri's description "enemies of God" thus called by "everybody," that is by Greek Orthodox and Catholics alike, makes more sense, when applied to Christian sectarians than with reference to Muslims or Jews in whose case it would be a mere truism. On his general unreliability, see the editor's preface, pp. vii ff.

24. Cf. the aforementioned Byzantine letter, ed. by Neubauer in his "Egyptian Fragments, II" in *JQR*, [o.s.] IX, 26 ff.; with Kaufmann's German translation and comments in *BZ*, VII, 83 ff.; also comments by J. Mann in *Hatekufah*, XXIII, 253 ff. (reprinting Neubauer's text after collation with the Bodleian MS), and by Starr, *Byzantine Empire*, pp. 203 ff. No. 153; and *supra*, Chap. XIX, n. 23. This commotion in Salonica reflected the messianic movement of that crucial year which, starting in western Europe, spread through all the lands of Christendom. It is even possible that the conversion of "Archbishop" Andreas and his escape to "Constantinople" which had so impressed Johannes-Obadiah the Norman proselyte, was the effect of that movement stimulated by the preachment of the Christian Crusade. Curiously, it did not seem to affect the communities under Islam in either West or East. Cf. *supra*, Chap. XIX, n. 21; and *infra*, Chap. XXV, n. 67. That Byzantine Jewry, on the whole, escaped persecution at this juncture is evidenced not only by the silence on this score of contemporary chroniclers, but also by the continued disputes between the Karaite and the Rabbanite communities in Constantinople, "at the time of the arrival of the Germans." Cf. Aaron ben Elijah's *Gan 'Eden* (Garden of Eden; a Book of Precepts), 1.8, ed. by Y. Savsakan, fol. 8d; and Starr, *Byzantine Empire*, p. 208 f. No. 154. Like the designation "Franks," the term "Germans" (*Ashkenazim*) is used here, and in many other Near Eastern sources, for all Westerners; in this case principally for the Franco-Norman majority of participants in the First Crusade. Cf. *supra*, Chap. XIX, n. 53. On the background, cf. e.g., P. Charanis's "Aims of the Medieval Crusades and How They Were Viewed by Byzantium," *Church History*, XXI, 123–34, where however only the high policies of the imperial government are treated. Of even greater interest would be a similar study on the reaction of the Balkan and Ánatolian masses. See also A. Sharf, "An Unknown Messiah of 1096 and the Emperor Alexius," *JJS*, VII, 59–70.

25. Letter from the Syrian community, probably not far from Damascus, published from a Cairo MS by J. Mann in *Hatekufah*, XXIII, 260 f.; *Gesta Francorum*, x. 36, ed. by Bréhier in *Histoire anonyme*, p. 192. The chronicler's failure to mention Ramleh Jews among the evacués may be owing to their slight number. After the earthquake of 1067, speedily followed by the Seljuk conquest of 1071 and the sale into slavery of a great many captives, the Jewish community in that formerly important center of trade and administration never recovered its strength. Cf. *Sefer ha-Yishub*, II, 20 f. There is no evidence that the Damascus, or any other, community had to strain its resources for the redemption of Jewish captives in 1098–99, although sales of prisoners into slavery are occasionally reported by chroniclers (see n. 26). The Crusaders often gave no quarter to the non-Christian inhabitants of cities, but left most peasants undisturbed. This policy was dictated by the necessity of providing food for their own combatants who more than once were rescued from starvation only by the timely arrival of supplies in Italian ships.

26. William of Tyre, *Historia rerum in partibus transmarinis gestarum*, VIII.20, in *RHC*, Hist. occidentaux, I, 354 f.; and in E. A. Babcock's and A. C. Krey's English translation, entitled *A History of Deeds Done Beyond the Sea*, I, 372; Abu Yaḥya Hamza ibn al-Qalanisi, *K. Mudhayyal tarikh Dimashq* (History of Damascus 363–555 A.H., Being a Continuation of the History of Damascus of Hilâl al-Sâbi), ed. by H. F. Amedroz, p. 137; and in H. A. R. Gibb's selections from *The Damascus Chronicle of the Crusades* in English translation, p. 48 (cf. also Gibb's "Notes on the Arabic Materials for the History of the Early Crusades," *BSOAS*, VII, 739–54, showing the superiority of Ibn al-Qalanisi's report over the later chronicles, including that of Ibn al-Athir); R. Le Tourneau's comments on his French version of Ibn al-Qalanisi's text in his *Damas de 1075 à 1154*, p. 43; and Albert of Aix' *Historia Hierosolymitana*, VI, 21–30, in *RHC*, Hist. occidentaux, IV, 478 ff. (in Hefele's German trans., *Geschichte des ersten Kreuzzugs*, I, 298ff.). Even pious Godfrey of Bouillon gloatingly reported to the pope that in the Temple area "our men rode in Saracen blood up to the horses' ankles." Fortunately for the Jews, their number had greatly declined since the conquest of Jerusalem by the Seljuks in 1071 and the recurrent attempts at its recapture by Egypt. On the disorders, and ultimately also diseases, which ruined the country, cf. now the graphic description in the letter of a would-be Jewish pilgrim to the Holy Land, recently recovered from a Genizah MS in Cambridge by S. D. Goitein. This pilgrim, probably writing in 1100, had already spent several years in Egypt, vainly awaiting the opportunity to visit the Holy Land in relative peace. See the Arabic text of the second Genizah document, ed. with a Hebrew trans., by Goitein in his "New Sources for the Fate of the Jews during the Conquest of Jerusalem by the Crusaders" (Hebrew), *Zion*, XVII, 144 ff.; and its English translation with substantially the same introduction, in his "Contemporary Letters on the Capture of Jerusalem by the Crusaders," *JJS*, III, 175 ff.

Curiously, the massacre of the Jerusalem Jews left few traces in Hebrew letters, unless it be in the nearly contemporary Persian "Apocalypse of Daniel," as suggested by J. Darmesteter in "L'Apocalypse persane de Daniel," *Bibliothèque de l'Ecole pratique des hautes études*, LXXIII, 416 f.; and Ibn Shemuel's *Midreshe ge'ulah*, pp. 199 ff., 221 f. But if this writer should indeed have had in mind Godfrey of Bouillon as the last of the twenty-five rulers here enumerated, his claim that not only was a multitude of Jews massacred but that circumcision, Sabbath observance, study of the Law and recitation of prayers were outlawed, would require further substantiation. Ibn Shemuel may, therefore, be quite right in denying the identification with Godfrey and in seeing in that twenty-fifth ruler but the old mythological figure of Armilus. At any rate, perhaps because it had affected only a relatively small number of Jews, was part of a military action, and was not repeated in other parts of the country, the impact of the Crusaders' conquest of Jerusalem on the rest of Near Eastern Jewry was quite limited. See next note.

27. Baudri, *Historia*, iv.14, in *RHC*, Hist. occidentaux, IV, 103 n. 7 (see, however, *supra*, n. 23); *Tefillat R. Shimeon bar Yoḥai* (Simon bar Yoḥai's Prayer), in Ibn Shemuel's *Midreshe ge'ulah*, pp. 281 f. Modern scholars have long agreed that most passages in that composite prayer date from the age of the Crusades, but there still is great uncertainty about the attribution of individual sections to a particular phase of that conflict. Although arguing in favor of an earlier date of some other sections (see *supra*, Chap. XVII, n. 27), B. Lewis has plausibly ascribed the paragraph here quoted to Palestine's occupation in 1099. See "An Apocalyptic Vision of Islamic History," *BSOAS*, XIII, 311, 318, 337. However, his assertion that "every line suggests the horror of a contemporary witness," appears too sweeping.

28. Albert of Aix, *Historia*, vii.22–25 in *RHC*, Hist. occidentaux, IV, 521 ff. (Hefele's trans., II, 22 ff.); and the first Genizah document published by Goitein in *Zion*, XVII, 136 ff.; and in *JJS*, III, 171 ff. The prohibition for Jews (and Muslims) to dwell in Jerusalem, probably a conscious or unwitting renewal of the old Hadrianic exclusion, is mentioned by William of Tyre in his *Historia rerum*, xi.27, in *RHC*, I, 500 f.; and in Babcock and Krey's English translation, I, 507. Writing in the 1120's Abraham bar Ḥiyya (Savasorda) claimed that "not a single Jew is found in Jerusalem at this time." Cf. his *Megillat ha-megalleh* (Scroll of Disclosure), iv, ed. by A. Poznanski, pp. 99 f. Albert of Aix' extensive description makes it clear that in Haifa the Jews were the main defenders of the city assaulted by Tancred's army on land, and by a Venetian fleet from the sea. "All that were found in the city were slain." Cf. A. Mentsher's "Jewish Haifa in the Period of Crusades" (Hebrew), *Karmelit*, II, 233–40. Cf. also Mann, *Jews in Egypt*, II, 198 ff. including the text of a letter in which an unknown writer asks for an introduction to the authorities of Ascalon, "if I should wish to go from Ḥazor to Ascalon in an emergency, since she is stronger and more fortified than Ḥazor."

The tragic effects of the Crusaders' conquest of the Holy Land on the local Jewish communities, which had been declining during the preceding several decades, was first told in a consecutive fashion by B. Z. Dinaburg in "A Study of the History of Jews in Palestine during the First Crusade" (Hebrew), *Ṣiyyon*, II, 38–66. Cf. also the excerpts assembled in his *Yisrael ba-golah*, II, 118 ff. Additional data were supplied by J. Prawer in "The Jews in the Latin Kingdom of Jerusalem" (Hebrew), *Zion*, XI, 38–82; and more briefly, but in a broader context, in his *Mamlekhet Yerushalayim ha-ṣalbanit* (The Latin Kingdom of Jerusalem, 1099–1291), pp. 50 ff. The often highly confusing succession of rulers in the various principalities established by the Crusaders is lucidly presented in J. L. LaMonte's "Chronology of the Orient latin," *Bulletin of the International Committee of Historical Sciences*, XII, 141–202.

29. Goitein's documents in *Zion*, XVII (or *JJS*, III), *passim*; *Sefer ha-Yishub*, II, 36, No. 9. Cf. *infra*, Chap. XXVI, n. 75 (also on the technical use of the term,

maskil). On the location of the Karaite quarter in 1099, cf. J. Prawer's data in "The Vicissitudes of the Jewish and Karaite Quarters in Jerusalem during the Arab Period (640–1099)" (Hebrew), *Zion*, XII, 141 ff.

30. Mann, *Jews in Egypt*, I, 169 f., 199 f. (cites the Karaite colophon, first published by Harkavy in 1875); II, 198 ff. Mann is right in assuming both the genuineness of the colophon and Solomon's likely descent from 'Anan, but he argues rather too rashly for the spuriousness of various other references to the relations between the Karaites and the early Latin rulers. These data ought to be reexamined now in the light of the apparently more friendly attitude of the conquerors toward these sectarians.

31. Isaiah ben Maṣliaḥ's letter, ed. by Goitein (line 24: "The accursed ones who are called *Ashkenaz*"; see *supra*, n. 24); R. Röhricht's *Regesta Regni Hierosolymitani (MXCVII–MCCXCI)*, No. 1114 p. 291. Because of the relative moderation during their occupation of Syria, the Crusaders found that the local population at first reciprocated and often actually welcomed the invaders, as during the conquest of Antioch. Cf., for instance, the testimony of the Armenian chronicler, Hovannes (Joannes), published in Latin translation by P. Peeters in "Un Témoignage autographe sur le siège d'Antioche par les Croisés en 1098," in *Miscellanea historica in honorem Alberti de Meyer*, I, 373–90.

32. Benjamin, *Massaʿot*, pp. 20 f., 23 (Hebrew), 18 f., 22 (English); Ibn al-Qifṭi's *K. Taʾriḥ al-ḥukamaʾ* (History of Scholars), ed. by Lippert, p. 218. In view of the continued prohibition for Jews to reside in Jerusalem, the reading *dalet* (four) instead of *resh* (200) families in Benjamin's travelogue appears decidedly preferable. A decade later Petaḥiah found there only one Jew, "Abraham the dyer [who] pays a heavy tax to the king to be permitted to remain there." See his *Sibbub*, ed. by Grünhut, p. 32; and in Benisch's English trans., pp. 60 f. On the Maimonidean episode, cf. also C. Cahen's "Indigènes et Croisés. Quelques mots à propos d'un médécin d'Amaury et de Saladin," *Syria*, XV, 353; and *infra*, Chap. XXXVI.

33. A. S. Tritton, "The First and Second Crusade from an Anonymous Syriac Chronicle," *JRAS*, 1933, 291 (trans. of text in *CSOC*, 3d ser. XV); Runciman, *History*, II, 101, 239. In his "Saladin and the Jews," *HUCA*, XXVII, 325, E. Ashtor-Strauss intimates that the figure of 300 Jewish families settled in Edessa may be exaggerated. But replacement of a substantial Armenian population could hardly be meaningful, if fewer Jews had been resettled. The great shortage of manpower and the ensuing "Colonization Activities in the Latin Kingdom of Jerusalem," are described in J. Prawer's pertinent essay in *RBPH*, XXIX, 1063–1118; and in his study of "The Settlement of the Latins in Jerusalem," *Speculum*, XXVII, 490–503. Such shortages must also have favorably influenced the attitude of rulers to their Jewish subjects.

34. Röhricht, *Regesta Regni Hierosolymitani*, p. 167 No. 633; J. L. LaMonte, *Feudal Monarchy in the Latin Kingdom of Jerusalem*, pp. 180 f. This novel national tax undoubtedly influenced also the so-called Saladin tax in England and similar Continental levies five years later. But the difference is equally significant: in England, as we recall, Jews had to contribute funds at the absolutely ruinous rate of 25 percent of their property, whereas the rest of the population paid only

10 percent. Cf. *supra*, Chap. XX. n. 106. In his "Etude préliminaire sur les sources et la composition du 'Livre de assises des bourgeois,'" *RHDF*, 4th ser., XXXII, 362, J. Prawer has pointed out that, according to that contemporary author, Jews and Samaritans enjoyed equal burghers' rights with Syrians, Nestorians and Saracens. Cf. also, more generally, the well-documented studies by J. Richard, *Le Royaume Latin de Jérusalem* (a mimeographed index was supplied only on special request); and P. Rousset's succinct comparison between Sicily under Roger II and Syria under Baldwin I in his "Deux expériences pluralistes dans l'Europe du XIIe siècle," *Zeitschrift für schweizerische Kirchengeschichte*, XLVI, 113–29. In his review of Richard's volume (in *HZ*, CLXXIX, 397–98) B. Spuler mentioned also an unpublished Hamburg dissertation by A. Lüders, *Die Kreuzzüge im Urteil syrischer und armenischer Quellen*. Other pertinent monographs are W. Hotzelt, *Kirchengeschichte Palästinas im Zeitalter der Kreuzzüge*; G. Beyer, "Die Kreuz-fahrergebiete Südwestpalästinas," *Beiträge zur Biblischen Landes- und Altertums-kunde*, LXVIII, 249–81; and for the sake of comparison, C. Cahen, *La Syrie du Nord á l'époque des Croisades et la principauté franque d'Antioche*. The enormous older literature is conveniently listed in P. Thomsen's successive volumes of *Die Palästina-Literatur*.

35. Yehudah ben Solomon al-Ḥarizi's *Taḥkemoni* (Maqamae), XLVI, ed. by Lagarde, pp. 167 f.; ed. by Toporowski, pp. 349 f.; Abraham bar Hillel's *Scroll*, ed. by A. Neubauer in his "Egyptian Fragments," *JQR*, [o.s.] VIII, 549. Cf. Mann, *Jews in Egypt*, I, 236 n. 1. Of considerable interest are also the "Letters from Palestine in the Age of Crusades" published by S. D. Goitein in a Hebrew essay in *Yerusha-layim*, II–V, 54–70, where Letter II, written after 1187, reveals the attachment of Egyptian Jews to Palestine. Goitein upholds here also the historicity of Saladin's invitation to the Jews to return to Jerusalem. Although in his address to the Christian delegation during the Third Crusade, Saladin is reputed to have empha-sized the holy character of Jerusalem also to the Muslims, he evidently did not mind restoring the Jewish status which had existed in the early Muslim period. That this policy of toleration extended even to Christians is the more remarkable as Saladin had fought a "holy war" and informed the other Muslim sovereigns of his success in "purifying" the Holy City from the uncleanliness of its infidel masters. When soon thereafter the Third Crusade gathered momentum, he appealed to the rabidly anti-Jewish, as well as anti-Christian, Almohades for naval assistance, especially against the powerful Sicilian fleet. See "Une Lettre de Saladin au caliphe almohade," ed. by M. Gaudefroy-Demombynes in *Mélanges René Basset*, II, 279–304; *Der Sturz des Königreichs Jerusalem (583/1187) in der Darstellung des 'Imād ad-Dīn al-Kātib al-Iṣfahānī*, ed. by J. Kraemer; H. A. R. Gibb's brief review of "The Arabic Sources for the Life of Saladin," *Speculum*, XXV, 58–72; and his succinct summary of "The Achievement of Saladin," *BJRL*, XXXV, 44–60. It appears that, soon after the conquest, Saladin appointed Obadiah bar 'Ulla as chief of Syrian and Palestinian Jewry, thus hoping to promote an orderly internal administration of the Jewish communities under state supervision. To judge from 'Imad's flowery description of Saladin's conquest of Tiberias, the few Palestinian Jews, too, must have sustained severe losses during the campaign. The new administration was doubly interested, therefore, in speedily restoring the economic life of the country. Looking into the later evolution, however, E. Ashtor-Strauss correctly summarized his analysis of the relations between "Saladin and the Jews" by saying that "the

non-Muslim communities were not persecuted in his days, but he sowed the seed which resulted in their persecution" (*HUCA*, XXVII, 326). Cf. also A. S. Atiya's succinct observations on "The Crusades: Old Ideas and New Conceptions," *Journal of World History*, II, 469–75 ("from the point of view of Islam").

36. Solomon bar Simson's chronicle, in Neubauer and Stern ed., pp. 11 f. (Hebrew), 105 ff. (German); Habermann ed., pp. 36 f.; Ekkehard, *Chronicon universale*, ad 1098 in *MGH*, Scriptores, VI, 209; Clement III's letter of July 29, 1099, in Jaffé, *Monumenta moguntina*, pp. 377 ff. No. 32 (both summarized in Aronius, *Regesten*, pp. 94 ff. Nos. 205, 207); *supra*, n. 11; and Chap. XIX, n. 21. For greater emphasis the pope addressed his letter to the people, as well as to the clergy of Mayence. As lord of the city, the archbishop may have felt entitled to take over heirless Jewish property, but his behavior throughout the disturbances was obviously dictated by considerations for personal safety and financial gain, rather than for the maintenance of public order.

37. Sigmund Meisterlein's *Nieronbergensis cronica*, 1.14–15, ed. by D. Kerler, in *Chroniken deutscher Städte*, III, 205 ff:; Aronius, *Regesten*, pp. 97 ff. Nos. 212, 213, 215, 219. Meisterlein wrote his chronicle in 1488, and often reflected fifteenth-century opinions, rather than facts of the past. Cf. Kerler's observations, pp. 20 ff. His report about the city's surrender in 1105 is doubly suspect, as he claims that at that time there was "a great multitude" of Jews in the city and that "they placed their hopes in the junior" emperor against his father, Henry IV. All available evidence points, on the contrary, to the Jews' genuine allegiance to their tested benefactor, Henry IV, and their non-involvement in the struggle between the Papacy and the Empire, in which Henry V's conquest of Nuremberg represented a victory of the ecclesiastical party. Cf. also H. Tykocinski's "Nürnberg," in *Germania judaica*, p. 249; and, on the legal and moral issues involved in Henry V's rebellion against his father, H. F. Haefele's dissertation, *Fortuna Heinrici IV. imperatoris*, pp. 90 ff. On the religious debates of the period, cf. *infra*, Chap. XXIV.

38. Cosmas, *Chronicon*, *supra*, n. 12; Aronius, *Regesten*, pp. 95 ff., Nos. 206, 214, 218, 220–21; Bondy and Dworsky, *Zur Geschichte der Juden*, pp. 6 f. Nos. 11–13. On the still obscure story of Jacob's rise and fall, cf. S. Steinherz's analysis of "Der Sturz des Vicedominus Jacob (1124)," *JGJČR*, II, 17–49. The complex problems of forced conversions which, as a rule were considered valid, though unlawful, and only under very special conditions could be declared null and void, will be discussed more fully in connection with the later medieval debates on this score by authoritative canon jurists, and the Inquisitorial procedures based on them. For the time being we need but refer here to J. Juster's *Empire romain*, I, 110 n. 1, 272 ff. (pointing out that Justinian introduced the first penalties for relapsed converts); and the first ed. of this work, II, 48 ff.; III, 109 ff. Cf. *supra*, Chap. XVI, n. 47.

39. Ephraim bar Jacob of Bonn's *Sefer Zekhirah* or *Zikhronot* (Book of Remembrance), ed. by Neubauer and Stern, pp. 58 ff. (Hebrew), 187 ff. (German); ed. by Habermann, pp. 115 ff. On the author, cf. the biographical data assembled by A. Aptowitzer in his *Mabo le-Sefer Rabiah*, pp. 319 ff. The Würzburg riots are of interest also because they had been provoked by the discovery of a wonder-working Christian corpse in the river and the accusation, readily believed, that Jews had

caused his death. This was but another link in the chain of evolution toward the full-fledged blood libel. See *infra*, nn. 56 ff. Cf. also M. Szulwas's data in *Die Juden in Würzburg*, pp. 9 ff. (with a rather inconclusive discussion of the misspelled name of the fortress, p. 11 n. 12). The identity of the three distant communities with Ham, Sully, and Carantan in France, suggested by Graetz and accepted by most scholars, is questionable. Certainly, the weighty objections raised by H. Gross (in his *Gallia judaica*, pp. 187, 434 ff.), and especially the absence of any other record of Jewish communities in these cities, have never been adequately answered. On the other hand, Gross's own suggested identification with Böhm (Bohemia), Saale (Halle) and Kärnten (Carinthia), has even less to commend itself. Since the copyists themselves were uncertain about the spelling of these names, and since only one of the extant manuscripts goes back to the fourteenth century, the readings are obviously corrupt. It may not be too venturesome to suggest, therefore, that we have here a misspelling of the names Dreux, Saulieu, and Courson, each of which is recorded in connection with at least one outstanding rabbi of the twelfth century. Cf. the data, including some pertinent misspellings, cited by Gross himself, pp. 171 ff., 574f., 645 f. At any rate it should be noted that the largest communities, not only in the south, but also in northern France, including Paris and Troyes, escaped persecution during both Crusades.

40. Otto of Freising, *Gesta Friderici*, 1.37–39, in *MGH*, Scriptores, XX, 372; in C. C. Mierow's English trans., entitled *The Deeds of Frederick Barbarossa*, pp. 74 f.; Ephraim of Bonn's report; and Bernard of Clairvaux's *Sermones in Cantica*, LXIV.8, in *PL*, CLXXXIII, 1086 f. The differences between the two accounts concerning Conrad's alleged intervention and the convergence of Jewish refugees on Nuremberg, is pointed up by Aronius, *Regesten*, p. 108 No. 233. However, the Hebrew chronicler's failure to mention Nuremberg as a place of refuge is far from conclusive, while his complaint that "in those days there was no king to rescue Israel from the Crusaders, for King Conrad himself signed up, took the cross, and went to Jerusalem" (pp. 61, 192), is palpably anachronistic. It was only during the Christmas season of 1146, that St. Bernard finally persuaded Conrad to join the Crusade. By that time most of the damage had already been done and, except for Würzburg and Bachrach, public order was fairly well maintained. Nothing is known about attacks on Jews after the king's departure from Germany at the end of May, 1147.

41. St. Bernard, *Epistolae*, Nos. 363, 365, in *PL*, CLXXXII, 567 f., 570 f. (cf. also some variants in the MS letter to the English people preserved in the Bibliothèque Nationale and reproduced in English translation by B. S. James in his *St. Bernard of Clairvaux Seen through His Selected Letters*, pp. 268 f.); Otto of Freising, *Gesta Friderici, loc. cit.* According to a newly discovered letter of 1147, Bernard not only restrained Radulph, but generally forbade Cistercian monks to participate in the Crusade. "If you wish to retain your place in the order," he declared, "why sew on your garment the sign of a cross, which you ought never to cease wearing in your heart?" Cf. L. Grill's ed. of "Ein unbekannter Brief Bernhards von Clairvaux," *MIOG*, LXI, 383–84. In his *De Consideratione* (III.1.3, in *PL*, CLXXXII, 759) Bernard also taught that, unlike other infidels, Jews were excused by Time: "Their time limits [for ultimate conversion] are set and cannot be advanced. All the masses of pagans must come first." Cf. also some of the numerous recent octocentennial works on the saint, such as the *Mélanges Saint Bernard*, published by

the Association des amis de Saint Bernard in Dijon; or *Bernard de Clairvaux* (with a Foreword by T. Merton) published by the Commision d'histoire de l'Ordre de Citeaux (both include rather lame apologias for Bernard's role in the controversy between Anacletus II and Innocent II); W. Williams's English biography of *Saint Bernard of Clairvaux;* and, more generally, G. Constable's searching analysis of "The Second Crusade as Seen by Contemporaries," *Traditio,* IX, 213–79, especially pp. 245 n. 170, 276 ff.

42. Bernard of Clairvaux's *Sermones in Cantica,* LX, LXXV.10, in *PL,* CLXXXIII, 1066 ff., 1149. It was misleading enough if, in the aforementioned Raffelstetten toll ordinance of 906, Jews were sweepingly identified with merchants (*mercatores, id est Judei et alii mercatores*). Here the use of the term *iudaizare* as a synonym for extorting usury, introduced a novel term of opprobrium. On the economic activities of Jews in the mid-twelfth century, and the relatively small role their moneylending still played in Germany and France, cf. *infra,* Chap. XXII, n. 72. On Bernard's struggle against Anacletus, from the outset conducted on a personal level, see note 41; *supra,* Chap. XX, n. 8; and W. Williams, *Saint Bernard,* pp. 96–158.

43. Peter the Venerable's letter (XXXVI) to Louis VII, and his *Tractatus adversus Judaeorum inveteratam duritiem,* Introduction, in his *Opera,* in *PL,* CLXXXIX, 366 ff., 509 (both also summarized in A. L. Williams, *Adversus Judaeos,* pp. 384 ff.). Peter, generally considered the last of the seven great abbots of Cluny, had headed the famous monastery for nearly a quarter of a century when Eugenius III issued his call to the Second Crusade. Perhaps he was still smarting under the memory of the great hardships he had suffered when, in 1122, he assumed the management of the monastery, then in great financial straits. Cf. his *Dispositio rei familiaris cluniacensis,* in *PL,* CLXXXIX, 1047 ff.; W. Williams's *Saint Bernard,* pp. 267 f., 388 ff. Like Agobard, Peter was principally a statesman and organizer, rather than a theologian. Hence his strong interest in, if not full understanding of the economic problems of his time. In his polemics against Judaism he did not go beyond the old clichés, although he generally believed that in order to convert non-Christians one must first understand their point of view. For this purpose he even organized a group of scholars at Cluny to translate the Qur'an and other Arabic works relating to Mohammed. Cf. M. T. d'Alverny's "Deux traductions latines du Coran au moyen âge," *AHDL,* XXII–XXIII, 69–131; and, more generally, J. Leclercq's admiring biography, *Pierre le Vénérable.* On Peter's friendship with St. Bernard, see also the data culled from their writings by J. de la Croix Bouton in his "Bernard et l'Ordre de Cluny," in *Bernard de Clairvaux,* published by the French Cistercians, pp. 210 f.

44. Peter's proneness to generalize is evidenced also by his sweeping assertion that all Church objects found in Jewish possession must have come from thieves. Cf. his letter to the king, in *PL,* CLXXXIX, 368. He clearly underestimated the number of clerics who, out of dire necessity or prompted by avarice, parted with consecrated objects. Precisely the frequency of such transactions had inspired already a Carolingian prohibition for Jews to handle these objects. But the ineffectiveness of this embargo is demonstrated by its constant reiteration by rulers and church councils, as well as by rabbis. These and other theologico-economic arguments of

the Abbot of Cluny will be better understood against the general background of the economic changes and the religious controversies of the age of the Crusades, treated more fully *infra*, Chaps. XXII (esp. n. 67) and XXIV. On the difficulties of financing such a vast international enterprise as the Crusades, cf. M. Villey's succinct observations in *La Croisade. Essai sur la formation d'une théorie juridique*, pp. 135 ff.

45. Needless to say, despite this trend toward secularization, the religious enthusiasm still remained a potent force. In fact, Jewish messianic speculations seem to have contributed at that time a novel ingredient to the popular excitement also among Christians, as attested by the anti-Jewish chronicler, Rigord. One of these computations, as we shall see, had long predicted the coming of the Messiah in 1186. The messianic tension, rather than dying down after the passing of that year, received new nourishment from the happenings in the Holy Land. Cf. F. Baer's ingenious reconstruction of "Eine jüdische Messiasprophetie auf das Jahr 1186 und der dritte Kreuzzug," *MGWJ*, LXX, 113–22, 155–65; and *infra*, Chap. XXV, n. 70. Baer's hypothesis remains substantially valid even if we relate the pertinent passages in Simon bar Yoḥai's *Prayer* to the First, rather than the Third Crusade. See *supra*, n. 27.

46. Ephraim bar Jacob's "Book of Remembrance" Appendix, ed. by Neubauer and Stern, pp. 69 f. (Hebrew), 204 f. (German); ed. by Habermann, p. 127; Menaḥem bar Jacob's poem, *Alelai li* (Woe unto Me), ed. by Habermann, pp. 147 ff.; that by Joseph bar Asher of Chartres, *Elohim b'ulunu* (O God! Other Masters Have Possessed Us), *ibid.*, pp. 152 ff.; William of Newbury's *Historia rerum anglicarum*, IV.1, ed. by R. Howlett, I, 294 ff. The latter account, and those by several other contemporary English chroniclers are fully excerpted by Jacobs in *The Jews of Angevin England*, pp. 99 ff., with comments by him *ibid.*, and in Appendix XIV on "The York Riots" (pp. 385 ff.). On Joseph of Chartres and his poem, see also Gross's *Gallia judaica*, pp. 603 f.; and B. (C.) Roth's observations in his edition in "An Elegy on the York Martyrs of 1190" (Hebrew), *Metsudah*, II, 116–21. On Jacob of Orléans, who rather confusingly was sometimes called Rabbenu Tam of Orléans, in emulation of his master, Jacob bar Meir Tam, cf. Urbach's *Ba'ale hatosafot*, pp. 122 ff.; and *infra*, Chap. XXII, n. 71. The peculiar Jewish stone houses in England were discussed *supra*, Chap. XX, n. 112.

47. The story of Benedict of York's conversion, briefly mentioned by William of Newbury (*loc. cit.*), is more fully reported, together with the story of his relapse and the archbishop's irate exclamation, by Roger Howden (Hovedene) in his *Chronica*, ed. by Stubbs, III, 12 f. (Jacobs, *Angevin England*, pp. 105 f.). It is repeated by such other chroniclers as Benedictus Abbas in *De vita et gestis Henrici II et Ricardi I*, II, 560 ff. Remarkably, the Jews of England were less tolerant of such repenting forced converts than were their Continental coreligionists. When shortly after these events Benedict died, apparently from the wounds inflicted on him during the massacre, the community of Northampton refused him burial in the Jewish cemetery, just as the Christians did not admit his body to a Christian graveyard; "the former because he had turned Christian, the latter, because, like a dog to his vomit, he had returned to the Jewish depravity" (Howden).

48. Ralph de Diceto (Disset), *Imagines historiarum*, ed. by W. Stubbs, II, 69, 75 f.; William of Newbury, *Historia*, IV.7–11, ed. by R. Howlett, I, 308 ff.; Richard

of Devizes, *De rebus gestis Ricardi Primi,* ed. by Howlett, p. 383; Ephraim bar Jacob, *loc. cit.* (Jacobs, *Angevin England,* pp. 112 ff.). Cf. S. M. Toyne's excerpt from Richard's chronicle in *The Angevins and the Charter (1154–1216),* pp. 72 f. The number of York victims, given by Ephraim as 150, probably in addition to the sixty sacrificially slain by Yom Tob of Joigny and other victims of the mass suicide compact, is raised by Ralph to 500. The latter also mentions 57 dead after the riots of Bury St. Edmunds. On R. Yom Tob, see the meager biographical data cited in Urbach's *Ba'ale,* pp. 124 f. Other names of individual martyrs are mentioned in Joseph of Chartres' poem (Benjamin, Asher, Jacob, Moses, Joseph, and Elijah), but without patronymics, and hence are difficult to identify. See Roth's observations in *Metsudah,* II, 121. In his note on Ralph's report (p. 113), Jacobs observed that there "probably" were also some riots in Colchester, Thetford, and Opspringe and that "Winchester seems to have been the only exception." The former assertion is based on some questionable entries in the *Pipe Rolls,* while the latter is definitely untrue, despite Richard of Devizes' testimony. In the score of communities which contributed to the Northampton *donum* of 1194 only that of York and Bury St. Edmund are conspicuous by their absence. The latter, as we recall, had suffered from both the massacre and a subsequent expulsion. See *supra,* Chap. XX, n. 111. The others, including the larger ones mentioned in the text, seem either to have suffered no losses, or else, like those of London and Norwich, to have speedily recovered from the shock. Cf. I. Abrahams's list, "The Northampton 'Donum' of 1194," in *Miscellanies JHSE,* I, pp. lxii ff., and the local data, or rather lack of data, referred to by M. Adler in his *Jews of Medieval England,* pp. 55 f. (Canterbury), 199 f. (Bristol); H. P. Stokes in his *Studies in Anglo-Jewish History,* pp. 131 f. (Cambridge); C. Roth in *The Jews in Medieval Oxford,* pp. 9 f. The background and purpose of Art. V of the Assize of Arms, enacted by Henry II in 1181 (cf. Howden, *Chronica,* II, 261; Jacobs, *Angevin England,* p. 73), still is unclear. The explanation offered in the ordinance, that the weapons were to be removed from Jews "in such a fashion that they remain in the service of the king of England," is of little help, since one cannot see how the king's forces could be directly aided by arms freely sold or given away by Jews to any Gentile, which the law specifically permitted them to do. One may perhaps note here the reflection of a trend clearly developing in Germany at that time and aiming at disarming both Jews and the clergy, as classes already protected by the king's "peace." Cf. G. Kisch, *Forschungen zur Rechts- und Sozialgeschichte der Juden,* pp. 32 ff.

49. William of Newbury, *loc. cit.* Jacobs, following Stubbs, seems to go too far, however, in attributing the entire York massacre to a cabal of noble debtors of Jews, led by Richard de Malbys. To be sure, in a deed of 1182 we find Richard owing a "great debt" to Aaron of Lincoln. Cf. M. D. Davis's *Shetarot: Hebrew Deeds of English Jews before 1290,* p. 288 (Jacobs, *Angevin England,* p. 77). However, Aaron had died in the meantime and all the debts owed his estate were being collected for the benefit of the Treasury. On the other hand, this may have precisely been the reason why some of these writs of indebtedness were kept in the Church, and why Richard I was doubly angered by the riots.

50. William of Newbury, *Historia,* IV.1, 11, Howlett ed., I, 298 f., 323; Davis, *Shetarot,* p. 288; Jacobs, *Angevin England,* pp. 28, 77, 104, 131 ff., 385 ff.; Stokes, *Studies,* p. 126; Ephraim of Bonn, *loc. cit.* Probably under the stimulus of the disturbances—possibly even the news of what was happening in York during the

preceding several days—Richard renewed Henry II's general charter in favor of the
Jews of England (March 18, 1190). Upon his return in 1194, he first decreed that
"all the pledges and debts of the slain Jews are to be taken into the King's hands,
and those who were present at the slaying of the Jews and have not made fine
with our lord the King or his justiciars, shall be arrested and not liberated except by
our lord the King or his justiciars." Subsequently, in order to prevent further
losses to the Crown's property by the destruction of deeds of indebtedness owed to
its Jewish subjects, he introduced, as we recall, the new system of public registration
of all such deeds in special chirograph offices. Cf. the *Capitula placitorum*, Arts.
IX, XXIV, XXV, cited in Howden, *Chronica*, III, 263, 266 f. (Jacobs, *Angevin England*,
pp. 155 ff.); and *supra*, Chap. XX, n. 109.

51. Anonymous chronicler of Laon in Bouquet, *Recueil*, XVIII, 707 f.; Ephraim
of Bonn's "Book of Remembrance," ed. by Neubauer and Stern, pp. 70 (Hebrew),
205 f. (German); ed. by Habermann, p. 128; Rigord's *Gesta Philippi Augusti*, in
Bouquet, *Recueil*, XVII, 36; Guillaume Brita, *Gesta, ibid.*, p. 71; and *supra*, Chap.
XX, n. 81. Because of this formidable array of contemporary testimonies, these
accounts found general acceptance among modern scholars. H. Graetz merely questioned R. Yom Tob of Joigny's role in these events, which is reported by Ephraim
in exactly the same words in his preceding account of the York massacre. That
rabbi could not have performed the sacrificial slaughter on sixty persons including
himself in York in 1190, and in Bray in 1191. Cf. Graetz, *Geschichte der Juden*,
VI, 393 f. Of course, this one line, which in any case confuses the account of the
Bray cremation with a mass suicide, may have been inserted here by a careless
copyist from the preceding paragraph. It is, therefore, rightly omitted in the Habermann edition. But there seems to be no adequate answer to the more serious
chronological and legal difficulties mentioned in the text.

52. Eleazar bar Yehudah's "Memoires," ed. by Neubauer and Stern, pp. 76 ff.
(Hebrew), 214 ff. (German); ed. by Habermann, pp. 161 ff. This autobiographical
narrative by the great mystic known as Eleazar of Worms and author of the *Sefer
Roqeaḥ*, is an eye-witness account of the events in Mayence, where he had lived
before moving to Worms. He had been among the refugees in the castle of Münzenberg. While there he received a letter from his brother-in-law, Moses bar Eliezer
ha-Kohen who had remained behind in Mayence, perhaps because, as communal
precentor, he felt obliged to conduct the services for the remaining members of the
congregation. Evidently not the entire community had been evacuated. It is from
Moses' letter, which Eleazar quoted in full, that we receive most of the factual
information, including the brief quotations from Frederick I's decree and the
bishops' circular letter. Neither text is attested by any other source. We have, however, some confirmation in another report by Eleazar relating to the danger the
Jews of Münzenberg had faced earlier (in March 1188). They had been accused of
the murder of a Christian woman, whose body had been recovered from a well.
They were saved by the intervention of the "high official" (*ha-sar*), probably on
orders of Emperor Frederick, rather than Duke Kuno I of Münzenberg. Cf. Eleazar's
report in his *Perush* (Commentary) on the Common Prayers in a Bodleian MS,
cited in A. Neubauer's *Catalogue of Hebrew Manuscripts in the Bodleian Library*,
pp. 418 f. No. 1204, and Aronius's *Regesten*, p. 146 No. 323b. Frederick's intercession is also confirmed by Ephraim bar Jacob's note in the Appendix to his

"Book of Remembrance." Here the Bonn chronicler described the danger to German Jewry arising from the agitation which followed the news about Saladin's conquest of Jerusalem. "But the Lord took pity on his people and caused them to be mercifully treated by their masters. He induced King Frederick to take only a little from their fortune, but nothing large. The king ordered the clergy not to speak ill about them, and defended them with all his power . . . so that the Jews were not harmed. And Jerusalem and the entire [Holy] Land has remained in the hands of the king of Ishmael for the last five years." Ed. by Neubauer and Stern, p. 73 (Hebrew), 209 (German); ed. by Habermann, p. 130. Remarkably undismayed, Eleazar continued in Münzenberg his literary activity and even, together with a local scholar, David, issued a responsum quoted by Meir bar Baruch of Rothenburg (in his *Resp.*, Prague ed., No. 872). Cf. I. Kamelhar's Hebrew biography of *Rabbenu Eleazar mi-Garmaiza ha-"Roqeah"* (R. Eleazar of Worms), pp. 13 ff.; and *supra*, Chap. XX, n. 90.

53. Joseph ben Joshua ha-Kohen, *Dibre ha-yamim le-malkhe Ṣarefat u-malkhe Bet 'Ottoman* (History of the Kings of France and Turkey, or of the West and the East), fol. 33ab; Gedaliah ibn Yaḥya, *Shalshelet,* Venice ed., fol. 111a; Nicetas Choniates, *Historia,* ed. by I. Bekker, pp. 730 f.; Geoffroi de Villehardouin's narrative of *La Conquête de Constantinople,* CLIX, CCIII, ed. and trans. by E. Faral, I, 158 f., 208 f., and Faral's notes thereon; Starr, *Jews in the Byzantine Empire,* p. 242 No. 196. Starr rightly points out that, contrary to previous assertions, the Crusaders destroyed the mosque, but not the Jewish quarter, of Constantinople. Cf. also A. M. Schneider's "Brände in Konstantinopel," *BZ,* XLI, 382–403, especially pp. 386 f. On the growing tension between the Greeks and the Latins cf. the data marshaled by L. Bréhier in *Le Monde byzantin,* I, 345 f.; and by A. Frolow in "La Déviation de la 4e Croisade vers Constantinople. Problème d'histoire et du doctrine," *RHR,* CXLV, 168–87; CXLVI, 67–89, 194–219.

54. *Chronica Adefonsi Imperatoris,* ed. by H. Florez in *España sagrada,* XXI, 398; ed. by L. Sanchez Belda, p. 160; the poem appended to it, a fragment of which was published by L. T. Belgrano in *Atti della Società Ligure di Storia Patria,* XIX, 400, verses 44 ff.; Shem Tob Sonzolo, cited in Solomon ibn Verga's *Shebet Yehudah,* ed. by Wiener, p. 113 (German trans., p. 232); ed. by Shohet, p. 147. The foreign influences on the spread of southern French heterodoxies are well illustrated in C. Touzellier's "Hérésie et Croisade au XIIe siècle," *Revue d'histoire ecclésiastique,* XLIX, 855–72. Cf. also H. C. Lea's data on Pedro II's attitude in *A History of the Inquisition,* I, 132, 140, 157, 170, 177; and *supra,* Chap. XX, n. 72. The events in Lisbon are narrated by the Latin chroniclers, Osbern (or Osbert) and Arnulf. See the texts, ed. with a Portuguese trans. by J. A. de Oliveira, under the title *Conquista de Lisboa aos Mouros (1147);* the former also with English trans. by C. W. David, *De expugnatione Lyxbonensi: The Conquest of Lisbon,* especially, pp. 176 ff. They are also reflected in the aforementioned elegy by Abraham ibn Ezra, trans. and analyzed by S. Schwarz in *A tomada de Lisboa conforme documento coevo de un codice hebraico de Biblioteca Nacional.* The Spanish Crusaders' intervention in behalf of threatened Toledan Jewry in 1212 is reported, with some satisfaction, by Alphonso X in his *Estoria de Espanna,* III. Cf. also the *Anales Toledanos,* I (under the date of 1211), ed. by H. Florez in his *España sagrada,* XXIII, 395. These developments, which were connected with the Albigensian Crusade and the Jewish

role in it, both active and passive, extend chronologically beyond the scope of the present treatment. See L. I. Newman's *Jewish Influence on Christian Reform Movements*, pp. 131 ff.; and F. Niel's "Béziers pendant la croisade contre les Albigeois," *Cahiers d'études Cathares*, IV, 139–51. Cf. also G. Constable's observations in *Traditio*, IX, 226 ff.

55. Ephraim bar Jacob's "Book of Remembrance," ed. by Neubauer and Stern, pp. 69, 73 ff. (Hebrew), 203 f., 209 ff. (German); ed. by Habermann, pp. 126 f., 130 ff. Cf. also Menaḥem bar Jacob's aforementioned elegy, *Alelai li* (Woe unto Me) on the Boppard martyrs, ed. by Habermann, pp. 147 ff. Ephraim is a doubly reliable witness for the incredible retaliations in Boppard and Neuss, as he was residing in the latter community, while his former community of Bonn had had to share in the payment of the huge fines in 1179. Fortunately for him, and perhaps also for the preservation of the memory of that mournful historic episode, he had left Neuss three days before the tragedy and visited neighboring Cologne. He escaped therefore unscathed, except for the property losses which he, too, sustained during the general burning and pillage. Cf. also M. Brann's reconstruction of "Das zweite Martyrium von Neuss," *MGWJ*, XXXVIII, 318–22 (plausibly arguing for 1197 rather than 1187). That the tragedy in Spires occurred in 1195, rather than 1196, seems evident from the computation of Henry VI's return from Italy. Cf. Aronius, *Regesten*, pp. 151 f. No. 337. On R. Isaac bar Asher ha-Levi, called *ha-Baḥur*, the Younger, in contradistinction to his even more famous grandfather and namesake, see M. Brann *et al.*, "Speyer" in Brann's *Germania Judaica*, pp. 342, 360 f.; and Aptowitzer's *Mabo*, pp. 370 f.

56. A fuller analysis of the origin, growth, and ramifications of the "blood accusation" must be reserved for a later volume, since the first full-fledged investigation was made by a royal commission appointed by Emperor Frederick II after its first appearance in Germany in 1235. According to the commission's unanimous findings Frederick II denied that there was any truth in that accusation. His declaration was followed by a similar statement of Pope Innocent IV in 1246. For the time being we need but refer to the data assembled more than sixty years ago by H. L. Strack in *The Jew and Human Sacrifice*, English trans. Cf. also V. Manzini's "historical-sociological researches" in *L'Omicidio rituale e i sacrifici con particolare riguardo alle accuse contro gli Ebrei;* and the violently Nazi historical survey of *Der jüdische Ritualmord* by H. Schramm (concentrating on the last hundred years). The latter work is mainly interesting as an illustration of the mental processes which led medieval men gullibly to accept such uncontrolled rumors.

57. H. A. Rositzke's translation of *The Peterborough Chronicle*, p. 161 (the continuator speaks here vaguely of the Norwich events transpiring in King Stephen's time); Jacobs, *Angevin England*, pp. 19, 256 ff.; Thomas of Monmouth, *The Life and Miracles of St. William of Norwich*, ed. from a Cambridge MS by A. Jessopp and M. R. James, pp. 93 f., and the Introduction, pp. lxxi, lxxix n. 1; and Jacobs's review of that volume in *JQR*, [o.s.] IX, 748–55 (also answering I. Zangwill's strictures against the historicity of Theobald). Cf. Stokes, *Studies*, pp. 125 f. Theobald's fertile imagination might have been stimulated by his knowledge that in that period French rabbis often convoked synods to discuss a variety of legal and communal affairs. Although they never met in Narbonne, the impact of that old seat

of Jewish learning made itself felt in the deliberations. See *infra,* Chap. XXIII, n. 79.

58. Cf. W. H. Hart's ed. of *Historia . . . monasterii Sti. Petri Gloucestriae,* pp. 20 f.; Jocelin of Brakelond's *Cronica,* ed. and trans. by H. E. Butler, p. 16 (Jocelin's fuller treatise is not extant); Richard of Devizes, *De rebus gestis Ricardi Primi,* ed. by Howlett, pp. 435 ff. (Jacobs, *Angevin England,* pp. 45 ff., 75, 146 ff.); M. Adler, *Jews of Medieval England,* pp. 185 f.

59. Přemysl Ottokar II's statute of 1254, in Bondy and Dworsky, *Zur Geschichte der Juden,* I, 21. On the indiscriminate use of the term "Jew" for religious adversaries of any kind, cf. the biographer's report concerning Emperor Henry VI's refusal, in 1192, to confirm the election of Bishop Albert of Liège. The pope, we are told, ordered the archbishop of Cologne nevertheless to proceed with the consecration. Should the latter refuse, "because of his fear of the Jews," that is the emperor's partisans, the archbishop of Reims should perform the ceremony. Cf. the anonymous *Vita Alberti episcopi Leodiensis,* 14, ed. by J. Heller, in *MGH,* Scriptores, XXV, 148 (Aronius, *Regesten,* p. 150 No. 335). Cf. also *supra,* Chap. XVI, n. 1. Nonetheless these recurrent denunciations revealed a dangerous state of mind of the Christian public, and its readiness to accept at their face value the most incredible stories about the Jews.

60. In contrast to the English incidents the tragedy of Blois is known to us exclusively from Jewish sources, especially Ephraim bar Jacob's "Book of Remembrance," his poem, *Le-mi Oy* (Woe unto Whom); and his brother Hillel's poem, *Emune Shelumme Yisrael* (The Staunch and Unwavering of Israel). There also are some additional notes from an unknown writer appended to the London MS of Solomon bar Simson's chronicle. See Neubauer and Stern ed., pp. 32 f., 66 ff. (Hebrew), 144 ff., 199 ff. (German); Habermann ed., pp. 124 ff., 133 ff., 137 ff. The two strophes cited in the text are taken from the last mentioned poem, vv. 21 ff., 65 ff. There probably were many more such poems. In concluding his pertinent account, Ephraim himself mentioned still another poem, Ḥatanu Ṣurenu (We Have Sinned, O Our Rock), and added the somewhat cryptic remark, "And this matter is written up above in the penitential poems relating to the persecution in Blois." Very likely there was such a special collection within the general *Maḥzor* (Prayerbook for Festivals) in use in Bonn and elsewhere. Perhaps Ephraim's entire "Book of Remembrance," was conceived as but an appendix to his commentary on that liturgical collection. Cf. Habermann's notes, pp. 115, 157. On the origin and liturgical significance of the *'Alenu* prayer (quoted here in a variant of the English translation in the *Sabbath and Festival Prayer Book* of the Rabbinical Assembly of America, p. 37), cf. I. Elbogen's data in *Der jüdische Gottesdienst,* pp. 80 f., 143, 524 n. 10; and *infra,* Chap. XXXI. Cf. also S. Spiegel's remarks in his Hebrew essay on "The Legend of Isaac's Slaying and Resurrection," *Marx Jub. Vol.,* Hebrew Section, pp. 471–547 (with special reference to a poem by Ephraim of Bonn); and especially his *"In Monte Dominus Videbitur:* the Martyrs of Blois and the Early Accusations of Ritual Murder," *Mordecai M. Kaplan Jubilee Volume,* Hebrew vol., pp. 267–87. In this ingenious reconstruction, Spiegel not only postulates two earlier blood accusations in Pontoise and Janville in France's royal domain, but also explains the gravity of the danger confronting all of French, perhaps European, Jewry if the accused had

yielded to the tortures and confessed their alleged crime. Because their self-sacrificing loyalty had averted that danger, they merited, in Jacob Tam's opinion, a great commemorative fast day in their honor. Spiegel also republishes (pp. 285 ff.) from a Parma MS a letter by one Obadiah son of Makhir, describing the events in Blois and incidentally adding an interesting observation on the limits of the legitimate royal legislation beyond which Jews need not respect the "law of the kingdom." See *supra*, Chap. XX, n. 82.

61. The nexus between the burning of Haman's effigy and the blood accusation was first suggested by S. Cassel in his article "Juden" in J. S. Ersch and J. G. Gruber, *Allgemeine Encyklopädie der Wissenschaften*, II, 78 f. It was more fully elaborated by C. Roth in "The Feast of Purim and the Origins of the Blood Accusation," *Speculum*, VIII, 520–26. However, our main source, the geonic responsum published by L. Ginzberg in his *Geonica*, II, 3, expressly refers to it as a custom practiced among Babylonian and Elamitic Jews. Neither did Nathan ben Yeḥiel in his talmudic dictionary, the *'Arukh*, where he indirectly quoted that responsum, intimate any such observance among his Italian or, for that matter, any other European coreligionists. Cf. his entry under *Shur*, in A. Kohut's ed. of the *'Arukh ha-shalem* (Aruch completum, a Lexicon), VIII, 42; and S. Krauss's additional note in his *Tosefot he-'Arukh ha-shalem* (Additamenta to the 'Arukh), p. 393.

62. These irrational factors in medieval Jew-baiting are aptly described by J. Trachtenberg in *The Devil and the Jews: The Medieval Conception of the Jew and Its Relation to Modern Antisemitism*. Cf. also, from other angles, C. Roth's brief analysis of "The Medieval Conception of the Jew," reprinted in his *Personalities and Events in Jewish History*, pp. 53–68; and M. Hay's eloquent summary, *The Foot of Pride; The Pressure of Christendom on the People of Israel for 1900 Years*, where the impact of the Catholic Church is decidedly overstressed. Since these magic and other ingredients of medieval anti-Judaism were to come to full fruition only in the thirteenth century and after, their more detailed analysis must be relegated here to a later volume.

63. Albert of Aix, *Historia*, 1.25–29, in *RHC*, Hist. occidentaux, IV, 291 ff. (in Hefele's trans. I, 32 ff.); Ekkehard, *Chronicon universale* ad 1123, in *MGH*, VI, 261; William of Newbury, *Historia*, IV. 1. ed. by Howlett, I, 298; Richard of Devizes, *De rebus gestis* ed. by Howlett, p. 383; Robert of Gloucester's *Metrical Chronicle*, II, verses 9914–21, ed. by W. A. Wright, p. 691 (Jacobs, *Angevin England*, pp. 103, 106 f.; Toyne, *The Angevins*, pp. 72 f.). Most of the German chroniclers, in particular, were silent, noncommittal, or outrightly hostile. Even a judicious writer like Eike von Repgow, who in his *Sachsenspiegel* impartially analyzed the Jewish status in thirteenth-century Germany, spared only a few meaningless words of censure for Peter the Hermit's followers in his *Sächsische Weltchronik*, cxci, ed. by L. Weiland in *MGH, Deutsche Chroniken*, II, Part 1, p. 179. Cf. G. Kisch's *Jews in Medieval Germany*, pp. 38, 385 n. 22. A closer examination of the far from numerous references to the massacres in both chronicles and belles lettres will undoubtedly show that there was not even a forced effort to forget, but that most writers either simply shrugged off these happenings as acts of irresponsible individuals, or else put the entire blame on the Jews themselves. This is the more remarkable as there existed at all times some opponents of the idea of Crusades. Already intimated

by Albert (1.29, p. 295) and Ekkehard (in his *Hierosolomita*, XII, in *RHC*, Hist. occidentaux, V, 20 f.), this opposition became quite articulate during the Third Crusade in the writings of Ralph Niger, and swelled into a chorus in the thirteenth century. Cf. P. A. Throop's *Criticism of the Crusade: a Study of Public Opinion and Crusade Propaganda;* G. B. Flahiff's *"Deus non vult,* a Critic of the Third Crusade," *Mediaeval Studies,* IX, 162–88. And yet even in those circles one heard little condemnation of the anti-Jewish outbreaks.

64. The Mayence Anonymous, Neubauer and Stern ed., pp. 48 (Hebrew), 171 f. (German); Habermann ed., pp. 94 f. On the other hand, some far-sighted leaders sensed the jealousies created by the display of Jewish wealth, and at least on certain occasions tried to curb it. For this reason foundations began to be laid in the crusading age for the future evolution of a ramified sumptuary legislation, which will be analyzed in a later volume. Cf. my *Jewish Community,* II, 301 ff.; III, 200 ff.

65. Neubauer and Stern ed., pp. 30 (Hebrew), 141 f. (German); Habermann ed., pp. 59, 105 f. Solomon's tirade is a mosaic of biblical phrases, taken from Jer. 12:3, Ps. 79:12, Lam. 3:64–66, Isa. 34:8, 45:17. Since many of these phrases had long become part and parcel of Jewish liturgy, they had a familiar ring to all Hebrew readers. The poem *Titnem* is sometimes compared with an equally vindictive, though more concise, verse by Joseph ben Isaac ibn Abitur, first published by I. Davidson in *Ginze Schechter* (Genizah Studies in Memory of Solomon Schechter), III, 320. But the difference between the heaping of curses on an individual, indulged in by Ibn Abitur in the relatively quiescent tenth century, and the revengeful outpouring of the Ashkenazic penitential poem addressed to the entire Gentile world (Ishmael is mentioned for good measure toward the end), is quite marked. On the attribution of the latter poem to Rashi, see the observations of its first editor, A. H. Freimann in *"Titnem le-herpah,* An Imprecatory Poem by Rashi" (Hebrew), *Tarbiz,* XII, 70–75.

66. Solomon's and Eliezer bar Nathan's chronicles, Neubauer and Stern ed., pp. 2, 8, 37, 39 (Hebrew), 83, 98, 154, 158 (German); Habermann ed., pp. 25, 32, 75. It stands to reason that Eliezer had before him Solomon's account, and repeated both his impressive query and his emphasis on the chosen generation. Cf. also his and Ephraim bar Jacob's more elaborate descriptions of the martyrs' eternal bliss, based on the Aggadah, Neubauer and Stern ed., pp. 46, 65 f. (Hebrew), 167 f., 198 (German); Habermann ed., pp. 123, 82. Here and there one also perceives a mild echo of the Jobian questioning of divine justice, which probably was more frequently heard than is recorded in our sources. But there was no recorded Jewish counterpart to those South-Italian Crusaders, who were still in Asia Minor in 1098, when the first, rather exaggerated, news about the Saracen victories in Syria reached them. Their commanding officer, Wido, Bohemund's brother, questioned God's right to abandon the fighters for the liberation of the Holy Sepulcher. "If it be true," Wido exclaimed, "what we hear from these most reprobate men, we, and other Christians, shall leave Thee. We shall no longer remember Thee, and none of us will hear the other invoke Thy name." According to the author of the *Gesta Francorum* (XXXVII; in *RHC*, Hist. occidentaux, III, 149), the chronicler of these events, no knight, bishop, or abbot dared, for several days thereafter,

to invoke the name of Christ. Cf. L. Bréhier's ed. of *Histoire anonyme*, pp. 142 ff. (Bréhier himself considers this account exaggerated); and A. Waas's comments thereon in *Die Welt als Geschichte*, XI, 225. In the face of much greater trials, most Jews simply seem to have bowed their heads before God's inscrutable decrees.

67. Kalonymus bar Yehudah's penitential poem, *Mi yitten* (Oh, that My Head Were Waters; after Jer. 8:23) reprinted by Habermann, p. 68; Naṭronai Gaon's and Hai Gaon's decisions reproduced in B. M. Lewin's *Otzar ha-gaonim*, VII, Part 1, 140 f.; Jacob ben Asher's and Joseph Karo's law codes (*Ṭurim* and *Shulḥan 'Arukh*), O.Ḥ. 493, with David ha-Levi's commentary on the latter, entitled *Ṭure zahab*. The nexus with the tragic events of the crusading age was first clearly spelled out by the later Italian author of the *Minhag tob* (Good Conduct; a custumal). The custom not to cut one's hair or nails, nor to enjoy bathing or wearing new clothes during the period between Passover and the Festival of Weeks is moti- vated by the mourning "in honor of the humble and righteous pious men who sacrificed their lives for the sanctification of the name of the Lord." Cf. the text, ed. from a Kaufmann MS by M. Z. Weiss in *Ha-Zofeh*, XIII, 231 No. 61. But this author undoubtedly quoted here, as elsewhere, earlier German sources. Cf. also L. H. Silberman's study of "The Sefirah Season," *HUCA*, XXII, 221–37. On the other hand, the attribution of the famous prayer, *U-netaneh toqef* (Let us extol the profound holiness of the day), to a martyr of the First Crusade, R. Amnon of Mayence, is legendary. Although reported from a MS by Ephraim bar Jacob of Bonn by the Viennese Isaac bar Moses in his *Sefer Or zaru'a*, II, No. 276 fol. 125b, its style and its acceptance in the Mediterranean countries make it more likely that it was composed in the earlier period of the *piyyuṭ*. Cf. I. Elbogen's note in *Der jüdische Gottesdienst*, p. 565. The name of the books of remembrance was apparently derived from the centrally located *almemar* of the synagogues, on which they were displayed for public inspection. The most important of these collections is the early "Nuremberg" *memor* book, essentially of Mayence origin. It was edited by Salfeld in *Das Martyrologium*. These books proliferated later, al- though they widely differed in the extent of historically valuable information they were able to preserve. Cf. especially M. Weinberg's "Untersuchungen über das Wesen des Memorbuches," *JJLG*, XVI, 253–322 (on its origin in the Rhinelands, pp. 308 ff.); his "Memorbücher," *Menorah*, VI (1928), 697–708; and other literature listed in my *Jewish Community*, III, 152 n. 23.

68. Yehudah the Pious, *Sefer Ḥasidim* (Book of the Pious), ed. by Wistinetzky, pp. 74 f. No. 198. In his *Yisrael ba-golah*, II, 21 n. 5, B. Z. Dinaburg suggested that Yehudah had here in mind the apostasy of Micheas of Treves (see *supra*, n. 21). This is unlikely. The main point of the pietist's story was that the weak- kneed rabbi had been sincere about his expectation to return to Judaism at the earliest possible moment, and yet was punished by the subsequent apostasy of his children. Micheas remained a Christian even after Henry IV's permission to retract, and no one had to be told that his descendants also professed Christianity. On the progressively less charitable views held about returning forced converts, see *supra*, n. 45; and, for the later period, the independently written and, hence, often repetitious data, assembled by H. J. Zimmels in *Die Marranen in der rabbinischen Literatur;* and by S. Assaf in his "Spanish and Portuguese Marranos in the Responsa Literature" (Hebrew), reprinted in his *Be-Ohole Ya'aqob*, pp. 145–80.

69. Yehudah Halevi, *K. al-Khazari*, ii.33, 36, iii.11 end, ed. by Hirschfeld, pp. 102, 162; in his English translation, pp. 107, 109, 150; and D. Cassel's comments thereon in his ed. of Yehudah ibn Tibbon's Hebrew version, with a German translation, pp. 145 ff., 226. Cf. more fully my "Yehudah Halevi: An Answer to an Historic Challenge," *JSS*, III, 243–72; and *infra*, Chap. XXXIV. From his Spanish vantage point, Halevi saw his people ground between the millstones of the perennial conflict between Christendom and Islam. In a famous poem, *Yedidi ha-shakhaḥta* (My Love Hast Thou Forgotten?), where he queried why Israel was sold "for ever for them that enslave me," he complained, "Thrust unto Seir [Christendom], cast out unto Kedar [Islam], / Tested in the furnace of Greece [Byzantium], afflicted under the yoke of Media [Turks?] / Is there, beside Thee, a redeemer or, beside me, a captive of hope?" Cf. his *Diwan*, ed. by H. Brody, III, 4 No. 3; and in N. Salaman's English translation of his *Selected Poems*, p. 96 No. 47. In the long run it was this dedication, or as Halevi calls it, captivity to the messianic hope, which made the Jewish people survive these endless tribulations. On the messianic movements stimulated by the Crusades, cf. *infra*, Chap. XXV, n. 64.

70. Cf. Henry III's order in *Pipe Rolls*, 1218, p. 157; *Annales Egmundani*, Anno 1152, ed. by G. H. Pertz, in *MGH*, Scriptores, XVI, 458, summarized by Aronius, *Regesten*, pp. 115 f. No. 254. Henry's order was part of an elaborate action designed to stave off the repetition of anti-Jewish riots in connection with the new Crusade preached by Innocent III and the Fourth Lateran Council since 1215. Cf. also the list of some forty German communities recorded in the "Nuremberg" *memor* book, ed. by Salfeld, pp. 3 f. This obviously incomplete list presumably recorded only communities affected by persecutions at one time or another, but all apparently still existing in the days of the *memor* book's compilers.

71. Cf. P. Lehmann's pertinent observations on "Die Vielgestaltigkeit des zwölften Jahrhunderts," *HZ*, CLXXVIII, 225–50. Although written largely from the standpoint of medieval Latin literature, this essay indirectly points up many facets of Jewish history during that crucial century. "The Idea of a Twelfth-Century Renaissance," first introduced by C. A. Haskins, was debated anew by U. T. Holmes in *Speculum*, XXVI, 643–51. Cf. also E. M. Sanford's further remarks on "The Twelfth-Century: Renaissance or Proto-Renaissance?" *ibid.*, pp. 635–42 (prefers to use neither term). Whatever the merits of this semantic controversy may be, there is no question of the great economic and cultural upsurge of Spanish and other European Jewries in the course of the twelfth century. The fuller picture of these changes will unfold in the following chapters.

CHAPTER XXII: ECONOMIC TRANSFORMATIONS

1. The two centuries preceding and following the rise of Islam belong to the darkest periods of Jewish economic history. The general paucity of Hebrew sources and the scarcity of references to Jews in the non-Jewish writings are aggravated here by their almost exclusive concentration on religious and political problems. Economic facts are mentioned but incidentally, if at all. From the ninth century on, legal decrees, letters, business documents, as well as theological writings, begin to flow more richly and offer many more glimpses into the economic environment. But we must beware of equating purely normative statements with economic actualities. The difficulties of the Jewish economic historian are further increased by our inadequate knowledge of the general economic evolution of the Muslim world. While all phases of economic endeavor in western Europe and, to a lesser extent, in the Byzantine Empire have been gone over with meticulous care by three or four generations of competent scholars (cf. the bibliographies cited in the respective chapters of the *Cambridge Economic History of Europe*, ed. by J. H. Clapham, *et al.*), very little has thus far been accomplished in the elucidation of fundamental economic facts and trends in medieval western Asia, North Africa, or even Muslim Spain. Alfred Kremer or Carl Becker, to whom we owe most of our socioeconomic data for that area, were essentially linguists, interested in Arab culture in all its manifestations, but hardly specialists in economic history. There also are some interesting chapters in Mez's *Renaissance*, Reuben Levy's *Introduction to the Sociology of Islam,* and particularly A. Mazahéri's more popular but documented survey, *La Vie quotidienne des Musulmans au moyen âge, Xᵉ au XIIIᵉ siècle* (esp. pp. 166–305). Since down to the twelfth century the overwhelming majority of the Jewish people lived under Islam, this insufficiency of background information alone would exculpate many of the shortcomings of Jewish economic historiography. A mere glance into the pertinent works by G. Caro (his *Sozial- und Wirtschaftsgeschichte*) and I. Schipper (his Yiddish work, *Yidische Geschichte: Virtshaftsgeshichte;* or, in the Hebrew translation, *Toledot ha-kalkalah ha-yehudit*), will show that, except for largely reproducing the acute observations of Benjamin of Tudela, these scholars were able to contribute little to the knowledge of Jewish economic structure in the Muslim world. Even more specialized is, of course, A. Milano's monograph on *Vicende economiche degli Ebrei nell' Italia meridionale ed insulare durante il medioevo* (see esp. pp. 39 ff.). Other recent monographs, to be sure, have shed much light on certain phases of Jewish trade and banking during that period—these will be mentioned in the following notes—but they have merely broken the ground for the comprehensive analytical treatment which ought soon to be undertaken by a well-trained economic historian equipped with the necessary, rather complex, linguistic tools. On the conditions prevailing in the outgoing period of antiquity, cf. *supra,* Vol. II, pp. 241 ff., 413 ff.

2. Cf. C. Cahen "La Fiscalité sous les premiers 'Abbasides," *Arabica,* I, 144; the data succinctly reviewed by W. Marçais in "L'Islamisme et la vie urbaine," *CRAI,* 1928, pp. 86–100; my *Essays on Maimonides,* pp. 168 ff.; and *infra,* n. 14. On the

landflight from Palestine, see Baladhuri's *K. Futûh al-buldân*, 144; in Hitti's English trans. in *The Origins of the Islamic State*, I, 221; and, more generally, E. Pröbster's "Privateigentum und Kollektivismus im mohammedanischen Liegenschaftsrecht, insbesondere des Maghrib," *Islamica*, IV, 343–511; and G. E. Heyworth-Dunne's brief review of *Land Tenure in Islam 630 A.D.–1951 A.D.* (includes a translation of a pertinent *fatwa* of 1948; pp. 30 ff.). The collective responsibility is recorded in *Teshubot geone mizrah u-ma'arab* (Responsa of Eastern and Western Geonim), ed. by J. Müller, fol. 40b No. 165. While the editor is inclined to attribute this responsum to Meshullam bar Kalonymos of tenth-century Lucca, or some other contemporary in a Christian country, he admits that, on purely literary grounds, the Cordovan scholar Moses ben Ḥanokh or his son Ḥanokh (Enoch), is its more likely author. Nor can one rule out its authorship by a North African or eastern scholar.

3. *Yoṣer ra'ash shebi'i* by an anonymous liturgical poet, ed. by M. Zulay in his "Liturgical Poems on Various Historical Events" (Hebrew), *SRIHP*, III, 153 f., with reference to Mann, *Jews in Egypt*, I, 156 ff.; II, 176 ff. Not surprisingly, we find only one somewhat equivocal record of the ninth or tenth century relating to landed property left behind by a Jew in the Shefelah, although the latter area extended to the vicinity of the populous communities of Ramleh and Lydda. See the document ed. by S. Assaf and republished in his *Meqorot u-mehqarim*, p. 29 No. 4. Cf. also *ibid.*, p. 26.

4. Benjamin, *Massa'ot*, pp. 12 (Hebrew), 10 (English). "On the Importance of Land Tenure and Agrarian Taxation in the Byzantine Empire from the Fourth Century to the Fourth Crusade," see K. M. Setton's succinct analysis in the *American Journal of Philology*, LXXIV, 225–59. Cf. also *supra*, Chap. XIX, n. 23.

5. IV Lateran Council, canon 67; Council of Narbonne of 1227, canon 4, in Mansi, *Collectio*, XXII, 1054; XXIII, 22 (Hefele, *Histoire*, V, Part 2, pp. 1385 f., 1452); and in S. Grayzel's English trans. in *The Church and the Jews*, pp. 309, 319. Cf. also *ibid.*, pp. 36 ff.; Caro, *Sozial- und Wirtschaftsgeschichte*, I, 291 f., 496 f.; E. Melichar's study of "Der Zehent als Kirchensteuer bei Gratian," *Studia Gratiana*, II, 387–407 (pointing out that the distinguished canonist already treated the tithe as a tax by virtue of the Church's position in public law); and C. E. Boyd, *Tithes and Parishes in Medieval Italy, passim*. The decision of the Council of Narbonne of 1227 contrasted sharply with the privilege issued in 1048 by Archbishop Guifred and Count Bérenger in favor of the Cathedral of Narbonne. Here the church was given the right to collect a tithe from the salt produced in the whole area between Narbonne and the Villa Judaica, "except the salt being extracted from the Jewish *allodium* which they [the Jews] possess today." Devic and Vaissete, *Histoire de Languedoc*, V, 454 f. No. cxciii. Cf. also *supra*, Chap. XX, n. 11.

Nor was the issue of levitical tithes and priestly heave-offerings demanded from Jewish landowners by the biblical legislation completely resolved in the minds of medieval pietists. The majority agreed that these imposts were not obligatory outside Palestine. Some rabbis rationalized that Jewish land in the dispersion was free from priestly dues because it had all been acquired from Gentiles—an argument disputed among others by R. Simson of Sens, who thought that previous Gentile ownership did not liberate the land from tithes—or because it was held by Jews only under the king's eminent domain. Cf. *Tosafot* on Ḥullin 6b *s.v. Ve-hittir*, toward end; Simson of Sens, *Commentary* on M. Demai II.1, III.4. Yet R. Eliezer bar Samuel of Metz could write that "in some such places in the dispersion as Spain," Jews did not separate tithes from their produce, as if elsewhere the prevailing practice had been to do so. Cf. his *Sefer Yere'im ha-shalem* (Book of the God-fearing; a Halakhic Treatise), p. 148 No. 53. His older contemporary, R. Abraham bar Isaac of Ratisbon, actually segregated the heave-offering from his vineyard and gave it to children of priests. However, this clearly was an act of pietistic supererogation. Cf. also other twelfth-century sources in L. Rabinowitz's *Jews of Northern France*, pp. 186 f.; and Urbach's *Ba'ale ha-tosafot*, pp. 175, 257 f. Obviously these conscientious scruples had but little bearing on Jewish landownership.

6. Peter of Cluny's epistle to King Louis VII, in *PL*, CLXXXIX, 366 ff. Writing in a period when pagan slaves were still freely available, Amulo had merely suggested that Jews be made to use such slaves alone in both cities and villages. Cf. his *Contra Judaeos*, XLIII, in *PL*, CXVI, 171.

7. Jacob Tam, cited by Mordecai bar Hillel ha-Kohen in his *Sefer Mordecai* (Halakhic Commentary), on Giṭṭin, section 401. Our negative assertions are made here with considerable diffidence, for the *argumentum a silentio* is doubly inconclusive in this area. How much information do we find in the Muslim, Byzantine, or even Western sources about the innumerable non-Jewish agricultural laborers? Completely inarticulate, these vast masses, whether consisting of villeins or free workers, did not speak up for themselves. They are mentioned but casually, often inferentially, in the extant records, except for the relatively few legal enactments and papyrological or other contracts.

8. Cf. *Leges Visigothorum*, XII.2.18, ed. by Zeumer, p. 427; *supra*, Chaps. XVI, nn. 47 and 55; XX, n. 80. We have fuller information only about the depressed prices of Jewish holdings after the later medieval expulsions, as will be shown in a forthcoming volume. But, under the far more restricted demand in the earlier Western economies, any such sudden oversupply must have yielded even less revenue to Jewish owners or their Christian successors.

9. Sherira's or Hai's resp. in *Teshubot ha-geonim*, ed. by Harkavy, pp. 5 No. 11, 224 ff. No. 431; Hai's resp. in *Sha'are ṣedeq*, 1.6.3, fol. 23b; Third Council of Orléans (538) canon 28, and that of Narbonne (589) canon 4, in Mansi, *Collectio*, IX, 19, 1015 (Hefele, *Histoire*, II, Part 2, p. 1162; III, Part 1, p. 229; in the English trans. by Clark, IV, 208 f., 422; in both cases the prohibition for Jews is merely implied); *Chronicle of Ahimaaz*, ed. by Salzman, pp. 5 (Hebrew), 68 (English); ed. by Klar, p. 18. The latter source, however, need not refer to farmers arriving for Sabbath services, or for that matter even to Jews. The *burgus Judaicus*, recorded near Nîmes, and similar localities near Posquières, Franquevaux, and elsewhere, give the impression of Jewish agricultural settlements, although they, too, may connote merely Jewish landownership. Cf. A. Dupont, *Cités de la Narbonnaise première*, p. 529. As in many other areas, Visigothic law outdid the older canonical provisions, and threatened with a fine of 100 gold solidi Jews permitting Christian servants to perform on Sundays or specified holidays even purely domestic chores, "except in

so far as such work is permitted by the honest custom of noble Christians." Cf. *Leges Visigothorum*, xii.3.6, in *MGH*, Leges I, 434 f. Apart from the regular holidays the numerous Jewish fast days must also have interfered with the arduous work in fields. Some pious Jews may even have had compunctions to attend to their sowing or harvesting on the half holidays of Passover and the Feast of Tabernacles, although Naṭronai and other geonim specifically permitted vinters to employ Jewish, as well as Gentile, workers to tend their vineyards on those days. Cf. Müller's ed. of *Teshubot geone mizraḥ u-maʿarab*, fol. 20b No. 86.

10. Rashi's *Commentary* on Shabbat 33b *s.v. Ve-ʿoseqin;* Joseph Bonfils, cited *infra*, n. 14; Eliezer bar Nathan, *Eben ha-ʿEzer* (Legal Treatise), Nos. 290–91, ed. by S. Albeck, pp. 131 f.; ed. by S. Z. Ehrenreich, fol. 125a; and the sources cited by A. Schwarz in "Das Verhältnis Maimuni's zu den Gaonen," in *Moses ben Maimon*, ed. by J. Guttmann *et al.*, I, 362. Cf. *supra*, Vol. II, pp. 124 f. The problem of dairy products often agitated the minds of medieval rabbis. The Babylonian Talmud had permitted the consumption of butter produced by non-Jews, and Babylonian Jewry is recorded to have long adhered to this practice, which was at variance with that accepted in Palestine. Cf. M. Margulies's ed. of *Ha-Ḥilluqim she-ben anshe mizraḥ u-bene Ereṣ Yisrael* (The Differences between Babylonian and Palestinian Jews), pp. 78 f., 112 ff. (extensively citing also the views of later medieval rabbis); and *infra*, Chap. XXIII, n. 27. But the later geonim took a more rigid stand. Disturbed by the observation that many producers of butter cheapened their product by the admixture of animal fats, which in some cases cost as much as 80 percent less, they forbade Jews, under the threat of excommunication, to use any butter produced by non-Jews. See the responsum published by S. Assaf in his *Teshubot ha-geonim*, 1942, pp. 91 ff. No. 87, with his introductory remarks. The rabbis' concern was truly justified, inasmuch as fraudulent admixtures in foods and drugs spread ever more widely throughout the Muslim world, inducing Abu'l Jafar al-Dimashqi to devote a large section of his commercial treatise to these "falsifications." See *infra*, n. 89.

Clearly, such a prohibition could more effectively be upheld in the eastern lands with their large populations, which included a substantial number of Jewish cattle breeders, than in western Europe. According to the testimony of one of Jacob Tam's Central European pupils, Isaac bar Jacob ha-Laban (the Blond), his master had allowed free use of Gentile butter in France. This testimony is cited by Eliezer bar Joel ha-Levi in his *Sefer Rabiah*, No. 1078. Cf. Aptowitzer's *Mabo* to the latter, p. 296; and Tam's parallel decision concerning the permissibility of cheese made by Gentiles, cited by *Tosafot* on 'A.Z. 35a *s.v. Hada.* Though the Tosafists quoted here also the sages of Narbonne among those taking the lenient view, Tam's decision ran counter to clearly expressed geonic views (for instance, Ṣemaḥ Gaon's curt declaration in *Shaʿare teshubah*, No. 247), followed by Rashi's overt reversal of an earlier more liberal opinion (in his *Commentary* on Ḥullin in 116b *s.v. Hare*). Tam's leniency caused, therefore, considerable eyebrow-raising among later rabbis who lived at a time when the increase in Europe's Jewish population made such liberality less urgent. Isaac Or Zaruʿa of Vienna succinctly warned, "Let any godfearing person beware of permitting such a thing, since this prohibition had been adopted in all lands of Canaan [Slavonic Central Europe]." Cf. the discussion in his *Or zaruʿa*, 'A.Z. No. 186 (Jerusalem ed., IV, 51 f.); and Joseph Karo's comments on Jacob ben Asher's *Ṭurim*, Y. D. cxv (citing also the more stringent views of

Benjamin of Canterbury and Perez of Corbeil). Facing a different social situation, Or Zaru'a could limit the permission of using non-Jewish dairy products to cases when considerable financial losses would accrue to Jewish merchants or consumers. Cf. also the divergent opinion expressed by S. Albeck in his recent "Rabbenu Tam's Relations to the Problems of His Time" (Hebrew), *Zion*, XIX, 124.

11. Baer, *Juden im christlichen Spanien*, I, Part 1, pp. 2 Nos. 2, 4; 20 No. 31; 34 f. No. 45; Part 2, pp. 94 f. No. 100 Art. 26; R. Straus, *Juden im Königreich Sizilien*, p. 66, citing also earlier sources. The theory long held by N. Tammassia and others that Salernitan Jewry was early forbidden to own land has been effectively disproved, with new documentation, by A. Marongiu in "Gli Ebrei di Salerno nei documenti dei secoli X–XIII," *Archivio storico per le provincie napolitane*, LXII, 238 ff. Cf. also the interesting data assembled by Vallecillo Ávila in "Los Judíos de Castilla," *CHE*, XIV, 92 ff. In view of the availability of much source material here and in Provence, as well as the extensive research done by Spanish, Italian, and French scholars on the general agricultural evolution before and after 1200, a full-length monograph on the Jewish share in the development of the agricultural resources of the Iberian Peninsula and the adjoining Italian and French regions should prove extremely rewarding. A good background study is now available in C. E. Dubler's *Ueber das Wirtschaftsleben auf der Iberischen Halbinsel vom XI. zum XIII. Jahrhundert.*

12. Muhammed abu-Naṣr al-Farabi, *Risala fi . . . ara' ahl al-madina* (Abhandlung, der Musterstaat), ed. by F. Dieterici, p. 51; *Teshubot ha-geonim Ḥemdah genuzah*, ed. by Z. W. Wolfensohn and S. Z. Schneursohn, fol. 13b No. 65; and, more generally, in L. Gardet's comprehensive study of *La Cité musulmane; vie sociale et politique;* G. E. von Grunebaum's stimulating observations on "The Structure of the Muslim Town" (*supra,* Chap. XVIII, n. 29); and my *Essays on Maimonides,* pp. 168 f. Not that Mamonides personally welcomed this growing alienation of the Jews from the soil even in his own state-capitalistic Egypt. Observing his family's business reverses, he actually went beyond his talmudic sources in extolling the merits of landownership. In his Code he counseled that a man "should not sell a field and purchase a house, sell a house and acquire a movable object, or use the purchase money to engage in business, but should rather convert movables into landed property. In general he should aim to acquire wealth by converting the transitory into the permanent." Cf. *M.T.* De'ot v.12; Naḥlot xi.6; and his letter to Yefet ben Elijah in his *Quobeṣ teshubot* (Collection of Responsa and Epistles), ed. by A. L. Lichtenberg, II, fol. 37d. This private predilection did not prevent the Fusṭaṭ jurist from following the Talmud in offering preferential rights to the city purchaser of a parcel of land for the erection of a building, as against the village neighbor who wished to place it under cultivation. *M.T.* Shekhenim xiv.1.5. On the rabbinic sources and medieval opinions related to these doctrines, see my *Essays,* pp. 165 ff. The considerable number of formulas, on the other hand, relating to agricultural transactions included in the Books of Deeds by Hai Gaon or Yehudah bar Barzillai undoubtedly reflected an existing need. The preserved portion of one of the oldest of these compilations, namely that prepared in Lucena in 1021, contains brief contracts for tenancy in vineyards, sharecropping in raising sheep, the sale of cattle, and the like. Cf. S. Assaf's "Sources for the History of the Jews in Spain" (Hebrew), reprinted in his *Meqorot u-meḥqarim,* pp. 100 ff.

13 F. de Bofarull y Sans's data in *Los Judios en el territorio de Barcelona* (*siglos* X al XIII), *passim;* Dubler, *Ueber das Wirtschaftsleben*, pp. 102 f.; *Teshubot Rashi*, ed. by I. Elfenbein, p. 283 No. 242; Bouquet, *Recueil*, VI, 624 No. ccxxxii (Aronius, *Regesten*, pp. 42 f., No. 102). In his well-known privileges for the Jews of Spires and Worms of 1090, Henry IV likewise emphasized the possession by Jews of "hereditary rights in manors, houses, gardens, vineyards, fields, slaves, and other immovable and movable property." Cf. *supra*, Chap. XX, nn. 86–87. Such pride of possession was naturally even stronger in Palestine. In a greatly mutilated autograph letter, Solomon ben Yehudah, the Palestinian gaon, referred to the pathetic case of a Jew who had "to sell a field, the inheritance of his forefathers." Cf. Mann, *Jews in Egypt*, I, 124 ff.; II, 144. On the various Jewish villages in Spain, see the sources cited by Baer in his *Toledot ha-Yehudim bi-Sefarad*, I, 310 n. 4. Cf. also *supra*, n. 9; and Chap. XVII, n. 42. An interesting illustration of the cooperation between the clergy and the Jews is the contract recorded in 1192, wherewith the archbishop and chapter of Tarragona, jointly with Bonafos ben Yehudah acting as royal bailiff, transferred a mill in the vicinity of Tarragona. As was customary in that period, Bonafos countersigned his name in Hebrew. The same signature appears in still another official document, issued fifteen years later. Cf. Baer, *Juden*, I, Part 1, pp. 45 f. No. 54, with the notes thereon.

14. S. Assaf's ed. of *Teshubot ha-geonim mi-tokh ha-genizah* (Geonic Responsa from Geniza Manuscripts), 1928, p. 172 No. 144; *Teshubot ha-geonim*, ed. by Harkavy, p. 4 No. 10; Abraham ben David's *Temim de'im* (Perfect in Knowledge; a Halakhic Treatise), Lwow ed., 1811, fol. 16cd No. 133; Caro, *Sozial- und Wirtschaftsgeschichte*, I, 250; Raphael Levy's philological data in *The Astrological Works of Abraham ibn Ezra* ("Johns Hopkins Studies in Romance Literatures and Languages," Vol. VIII), p. 82. Cf. also Joseph Tob 'Elem's (Bonfils) collection in *Teshubot geonim qadmonim* (Rechtsgutachten der Geonim), ed. by D. Cassel, fol. 8b No. 44. On a Jewish palm grove within the city of Palermo, see *supra*, n. 11. As Assaf pointed out (p. 153), the author of the geonic responsum cited in the text was Naṭronai Gaon of the ninth century. Although basing his decision on a talmudic source (Berakhot 22a; Qiddushin 39a), the gaon could now emphasize this universal relaxation of the biblical prohibition. Cf. *supra*, Vol. I, p. 253. On R. Jacob Tam, see his responsa in *Sefer ha-Yashar* (Book of the Righteous), ed. by F. Rosenthal, p. 73 No. 42; and, more generally, Urbach's remarks in his *Ba'ale ha-tosafot*, p. 57; and *infra*, n. 16.

The importance of vineyards for both the royal and ecclesiastical administrations in medieval France has recently been stressed by R. Dion in his "Viticulture ecclésiastique et viticulture princière au moyen âge," *RH*, CCXII, 1–22. As here pointed out, the location of many monasteries and episcopal sees was determined by the presence of vineyards. Under these circumstances the early concentration of northern French Jewry in the cities of Champagne, long before these became major commercial centers through their famous fairs, may likewise have been owing to the impact of viticulture in that region. Cf. my remarks in *Rashi Anniv. Vol.*, pp. 47 ff.; and *infra*, n. 30. Much material on Jewish agricultural endeavor in the Middle Ages is found in I. Löw's comprehensive work on *Die Flora der Juden*, with good indexes. On the other hand, in *Der Geldhandel der deutschen Juden während des Mittelalters bis zum Jahre 1350*, pp. 3 ff., M. Hoffmann but painfully assembled a few data from rabbinic and other sources concerning Jewish landholdings in Germany.

15. J. M. Rigg, *Select Pleas, Starrs and Other Records from the Rolls of the Exchequer of the Jews, A.D. 1200–1284,* p. 1; Rymer, *Foedera,* I, 292; Jacobs, *Angevin England,* pp. 134 f., 212 ff.; A. N. Poliak, *Feudalism in Egypt, Syria, Palestine, and the Lebanon, 1250–1900;* his *Toledot ha-yeḥasim ha-qarqaiyim* (A History of Agrarian Conditions in Egypt, Syria and Palestine at the End of the Middle Ages and in Modern Times); and G. Ostrogorsky, *Pour l'histoire de la féodalité byzantine.* See *supra,* n. 8. Although Near Eastern feudalism was both younger and less watertight, and hence also less antagonistic to Jewish landholdings than its European counterpart, its long-range impact necessarily reduced further the Jewish share in agriculture. Antecedents of the new forms of exploitation were clearly noticeable already in the twelfth century, especially in the areas under the domination of Crusaders. Cf. the data assembled by G. Beyer in his detailed review of "Das Gebiet der Kreuzfahrerherrschaft Caesarea in Palästina," *ZDPV,* LIX, 52 ff., 60 ff.; and J. Prawer in "Etude de quelques problèmes agraires et sociaux d'une seigneurie croisée au XIIIᵉ siècle," *Byzantion, XXII,* 5–61; XXIII, 143–70, referring also to earlier developments.

16. Cf. the data cited by Albeck in *Zion,* XIX, 124; *supra,* n. 14; and *infra,* n. 90. Unfortunately, the responsum relating to the right of a Jewish innkeeper to accept Gentile guests (Assaf, *Teshubot,* 1928, p. 116 No. 203) is incomplete and we do not know the gaon's decision. But if negative, it probably remained quite ineffectual. Cf. also Tritton, *Caliphs,* pp. 110 f., 149 ff., 193 ff.; Rashi's resp. concerning forced converts cited *supra,* Chap. XXI, nn. 21 and 38. Jews, nevertheless, often refrained from offending the sensitivities of their Muslim neighbors, especially such extremists as the Almohades. See the letter published by E. Lévi-Provençal in his *Trente-sept lettres officielles almohades,* pp. 164 ff. No. xxviii; and his comments thereon in *Hespéris,* XXVIII, 56 f. The need of extreme caution is quite apparent in Maimonides' medical treatise on fits. While prescribing the drinking of wine as a remedy, the author apologized that he merely mentioned the most effective remedy without urging his patients to break the temperance laws. Cf. *infra,* Chap. XXXVI.

It may also be noted that, following talmudic traditions, the medieval rabbis considered wine, as well as oil and flour, among the necessities of life, much more than meat or even bread. Cf. the sources cited in my *Essays on Maimonides,* pp. 175 f., 182. Remarkably, we find in Jewish sources no complaints about the widespread practice in Muslim mills fraudulently to mix in inferior materials. Cf. E. Lévi-Provençal, *Histoire de l'Espagne musulmane,* III, 273; and, more generally, Mazahéri, *Vie quotidienne,* pp. 269 f. Perhaps this practice explains the establishment of royal mills in Aragon. Of course, in such cases the fiscal aspects were never overlooked. That is why when, in 1062, King Sancho Ramirez granted the citizens of Jaca a general exemption from the obligation to have their flour milled in the royal establishment, he did not extend that exemption to either Jews or professional bakers. Cf. Baer, *Juden,* I, Part 1, p. 3 No. 6. This discriminatory clause was dropped, however, at the renewal of that privilege in 1134.

17. J. Finkel's ed. of "A Risala ot Al-Jaḥiẓ," *JAOS,* XLVII, 311–34; Muqaddasi's *K. Aḥsam at-taqasim,* ed. by De Goeje, p. 183; in Le Strange's English translation of his *Description of Syria,* p. 77. The latter author discusses here only the Syro-Palestinian situation in his time (about 985), but these occupations were doubtless strongly represented also among other Near Eastern Jews. In Isfahan, with its

old Jewish quarter, Abu Nuaim observed many Jews in the lowliest occupations of cupping, tanning, and fulling. Cited from a Leiden MS by Mez in his *Renaissance*, p. 39 n. 6. See also W. J. Fischel's observations in "Isfahān," in *Starr Mem. Vol.*, pp. 115 f.

18. Michael Choniates, cited by Starr in *The Jews in the Byzantine Empire,* pp. 224 f. No. 176; Benjamin, *Massa'ot*, pp. 16 f. (Hebrew), 14 (English); Baer, *Juden*, I, Part 1, p. 43 No. 52; M. Ketubot VII.10; Assaf, *Teshubot ha-geonim*, 1928, p. 93 No. 179. We hear much less about objections to Jewish tanners in the later Middle Ages, particularly in the Western countries. Possibly the rabbis themselves recognized the growing need for leather goods, including parchment, on which most of their precious books were written. In view of the extremely high cost of books (see *infra*, n. 21, and Chap. XXXII, n. 4), further discouragement of Jewish or other suppliers of this important writing material could only handicap literary production. On the problem of the tanneries in Troyes and their bearing on Rashi's writings, see my remarks in "Rashi and the Community of Troyes," in *Rashi Anniv. Vol.*, pp. 50 f.

19. Ibn 'Abd Allah Yaqut's *K. Mu'jam al-buldān* (Geographical Dictionary), ed. by F. Wüstenfeld, I, 295; and other data cited by Fischel, "Isfahān," in *Starr Mem. Vol.*, p. 115; Sahl ben Maṣliaḥ and Hai, as cited *infra*, Chap. XXV, n. 40; Maimonides, *M.T.* Talmud torah 1.9; and his *Commentary* on M. Abot 1.10. Cf. *supra*, Vol. I, pp. 278 ff.; II, 242. Among the weavers there were a few large-scale entrepreneurs who used their discretion in dealing with merchants. Cf. the description of such a transaction in the letter of one Jewish partner to another, published by R. Gottheil and W. H. Worrell in their *Fragments from the Cairo Genizah*, pp. 160 f. No. xxxv. Needless to say, not all artisans were illiterate. But their very long hours of labor placed them at a disadvantage toward traders and moneylenders with respect to time devoted to study. On the interrelations between the Jewish people's growing intellectualization and its occupational distribution, see *infra*. n. 94.

20. Cosmas Indicopleustes, *Topographia*, III.180, in *PG*, LXXXVIII, 172, with reference to Exod. 31:3 ff. (cf. E. O. Winstedt's ed., p. 121); Benjamin, *Massa'ot*, pp. 11, 20, 23 (Hebrew), 9, 18, 22 (English); A. Grohmann's "Ṭiraz," *EI*, IV, 785–93, with additions in Fascicle N; and the data assembled by J. Starr in "The Epitaph of a Dyer in Corinth," *Byzantinisch-neugriechische Jahrbücher*, XII, 42–49 (publishing an inscription dating between the ninth and the twelfth centuries). Cf. also Gottheil and Worrell, *Fragments*, pp. 152 f. No. xxxiii; and S. D. Goitein, "Petitions to Fatimid Caliphs from the Cairo Genizah," *JQR*, XLV, 32 f. ("the artisans of this profession are Jews, but I am the only Karaite among them"). On early Jewish glass blowers in Constantinople and Emesa, see the miracle stories narrated in Euagrius Scholasticus' *Historia ecclesiastica*, IV.36, in *PG*, LXXXVI, Part 2, col. 2769; and in *Vita Simeonis Sali*, VIII.54, in *Acta sanctorum*, ed. by J. Carnandet, under July 1, p. 146. Cf. Caro, *Sozial- und Wirtschaftsgeschichte*, Index, *s.v.* Gewerbe and Handwerk; R. Straus, *Juden im Königreich Sizilien*, pp. 69 ff.; and *supra*, Chap. XX, n. 21. On the important silk manufacture and trade (the same persons usually acquired the raw materials, processed and sold them) of that period, in which Jews took an active part, see the monographs by R. S. Lopez, "Silk

Industry in the Byzantine Empire," *Speculum*, XX, 1–42, especially pp. 23 f.; A. Herrmann, *Die alten Seidenstrassen zwischen China und Syrien* (mainly from Chinese sources of the Han period); and E. Lévi-Provençal, *L'Espagne musulmane au Xe siècle*, pp. 183 f. (emphasizing the high quality of the silk and silk garments produced in Spain). Here the story told by Abraham ibn Daud about the brothers Jacob and Joseph ibn Jau, who "had become strong in the manufacture of silk and made beautiful garments" has a kernel of historic truth, despite some legendary accretions. Cf. Ibn Daud's chronicle in Neubauer's ed., *MJC*, I, 70.

21. Muqaddasi, *Aḥsam*, pp. 180, 238 (Le Strange trans., pp. 28, 70); Baer, *Juden*, I, Part 1, pp. 112 No. 103, 120 No. 108 (showing that in the 1270's the community of Jativa was subject to substantial tax assessments), and so forth. Cf. S. Klein's "Paper and Paper Industry in Ancient Palestine" (Hebrew), in *Ha-Mishar ve-ha-ta'asiyah*, ed. by S. Yeivin, pp. 83 f. While chiefly concerned with the ancient evolution, Klein suggested here that the author of *Pirqe de-R. Eliezer* in his aforementioned prophecy attributed to R. Ishmael (xxix, end) may already have had in mind the new processes. See Higger's edition in *Horeb*, X, 193 f. (Friedlander's trans., p. 221); and *supra*, Chap. XVII, n. 27. This seems unlikely. That midrash was probably composed in the eighth century, whereas the new technique could hardly have reached Palestine before the latter part of the ninth century. Curiously, paper did not come into common use even in Constantinople, the great emporium of trade and culture, until the middle of the eleventh century. For a long time thereafter it was sometimes called there the "Baghdadian" product according to J. Irigoin in "Les Debuts de l'emploi de papier à Byzance," *BZ*, XLVI, 314–19.

22. Abu 'Ubaid al-Bakri's *K. al-Masalik w'al-mamalik* (Book of Routes and Kingdoms), in the part ed. by W. M. de Slane under the title *Description de l'Afrique septentrionale*, p. 284; Jacobs's *Angevin England*, pp. 206 f.; and *supra*, Chap. XVIII, n. 32; XX, n. 112. Our information about the Jews in the building trades leaves much to be desired. Their importance is evident from the frequency with which Jewish real estate transactions are recorded in the rabbinic and other sources in both East and West. But owing to their preeminently legal orientation, these sources record sales of houses more frequently than matters relating to their construction. In the latter category, too, such problems as the right to use Gentile contract labor for work on Sabbath, or the extent to which the rights of Jewish neighbors may be infringed upon, loom much larger than the purely factual and economic facets. Yet one may learn a great deal, especially from the numerous Hebrew deeds recording real estate acquisitions and sales recovered from the municipal records of medieval Cologne and Vienna. Cf. *Das Judensschreinsbuch der Laurenzpfarre zu Köln*, ed. by R. Hoeniger, in collaboration with M. Stern; and *Urkunden aus Wiener Grundbüchern zur Geschichte der Wiener Juden im Mittelalter*, ed. by R. Geyer and L. Sailer (which, however, begins only in 1381). No such records are available from the much larger and more populous cities in the Near East. One must be grateful, therefore, for such stray finds as a Hebrew-Arabic lease, found on the back of an Arabic papyrus, and published in the *Corpus Papyrorum Raineri Archiducis Austriae*, III, Series Arabica, ed. by A. Grohmann, I, No. 354; or "A Judeo-Arab House-Deed from Ḥabbān," published by R. B. Sergeant in *JRAS*, 1953, 117–31. Stemming from the later Waḥidi sultanate, where Jewish life had retained its wholly medieval character, the latter deed

doubtless resembled many others written in other areas and periods. Somewhat less informative for actual industrial life are the numerous formularies for such contracts included in the various medieval Hebrew "Books of Deeds" by Hai Gaon, Yehudah bar Barzillai, and others. Cf. *infra*, Chap. XXVII, nn. 79 and 81.

23. Emperor Leo VI's important *Eparkhikon Biblion* (Book of the Prefect) was edited from a Geneva MS, with a Latin translation, by J. Nicole; and it was later provided by him with a French translation, introduction, and notes. Reprinted in Zépos and Zépos, *Jus graecoromanum*, II, 371–92, it is also available in E. N. Freshfield's English trans. in his *Roman Law in the Later Roman Empire: Byzantine Guilds*. A new edition of the text with an up-to-date French commentary is now in preparation by P. Lemerle, according to his aforementioned "Etudes d'histoire de Byzance," in *Annales*, X, 545. Neither is our information about general wages and conditions of labor in Byzantium or the Caliphate altogether adequate. G. Ostrogorsky's "Löhne und Preise in Byzanz," *BZ*, XXXII, 293–333, is a laudable pioneering effort, but will have to be followed up by many monographic studies before the constant changes in this field will be more fully clarified. For the countries of Islam we do not possess even such preliminary studies. The sources, too, are very inarticulate in this respect. We seem to possess but one reference to wages in the entire Islamic literature relating to the eastern provinces, and that only because its recipient later turned out to have founded a dynasty. Ya'qub aṣ-Ṣafar, we are told, had earned as a coppersmith in his youth only 15 dirhems a month. Obviously, such a low monthly income, approximately $2.50, could sustain a person only if he received in addition free board and lodging from his master. Cf. B. Spuler's *Iran in frühislamischer Zeit*, pp. 510 f. While it is possible that the wage scale in the western provinces of the Caliphate, and especially for Jewish workers, was substantially higher, this cannot be proved by documentary evidence. We learn only that a mason, probably of more than average skill, earned the equivalent in money of some 20 cents a day in Baghdad in 763 and 813, and some 30 cents a day in Cordova a century later. Cf. H. Sauvaire's older and far from satisfactory *Matériaux pour servir à l'histoire de la numismatique et de la métrologie musulmanes* (takes little cognizance of changes in weights and values in different periods), in part summarized by Mazahéri in *La Vie quotidienne*, pp. 212 ff. On the later period, see especially E. Strauss's "Prix et salaires à l'époque mamlouke," *Revue des études islamiques*, 1949, pp. 49–94; and, on prices, *infra*, n. 73.

24. The interplay of ethnic-religious with occupational quarters in the cities of Muslim Spain is well illustrated by L. Torres Balbás in "Estructura de las ciudades hispanomusulmanas, la medina, los arabales y los barrios," *Al-Andalus*, XVIII, 149–77. Similar conditions doubtless prevailed also elsewhere under Islam. Our information concerning Jewish guilds, their relation to non-Jewish associations in the same branches of production, and the admission of individual Jewish artisans to general corporations, is likewise extremely limited. Many discussions in the medieval rabbinic literature are but theoretical speculations based upon the better known realities of the talmudic age, on which see *supra*, Vol. II, pp. 260 f., 417 nn. 36–37. But at least our knowledge of the general background is somewhat more detailed. For Byzantium the Book of the Prefect has furnished much first-hand information, which has been frequently analyzed together with other relevant

sources. Cf. especially A. Stöckle's *Spätrömische und byzantinische Zünfte* (also arguing for dating the Book of the Prefect after 911 but before 968, perhaps under Nicephoros Phokas; pp. 142 ff.); and the other literature listed by Ostrogorsky in his *Geschichte*, pp. 174 n. 8, 203 f. Less information dating from the medieval period is available for the Islamic guilds, on which see the three early modern documents translated by A. M. Kassim and communicated by L. Massignon in his "Etudes sur les corporations musulmanes indo-persanes," *Revue des études islamiques*, I, 249–72; some earlier data assembled by him in "Le 'Futuwwa' ou 'pacte d'honneur artisanal' entre travailleurs musulmans au moyen-âge," *Nouvelle Clio*, IV, 171–98; and by B. Lewis in "The Islamic Guilds," *Economic History Review*, VIII, 20–37. Cf. also Dubler's *Ueber das Wirtschaftsleben auf der iberischen Halbinsel*, pp. 134 ff., 138; and *infra*, n. 42. Apart from pointing out the deeply mystical Ismaelian background of some of these associations, Lewis has shown that, unlike their European counterparts, these guilds usually arose spontaneously from the rank and file, and had less of a hierarchical structure. Most significantly, they were as a rule interdenominational, and hence Jewish artisans had less need to organize their own associations. Cf. also my *Jewish Community*, I, 364 ff.; III, 94 f. This subject, too, will have to be more fully analyzed in a later volume in connection with the far better known structure of Jewish guilds in later medieval Spain and other countries.

25. E. Strauss, *Toledot ha-Yehudim be-Miṣrayim ve-Suriah taḥat shilṭon ha-Mameluqim* (History of the Jews in Egypt and Syria under Mameluk Rule), pp. 172 ff., 176 ff. These lists have the additional disadvantage of belonging to a somewhat later age than that here under review. Cf. also the compilation of data relating to Jewish craftsmen in Egypt in D. Neustadt's pioneering "Contributions to the Economic History of the Jews in Egypt in the Middle Ages" (Hebrew), *Zion*, II, 237 f. Jews participated also in such borderline activities between industry and agriculture as the building of canals. Cf., for instance, the story told about Solomon Abu'l Munajja, *supra*, Chap. XVIII, n. 39.

26. J. H. Kramers in his "Geography and Commerce," in *Legacy of Islam*, ed. by T. Arnold and A. Guillaume, p. 97; Sherira Gaon's resp. cited in Yehudah bar Barzillai's *Sefer ha-'Ittim*, p. 76; Qur'an 55:19–20 (also 25:55). Cf. C. Courtois's suggestive observations on "Les Rapports entre l'Afrique et la Gaule au début du moyen-âge," *Cahiers de Tunisie*, II, 127–45.

27. Ibn Parḥon's *Maḥberet he-'Arukh*, end; Ibn Khurdadhbah's *K. al-Masalik w'al-mamalik* (Book of Routes), ed. by De Goeje, pp. 124 ff., (French), 162 f. (Arabic); E. N. Adler's observations thereon in "A Jewish Merchant in China at the Beginning of the Tenth Century," *Abhandlungen Chajes*, pp. 1–5 (he believes that Sallam the interpreter was an Andalusian Jew); Dunlop's *History of the Jewish Khazars*, pp. 190 f. (he suggests Sallam's possible Khazar origins). On Isaac's and Ibrahim's missions, see *supra*, Chaps. XIX, n. 57; XX, n. 57. Cf. F. W. Buckler's *Harunu'l-Rashid and Charles the Great;* W. Björkman's review thereof in *OLZ*, XXXVI, 693–95 (the latter's denial of the very diplomatic exchanges between the two monarchs merely because no Arabic source refers to them is not justified); and B. Spuler's "Ibrāhīm ibn Ja'qūb, Orientalistische Bemerkungen," *Jahrbücher für Geschichte Osteuropas*, III, 1–10. One should not exaggerate the silence, how-

ever astonishing, of Arab historians with respect to Charlemagne's embassy and the Eastern missions to the West. In their eyes an embassy from a distant and barbarous country like the Frankish Empire of that time, was little more than another exotic interlude in a constant procession of foreign and provincial visitors. The almost total disappearance of the Syrian trader in Western countries after the seventh century has been forcefully restated by H. Pirenne in "Le Fin du commerce des Syriens en Occident," *Annuaire*, II, 677–87. The new status of the Hebrew language and its effect on the upsurge of linguistic studies among Jews will be discussed *infra*, Chap. XXX. We must bear in mind, however, that long before the Islamization of the Syrians, we hear of a Jewish merchant traveler who, for a modest 10 percent commission, undertook to sell cloth valued at 144 gold pieces (bezants) in Africa and in Gaul for a wealthy businessman in Constantinople. Cf. Jacob son of Tanumas' *Doctrina Jacobi nuper baptizati*, ed. by Bonwetsch, p. 90.

28. A. Mez, *Renaissance of Islam*, p. 478; H. Hirschfeld, "Some Judaeo-Arabic Legal Documents," *JQR*, XVI, 280 f., with additional comments by J. Mann, *ibid.*, XVII, 83–85; S. D. Goitein, "From the Mediterranean to India," *Speculum*, XXIX, 186 f.; Gottheil and Worrell, *Fragments*, pp. 44 ff. No. ix. Interesting illustrations of Jewish commercial activities in the eleventh and twelfth centuries may be found in the letters published by J. Starr in his "Contribution to the Life of Naharai ben Nissim of Fusṭaṭ" (Hebrew), *Zion*, I, 436–53; another "Jewish Merchant's Letter from the Eleventh Century" (Hebrew), ed. by I. Ben-Zvi, *ibid.*, III, 179–82 (dated Aleppo in 1060, this letter gives an inkling of its author's business trips and money transfers); and the "Early Letters and Documents from the Collection of the Late David Kaufmann" (Hebrew), ed. by S. D. Goitein in *Tarbiz*, XX, 191–204. Of interest also are such archaeological finds, possibly originally imported by international Jewish traders, as are analyzed in E. Combe's "Natte de Tibériade au Musée Benaki à Athènes," *Mélanges Dussaud*, II, 841–44 (this fine sample of the Tiberian textile industry dates from 961; there is also a brief review of other data concerning that industry).

29. Cf. S. D. Goitein's essay in *Speculum*, Vol. XXIX, and his other studies mentioned above. Even fuller information will be supplied by him in a forthcoming comprehensive documentary volume. Cf. also J. Braslavsky's older study of "Jewish Trade between the Mediterranean and India in the Twelfth Century" (Hebrew), *Zion*, VII, 135–39; and, more generally, G. F. Hourani's brief sketch of *Arab Sea-faring on the Indian Ocean in Ancient and Early Medieval Times;* N. Pigulevskaya's *Vizantiia na putakh v Indiiu* (Byzantium on the Road to India; From the History of Byzantine Trade with the East in the Fourth to the Sixth Centuries); and R. S. Lopez's "European Merchants in the Medieval Indies: The Evidence of Commercial Documents," *Journal of Economic History*, III, 164–84 (dealing mainly with the later Middle Ages from Marco Polo on). On the China trade, see J. Kuwabara's "On P'u Shou-Keng . . . with a General Sketch of Trade of the Arabs in China during the T'ang and Sung Eras," *Memoirs of the Research Department of the Toyo Bunko (The Oriental Library)*, II, 1–79; VII, 1–104; C. E. Dubler's data on "El Extremo Oriente visto por los Musulmanes anteriores a la invasión de los Mongoles en el siglo XIII," *Homenaje a Millás Vallicrosa*, I, 465–519; and *supra*, Chap. XVII, nn. 49–51.

The story of the Jews' entry into large-scale international trade is yet to be told in full detail, especially in so far as it relates to the Eastern Jews. Unfortunately, neither the foreign nor the domestic commerce of the Muslim countries themselves even in the period of their greatest power and affluence, has been satisfactorily investigated. There is, to be sure, abundant Arabic as well as Jewish source material available, but only a fraction of the extant records is thus far accessible in print. Numerous monographs are needed to elucidate this enormously important phase of general and Jewish history. For the time being, the articles in *EI*, the surveys of Mez, Hitti, Poliak, and others are very helpful. Only for Egypt do we possess the careful analyses by C. H. Becker in his *Beiträge zur Geschichte Aegyptens unter dem Islam*, his *Islamstudien*, and other works. Cf. also the recent broad surveys by J. Somogyi, "The Part of Islam in Oriental Trade," *IC*, XXX, 179–89; and by the outstanding worker in this field, C. Cahen, "L'Histoire économique et sociale de l'Orient musulman médiéval," *Studia Islamica*, III, 93–115 (referring to his own earlier researches, some of which have been, or will be mentioned in our notes). With the materials recovered from the Egyptian *Genizah* by Mann, Goitein, and others, one may reconstruct at least partially the Jewish commercial activities in that country. Cf. D. Neustadt's aforementioned essay in *Zion*, II, 216–55. Cf. also the stray references to Egyptian Jewry's economic life and thinking in Maimonides' writings analyzed in my *Essays on Maimonides*, pp. 127 ff.

30. Gregory of Tours, *Historia Francorum*, III.19, in *MGH*, Scriptores rerum merov., I, 129 f.; in O. M. Dalton's English trans., p. 103 (with the comments thereon by P. Gras in "Chalon ou Ascalon," *Annales de Bourgogne*, XXIV, 52–54; and E. Salin's *Civilisation mérovingienne*, I, 135, 443, 463 f., where other passages relating to wines of Gaza are assembled; Gras's hypothesis is not seriously weakened by R. Dion's mention of an early MS reading: *Cabillonum, Annales, loc. cit.*, p. 160); Ephraim bar Jacob's "Book of Remembrance," ed. by Neubauer and Stern, in *Hebräische Berichte*, pp. 71 f. (Hebrew), 206 ff. (German); ed. by A. M. Habermann in *Sefer Gezerot Ashkenaz*, pp. 128 ff.; Agobard's *De insolentia Judaeorum*, v, in *PL*, CIV, 75. The unsurpassed quality of some Palestinian grapes, grown especially in the vicinity of Hebron, from where they might have been exported to the West through Ascalon, was emphasized several times also by Muqaddasi in his *Description of Syria*, ed. by De Goeje; in Le Strange's English trans., pp. 69 ff. (with the translator's note thereon, p. 69 n. 3). On the importance of wine trade in medieval France, see especially Y. Renouard's recent study, "Le Grand commerce du vin au moyen âge," *Revue historique de Bordeaux*, n.s. I, 5–18; the debate on this score between J. de Sturler and R. Doehaerd in *Moyen Age*, LVII, 93–128, 359–81; and *supra*, n. 14.

At the Cologne fair, Jews played a sufficiently important role already in the days of Gershom bar Yehudah for him to specify in a reply to Jacob bar Yaqar that the practice of lending 12 ounces for the fair and receiving 13 in return in Mayence or Worms was permissible only if the lender shared the risk of the transportation and sale of goods. Cf. *Ma'aseh ha-geonim* (Precedents of Early Rhenish Rabbis), ed. by A. Epstein, p. 70; and Rashi's *Pardes*, ed. by Ehrenreich, p. 73. On the considerable role played by Jews also in the later famous fairs of Troyes and Provins in the Champagne, see M. A. Gerson's brief data in "Les Juifs en Champagne," *Mémoires de la Société académique d'agriculture . . . du départment de l'Aube*, LXIII, 244 ff.; my remarks in *Rashi Anniv. Vol.*, pp. 47 ff.; *infra*, n. 75; and, more generally, F. Bourquelot's *Etudes sur les foires de Champagne*, II, 154 ff.; and E. Chapin's detailed study of *Les Villes de foires de Champagne des origines au début du XIVe siècle.* Jews seem also to have actively participated in the early fairs held in the city of Orléans. This seems at least to be the meaning of a passage in Rashi's *Teshubot,* p. 274 No. 241. To be sure, this may have been merely a local market (unlike the term *yerid,* the word *shuq* may refer to either), although the presence there of representatives of "communities" would seem to indicate a regional gathering. On the other hand, it is not likely that the claimant should have submitted a perfectly simple litigation to a full-fledged rabbinic synod. At any rate, in his notes on this responsum the editor not only inexactly quotes my remarks, but also assumes that Orléans belonged to the counts of Champagne, whereas the city permanently was part of the royal domain. In fact, according to Glaber, it served as "the principal residence of the king" who in certain administrative matters, including the supervision of fairs, conceded the bishop a share in his jurisdiction. Cf. R. Crozet's *Histoire de l'Orléanais,* pp. 67 f., 100; and more generally the literature listed *supra,* Chap. XX, n. 81. At times conscientious Jews were disturbed by certain taxes imposed upon all sales at such fairs for the benefit of churches. These fears were dispelled by a somewhat forced argument by Baruch bar Isaac of Worms in his *Sefer ha-Terumah* (Legal Code), No. 137 (Zolkiew ed., 1811, fol. 10d). R. Baruch finally expressed the hope that the revenue might be used for charity rather than worship. See Urbach, *Ba'ale ha-tosafot,* pp. 290 f. Privileges for free trading were also extended to Jews, as well as to Christians and Moors, in some of the city statutes in northern Spain. Cf., e.g., B. Checa's ed. of the *Fuero de Plasencia.* Cf. also S. A. della Torre's additional data in "Noticias de viajes . . . ," *CHE,* XII, 102 ff. On the other hand, we have little information about the Jewish role in the Muslim fairs, which may likewise have been quite considerable, since our general knowledge of the operation of such fairs under medieval Islam is quite limited. Cf. R. Brunschvig's concise summary, "Coup d'oeil sur l'histoire des foires à travers l'Islam," *Recueil de la Société Jean Bodin,* V, 43–47.

31. Frederick's privilege, ed. by P. Scheffer-Boichorst in *MIOG,* X, 459 f. (Aronius, *Regesten,* pp. 139 ff. No. 314a). Frederick's decree was but a link in the chain of his and his successors' mercantile measures, which included the promotion of Jewish settlement in eastern Germany and the reestablishment of royal control over the entire Rhenish trade, in which the Mayence and Cologne Jewish communities played a significant role. Cf. *supra,* Chap. XX, n. 97; and H. Borchers, "Beiträge zur rheinischen Wirtschaftsgeschichte," *Hessisches Jahrbuch für Landesgeschichte,* IV, 64–80. Our knowledge of the important German trade with eastern Europe, and the Jewish role therein, is largely limited to a few stray references in rabbinic sources. Only because they happened to arrive in Hungary from Russia with their wagons laden late one Friday afternoon, and hence possibly infringed on the Sabbath rest commandment, the case of one Abraham bar Ḥiyya of Ratisbon and his brother Jacob, was brought to the attention of the rabbinic authorities. It was subsequently reported by Zedekiah ben Abraham Anav in his *Shibbole ha-Leqeṭ,* ed. by S. Buber, pp. 47 f. No. 60. Cf. further data assembled by J. Brutzkus in "Der Handel der westeuropäischen Juden mit dem alten Kiev," *ZGJD,* III, 97–110; and, again, in his "Trade with Eastern Europe, 800–1200," *Economic History Review,* XIII, 31–41. Perhaps more could be learned from a fresh reexamination of the available numismatic evidence, such as was done in G. Shalsky's more general review of "The Bohemian Trade in the X–XI Centuries in the Light of Coins" (Czech), *Numismatický Sborník,* I, 13–43.

Nor are we much better informed about the Jewish traders who exchanged goods between Slavonic eastern Europe and Byzantium. Some such Russian Jewish merchants are mentioned as arriving in a Byzantine city (Constantinople or Salonica) and taking part in a local communal controversy. Cf. the otherwise unidentifiable letter, probably written in the eleventh century, and published in Mann's *Texts and Studies*, I, 45 ff., 48 ff.; and Starr's comments thereon in *The Jews in the Byzantine Empire*, pp. 182 ff. No. 125. Cf. also *infra*, n. 34. Such Jews may, indeed, have been instrumental in bringing Russian linen to Byzantium and in shipping it further all the way to India, where it was much sought for at that time. Cf. Goitein's comments in "From the Mediterranean to India," *Speculum*, XXIX, 192 n. 20; and, more generally, A. Vasiliev's "Economic Relations between Byzantium and Old Russia," *Journal of Economic and Business History*, IV, 314–34.

32. S. Assaf, "Relations between the Jews of Egypt and Aden in the Twelfth Century" (Hebrew), *BJPES*, XII, 116–19; and S. D. Goitein, ed., "A Document from the African Port of Aidhab in the Age of the Head of Academy Joshua ben Dosa" (Hebrew), *Tarbiz*, XXI, 185–91. This basic identity of law and its administration was little disturbed by the numerous local variations and occasional dissensions between communities. Cf. also O. Löfgren, *Arabische Texte zur Kenntnis der Stadt Aden im Mittelalter* (publishing and commenting on Abu Maḥrama's "History of Aden" and related texts); and *infra*, Chaps. XXIII, nn. 47 and 50; and XXVII, nn. 140 ff.

33. Cf. Goitein's data in *Speculum*, XXIX, 197; the interesting document of 1046, published by Assaf and reprinted in his *Meqorot u-meḥqarim*, pp. 137 ff.; and *infra*, n. 42. Here we find a Jew of Tahort, Algeria, appearing before a Cairene court with a deed confirmed by the regular Jewish court of Kairuwan. It related to money owed the claimant's brother by a Jew who had interveningly lost his life on a journey from Sicily to Egypt, but had funds on deposit in Cairo.

34. Maimonides, *M.T.* Matenot 'aniyyim, viii.10; his *Responsa*, No. 379, p. 86; Alfasi's *Resp.*, fol. 19b No. 132; Mann, *Jews in Egypt*, I, 87 ff., 241 f., 244; II, 87 ff., 306 f., 316 f., 344 f.; his *Texts and Studies*, I, 136 ff., 348 ff., 366 ff.; *supra*, Chap. XX, n. 79; and, more generally, my *Jewish Community*, II, 333 ff.; III, 213 f. Interesting data on the ransom of Jewish captives by Byzantine communities are also supplied in the "New Documents concerning Proselytes and a Messianic Movement" (Hebrew), published by S. Assaf in *Zion*, V, 113 ff. In her letter, Maliḥah intimated that on their journey to Byzantium her brothers could take along some merchandise to cover their expenses. Cf. also Rashi, *Teshubot*, ed. by Elfenbein, pp. 262 f. No. 234, concerning a partner who on a business trip had been robbed of all his merchandise, and had to pay in addition much ransom money. Rashi rejected his claim for restitution, by the other partner, of half that sum as a business expense. This must have been a rather rare occurrence in eleventh-century France or Germany, however. The fine reception extended everywhere to such travelers as Benjamin, Petaḥiah, and Al-Ḥarizi is indicative of the advantages enjoyed also by Jewish businessmen in a divided world.

35. The greater importance of Jews in the international trade of the Western countries has long been recognized. It remains unimpaired by the controversy between the schools of Pirenne and Dopsch as to whether, concomitant with the

rise of Islam, trade in the Merovingian and Carolingian empires was on the down-grade (Pirenne), or on the upswing (Dopsch). Reference has already been made (*supra*, Chap. XX, n. 55) to the political implications of Pirenne's theories, and the extensive debates on this score in recent historical literature. Pirenne's sweeping contention that under the Carolingian "there was no longer a class of professional merchants, [and] that Oriental products (papyrus, spices, silk) were no longer imported" (*Mohammed and Charlemagne*, p. 242), has definitely been disproved through literary as well as archaeological evidence. Pirenne himself admitted (pp. 255 ff.) that Jews were an exception. Certainly, Jewish merchants remained active in the importation of textiles of all kinds, on which cf. E. Sabbe's data in "L'Impor-tation des tissues orientaux en Europe occidentale au haut moyen-âge," *RBPH*, XIV, 811–48, 1261–88. The importation, by Spanish Jews, of scarlet (*siglatun*) tissues and *Iraqi* vases from Baghdad, Cairo, and Byzantium is attested by Spanish-Arab poets, cited by H. Pérès in his *Poésie andalouse*, p. 327. Of interest for the early period is also H. Laurent's "Marchands du palais et marchands d'abbeys," *RH*, CLXXXIII, 281–97. Laurent's insufficient consideration, however, of the Carolingian privileges for Jewish merchants, which in many ways served as prototypes for those granted to their Gentile counterparts (see *supra*, Chap. XX, n. 62) has rightly been criticized by F. Rörig in his "Magdeburgs Entstehung und die ältere Handels-geschichte," in the Berlin Academy's *Miscellanea Academica Berolinensia*, II, 107 n. 4, 108 n. 1.

In certain regions, to be sure, Jews were outstripped by their Christian competi-tors, the Frisians. Cf. the mutually complementary recent studies by H. Jankuhn, "Der fränkisch-friesische Handel zur Ostsee im frühen Mittelalter," *VSW*, XL, 193–243, and D. Jellema, "Frisian Trade in the Dark Ages," *Speculum*, XXX, 15–36. But the preponderance of Jews in the southern trade, especially with the Muslim countries, remains uncontested. Cf. also R. S. Lopez's general observations on "L'Evolution de la politique commerciale au moyen-âge," *Annales*, IV, 389–405 (chiefly concerned with promotion of, or barriers to, international trade); and the interesting selected documents, included by him and I. W. Raymond in their *Medieval Trade in the Mediterranean World*.

36. Petaḥiah's *Sibbub*, xxi, ed. by Grünhut, pp. 29 (Hebrew), 41 (German); in Benisch's English trans., p. 55. On the respective roles of the *muḥtasib* and the Jewish market police, cf. Lévi-Provençal's *Espagne musulmane*, pp. 185 ff.; *infra*, n. 44; and Chap. XXIII, n. 80. Occasionally shopkeepers, too, entered partnerships, their controversies being recorded in contemporary rabbinic letters; for instance, that of two silk merchants in Spain or Morocco brought to Alfasi's attention. Cf. his *Resp.*, fol. 12 No. 77.

37. Cf. Baer, *Juden*, I, Part 1, pp. 10 No. 17, 29 No. 39, 82 f. No. 83; Part 2, pp. 13 No. 27, 30 No. 56 note; the anonymous tenth- or eleventh-century Genizah fragment published by Assaf in his *Meqorot*, p. 22; and the somewhat overdrawn picture of Jerusalem's dependence on Ramleh in the Jerusalem letter, dated 1025, in Mann's *Jews in Egypt*, II, 181. A "Jewish market" is recorded also in Tiberias. Cf. J. Bras-lavsky's remarks in "The Jews of Khaibar in Palestine," *BJPES*, VII, 80. Cf. also other scattered sources, excerpted by Dinaburg in his *Yisrael ba-golah*, I, 118 ff.; and the occasional references in the general works by Mez, or Spuler (e.g., *Iran*, pp. 400 ff.). The story of petty Jewish merchants and peddlers, whose number at

all times greatly exceeded that of their more impressive international confreres, is yet to be told in detail. True, the sources are not only widely scattered, but also oriented toward legal, rather than economic aspects. Very frequently they are neither precisely datable, nor geographically well defined. Nonetheless a careful monographic review of the considerable material extant in Jewish and non-Jewish sources, in combination with what little is known about the non-Jewish petty traders of the period, ought to prove quite rewarding.

38. Ginzberg, *Geonica*, II, 74, 80; Alfasi's *Resp.*, fol. 18a No. 119. On the *commenda* contracts, cf. E. E. Hildesheimer's analysis in *Das jüdische Gesellschaftsrecht*, pp. 113 ff.; S. D. Goitein, "What Would Jewish and General History Benefit by a Systematic Publication of the Documentary Geniza Papers?" *PAAJR*, XXIII, 34; my *Essays on Maimonides*, pp. 217 ff.; and *infra*, n. 64. The business documents included in Gottheil and Worrell's *Fragments*, shed considerable light on Jewish trade of the period, despite their frequently unsatisfactory preservation and edition. Cf. especially pp. 32 ff. No. VII (a memorandum of 1150, relating to a litigation between two Jews before an Arab *qadhi;* the controversy centered about the question whether the writer had been the plaintiff's partner, or mere agent); 72 ff. No. XIV, 164 ff. No. XXXVI (accounts showing many and varied expenses, including multifarious bakshish, which tremendously increased the cost of doing business, necessitating a higher rate of profit); 160 ff. No. XXV (complaint about a partner's inefficiency in dealing with weavers, and the like).

39. Ibn Khurdadhbah, *K. al-Masalik*, ed. by De Goeje, pp. 153 ff. (Arabic), 114 ff. (French), in E. N. Adler's English trans. in *Jewish Travellers*, p. 2; Ibn Ḥauqal, *K. al-Masalik*, or *Ṣurat al-ardh* (Opus geographicum), ed. by De Goeje, p. 281; ed. by Kramers, pp. 392 f.; and Ibn al-Ḥusayn (probably echoing Ibn Rustam) in the excerpt commented on by Minorsky in "The Khazars and the Turks . . . ," *BSOAS*, IX, 141 ff. Ibn Khurdadhbah's oft-quoted passage is annotated in Lopez and Raymond, *Medieval Trade in the Mediterranean World*, pp. 30 ff. On Khazar trade with western Asia, see Mez, *Renaissance*, pp. 472 f. It seems unlikely, however, that before the weakening of their empire and the destruction of their metropolis in 969, as reported by Ibn Ḥauqal (*loc. cit.*), the Khazars should have been satisfied with mere tolls on goods in transit as described by Mez. More probably they themselves actively participated in their foreign trade, although Ibn Khurdadhbah wished to call attention principally to the arrival in Baghdad of the even more exotic Russo-Normans. Khazar-Jewish traders were doubtless included by him in that motley group of "Radhanites" which, by virtue of the languages spoken in its midst, must have come from various lands. Despite the occasional appearance of exceptional linguists like Sallam the interpreter, we certainly cannot assume that all the Radhanites were traveling polyglots at a time when even familiarity with two such important languages as Arabic and Latin was limited to relatively few individuals. That is why the recurrent attempts to connect Ibn Khurdadhbah's term, *Radhaniyya*, with their particular place of origin (for instance, Radanat in the district of Samarra, or in the district of Jukha; see J. Obermeyer's *Landschaft Babylonien*, p. 126; or the Rhone Valley, as suggested in 1907 by D. Simonsen) seems so untenable. De Goeje's old explanation that Ibn Khurdadhbah, a Persian, merely borrowed here the Persian term *rahdan*, meaning merchant-traveler, appears far less remote. Cf. Simonsen's note, "Les Marchands juifs

appelés 'Radanites,'" *REJ*, LIV, 141–42; L. Rabinowitz's observations on "The Routes of the Radanites," *JQR*, XXXV, 251–80; his *Jewish Merchant Adventurers*, pp. 93 ff.; C. Cahen's review thereof in *RH*, CCV, 119–20; and, for the routes from and through Byzantium, W. Tomaschek's older but still useful analysis of "Die Handelswege im 12. Jahrhundert nach den Erkundigungen des Arabers Idrisi," *SB* Vienna, CXIII, 285–373. In his *Khazariyyah*, pp. 86 ff., Poliak suggested that Khazaria's trade with the Eastern countries, which had inherited the Sassanian silver currency, was so great that the Khazars required no minting of their own before the tenth century, when the export of silver coins to Khazaria had begun to create a monetary crisis in the East.

40. See the data cited by Abu Yusuf in *K. al-Kharaj*, pp. 76 ff. (in Fagnan's French trans., pp. 204 ff.); Tritton in his *Caliphs*, pp. 142, 218 ff.; Goitein in "From the Mediterranean to India," *Speculum* XXIX, 188; L. Ménard in his *Histoire civile, ecclésiastique, et littéraire de la ville de Nîmes*, I, 412; and Lévi-Provençal in his *Histoire*, III, 32. The story of Isḥaq, the Jewish merchant who reached tenth-century China, is filled with episodes of attempted extortion and the merchant's efforts to evade them. He ended tragically when the Sultan of Sumatra, to whom he had refused to pay 20,000 dinars, ordered his assassination. Cf. E. N. Adler's trans. in *Abhandlungen Chajes*, pp. 2 ff. Jewish merchants often also had to contend with recurrent outbreaks of xenophobia in other countries. In an eleventh-century letter, one Israel ben Nathan informed his cousin Naharai ben Nissim of his rescue from a Constantinople prison. His preceding curses hurled at the country of his "great tribulations" indicate that he considered his imprisonment inspired by an anti-alien or anti-Jewish animus. Cf. Starr's edition of that letter in *Zion*, I, 443; II, 92; and his additional comments in *The Jews in the Byzantine Empire*, pp. 199 f. No. 146. Cf. also *supra*, n. 29; and, more generally, M. Awad's *Al-Ma'assir: Land and Sea Toll Barriers in the Byzantine and Moslem Empires*.

41. Louis the Pious' privileges in *Formulae imperiales*, Nos. 30, 31, 52, ed. by Zeumer in *MGH*, Leges V: *Formulae*, pp. 309 f., 325 (Aronius, *Regesten*, pp. 30 ff. Nos. 81–83); Charles the Bald's *Capitulare Carisiacense*, xxxi, ed. by A. Boretius and V. Krause, in *MGH*, Capit., II, 361. Cf. *supra*, Chap. XX, n. 62; L. Brunschvicg's archival excerpt in "Les Juifs d'Anger et du pays angevin," *REJ*, XXIX, 231 n. 1; Bourquelot's *Etudes sur les foires de Champagne*, II, 154 ff., 160 f. Of course, then as always, merchants sought means of evading burdensome surcharges. In his *Commentary* on the Mishnah, Simson of Sens (about 1200) noted the practice of contemporary traders to avoid the payment of duty on metals by turning them into clumsy utensils. As such they could be imported free of duty, and subsequently melted into whatever other objects were desired. Cf. his comment on M. Kelim xi.3. Although quoting T.B.M. ii.1.373, this interpretation has a contemporary ring.

42. Leo VI's *Book of the Prefect*, ed. by Nicole, vi.15, p. 33 (in the French trans., p. 39; ed. by Zépos and Zépos in *Jus graecoromanum*, II, 379; and in Freshfield's English trans. in his *Roman Law in the Later Roman Empire: Byzantine Guilds*, p. 23); the Monk of St. Gallen (Monachus Sangallensis), *De gestis Karoli imperatoris*, ii.14, ed. by G. H. Pertz, in *MGH*, Scriptores, II, 757 (on the date, see Aronius, *Regesten*, p. 27 No. 74); *Sefer Ma'aseh ha-geonim*, ed. by A. Epstein and J. Freimann,

p. 31 No. 47; Eleazar of Worms, *Sefer ha-Roqeaḥ*, No. 304, Warsaw ed., fol. 72b; Mahruz's letter published in facsimile and analyzed by S. D. Goitein in "The Jewish India-Merchants of the Middle Ages," *India and Israel*, V, No. 12, pp. 36–37; *supra*, Vol. II, p. 249. According to R. S. Lopez, the unusual restriction of the Book of the Prefect, originally promulgated in 911–12, was, like that entire decree, connected with the monetary difficulties in Byzantium. Cf. "La Crise de besant au Xe siècle et la date du Livre du Préfet," *Annuaire*, X, 403–18. See *supra*, n. 24, however, for a divergent date. Cf. also Starr's comment in *Byzantine Empire*, p. 163 No. 108; and on many technical aspects, including terminology, of "Arab Navigation," S. S. Nadavi's detailed analysis in *IC*, XV, 435–48; XVI, 72–86, 182–98, 404–22; S. M. Yusuf's "Al-Ranaj: The Route of Arab Mariners across the Bay of Bengal and the Gulf of Siam in the 3d and the 4th Centuries A.H.," *ibid.*, XXIX, 77–103; and G. F. Hourani's *Arab Seafaring in the Indian Ocean in Ancient and Early Medieval Times*. In a case known to us through the intervention of Pope Gregory the Great, a Sicilian Jew, Nostamnus (or Tamnus), was deprived of his ship by the papal *defensor* in Gaul in connection with a litigation. Cf. Gregory's *Epistolae*, IX.40, ed. by L. M. Hartmann, in *MGH*, Epistulae, II, 68. On medieval Jewish seafaring from the harbor of Marseilles, cf. the studies by A. Crémieux, "Les Juifs de Marseilles au moyen-âge," *REJ*, XLVI, 1–47, 246–68; XLVII, 62–86, 243–61 (mainly concerned with the later period); and *Histoire du commerce de Marseille*, ed. by G. Rambert *et al.*, Vols. I–II.

43. F. Barlow, *The Feudal Kingdom of England, 1042–1216*, p. 122; Maimonides' *Resp.*, pp. 156 f. No. 159; Gershom's resp. in J. Müller's *Teshubot ḥakhme Ṣarefat ve-Lotar*, pp. 58 ff. No. 101; a geonic resp. (by Saadiah?) in *Sha'are Ṣedeq*, II.11, fol. 12a. The problem of '*agunot*, created by a husband's probable, but unprobable, demise, became particularly significant in that period of both perilous journeys and large-scale massacres of Jews. It increasingly engaged the attention of Jewish jurists.

44. Cf. G. Caro, *Sozial- und Wirtschaftsgeschichte*, I, 434 f.; L. Massignon's concise remarks on "Guilds: Islamic," *Encyclopaedia of the Social Sciences*, VII, 214–16; and *supra*, nn. 24 and 36. On the *ḥisba*, in its legal and economic importance, see the various Arabic treatises discussed in M. Gaudefroy-Demombyne's "Sur quelques ouvrages de *ḥisba*," *JA*, CCXXX, 449–57. Cf. also C. Cahen's careful comparative study of "L'Evolution de l'iqta du IXe au XIIIe siècle," *Annales*, VIII, 25–52. On the Western evolution, see F. Sevillano Colom's preliminary study, "De la institución del mustaçaf de Barcelona, de Mallorca y de Valencia," *AHDE*, XXIII, 525–38; F. Rörig's data in "Magdeburgs Entstehung und die ältere Handelsgeschichte," in *Miscellanea Academica Berolinensia*, pp. 103–32; and the sources and literature briefly reviewed by E. Coornaert in "Les Ghildes médiévales (Ve–XIVe siècle)," *RH*, CXCIX, 22–55, 208–43. On Byzantium, see Lopez's observations in "Silk Industry in the Byzantine Empire," *Speculum*, XX, 3 ff.

45. See L. Rabinowitz's pertinent essay on "The Medieval Jewish Counterpart of the Gild Merchant," in *Economic History Review*, VIII, 180–85. Cf. also *The Herem Hayyishub, passim;* my remarks in *Rashi Anniv. Vol.*, pp. 62 ff.; J. Rabinowitz's comparative study of "The Title *De migrantibus* of the *Lex Salica* and the Jewish *Herem Hayishub*," *Speculum*, XXII, 46–50 (postulating the former's

indebtedness to the latter); *supra*, Chap. XX, n. 91; and *infra*, Chap. XXIII, n. 78. On the much-debated institution of *ma'arufia,* whose very etymology is doubtful, see S. Eidelberg's "'Maarufia' in Rabbenu Gershom's Responsa," *HJ*, XV, 59–66. The author's observations (pp. 63 ff.), however, on my succinct summary in *Jewish Community*, II, 80, are pointless; indeed controverted by Gershom's *Resp.* reproduced in Müller's *Teshubot ḥakhme Ṣarefat ve-Lotar*, p. 49 No. 88, and trans. by Eidelberg, pp. 63 ff. Cf. also the latter's recent edition of Gershom's *Resp.*, pp. 159 ff. Nos. 68–69. The evolution of these two significant legal institutions were to become clearer at the height of Jewish self-government and feudal regimentation in later medieval Europe.

46. Mahruz's aforementioned letter published by Goitein in *India and Israel*, V, No. 12; the latter's data in "From the Mediterranean to India," *Speculum*, XXIX, 188, 197; *M.T. Sheluḥin ve-shutefin* v.10. Although based on the talmudic fear lest some ensuing controversy force the Jewish partner to exact a pagan oath from the Gentile, and although upheld by such distinguished medieval teachers as Sar Shalom Gaon and Alfasi, the prohibition of interdenominational partnerships was not sharply enforced. Cf. *Teshubot geone mizraḥ u-ma'arab*, ed. by Müller, fol. 27a No. 102. Since the talmudic sages themselves were not altogether unanimous and consistent, Jacob Tam, facing the social situation of the slight Jewish minority in western Europe, greatly relaxed that prohibition by arguing that, after all, Christians swear to the same Maker of heaven and earth. Cf. *Tosafot* on Bekhorot 2b *s.v. Shemma;* and on Sanhedrin 63b *s.v. Asur.* Even in the East the prohibition was frequently honored in its breach, as is attested by several geonic responsa themselves. Cf. the illustrations cited by Mann in *JQR*, X, 331 f. Joseph Gaon tried to outlaw at least the joint ownership of a shop by Jew and Gentile, not because of the ensuing social intimacy but rather because of the opportunities it might offer to the Jewish partner to evade the Sabbath rest commandment. Cf. his resp. cited in *Kol bo* (Halakhic Collectanea), Fürth ed., 1782, fol. 14bc.

This more rigid theoretical stand of the geonim may have been but a reaction to some uncompromising decisions of Muslim jurists. Malik, for instance, demanded that in all business partnerships with *dhimmis* the Muslim partner be present at every transaction, obviously an untenable requirement. See Tritton, *Caliphs*, p. 190; and, more generally, G. Bergsträsser, *Grundzüge des islamischen Rechts,* ed. by J. Schacht, pp. 44 ff. Cf. also other data cited in my *Essays*, p. 228 n. 165. Needless to say that Muslim, as well as Jewish and Christian, extremists viewed with disfavor even more informal relations between members of their faiths and "infidels." Ibn 'Abdun, a twelfth-century Sevillian, actually advised his readers not to sell scientific books to Jews. Cf. E. Lévi-Provençal's ed. of "Un Document sur la vie urbaine et les corps de métier à Seville au début du XIIᵉ siècle: Le Traité d'Ibn 'Abdun," *JA*, CCXXIV, 248; and in his French trans., *Seville musulmane*, p. 128 No. 206. But such excessive zeal was never shared by either the masses or the governments.

47. Ginzberg, *Ginze Schechter*, II, 158 f. The high-handed methods of the Amalfitans had sufficiently provoked the populace of Cairo as early as 996 for it to stage a bloody riot against these exacting foreigners. Cf. C. Cahen's analysis of "Un Texte peu connu relatif au commerce oriental d'Amalfi au Xᵉ siècle," *Archivio storico per le provincie Napolitane*, LXXIII, 61–66 (with reference to Yaḥya of

Antioch's Chronicle in *PO*, XXIII, 457 f.). We de not know whether Jews were involved in these disturbances, though the smallness of the Amalfitan Jewish community, in contrast to those of the neighboring cities, may have reflected some early enmity between the two groups. Similarly, the participation of the Genoese fleet in the Crusaders' reconquest of parts of Spain in 1146–47 and the treaty provisions for partial control over the occupied territories and free trade therein by these Italian merchant-mariners boded ill for the Jewish survivors there. Cf. these treaties in C. Imperiale di Sant' Angelo, *Codice diplomatico della Repubblica di Genova*, I (in *Fonti per la storia d'Italia*, Vol. LXXVII), pp. 204 ff. Nos. 166–69. Genoese influence may also have been responsible, in part, for both the weakness of the Jewish settlement in Almeria and the initial difficulties encountered by the community of Tortosa after its incorporation in Aragon. Cf. *supra*, Chap. XX, n. 32; and, more generally, A. R. Lewis's *Naval Power and Trade in the Mediterranean A.D. 500–1100*; and, for the later period, P. Charanis's "Piracy in the Aegean during the Reign of Michael VIII Palaeologus," *Annuaire*, X, 127–36 (showing how Pisan and other Italian pirates replaced the Arab corsairs).

Curiously, this antagonism between the Italian and, to a lesser extent, the Hanseatic merchants and their Jewish competitors did not interfere with the growth of the Jewish communities in these western centers themselves. The same Republic of Venice which tried to curtail international Jewish commerce apparently welcomed Jewish traders to her own shores, since these were likely to increase her commerce. See *supra*, Chap. XX, n. 26; and *infra*, n. 57. However, no definitely Jewish names could be identified in the extensive collection of *Documenti del commercio veneziano nei secoli XI–XIII*, Vols. I–II, compiled by R. Morozzo della Rocca and A. Lombardo. Even Genoa accommodated in the thirteenth century a substantial number of Jews, if we may judge from several documents published by C. Roth in his "Genoese Jews in the Thirteenth Century," *Speculum*, XXV, 190–97. While the Hansa, except for the city of Cologne, seems to have been less encouraging, we must bear in mind that the main development of most of these northern communities, including that of Hamburg, which was to play a major role in modern Jewish history, came only after the formation of the League. Certainly the Jewish merchants had never become entrenched in that northern trade, and hence did not have to be uprooted by any violent action of these expansive burghers' commonwealths. But that story, too, fully unfolded only after 1200.

48. Amram Gaon's resp. in *Sha'are Ṣedeq*, 1.5.18, fol. 25b; that of Sar Shalom in *Sha'are teshubah*, No. 255; and *supra*, Chaps. XVI, n. 37; XIX, n. 15; XX, nn. 6 and 16; and Vol. II, pp. 259, 416 n. 35. Cf. Ali Abd Elwahed (Al-Waḥid), *Contribution à une théorie sociologique de l'esclavage*, pp. 31 ff., 111 ff., stressing the fact that under medieval Islam the ancient methods of acquiring slaves through rapine, court judgment, sale by parents, or self-sale had legally been abandoned, and that, apart from unfree birth, only capture in war constituted a legitimate cause for slavery. The same legal theory, with minor variations, had earlier been adopted by Jews and Christians. Hai's decision was an alleviation of the ancient talmudic regulation which demanded that even a provisionally uncircumcised slave must observe at least the seven Noahide commandments. If he refused, he was subject to immediate execution. While unqualifiedly restating this talmudic law, Maimonides was certainly aware of its purely theoretical nature in his day, and Abraham ben David's vigorous objection, "We cannot execute any-

body now," applied even to the few areas where, as in Spain, Jews still enjoyed capital jurisdiction. Cf. *M.T.* Milah 1.1.6; Melakhim IX.2; with Abraham ben David's comment on the former; and my *Essays on Maimonides,* p. 236 n. 174. In reality, many pagan slaves were retained for longer or shorter periods in the possession of Jewish owners, especially traders, and Maimonides himself had to compromise with the existing facts in many of his *Resp.* and in his Code, 'Abadim VIII.12. On the other hand, even in thirteenth-century Germany, R. Baruch bar Isaac of Worms could still speak of the acquisition of Gentile slaves, their circumcision and ablution, and their immediate serving of wine at the tables of their masters as if it were a widespread custom. Cf. his *Sefer ha-Terumah,* fol. 60c No. 169. But this probably was a rare occurrence at that time. Cf. also, more generally, B. Z. Wacholder, "The Halakah and the Proselyting of Slaves during the Gaonic Period," *HJ,* XVIII, 89–106.

49. Mansi, *Collectio,* XI, 37 ff. canon 7 (Hefele, *Histoire,* III, Part 1, p. 295; in the English trans. by Clark, IV, 475). In all these debates, it may be noted, slavery as such was not an issue. Churchmen, *'ullama,* and rabbis alike took that institution for granted. Cf., for instance, the apologetically tinged analyses by Sister Margaret Mary, "Slavery in the Writings of St. Augustine," *Classical Journal,* XLIX, 363–68; and A. Calvanese, *La Chiesa e la condizione sociale dei servi nell' alto medioevo.* The dominant faiths merely wanted to make sure that they would not lose adherents via the conversion of slaves to their masters' religion. On the early Muslim attitudes, see A. N. Poliak's comments in "L'Arabisation de l'Orient sémitique," *Revue des études sémitiques,* XII, 39 f.

50. Canon 16 of the First Council of Mâcon, in Mansi, *Collectio,* IX, 935; Hefele, *Histoire,* III, Part 1, p. 204 (English trans. by Clark, IV, 405); and Innocent's letter reproduced in Grayzel, *The Church and the Jews,* pp. 112 f. On the latter's background, see also *supra,* Chap. XX, n. 53. Prices of slaves were undoubtedly much lower in the West than in the Orient. But twelve solidi must have approximated the market price only in sixth-century France with its generally low standard of life and small demand for slaves.

51. Mordecai bar Hillel ha-Kohen, *Halakhot* (Legal Commentary on the Talmud), on Yebamot No. 41; Second Council of Nicaea, canon 8, in Mansi, *Collectio,* XIII, 427; Hefele, *Histoire,* III, Part 2, p. 782 (in Clark's trans. V, 381) and *supra,* Chap. XVI, n. 37. Cf. also the succinct summaries by Starr in his *Byzantine Empire,* pp. 9, 19; and by S. Katz in *The Jews in the Visigothic and Frankish Kingdoms,* pp. 96 ff.

52. *M.T.* 'Abadim VIII.6–11; *Tosafot* on Ketubot 110b *s.v. Hakhi;* Deut. 23:16; *Sha'are ṣedeq,* III.6.29, 36, fols. 26b, 27b. Cf. also Mez, *Renaissance,* p. 166; and my *Essays on Maimonides, loc. cit.* We must bear in mind, however, that whether or not slaves found out about these provisions of Jewish law, we never hear of their large-scale immigration to Palestine. The temptation, on the other hand, to give slaves a good general, if not Jewish, education must have been very great, since it considerably enhanced the slave's value on the market. Muslim slaveholders, even if extremely proud of their own Arab descent, had no compunctions, therefore, about making available their educational facilities to slaves who, especially after their liberation, played a significant role in spreading Muslim culture. Cf. in

general I. Goldziher's pertinent observations in his *Muhammedanische Studien*, I, 101 ff.; and A. Wesselski's mainly ninth-century illustrations of "Die gelehrten Sklavinnen des Islams und ihre byzantinischen Vorbilder," *Archiv Orientalni*, IX, 353–78.

53. The correspondence between emperor and caliph, trans. from a Vienna Arabic MS by G. Schlumberger in *Un Empereur byzantin au dixième siècle*, pp. 427 ff., 432. Curiously, in his report on the Byzantine raid on Damietta in 853, *Ṭabari* (ed. by De Goeje, III, 1417 f.), mentioned both Muslim and Coptic, but not Jewish, women among the prisoners. Cf. A. Vasiliev, *Byzance et les Arabes*, I, 316. Al-Kindi, however, spoke more generally of *dhimmis* being taken into captivity, along with Muslim women and children. Cf. Mann, *Jews in Egypt*, I, 14. Jewish reticence toward female slaves led to an interesting inquiry addressed to Isaac Alfasi. A Jewish owner of a Christian slave found her "faithful and worthy" and hence did not wish to dispose of her. Since many Christians visited in the house on business, she asked to be allowed to associate with one of them, or else be sold to another household. The rabbi decided that her request be granted, provided that she had stipulated in advance of her sale to the Jewish owner that she would not be converted to Judaism. Cf. Alfasi's *Resp.*, fol. 25a No. 166. Otherwise, rabbinic opinion was generally opposed to any sexual relations between a Gentile slave and a free non-Jew, once the former had undergone circumcision or ablution. Cf. the resp. of Abraham bar Isaac of Narbonne published in S. Assaf, *Sifran shel rishonim*, pp. 49 f. No. 48.

54. *M.T.* 'Abadim v.4–5, 17; Rashi and Alfasi on Qiddushin 25a; a geonic resp. in *Teshubot ha-geonim*, ed. by N. N. Coronel, p. 9, No. 78; *Basilika*, XIX.1.85, ed. by Heimbach, II, 269; Mez, *Renaissance*, pp. 353 ff. Cf. S. Assaf's Hebrew essay on "Slave and Slave Trade among Jews during the Middle Ages (From Hebrew Sources)," reprinted in his *Be-Ohole Ya'aqob*, p. 232 n. 62. We know from Ibn Khurdadhbah and some geonic sources of Jewish trade in eunuchs, but no unequivocal source tells us about Jews themselves performing that surgery. Muqaddasi's extensive description of the operation (ed. by De Goeje, p. 242) may refer to some Lucena Jews performing it, although he does not name them. Ibn Ḥauqal, too, is far from unequivocal. Cf. his *K. Ṣurat al-ardh* (or *K. al-Mamalik*), ed. by De Goeje, p. 75 (ed. by J. H. Kramers, pp. 109 f.). Liudprand's report (dating from approximately 949), which is most frequently mentioned in this connection, is even less conclusive. The bishop of Cremona referred only to "Verdun merchants [who] do it on account of the enormous profit, and usually export [these eunuchs] to Spain." Cf. his *Antapodosis*, vi.6, ed. by G. H. Pertz, in *MGH*, Scriptores, III, 338. Liudprand would most likely have named Jews expressly, had they played a prominent part in these transactions. Only the vastly exaggerated assumption of the role of French Jews in the slave trade of the tenth century could have led students of Frankish law and history, as well as Arabists like Dozy, to read into this statement a reference to Jewish traders. Cf. Aronius, *Regesten*, p. 155 No. 127; and R. Dozy, *Histoire des Musulmans d'Espagne*, rev. ed., II, 154. Curiously, on his mission to Constantinople in 948, Liudprand himself presented four eunuchs to the emperor. Cf. his *Antapodosis, loc. cit.* It may be noted that, in discussing a eunuch's conversion to Judaism through ablution alone, Naḥshon, or another gaon, seems to take it for granted that he had not previously belonged to a Jew and been circumcised. Cf. Assaf's ed. of *Teshubot ha-geonim*, 1928, pp. 191 f. No. 261.

55. Eustratios' martyrology, reported by Simon, thirteenth-century bishop of Vladimir in *Kievo-Pecherskii Paterik*, ed. by D. Abramovich, pp. 107 f., and summarized by Starr in *Byzantine Empire*, pp. 209 ff. No. 155; *Un Manuel hispanique de ḥisba* by Abu 'Abd Allah Muḥammad as-Saqaṭi, ed. by G. S. Colin and E. Lévi-Provençal, pp. 47 ff.; the latter's *Espagne musulmane*, p. 192 n. 2; Naḥshon Gaon's resp. in *Sha'are ṣedeq*, v.6.17, fol. 81b; Maimonides' *M.T.* Mekhirah xv.13 In his translation of the talmudic blemish of *qubiustus* by the harsh term "kidnaper," rather than the milder one connoting a professional gambler, Maimonides followed Gershom and Rashi, though they had been rightly opposed by Ḥananel and the Tosafists. Cf. *Tosafot* on Qiddushin 11b *s.v. qubiustus;* and S. Krauss's *Griechische und lateinische Lehnwörter im Talmud*, II, 501. On his philosophic prejudice against slaves, cf. his *Guide*, III, 39. Cf. also *supra*, n. 49.

56. Cf. I. Agus's ed. of *Teshubot ba'ale ha-tosafot*, p. 85 No. 26. Nor was Yehudah Halevi's friend, Abu Naṣr ben Elisha of Alexandria, an exception when he mourned the death of a female slave. Cf. Halevi's elegy, *Ha-Sar 'ateret* (O Lord, the Glory of All Thy Friends) in his *Diwan*, ed. by Brody, I, 40 f. No. 31 (ed. by Zemorah, III, 315). The poet himself, however, is far from complimentary to slaves.

57. Naḥshon Gaon's resp. in *Sha'are ṣedeq*, 1.6.27, fol. 26b, and Yehudah bar Barzillai's *Sefer ha-'Ittim*, p. 238; Louis the Pious' aforementioned privileges in *Formulae imperiales*, Nos. 30, 31, 52, in *MGH*, Formulae, pp. 309 f., 325 (cf. in this context the general prohibition of selling slaves abroad included in Charlemagne's capitulary of 779, Art. 19, in *MGH*, Capit. I, 51); Agobard's *De insolentia Judaeorum*, III, VI, in *PL*, CIV, 62 f., 76; the Slavonic "Legend of Naum," cited by F. Dvornik in *Les Slaves, Byzance et Rome au IXe siècle*, pp. 298 ff. (despite Dvornik's arguments, this legend includes too many hagiographic stereotypes to be given full credence); Ibrahim's and Benjamin's travelogues cited *supra*, Chap. XIX, nn. 53 and 57; and Aronius's *Regesten*, p. 52 No. 122. Cf. also T. Lewicki's lucid summary, "Slav Settlements and Slav Slaves in Muslim Countries according to Medieval Arabic Writers" (Polish), *Przegląd historyczny*, XLIII, 473–91. Spanish Moors seemed to have some reason to fear that, after their surrender to Christian powers, some of them might be sold as slaves to Jews. That is why they secured the outlawry of such sales in their treaties of capitulation in Tudela, Tortosa, and Saragossa. Cf. Muñoz, *Colección de fueros*, p. 417; Baer, *Juden*, I, Part 1, pp. 15 f. No. 27, 919 f. No. 569.

The manpower shortage already underlay the canonical prohibition of exporting slaves adopted by the Merovingian Church Council of Châlons (variously dated between 639 and 656), although the menace of thus losing a number of actual or potential believers must also have been ever present in these churchmen's minds. Hence they emphasized that such trade might result in the captivity of Christian slaves or, "what is worse," their being held by Jews. Cf. Mansi, *Collectio*, X, 1189 f. canon 9 (Hefele, *Histoire*, III, Part 1, p. 283; in Clark's English trans., IV, 464). C. Verlinden goes too far, however, in insisting that this economic factor outweighed the religious scruples also in the reiterated Church and state prohibitions of the ownership of Christian slaves by Jews, since the latter were very likely to export such slaves to other lands. Cf. "L'Esclavage dans le monde ibérique médiéval," *AHDE*, XI, 329 ff. Verlinden not only overstates here the importance of a temporary and local factor with respect to an old, deep-rooted, and universal attitude of the Church, but also far too glibly accepts the view that Jews dominated the international slave trade of the period. See *infra*, n. 59. In fact, a case could be made for the Crown actually deriving tangible benefits from Jewish slaveownership through its increasing controls over all Jewish property. At times this conflict of interests became quite apparent, as in the aforementioned correspondence between Innocent III and Alphonso VIII. See *supra*, n. 50.

Commerce in slaves generally declined in the following generations, although an ordinance, dating from about 1100 and regulating the tariff at the toll barrier of Rhenish Coblenz, which belonged to the Monastery of St. Simeon of Treves, still tersely provided that "Jews are to pay four denarii for every salable slave." But this provision may have been but a verbatim repetition of some earlier enactment, without direct reference to contemporary realities. Cf. Aronius's comments, *Regesten*, p. 96 No. 208. Nor did Slavonic slaves ever constitute more than a mere fraction of the slave supply in Muslim markets. In a typical formula of a deed of sale, included in Hai Gaon's *Sefer ha-Sheṭarot* (Book of Deeds), the more inclusive writing reads: "Indian, Canaanite [Slavonic], Roman [Byzantine], Lybian or Senegalese [Zanzibar] slave." Cf. S. Assaf's ed., pp. 27 f. There is no evidence for any active Jewish participation in this trade with non-European areas.

58. Abu Yusuf, *K. al-Kharaj*, p. 127 (in Fagnan's French trans., pp. 318 f.); Simon Qayyara, *Halakhot gedolot* (Legal Code), ed. by J. E. Hildesheimer, pp. 253 f., 259 ff.; Naṭronai Gaon's resp. in *Sha'are ṣedeq*, 1.5.13, fol. 25a (here entered as a resp. by Amram Gaon); and samples of contractual clauses cited by L. M. Epstein in *The Jewish Marriage Contract*, pp. 272 f. Cf. also his study of "The Institution of Concubinage among the Jews," *PAAJR*, VI, 182 ff. Children of a slave girl, even a captive princess, were considered slaves, unless their mother had been liberated before their birth. This fact became, after Bustanai, an important issue in the anti-exilarchic attacks. In practice, however, public opinion severely condemned a Jewish slaveholder who mistreated such a child and its mother, as is seen in the behavior of the Jews of Aidhab, described in the letter published by Goitein in *Tarbiz*, XXI, 186 ff. Another community celebrated a regular wedding between two slaves; their master brought their son to the synagogue and gave him the customary Jewish education. Ultimately, they were all censured by Sherira Gaon. Cf. his resp. in *Sha'are ṣedeq*, 1.6.29, fol. 26b. A curious sidelight on the position of Christian help, free or unfree, in Jewish households is shed by Moses of Coucy's explanation why French mourners no longer covered their heads and parts of their faces. According to R. Moses, this ritual was still observed in Spain, "But in these kingdoms they do not observe it, for it causes great ridicule among the Gentiles; servants, female and male, laugh at us." Similarly, the old custom of upsetting beds in a mourner's dwelling, was discontinued, lest the servants accuse their masters of magic practices. Cf. his *Sefer Miṣvot gadol* (Large Book of Commandments), Abelut, in the concluding section of the work, II, Venice ed., 1522, fol. 31/ivd. See also *supra*, n. 55.

59. *Sha'are ṣedeq*, III.6.6; *M.T.* Matenot 'aniyyim, x.17 with reference to M. Abot 1.5 (cf. Maimonides' briefer statement in his commentary thereon); and the text, ed. by Goitein in *Tarbiz*, XXI, 186 ff. The extent of the Jewish slave trade before 1200 is still debatable. Older scholars, familiar only with the recurrent attacks of Church councils which were really aimed at Jewish slaveholding much more than at slave trade, and such occasional references in Arabic literature as Ibn Khur-

dadhbah's description of Jewish trade routes, were inclined to exaggerate greatly the Jewish share in this branch of international commerce. Characteristic of these older views were the sweeping assertions in B. Hahn's otherwise still valuable study of *Die wirtschaftliche Tätigkeit der Juden im fränkischen und deutschen Reich*, and Caro's *Sozial- und Wirtschaftsgeschichte, passim*. Cf., for instance, the series of *non sequitur* arguments *ibid.*, I, 102 f.

In the meantime, much more material has become available from Muslim and rabbinic sources in the Near East and Spain, showing that there were relatively more Jewish slave owners than traders there. Even in Christian Spain, where the shortcomings of slaveownership were to be so gravely deplored by later moralists, practically no sources relating to Jewish merchants in this human commodity during the eleventh and twelfth centuries appear in the voluminous documentation assembled by Baer in his *Juden*. Among the remarkable documents published by A. González Palencia in *Los Mozárabes de Toledo en los siglos XII y XIII*, only three seem to refer to Jewish slaveholdings (Nos. 634, 934, 1003), and one to a Jew serving as agent in the sale of a slave (No. 690). None of these dates from the twelfth century. All the deeds relating to intra-Jewish business (Nos. 1132–51) refer to real estate transactions in the years 1248–82. These "Escrituras mozárabes de hebreos toledanos" were transcribed and translated for González by J. M. Millás Vallicrosa, *ibid.*, III, 561–95. Nor is any significant Spanish-Jewish material of that period included in C. Verlinden's aforementioned detailed studies in *AHDE*, XI–XII (XII, 397 ff., he merely restates the well-known data concerning Jewish trade in Central Europe, but offers no significant Spanish documentation); his *L' Esclavage dans l'Europe mediévale, passim*, esp. pp. 66 ff., 672 ff., 707 ff.; and in Aḥmad al-'Abbadi's *Los Esclavos en España*, despite the author's attempt to correlate slavery with the racial *shu'ubiya* movement under Spanish Islam. Regrettably, all these works, including Verlinden's highly meritorious analysis, suffer from their extreme paucity of factual documentation. Despite his effort to utilize occasional illustrations from the European notarial archives, Verlinden, too, had to rely principally on the normative and homiletical sources which more frequently reflect their authors' biases and wishes than existing realities. This shortcoming is particularly evident in his treatment of Spanish slavery and the Jewish role therein. And Spain, the borderland between the two civilizations, with its prosperous Jewish communities, had traditionally had, at least in the Visigothic and early Muslim periods, relatively the largest concentration of Jewish slaveowners!

In Byzantium, too, where slaveownership and slave trade continued to flourish for many centuries, Starr was able to marshal only a few meager data, apart from the repetitive canonical regulations. The small Jewish share was almost entirely limited to the Empire's periphery. Cf. his *Byzantine Empire*, pp. 31 f.; and, more generally, A. Hadjinicolaou-Marava's *Recherches sur la vie des esclaves dans le monde byzantin*. Reviewing the Western records alone, E. Täubler had rightly concluded that "our evidence points only to the existence of Jewish slave traders in Italy and even there slave trade lagged far behind slave ownership for personal use." Cf. his "Zur Handelsbedeutung der Juden in Deutschland vor Beginn des Städtewesens," *Philippson Festschrift*, pp. 381 ff., 392.

Obviously, the combination of hostile laws enacted by Christian rulers and churchmen and the severe limitations of rabbinic law could not long be effectively defied. Only under particularly favorable economic conditions did some Jews in Visigothic Spain, the Carolingian Empire, and tenth-century Slavonic eastern

Europe, successfully overcome these formidable legal obstacles. But far more frequently they merely belonged to the slave traders' customers.

60. Mann, *Jews in Egypt*, I, 14; Mez, *Renaissance*, pp. 478 ff.; and *supra*, n. 17. Cf. E. Cohn's analysis of *Der Wucher (ribâ) im Qor'ân, Chadîth und Fiqh;* and A. H. M. Muhiy-ud-Din's succinct discussion of the "Islamic Prohibition of Riba (Usury) as a Basic Principle of Economics," *Islamic Review*, XLI, No. 6, pp. 9–11 (arguing for a clear-cut distinction between *ribah* and *mudharaba* or "partnership, with a two-sided risk," as helpful also for modern economic relations). Investigations concerning Jewish banking under the Caliphate have received new impetus through the studies by L. Massignon, "L'Influence de l'Islam au moyen âge sur la fondation et l'essor des banques juives," *Bulletin d'études orientales de l'Institut Français de Damas*, I, 3–12; and especially by W. Fischel, *Jews in . . . Medieval Islam*, supplemented in part by J. Mann's remarks in his "Varia on the Gaonic Period" (Hebrew), *Tarbiz*, V, 148–79. Cf. also A. Cohen's observations on "Die wirtschaftliche Stellung der Juden in Bagdad im 10. Jahrhundert," *MGWJ*, LXXIX, 361–81 (a rather inadequate elaboration of Fischel's and Massignon's essays by an economist); and, more generally, W. Björkmann's "Kapitalentstehung und -Anlage im Islam," *Mitteilungen des Seminars für orientalische Sprachen der . . . Universität Berlin*, XXXII, Part 2, pp. 80–98.

61. Justinian's *Codex*, IV.32–33; X.8.1–3, ed. by Krüger, pp. 171 ff., 397; Ostrogorsky, *Geschichte des byzantinischen Staates*, pp. 153 f.; and, more generally, G. Cassimatis's analysis of *Les Intérêts dans la législation de Justinien et dans le droit byzantin* (showing the persistence of Justinian's legal theory to the end of the Empire, but also the gradual adjustments inexorably made in the following centuries by the "collective conscience" reacting to changing needs). Cf. also S. Giet's "De Saint Basile à Saint Ambroise. La condamnation du prêt à intérêt au IVe siècle," *Science religieuse* (wartime ed. of *RSR*), 1944, pp. 95–128. As pointed out by Starr (in his *Byzantine Empire*, p. 34), there is only one equivocal reference to a Jew Abraham who had advanced money to a Christian Theodore. This excerpt from a typical conversion story, perhaps dating from the eighth century (published from a British Museum MS by A. Mussafia in his "Studien zu den mittelalterlichen Marienlegenden, III," in *SB*, Vienna, CXIX, Part 9, p. 5) may simply mean that the Jew and the Christian entered one of the then usual partnerships in shipping goods, with the capitalist reserving for himself in advance a certain specified rate of profit. Cf. Heinrich Loewe's general analysis, "Die Juden in der Marienlegende," *MGWJ*, LVI, 257–84, 385–416, 612–21 (esp. pp. 272 ff.).

62. Maimonides, *M.T.* Malveh ve-loveh, v.1–2, with reference to *Sifre* on Deut. 263, ed. by Friedmann, fol. 121b (ed. by Finkelstein, p. 285, also quoting many medieval sources); the responsa of the two geonim in *Sha'are ṣedeq*, IV.2.7, fol. 35b; 20, fol. 40a; and Mez's *Renaissance*, pp. 478 f. (citing Maqrizi). Maimonides' interpretation of the *Sifre* was rejected by Abraham ben David, *ad loc.*, and most other rabbis. The historical background and implications of these biblical laws have recently been reexamined by E. Neufeld in "The Prohibitions against Loans on Interest in Ancient Hebrew Laws," *HUCA*, XXVI, 355–412. On outright Jewish partnerships with Gentiles, cf. *supra*, n. 46; and *infra*, n. 64. We must note, however, that in his dramatic description of the abuses of moneylenders in their relations

with taxpaying farmers, Denys (Dionysius) of Tell-Mahré fails to mention Jews. Cf. his *Chronique*, ed. by Chabot, pp. 151 f.

63. Sar Shalom's resp. in *Sha'are ṣedeq*, IV.2.3, fol. 34a; *M.T.* Malveh ve-loveh, 1.2; and my *Essays*, pp. 211 ff. In the later Middle Ages the practice of *prosbol* became ever more sporadic. On his arrival in Spain in 1303, Asher ben Yeḥiel was shocked by the creditors' lackadaisical attitude toward thus securing the continued validity of their loans beyond the Sabbatical year. Cf. his *Resp.*, LXXVII.2, Venice ed., 1587, fol. 123b; and on his general difficulties with the local opposition A. Freimann's "Ascher ben Jechiel. Sein Leben und Wirken," *JJLG*, XII, 260 ff. In other countries, however, the practice continued, in part down to the nineteenth century. Cf. also *supra*, Vol. II, pp. 302 ff., 417 n. 39.

64. Geonic responsa offer numerous illustrations of both genuine partnerships and evasive contracts. For example, one contract called for the silent partner to contribute but 40 percent of the capital, and share in both the profits and losses to the extent of five twelfths. In Kairuwan the rabbis prohibited borrowings on land and houses if the creditor was to collect the produce or rents. But they could not prevent "sales" of such property with the proviso that the "seller" was to repurchase it at the same price, allowing the new owner to enjoy the revenue in the interim. Cf. *Sha'are ṣedeq*, IV.2.12, fols. 36a ff.; v.8.2, fols. 96b ff. On the various legal means of evasion, see the data analyzed by E. E. Hildesheimer in *Das jüdische Gesellschaftsrecht*, pp. 87 ff.; M. Hoffmann in *"Sheṭar 'Isqa und Contractus Trinus," Festschrift . . . David Hoffmann*, pp. 383–86; J. H. Rappaport in his dissertation, *Das Darlehen nach talmudischem Recht*, pp. 128 ff., 136 ff.; J. J. Rabinowitz in "Some Remarks on the Evasion of Usury Laws in the Middle Ages," *HTR*, XXXVII, 49–59 (with reference to a Hellenistic practice); and especially in my *Essays on Maimonides*, pp. 209 ff. On the much-debated *commenda* contract, see G. Astuti's *Origini e svolgimento della commenda fino al secolo XIII*, where however the Jewish and Muslim evolutions are not mentioned. Cf. also M. Hoffmann's comprehensive study of *Der Geldhandel der deutschen Juden während des Mittelalters* (still the fullest monograph on medieval Jewish moneylending anywhere; includes also numerous excerpts from rabbinic sources in German translation); I. Bernfeld's more popular survey of *Das Zinsverbot bei den Juden nach talmudisch-rabbinischem Recht;* R. Ruth's Nazi-colored "Wucher und Wucherrecht der Juden im Mittelalter," *Deutsche Rechtswissenschaft*, II, 111–57; G. Kisch's critique thereof in his *Forschungen*, pp. 256 ff.; and the more recent studies by J. Rosenthal, "The Law of Usury Relating to Non-Jews" (Hebrew), *Talpioth*, V, 475–92; VI, 130–52; and by S. Stein "Interest Taken by Jews from Gentiles: An Evaluation of Source Material," *Journal of Semitic Studies*, I, 141–64 (mainly deals with the fourteenth century and after). By their very nature these studies are greatly repetitious, but in their diverse ways they clearly illustrate the manifold adjustments of the law to the exigencies of life—a process which in the banking domain had been fully under way already in ancient times. Cf. *supra*, n. 62; Vols. I, pp. 346 n. 11, 409 n. 15; II, pp. 414 f. n. 29; and *infra*, Chaps. XXIV, nn. 58–59; and XXVII, n. 171. On the long and heatedly debated evolution of the anti-usury laws in the Christian world, see B. N. Nelson's well-documented analysis of *The Idea of Usury: From Brotherhood to Otherhood;* supplemented by "The Usurer and the Merchant Prince: Italian Businessmen and the Ecclesiastical Law of

Restitution, 1100–1550," *Journal of Economic History*, VII, Supplement, pp. 104–22; T. P. McLaughlin's detailed analysis of "The Teaching of the Canonists on Usury (XII, XIII and XIV Centuries)," *Mediaeval Studies*, I, 81–147; II, 1–22 (includes a review of the canonists' debate over the applicability to Jews as the enemies of Christianity of the principle, annunciated by Saint Ambrose, *ubi jus belli ibi jus usurae;* I, 137 f.); and by K. Weinzierl's detailed analysis of "Das Zinsproblem im Dekret Gratians und in den Summen zum Dekret," in *Studia Gratiana*, ed. by Forchelli and Stickler, I, 549–76 (pointing out that one of Gratian's commentators, Huguccio, although liberal in other interpretations, wished to extend the prohibition of usury to Jews; cf. pp. 565, 569). On the medieval background of the figure of Shylock, cf. *infra*, Chap. XXIV, n. 58.

65. 'Ali ibn 'Isa's letter is cited from two slightly differing versions by Hilal aṣ-Ṣabi and At-Tanukhi in Fischel's *Jews in . . . Mediaeval Islam*, pp. 23 f. Cf. also *ibid.*, pp. 31 f. on other Jewish connections with Aḥwaz. Incidentally, at the time of his dismissal in 928, 'Ali left the treasury of Aḥwaz in possession of the substantial cash amount of 1,050,000 dirhems. Cf. H. F. Amedroz and D. S. Margoliouth's edition of Ibn Miskawaihi's Arabic chronicle, *The Eclipse of the 'Abbasid Caliphate*, I, 186 (Arabic); IV, 210 (English).

66. *Ibid.*, III, 282 (Arabic); VI, 300 (English); Tritton, *Caliphs*, p. 148; and other data cited by Fischel, p. 33 n. 1. Of course assassinations and riots were a frequent concomitant of political distinction. On the price generally paid by the Jewish community for the elevation of some of its members, see *supra*, Chap. XVIII, n. 44.

67. Gregory of Tours, *Historia*, VII. 23, in *MGH*, Scriptores rerum merov., I, 305 f. (in Dalton's English trans., pp. 302 f.); Dodona, *Liber manualis*, LXXI, in *PL*, CVI, 117; Charlemagne, *Capitula de Judaeis*, I–II, in *MGH*, Capit., I, 258. Cf. Aronius, *Regesten*, pp. 17 f. No. 47, 27 f. No. 76, 45 No. 104. On the doubts concerning the authenticity of Charlemagne's capitulary and some other pertinent data, cf. also Caro, *Sozial- und Wirtschaftsgeschichte*, I, 139 f., 471. On their part, the rabbis, too, tried to discourage moneylending on church objects, and more broadly all business transactions likely to promote non-Jewish worship. Yet Rashi had to admit that at least priestly vestments were fit objects for pledges. Cf. his *Teshubot*, p. 365 No. 364; the extensive literature cited in the editor's notes thereon; and, especially, Eliezer bar Nathan's *Eben ha-'Ezer*, fols. 124d f. No. 289. Considering the special ethics condoning the pious appropriation of relics and the frequency of their sales, this was indeed a major commodity likely to appear also on a pawnbroker's shelves. Cf. H. Silvestre's "Commerce et vol de reliques au moyen âge," *RBPH*, XXX, 721–39. Conversely, Jews viewed with disfavor the pawning of Hebrew books with Christian lenders. Cf. Yehudah the Pious' *Sefer Ḥasidim*, ed. by Wistinetzki, p. 180 No. 689. On the other hand, there was no objection to Jews' lending money on the security of a Hebrew Bible. One particularly precious copy was once pawned in a Spanish or North African community for a loan of 500 dinars (some $2,000), according to an inquiry recorded in Alfasi's *Resp.*, fol. 11b No. 74. Neither the questioners nor the rabbi saw any reason to comment on this high valuation. That it was not completely out of line with the prices charged for precious manuscripts may be seen from the report, probably exaggerated, that a copy of the Qur'an, allegedly prepared by Caliph 'Uthman himself, fetched in

1184 in Cairo the fabulous equivalent of some $160,000. Cf. Mazahéri, *Vie quoti-dienne,* p. 217; and, on books generally, *infra,* Chap. XXXII, nn. 2 and 4.

68. Ginzberg, *Ginze Schechter,* II, 200, 220 (a resp. by R. Meshullam); Jacob Tam's resp., cited in full from Sir Leon's MS in both Isaac bar Moses' *Sefer Or zaru'a,* on B.M. No. 202 (Jerusalem ed., III, 57 f.); and Meir bar Baruch of Rothenburg's *Resp.,* Prague ed., No. 796. On the other hand, Tam's predecessor Jacob bar Isaac ha-Levi, allowed only the full transfer by one Jewish creditor to another of a debt owed by a Gentile, together with its pledge, but not the borrowing on such a pledge on interest. Cf. his resp. in Agus's ed. of *Teshubot ba'ale ha-tosafot,* pp. 49 f. Nos. 5 and 7. Tam was generally aware of the economic necessity of banking, he himself probably living from moneylending as well as tax farming. Cf. his *Sefer ha-Yashar,* Nos. 579, 610; L. Finkelstein's *Jewish Self-Government in the Middle Ages,* pp. 46 f., 105 f. He exempted, therefore, these transactions from the general restrictions of rabbinic law on trading during the half-holidays of Passover or the Feast of Tabernacles. Cf. *Tosafot* on M.Q. 10b *s.v. Praqmaṭiah.* One of his most distinguished pupils, Eliezer bar Samuel of Metz, however, observed, "I have seen some persons abstaining from such loans, and for many years I have abstained myself. Nevertheless I believe that they are permitted, and I say with reference to both the abstainer and the lender, 'Thy people shall be all righteous' [Isa. 60:21]." Cf. his *Sefer Yere'im ha-shalem* (Halakhic Treatise), No. 304 end, ed. by I. Goldblum, p. 341; and Urbach's *Ba'ale ha-tosafot,* pp. 78 f., 136. Because of the frequency with which Jews used Christian intermediaries in placing pledges with Jewish lenders, precautions had to be taken against the real debtors subsequently claiming that the loans, being extended to fellow Jews, had been unlawful, and that hence the interest should be refunded. Yehudah bar Kalonymos of Mayence recorded, therefore, "We have seen daily instances of loans extended to fellow Jews on pledges of Gentiles. Our forebears have placed under excommunication any Jew misleading his neighbor by merely pretending that his pledges belong to Gentiles. Hence no one is believed when he states that the pledge had been his and that he had cheated the lender by concealing this fact, for 'a man does not declare himself an evildoer.'" Cited in Mordecai bar Hillel's *Halakhot,* on B.M. No. 338. Cf. also Rashi's pertinent decisions in his *Resp.,* pp. 42 No. 49, 103 No. 79, 198 f. No. 177.

69. *Chartres et diplômes,* published by the Académie des Inscriptions, VI, Part 2, pp. 132 f. No. 583; and *supra,* Chap. XX, nn. 80 and 109. The Hessian theologians' memorandum, submitted in 1534 in answer to an inquiry of Landgrave Philipp, is cited by L. Munk in "Die Judenlandtage in Hessen-Cassel," *MGWJ,* XLI, 507. That this graphic simile was used not for the defense of Jews, but rather to advise the Landgrave not to admit them at all, does not in any way diminish its validity. Cf. also the similar implication in Innocent III's letter cited *infra,* n. 73. On the English law of 1194, and its Continental imitations, see *supra,* Chap. XX, nn. 109 and 111; and K. Scott's juridical analysis of "The Jewish Arcae," *Cambridge Law Journal,* X, 446–55.

70. S. Painter's summary of data (principally in the various *Rotuli,* ed. by T. D. Hardy), in *The Reign of King John,* p. 140; Thomas de Burton's *Chronica monasterii de Melsa,* ed. by E. A. Bond, I, 306, 315; Jocelin of Brakelond's *Cronica,* ed. and

trans. by Butler, pp. 1 ff. (both also in Jacobs, *Angevin England,* pp. 59 ff., 177 f.). An early acquisition of feudal lords' estates by the Church via the payment of a mortgage held by Jews is recorded in tenth-century Narbonne. Here two villages, mortgaged to two Jews, Sabrono and Barala, by the Countess of Carcassonne and her sons between 957 and 970, were taken over, together with the mortgage deed, for 1,000 solidi by a nephew of Archbishop Aymeric. Cf. Devic and Vaissete, *Histoire de Languédoc,* V, 232 f. No. xci. According to J. de Malafosse, this transaction, including the transfer of the *carta pignorationis,* belongs to the oldest French records of real estate mortgages without the dispossess of the debtor. See his observations in his "Contribution à l'étude du crédit dans le Midi aux Xe et XIe siècles," *Annales de Midi,* LXIII, 117 f.

Of great interest is also one of the earliest English records pertaining to loans extended by various Jews to a nobleman. Here Richard de Anesti listed in detail the debts he had incurred in 1159–63, the number of months it took him to repay them, and the amounts to which they had grown. Remarkably, the rate of interest actually declined here from 86⅔ to 43⅓ percent, probably as a result of the competition between the Jewish lenders themselves, who were still feeling their way through this new line of business in a strange environment. Cf. the text in Jacobs, pp. 38 ff.; the facsimile of the original document in H. Hall's *Court Life under the Plantagenets,* facing p. 100, with the notes thereon, pp. 204, 209 ff.; and Caro's analysis in his *Sozial- und Wirtschaftsgeschichte,* I, 321 f. A loan of 70 shillings, or the equivalent of 14 cows and 12 stones of lard, granted in 1182 by Moses ben Isaac of Oxford to William son of Sweting, seems to have grown to £80 in the course of thirteen years. Cf. C. Roth's *Jews of Medieval Oxford,* pp. 7 ff.

71. Richard son of Nigel's *Dialogus de Scaccario,* trans. by C. Johnson, pp. 99 f.; *Chartres et diplômes,* of the Académie des Inscriptions, VI, Part 2, pp. 385 f. No. 806; Jacob of Orléans' formula, cited from his holograph in *Haggahot Mordecai* (Notes on Mordecai bar Hillel's *Halakhot*), on B.M. No. 455. Jacob's liberality aroused the amazement of later rabbis, unfamiliar with the universality of intra-Jewish moneylending in Angevin England. Cf. Joseph Karo, *Bet Yosef* (House of Joseph; Commentary on Jacob ben Asher's *Ṭurim*) on Y.D. CLXXVII (Warsaw ed., 1865, fol. 29a); the editor's sharp remark in the *Haggahot Mordecai,* Vilna ed., *loc. cit.;* and Urbach, *Ba'ale ha-tosafot,* pp. 122 f. In fact, when the "Exchequer of Aaron" liquidated Aaron of Lincoln's claims, it found a number of Jewish debtors among the deceased man's clients. Cf. Jacobs, "Aaron of Lincoln," in *Transactions JHSE,* III, 170 f. On the other hand, more than two hundred deeds included in M. D. Davis's ed. of *Sheṭarot: Hebrew Deeds of English Jews before 1290;* and the even more numerous documents included in *Starrs and Jewish Charters Preserved in the British Museum,* ed. by I. Abrahams, H. P. Stokes, and H. Loewe, in so far as they relate to loan contracts, reflect for the most part transfers to other Jewish creditors of existing loans previously extended to Gentiles.

Regrettably, almost all this material dates from the thirteenth rather than the twelfth century. It is difficult, therefore, to pursue the individual stages in the evolution of Jewish moneylending from the days of William the Conqueror. Nevertheless, one can learn much from these later materials also about conditions in the preceding century. Cf. G. J. Meisel (Mrs. Salo W. Baron), "Jewish Money Lending in Angevin England, 1066–1290" (Master's essay, Columbia University, 1933); and, for the thirteenth century, P. Elman's London thesis on *Jewish Finance in Thir-*

teenth-Century England, with Special Reference to Royal Taxation, briefly summarized in the *Bulletin of the Institute of Historical Research,* XV, 112–13; and "The Economic Causes of the Expulsion of the Jews in 1290," *Economic History Review,* VII, 145–54. These later developments will be more fully considered in a forthcoming volume.

72. Aronius, *Regesten,* pp. 68 ff. Nos. 164, 168, 170–71; 112 No. 244; 123 No. 280 (also *supra,* Chaps. XX, n. 96; XXI, n. 42); Peter of Cluny's and St. Bernard's aforementioned epistles, in *PL,* CLXXXIX, 366 ff.; CLXXXII, 567 f. As has long been recognized, the moneylenders of the early Middle Ages were recruited from all classes, including the artisans and the clergy. See, e.g., J. Lestocqoy, "Les Usuriers du début du moyen âge," *Studi in onore di Gino Luzzatto,* I, 67–77.

73. *Ordonnances des rois,* I, 36 ff., 44 f.; Grayzel, *The Church and the Jews,* pp. 106 f., with reference to Lam. 5:2. Philip Augustus' laws of 1206 and 1218 were influenced by the English legislation, although some related measures had already been adopted by his father in 1174. Here Louis VII had ordained for the benefit of the citizens of Chateau-Landon that no Jews be allowed to lend money to Christians on the security of a pawn, except in the presence of witnesses. Cf. the document reproduced in E. Martène and U. Durand, *Thesaurus novus anecdotorum,* I, 576, and summarized in A. Luchaire, *Etudes sur les actes de Louis VII,* p. 307 No. 658. That the far more sweeping controls of the early thirteenth century were enacted primarily for the benefit of the Treasury was fully recognized, for instance, by Innocent III. In his letter of 1208 to the count of Nevers, the mighty pope bitterly complained "that certain princes do not have their eyes upon the Lord, before Whom all things lie clear and open, for, while they themselves are ashamed to exact usury, they receive Jews into their hamlets [*villis*] and towns and appoint them their agents for the collection of usury." Innocent claimed that often, even after paying the principal of their debts, many Christians, with royal connivance, failed to receive back their pledges and even were thrown into prison until they paid the full usury. Cf. Grayzel, pp. 126 f.; and, on the changes in the meaning of the term *villa,* H. Dubled's "Quelques observations sur le sens du mot *villa,*" *Moyen âge,* LIX, 1–9.

74. C. A. González Palencia's documents in *Los Mozárabes de Toledo,* esp. III, 123 ff., Nos. 833–96, dating between 1202–98, with F. Baer's Hebrew review thereof in *Tarbiz,* V, 228–36; Baer, *Juden,* I, Part 1, p. 10 No. 17, Part 2, pp. 6 f. No. 14. On the Cid's Jewish contacts, see *supra,* Chap. XX, n. 31. It stands to reason that Jews engaged in some moneylending also in Muslim Spain, and that they continued to do so after the Christian reconquest. There is such an extreme dearth of information on this subject, however, that Lévi-Provençal saw no reason to devote to it a paragraph in either *L'Espagne musulmane,* or his *Histoire.* On the later evolution in Christian Spain, from which some deductions may perhaps be cautiously drawn also for the period before 1200, see the numerous entries listed in the two subject indexes of Baer's *Juden, s.v.* Darlehensgeschäfte; his observations in "Probleme der jüdisch-spanischen Geschichte," *Korrespondenzblatt* of the Akademie für die Wissenschaft des Judentums, VI, 9 f.; and his *Toledot,* I, 64, 82, etc.

75. Cf. H. Jenkinson, "A Money-Lender's Bonds of the Twelfth Century," in *Essays in History Presented to R. Lane Poole,* pp. 190–210; and, on the much-

debated Italian bankers, see the recent essays by R. S. Lopez, "An Aristocracy of Money in the Early Middle Ages," *Speculum*, XXVIII, 1–43; P. Wolff, "Le Problème des Cahorsins," *Annales de Midi*, LXII, 229–38; the careful case histories by R. de Roover, *Money, Banking and Credit in Medieval Bruges, Italian Merchant-Bankers, Lombards and Money-Changers;* and J. de Malafosse's aforementioned essay in *Annales de Midi*, LXIII, 105–48 (particularly concerned with the ensuing real estate transactions and mortgages). A Jew from Champagne and Italian merchants from Rome and Siena collaborated in extending to Countess Johanna of Flanders the substantial loan of 29,174 pounds, for which she promised to repay 34,626 pounds (1221). Apparently the creditors encountered some of the usual difficulties. Principally to protect the investment of their Jewish subject, Count Thibaut and Countess Blanche of Champagne threatened to forbid attendance at their fairs to all subjects of Countess Johanna unless the debt were paid in full. From E. Bassermann's data it appears, however, even at that late date this is the only mention of a Jewish moneylender, as against numerous records relating to Italian lenders at the Champagne fairs. Cf. *Die Champagnermessen. Ein Beitrag zur Geschichte des Kredits*, p. 55. Cf., however, Bourquelot's *Etudes*, II, 154 ff.

76. Cf. H. Bowen, '*Ali Ibn 'Isa*, pp. 209 f.; Fischel, *Jews in . . . Mediaeval Islam*, pp. 13 ff. On ancient banking, see the literature cited *supra*, Vol. II, p. 414 n. 29. The political aspects of the employment of the Baghdad Jewish bankers, especially those of the "House of Neṭira," have been discussed *supra*, Chap. XVIII, n. 36.

77. *M.T.* She'elah u-piqqadon, VII.6–7, based on Alfasi's interpretation of B.M. 43a; Saadiah's "Treatise on Pledges," mentioned in *Teshubot ha-geonim*, ed. by Harkavy, No. 454, with the editor's notes thereon, p. 322; and partially ed. by S. Schechter as well as by S. Assaf. Cf. the latter's *Mi-Sifrut ha-geonim* (Gaonica), pp. 32 ff. Cf. also J. Müller's comments in his edition of the juristic works by Saadiah in the latter's *Oeuvres*, IX, 146; and the reference in "A Fihrist of Sa'adya's Works," published by J. Mann in *JQR*, XI, 425. If Harkavy, citing Menahem Meiri, is right and this treatise was written as a reply to inquirers (see his ed., p. 393), such an inquiry would merely demonstrate the practical demand for elucidation of existing laws. Cf. also H. Malter's *Saadia Gaon*, pp. 163, 345; I. Werfel's translation and supplementary notes thereon in *Rav Saadya Gaon*, ed. by J. L. Fishman, pp. 596 f., 651; *infra*, Chap. XXVII, n. 76; and more generally, A. P. Usher's mainly Western sources relating to the *Early History of Deposit Banking in Mediterranean Europe*, Vol. I (dealing chiefly with the later Middle Ages).

78. The complicated talmudic discussions (in B.M. 44–49) of the mutual relations between gold and silver, their respective treatment as merchandise or currency, and the underlying difference between the substantive and nominalist approach to money, gave rise to numerous discussions in later rabbinic literature. On the views of the geonim, see especially the resp. included in *Sha'are ṣedeq*, IV.2.26–27, fols. 40b–41a; Lewin's *Otzar ha-gaonim*, IX, 75 ff.; and the editor's comments thereon. Cf. also Alfasi's summary of the talmudic provisions in his *Halakhot ad loc.;* the interesting analysis in his *Resp.*, fol. 36b No. 243; Rashi's succinct discussion of the effects on a debt of an intervening currency depreciation in his *Teshubot*, pp. 249 f. No. 222; Maimonides' *Commentary* on M. B.M. IV.1–2; his *M.T.* Mekhirah v.6, VI.1, VII.1–2; and my *Essays on Maimonides*, pp. 188 ff. The constant

changes in the currency in circulation are well illustrated by the eleventh-century mathematical treatise analyzed in C. Cahen's "Quelques problèmes économiques et fiscaux de l'Iraq buyide," *Annales de l'Institut d'Etudes Orientales* of the University of Algiers, X, 329 ff., 338 ff. Even the relationship between the silver dirhem and the gold dinar often fluctuated. Instead of the theoretical ratio of 1:12, one usually paid 14⅓ dirhems for one dinar. Going further Sar Shalom had to warn that creditors, lending defective coins and receiving in return regular coins, or lending silver bullion and receiving silver coins of the same weight, committed the two crimes of usury and deception. Cf. *Sha'are ṣedeq*, IV.2.3, fol. 34a. On the complications in business because of the frequent tampering with the coins' metallic content, see, for instance, Rashi's interesting *Teshubot*, pp. 249 f. No. 222, 272 ff. No. 241. Cf. also J. Z. Cahane's "Changes in the Value of Currency according to Jewish Law" (Hebrew), *Sinai*, XIII, Nos. 149-50, pp. 129-48; and W. Taeuber's "Geld und Kredit im Dekret Gratians und bei den Dekretisten," *Studia Gratiana*, II, 459 ff. In his *Waage und Geld in der Merowingerzeit*, pp. 26 ff., J. Werner has supplied interesting illustrations for the need of northern French and Rhenish merchants to weigh all coins before accepting them. But it required further expert knowledge to ascertain the degree of purity of the coins' metallic content. The monetary reforms under the Carolingians brought only temporary respite.

Medieval rabbis often had to go to great lengths in discussing the coins prescribed in talmudic law and figuring out their contemporary equivalents. In his twin essays on "The Value of the Marriage Contract as a Measure of the Wealth of Medieval Jews" (Hebrew), *Horeb*, V, 143-68; and "The Development of the Money Clause in the Ashkenazic Ketubah," *JQR*, XXX, 221-56, I. A. Agus has shown the frequent local adjustments to changing currency values with respect to the talmudically prescribed settlement of 100-200 *zuzim* for a widow or a virgin, respectively. The same held true also for the additional 100 pounds of silver adopted in western Europe as an early safeguard against rash divorces. Most of Agus's material dates from the thirteenth century or later, but the additional provision of 100 silver pounds was accepted some time in the tenth century or earlier. This fact is rightly adduced by him as proof for the relatively high standard of life among the Ashkenazic Jews of that period. We must not forget, however, that in that early period the tiny Western communities consisted largely of merchants, whether long-established or newly arrived from the East. On the frequent designation of merchants as "very wealthy men" at that time, cf. the illustrations cited by E. Sabbe in "L'Importation des tissues orientaux," *RBPH*, XIV, 1287 n. 3. Nonetheless this generous provision for widows or divorcées must have in many cases wrought hardships on children and other heirs. With the growth of Jewish population and its greater economic differentiation, these hardships became fairly widespread and forced the thirteenth-century rabbis, including Meir bar Baruch, to modify that requirement. Cf. also A. H. Freimann's arguments against Agus's theory in "The Amount of the *Kethubah* in Medieval Germany and France," *Marx Jub. Vol.*, Hebrew vol., pp. 371-85; and its defense by Agus in "The Standard Ketuba of the German Jews and Its Economic Implications," *JQR*, XLII, 225-32.

79. *Pirqe de-R. Eliezer*, XXIX, by Higger in *Horeb*, X, 193 f.; in Friedlander's trans., p. 221; Baer, *Juden*, I, Part 1, p. 4 No. 7; G. C. Miles's data in *The Coinage of the Umayyads of Spain*, I, 42 (doubting, however, the existence of a

Hebrew inscription on an early dinar, mentioned in 1851 by Antonio Delgado). On Masha'allah, see M. Steinschneider's data in *Die arabische Literatur der Juden*, pp. 19 f., and *infra*, Chap. XXXV. The fiscal aspects of the depreciation of currency and the ensuing responsibility of taxpayer or tax collector arose already in the early days of Islam. Cf. C. Leyerer's remarks in "Die Verrechnung und Verwaltung von Steuern im islamischen Ägypten," *ZDMG*, CIII, 44 f. The rabbis, too, had to take cognizance of certain legal aspects of minting, especially in connection with the frequent collaboration between Jews and Gentiles. Cf. Ginzberg, *Ginze Schechter*, II, 49 ff.

The scattered materials on Jewish minters and traders in bullion have never been brought together and subjected to close scholarly scrutiny. A. N. Poliak's "Jews and the Mint in the Days of the Mameluks and the Early Turkish Regime" (Hebrew), *Zion*, I, 24–36; supplemented by S. Assaf's notes thereon, *ibid.*, pp. 256 f., sheds but little light on the earlier period. L. A. Mayer deals only with "A Small Detail Relating to Jewish Influence on Muslim Coins" (Hebrew), *BJPES*, XVIII, 230–32, namely with the bare possibility that a Jewish minter placed a variant from the "Sayings of the Fathers" on an Indian-Muslim coin dating from 1325–51. Cf. also the resp. of an unnamed gaon in Ginzberg, *Ginze Schechter*, II, 49 ff. On the other hand, there is an enormous literature on the coins in circulation, their provenance from certain mints, and the locations where they were found. They furnish moot testimony to the existence of more or less intensive commercial exchanges between their countries of origin and those where they were found. See especially the numismatic catalogues and other researches listed in L. A. Mayer's *Bibliography of Moslem Numismatics, India Excepted;* some of the more recent publications, relating especially to Persia, listed in Spuler's *Iran*, pp. 532 ff.; the various recent monographs by G. C. Miles, including *Fāṭimid Coins in the Collections of the University Museum, Philadelphia and the American Numismatic Society;* and *Coins of the Spanish Mulūk al-Tawā'if;* W. Wroth's *Catalogue of the Imperial Byzantine Coins in the British Museum;* and P. Grierson's analysis and bibliographical references in "The Debasement of the Bezant in the Eleventh Century," *BZ*, XLVII, 379–94. Of the vast Western literature we need refer here only to A. Luschin von Ebengreuth's old standard work, *Allgemeine Münzkunde und Geldgeschichte des Mittelalters und der neueren Zeit*, 2d ed.; and the recent essays by P. Le Gentilhomme, "Le Monnayage et la circulation monétaire dans les royaumes barbares en Occident (Vᵉ–VIIIᵉ siècle)," *Revue numismatique*, 5th ser., VII, 45–112; VIII, 13–64; and by R. Doehaerd, "Les Réformes monétaires carolingiennes," *Annales*, VII, 13–20. Biblical, though not necessarily Jewish, influences made themselves felt throughout the Christian world. Cf. the numerous illustrations from both East and West assembled by J. Vandervoorst in *Les Légendes bibliques sur les monnais*.

80. Ibrahim aṭ-Ṭartushi's travelogue included in Zakariya ibn Muhammad al-Qazwini's *K. Athar al-bilād* (Monuments of Countries; Part II of his *Kosmographie*), ed. by F. Wüstenfeld, p. 409. More than half a century ago Werner Sombart, speculating on the origins of Jewish capital resources in the medieval West, came forth with the suggestion that Jews may have salvaged some of their possessions from ancient times. This theory was controverted by I. Schipper in his *Anfänge des Kapitalismus bei den abendländischen Juden im früheren Mittelalter*. After calming down for several decades the debate was resumed on a much broader plane,

especially in connection with the controversy over Pirenne's theory of Islam's impact on the economy of the Western world. M. Lombard, in particular, has argued vigorously in favor of the monetary basis of Arab supremacy. Cf. his stimulating paper, "Les Bases monétaires d'une suprématie économique: l'or musulman du VIIe au XIe siècle," *Annales*, II, 143–60. Cf. also M. de Boüard's "Sur l'évolution monétaire de l'Egypte médiévale," *L'Egypte contemporain*, XXX, 427–59; and Lombard's comments thereon, "Or, argent, et cuivre dans l'Egypte du moyen âge," *Annales*, II, 239–40. Lombard's theory that, because they were able to export gold, the Arabs controlled the maritime trade in the Mediterranean, could be expanded also to the Indian Ocean, despite S. D. Goitein's legitimate reservations in *Speculum*, XXIX, 188. After all, Goitein's own documents have shown that at least on some occasions the Jewish India merchants demanded payment in gold for their imports. Despite the supply of the Sudanese mines and continued despoliation of Pharaonic tombs, ultimately Egyptian gold followed the Gresham law and gave way to silver. Under the reign of Saladin the drain on gold became so severe that the Egyptians often substituted alum as a means of exchange. Cf. Becker's *Islamstudien*, I, 217. Nor have such exchanges of Muslim currency for West European commodities including slaves been seriously controverted by P. Grierson's "Carolingian Europe and the Arabs: the Myth of the Mancus," *RBPH*, XXXII, 1059–74. Even if the term *mancus*, mentioned already in Louis the Pious' charter of 815, should not be an Arabic loan word (this etymology still is the most acceptable; it also has importance for the Carolingian origins of the famous Spires privilege of 1084 relating to Jews; cf. *supra*, Chap. XX, n. 96), the fact of the importation of gold and silver coins from the Arab world has been evidenced by many archaeological finds. Cf. also E. Perroy's rather inconclusive discussion of S. Bolin and M. Lombard's pertinent theories in his "Encore Mahomet et Charlemagne," *RH*, CCXII, 232–38; and, with direct reference to Sombart's original theory, H. Aubin's "Stufen und Triebkräfte der abendländischen Wirtschaftsentwicklung in frühen Mittelalter," *VSW*, XLII, 1–39 (especially p. 29). Further insights may be obtained from J. Lestocqoy's essay (*supra*, n. 72); and from F. Lot's *Nouvelles recherches sur l'impôt foncier*, pp. 126 ff.

Be this as it may, the rise of Western Jewish "capitalism" did not entirely depend on the importation of gold but may as well have originated with such luxury articles as silk or pepper, both of which often played the role of currency in mercantile exchanges far more frequently than alum. Nor did Jews necessarily depend on their own imports. If there were capital accumulations in the hands of Frisian merchants or local grandees, Jewish settlers were able to transform their landholdings, even under pressure, into much liquid capital and then increase it rapidly through usual commercial profits.

81. *Teshubot ha-geonim*, ed. by Harkavy, No. 199 (including the summary of a letter of authorization). The talmudic discussion concerning the *dioqni* (B.Q. 104b; on the meaning of this term, which is still obscure, see S. Krauss, *Griechische und lateinische Lehnwörter*, II, 202 f.) was far less significant in this context. Samuel ben Ḥofni's *Sefer ha-Harsha'ot* (Book of Authorizations) was cited later by some inquirers seeking Maimonides' legal advice. Cf. the latter's *Resp.* No. 300; and, more fully, my *Essays on Maimonides*, pp. 202 ff. On the use in these and other legal instruments of the reference to every Jew's ideal claim to four ells of land in Palestine, see *infra*, Chap. XXIII, n. 29.

82. *Teshubot ha-geonim*, ed. by Harkavy, Nos. 423, 467 with notes by the editor, pp. 316, 327 (also in Lewin's *Otzar*, IX, 67 f. No. 163, with the editor's notes thereon); Alfasi's *Halakhot* on B.Q. 104b; and *supra*, n. 30. Cf. R. Grasshof's study, *Das Wechselrecht der Araber;* M. Pappenheim's negative review thereof in *Kritische Vierteljahrsschrift für Gesetzgebung*, XLIII, 12–17 (his strictures have in part been invalidated, however, by subsequent research); R. de Roover's mainly Western data on *L'Evolution de la lettre de change, XIVe–XVIIIe siècles;* and Fischel, *Jews in . . . Mediaeval Islam*, pp. 17 ff. The main objections of Jewish, as well as Muslim, traditionalists stemmed from their apprehension that the banker's charge for the letter of credit, as a rule amounting to a dirhem per dinar or some 4 percent of the writ's nominal value, might be construed as usurious gain for a loan of money. But, because of the risks involved, even the Western rabbis Gershom and Rashi recognized the legitimacy of an increment.

83. Cf. *supra*, n. 30. On the enormous size of imperial revenues, cf. *e.g.*, the data for the reign of Al-Mamun (813–33) cited from manuscript records by Ibn Khaldun in his *K. al-Muqaddima* (Prolegomènes historiques), ed. by M. A. Quatremère, pp. 155 f. (also in W. de Slane's French translation); and A. von Kremer's fuller analysis, "Ueber das Einnahmebudget des Abbasidenreiches vom Jahre 306 H. (918–19)," *Denkschriften der K. Akademie der Wissenschaften*, Vienna, XXXVI, 283–362, which although some seventy years old has not yet been superseded. Cf. also W. Lotz's more recent survey of *Staatsfinanzen in den ersten Jahrhunderten des Kalifenreiches* in *SB* Munich, 1937, No. 4; Levy's *Sociology*, pp. 343 ff.; Hitti's *History of the Arabs*, pp. 320 f. Because of maladministration of these huge resources—Muqtadir alone is said to have wasted 70 million dinars ($280 million)—the bankers' credit was often better than the Treasury's. Ibn Miskawaihi, pointing out this fact, also admired the great range of that credit which caused bankers' bills to be honored even in enemy lands. Cf. Amedroz and Margoliouth's ed. of his *Eclipse of the Arab Caliphate*, I, 138 f. (Arabic), IV, 268 f. (English).

84. *Ibid.*, I, 35, 66, 106, 239 (Arabic), IV, 39, 72, 118, 269 (English; here only 2 million dinars); Hitti, *History*, p. 344 (citing Kutubi); Ibn Daud's Chronicle, ed. by Neubauer, in *MJC*, I, 73; *supra*, n. 65; Jacobs, "Aaron of Lincoln," in *Transactions JHSE*, III, 168; W. Bacher's "Notes critiques sur la Pesikta Rabbati," *REJ*, XXXIII, 40 ff. (on Bari). The Jewish governor of Siraf on the Persian Gulf in 990, cited in Ibn Miskawaihi's *Eclipse*, III, 149 f. (Arabic), VI, 155 (English), probably also belonged to that city's wealthy class famed for its honesty. Before its decline in the eleventh century several of its members reputedly owned property valued at 5–10 million dinars each. Cf. Mazahéri, *Vie quotidienne*, p. 286. There is no way of comparing the relative wealth of these Jewish bankers, since we do not know what money could buy in either the East or the West. While luxury articles, particularly those imported from the Orient, were undoubtedly much more expensive in western Europe, the staple articles of native growth were much cheaper. Data on prices in the Caliphate, scattered in many sources and more frequently relating to emergency rather than to normal periods, still await their investigator. Such a comprehensive study has recently been promised by W. Hinz. Cf. his provisional findings in his "Lebensmittelpreise im mittelalterlichen Vorderen Orient," *Die Welt des Orients*, II, 52–70. On earlier scattered data, see e.g., E. Stefanski and M. Lichtheim, *Coptic Ostraca from Medinet Habu*, pp. 21 ff.; and

C. Cahen's data in *Annales* of the Univ. of Algiers, X, 342 ff. On the basis of Genizah letters preserved in the Kaufmann collection, S. D. Goitein has shown that poor Jewish workers often had to live on the pittance of three quarters of a dirhem (about 25 cents) a day. Cf. his discussion in *Tarbiz*, XX, 191 ff. It is doubly regrettable, therefore, that Masha'allah's aforementioned treatise is unavailable. Cf. also T. Lewicki's Polish essay "On Prices of Some Goods in East-European Markets in the Ninth to Eleventh Centuries" in *Kwartalnik historii kultury materialnej*, I, 112–28; and *supra*, n. 22. In any case, these Jewish grandees certainly were sufficiently high on the economic scale of their respective countries to arouse much envy among non-Jews and to contribute to the anti-Jewish feelings under both civilizations.

85. *M.T.* Mekhirah XIII.1; Abu'l Faraj 'Ali al-Isfahani, *Kitab al-Aghani* (Collection of Biographies), IV, 8. Business was not so specialized as to preclude a banker being simultaneously a jeweler, general merchant, and landowner as well. In an interesting litigation about dealings with the archbishop of Narbonne, Joseph Bonfils decided that the defendant could be forced to take an oath stating "whether he had made any profit in his trade with the bishop while supplying the latter's needs, whether he had received payment from Gentiles for his services, had collected interest on loans, or exchanged [from the plaintiff's] silver or gold at a higher price and counted it at a lower price," or *vice versa*. Cf. his resp. in *Teshubot geonim qadmonim*, ed. by D. Cassel, fol. 37b No. 140.

86. *Teshubot ha-geonim*, ed. by Assaf, 1942, pp. 114 ff. No. 110. Of course, there also were poets who were either financially independent, or else failed to secure the expected patronage. Such men could at times indulge in attacks on the whole wealthy class. In a noteworthy poem, *Lo he'emin amun* (The Man Raised on Scarlet Did Not Believe), Yehudah Halevi castigated the wealthy men of Seville for their lack of appreciation of intellectual achievements. "Why do you treat wisdom like a burning piece of coal?" he exclaimed, "When in your hands it might turn into a precious ring!" But even here the poet singled out his friend Abu'l Ḥasan Meir ibn Qammaniel for his extraordinary generosity. Cf. his *Diwan*, ed. by Brody, I, 127 ff. No. 88; ed. by Zemorah, III, 116 f.; and H. Schirmann's comments thereon in "Life of Yehudah Halevi" (Hebrew), *Tarbiz*, IX, 50 f. We shall see that praise or blame through well-turned verses could become a mighty weapon and occasionally force the hands of reluctant givers. Cf. *infra*, Chap. XXXII. Since most of these professions were intimately connected either with the operation of Jewish self-government or with one or another intellectual pursuit, their story will unfold more fully in these contexts. Cf. especially Chaps. XXIII, XXXI, XXXV and XXXVI.

87. Saadiah, *Beliefs and Opinions*, x.8, ed. by Landauer, p. 298; in Ibn Tibbon's Hebrew trans., ed. by D. Slucki, p. 206; and in S. Rosenblatt's English trans., p. 378; Abraham Maimonides, *K. Kifayat al-'abadin* (The High Ways of Perfection), ed. and trans. by S. Rosenblatt, I, 91; II, 182 ff. Of course, Eastern Jews had access to the works written in, or translated into, Arabic. Among these the *Oikonomikos* by "Bryson" enjoyed the greatest reputation. In "A Genizah Fragment of a Treatise on the Sciences in General," published by R. Gottheil in *JQR*, XXIII, 171, 178, this rather insignificant tractate is called "the most renowned book" on domestic

economy. It was considered sufficiently authoritative for Avicenna, Al-Dimashqi, and others to summarize and paraphrase it in their own discussions on economics. Cf. M. Plessner's noteworthy comments in his edition of the Arabic text, together with the fourteenth-century Hebrew translation and an incomplete Latin translation in *Der Oikonomikos des Neupythagoreers "Bryson" und sein Einfluss auf die islamische Wissenschaft;* F. Wilhelm's earlier review of "Die Oeconomica der Neupythagoreer Bryson, Kallikratidas, Pariktione, Phintys," *Rheinisches Museum,* LXX, 161–223; and my *Essays,* pp. 127 ff. Cf. also the studies by S. Mahmassani, *Les Idées économiques d'Ibn Khaldoun,* and E. Schreiber, *Die volkswirtschaftlichen Anschauungen der Scholastik seit Thomas v. Aquin,* which, though dealing with later Muslim and Christian theories, are primarily concerned with the doctrine of just price, shed light also on the earlier approaches; and, more generally, N. P. Aghnides' *Muslim Theories of Finance,* and Shaikh Mahmud Ahmad's *Economics of Islam* (A Comparative Study). Aghnides offers a detailed, primarily juridical analysis of the various taxes and the administration of public domain; the latter furnishes a rather lame apologia for Muslim doctrines in the light of modern realities. The rabbis' economic teachings have never yet received the scholarly scrutiny they so amply deserve. On ancient times, see *supra,* Vol. II, pp. 414 f. n. 29. Our necessarily brief remarks here will be supplemented by additional data relating to the general medieval Jewish social philosophy *infra,* Chap. XXXIV. The entire problem will be dealt with more fully in connection with the better known economic realities and debates of the later Middle Ages. Cf. also S. D. Goitein, "The Rise of the Near-Eastern Bourgeoisie in Early Islamic Times," *Journal of World History,* III, 583–604.

88. Abraham ibn Daud, *Emunah ramah* (Exalted Faith), III, ed. by S. Weil, pp. 98, 101 (Hebrew), 126, 130 (German; the translation here lacks precision); Maimonides, *Maqala fi-ṣinaʿat al-mantik* (Treatise on Logic), XIV, ed. in Arabic, with Moses ibn Tibbon's, Aḥitub's, and Joseph ibn Vivas's independent Hebrew versions and an English translation by I. Efros, pp. 63 f. (English), 60 ff., 97 ff., 127 ff. (Hebrew; this section is not extant in the Arabic original). This Maimonidean classification of the sciences, and its relation to similar classifications among the Arabs and in later Hebrew letters, will be discussed *infra,* Chap. XXXV.

89. Ibn Daud and Maimonides, *loc. cit.* (on the latter's text see also Efros's remarks, pp. 18 f.); and L. Strauss, "Quelques remarques sur la science politique de Maïmonide et de Farabi," *REJ,* Cbis, 8 ff. Although Muslim law was likewise pliable and subject to constant reinterpretation with the aid of a similar juristic technique, some Arabic writers, like Abu'l Jafar al-Dimashqi, felt prompted to consider certain practical aspects of the new economic life. In his *K. al-Ishara ila maḥāshin at-tijāra* (The Book of Demonstration of the Beauties of Commerce and the Knowledge of Good and Bad Merchandise and Falsifications), Al-Dimashqi was as much concerned with warning his readers against the numerous shoddy and falsified products then spreading through the Muslim world (see *supra,* n. 10) as with analyzing the virtues of commerce and its numerous ramifications. Even within the extremely rich Arabic literature of the period, his treatise remained a rather exceptional monument to scholarly curiosity about certain seamy aspects of life which must have disturbed innumerable customers. Cf. H. Ritter's introduction to his German translation of that treatise under the somewhat exaggerating title, "Ein